New Concepts in Latino American Cultures

Also edited by Licia Fiol-Matta and José Quiroga

Cosmopolitanisms and Latin Amer...*a: Against the Destiny of Place*,
   by Jacqueline Loss

Ciphers of History: Latin America...
   by Enrico Mario Santí

Remembering Maternal Bodies: M...*Melancholy in Latina and Latin American*...*can
Women's Writing,*
   by Benigno Trigo

New Directions in Latino American Cultures

A series edited by Licia Fiol-Matta and José Quiroga

Intellectual History of the Caribbean,
   by Silvio Torres-Saillant

New Tendencies in Mexican Art,
   by Rubén Gallo

Jose Martí: An Introduction,
   by Oscar Montero

The Letter of Violence: Essays on Narrative and Theory,
   by Idelber Avelar

*The Masters and the Slaves: Plantation Relations and Mestizaje
in American Imaginaries,*
   edited by Alexandra Isfahani-Hammond

Bilingual Games: Some Literary Investigations,
   edited by Doris Sommer

Tongue Ties: Logo-Eroticism in Anglo-Hispanic Literature,
   by Gustavo Perez-Firmat

Velvet Barrios: Popular Culture & Chicana/o Sexualities,
   edited by Alicia Gaspar de Alba, with a foreword by Tomás Ybarra Frausto

The Famous 41: Sexuality and Social Control in Mexico, 1901,
   edited by Robert McKee Irwin, Edward J. McCaughan, and Michele Rocío
   Nasser

New York Ricans from the Hip Hop Zone,
   by Raquel Rivera

Forthcoming titles

AN INTELLECTUAL HISTORY

OF THE CARIBBEAN

Silvio Torres-Saillant

AN INTELLECTUAL HISTORY OF THE CARIBBEAN
© Silvio Torres-Saillant, 2006.

First published in 2006 by
PALGRAVE MACMILLAN™
175 Fifth Avenue, New York, N.Y. 10010 and
Houndmills, Basingstoke, Hampshire, England RG21 6XS
Companies and representatives throughout the world.

PALGRAVE MACMILLAN is the global academic imprint of the Palgrave Macmillan division of St. Martin's Press, LLC and of Palgrave Macmillan Ltd. Macmillan® is a registered trademark in the United States, United Kingdom and other countries. Palgrave is a registered trademark in the European Union and other countries.

ISBN 1–4039–6677–X

Library of Congress Cataloging-in-Publication Data is available from the Library of Congress.

    Caribbean/Antillean world/West Indies—Intellectual history—Antilleanism Caribbean discourse—Civilization. Haiti—Dominican Republic—Surinam—Netherlands Antilles—History—Humanity—Literature—Criticism and theory Caliban—Western discourse—Pan-Caribbean approaches—Regionalism—Imperial imagination—Theoretical compulsions

A catalogue record for this book is available from the British Library.

Design by Newgen Imaging Systems (P) Ltd., Chennai, India.

First edition: January 2006

10 9 8 7 6 5 4 3 2 1

Printed in the United States of America.

Transferred to digital printing in 2006.

For
Antonio Benítez-Rojo, Silvano Lora, Gérard Pierre-Charles

In Memoriam

CONTENTS

Acknowledgments

In the writing of this book I profited from numerous dynamic interlocutors who over several years at fora of various kinds engaged me in conversation about the structure of life in the Caribbean. Their acceptance, encouragement, challenge, or amendment of my claims helped to bring into sharper focus the kind of intervention to which I in the end would commit myself. I cannot list donors whose financial support freed me from the burden of the classroom in order to think and write. It was not freedom from the demands of the job, but the privileged settings where those demands took me, which brought this book into being. I therefore must list, instead, the institutions, individuals, and constituencies that, in creating stimulating working environments or sponsoring spaces of productive reflection, gave me the opportunity to speak, listen, and learn while rehearsing the thinking that fills the pages of this book. I begin with the leadership of Syracuse University's College of Arts and Sciences that has supported my endeavors since former Dean Robert G. Jensen first recruited me to head the Latino-Latin American Studies Program. My current dean Cathryn R. Newton has fostered a climate of intellectual dynamism that I have found most nurturing, and Associate Deans Susan S. Wadley and Gerald Greenberg have sustained me with their sensitive guidance. I have been invariably stimulated by the passion with which my colleagues in the English Department engage in the deployment of ideas about the contours of the field and literariness.

Teaching my graduate seminar "Caliban Revisited: Current Perspectives on Caribbean Literature and Thought" has afforded me an enviable opportunity to converse regularly with estimable cadres of insightful young scholars at that point in their learning when they are still curious about the basic questions. Concurrently with the course and under the auspices of the Ray Smith Symposium of the College of Arts and Sciences, in Spring 2001 I organized the conference "Caribbean Writers Imagine the Millennium" with memorable repercussions. Prominent writers from the four major linguistic blocs of the Caribbean came to the Syracuse University campus to read, speak, and converse. An audience made up of students, faculty, and visitors who came from near and far spent good quality time with Antonio Benítez-Rojo, Edouard Glissant, Dany Laferrière, Cynthia Mc Leod, M. Nourbese Phillip, Gisèle Pineau, and Luis Rafael Sánchez, among many other luminaries of Spanish-, Dutch-, English-, and French-speaking Caribbean letters. The readings, panel discussions, and conversations that these writers graced with their participation formed a composite document of historic cultural and intellectual value. Subsequently, in the fall of 2003, through the University's Division of International Programs Abroad, I developed the course "Beyond the Beach" in collaboration with my colleague Linda Carty, then the Chair of the African American Studies Department. Our four-week course took a group of students to Jamaica and the Dominican Republic for an in-depth look at "social movements, tourism, and culture in the Caribbean," through an interdisciplinary array of guest lectures by first-rate scholars, artists, and political leaders from the region plus a carefully chosen menu of visits to sites of key historical importance. I found the caliber of that intellectual experience enormously energizing and as transformative for me as it was for my teaching partner and the students.

Since the mid-1990s I have had the good fortune of coordinating, cosponsoring, or participating in projects that have brought me into close contact with the leading figures and the most stirring issues of Caribbean thought. My collaboration with Daniel Shapiro, head of The Americas Society's Literature Department, has enabled me to interact memorably with the likes of Lorna Goodison, Wilson Harris, Diana Lebacs, Earl Lovelace, and Olive Senior. New York University's Timothy J. Reiss has generously made me part of unique conversations involving artistic and intellectual figures of the prominence of Kamau Brathwaite, Maryse Condé, and Orlando Patterson. At Hostos Community College of the City University of New York, Provost and Vice President Daisy Cocco de Filippis has honored me with leading speaking roles in her impressive yearly international conferences, which have created optimal conditions for my formulating a distilled line of reasoning concerning globalization and transnationalism particularly as they pertain to the Caribbean experience. The roles assigned to me by Arcadio Díaz Quiñones in the major seminars on the Caribbean he has put together at Princeton University have brought me into close contact with the work and the engaging personalities of Joan Dayan, Sylvia Molloy, and Doris Sommer, among a host of other protagonists of our intellectual community. Similarly, my esteemed colleagues in the French and Spanish programs at the City University of New York's Graduate School and University Center— Francesca Canadé Sautman, Lía Schwartz, and Malva Filer—treated me to a bountiful scholarly banquet when in April 2004 they sat me at the table of conversation with Edouard Glissant, Roberto González Echevarría, and Maximilien Laroche to discuss the Franco-Hispanic chapter of cultural encounters in the Caribbean.

I am grateful to Tomás Ybarra Frausto, deputy director of the Rockefeller Foundation's Division of Creativity and Culture, and his former colleague Lynn Szwaja, for backing an international symposium I proposed for June 2001 to take place sequentially in New York City and Santo Domingo. Entitled "Up from the Margins: Diversity as Challenge to the Democratic Nation," the event brought together Dominican, Haitian, Puerto Rican, and Cuban scholars from the United States, Puerto Rico, the Dominican Republic, and Europe, to discuss the multiple ways in which traditional ideas of nation ought to confront their damaging exclusions. In convening such a gathering I performed my closing act as I transitioned out of the headship of the CUNY Dominican Studies Institute to make way for its current director, the notable sociologist Ramona Hernández. Earlier in 2001 Tomás had chosen me to organize, on behalf of the Foundation, an interdisciplinary summit entitled "The Transnationalization of Everyday Life: The Impact of Global Transformations on Community Experience," which brought together some 20 specialists in topics relating to migration, diaspora, and transnationalism. Together, the two events featured some 75 learned voices that came to examine questions of identity, migratory flows, cultural diversity, the rapport of diasporas or expatriate communities with their ancestral homelands, and the implications of global transformations to the prospects for community formation and endurance. My privileged access to these conversations enriched me to a degree greater than I can consciously fathom.

Some of my Dominican colleagues with whom I have maintained an ongoing dialogue on the concerns expressed in this book—Miguel Decamps, Franklin Franco Pichardo, Franklin Gutiérrez, Blas R. Jiménez, Jacqueline Jiménez Polanco, Luis Francisco Lizardo, Agliberto Meléndez, Frank Moya Pons, Odalís Pérez, Avelino Stanley, Anthony Stevens-Acevedo, and Virtudes Uribe—have hosted me as a speaker in formal fora or informal conviviality offering my words a welcoming hearing and enhancing my thought with the relevant intelligence of their conversation. I have also benefited from solid exchanges of ideas with sociologist Carlos Dore Cabral especially in connection with my contributions to *Revista Global*, the premier journal that he edits for Fundación Global Democracia y Desarrollo. Similarly, I deeply appreciate the fruitful communication I have sustained with literary scholar and critic José Rafael Lantigua, at least since August 2004 when he became minister of culture of the Dominican Republic and proceeded to facilitate my participation in dialogues of national and regional import by hosting me for several guest lectures.

Jaime Muñoz Domínguez, the head of the Mexico City Office of the Government of Quintana Roo during the administration of Governor Joaquín E. Hendricks Díaz, put me in his debt when he recruited me to serve as a juror in the essay competition "Prizes to Caribbean Thought" for three years until June 2004. As part of the task, I found myself in fertile deliberations about Caribbean matters with interlocutors who are among the most accomplished specialists on the history and culture of the region, including Nara Aráujo, Germán Carrera Damas, Jean Casimir, Lancelot Cowie, Gérard Pierre-Charles, Susan Craig James, Pablo Maríñez, and Glenn Sankatsing. I am also particularly grateful to A. James Arnold of the University of Virginia at Charlottesville for enlisting my participation in a project that aspires to set up a Caribbean Literature Digital Archive. The group Arnold formed to develop his visionary initiative met in June 2004 at the Rockefeller Conference Center in Bellagio, Italy, to formulate the next stages of the project. The company of an impressive array of key players in the study and the production of Caribbean letters, such as Edward Baugh,

Antonio Benítez-Rojo, Roberto Márquez, Ineke Phaf-Rheineberger, and Wim Rutgers—against the breath-taking backdrop of Lake Como and the surrounding mountains—amounted to an abridged education, apart from granting me the priceless occasion to hang out with Antonio at his jovial best only six months before his death in early January 2005.

Since July 2001 the Colombian historian Alfonso Múnera Cavadía has made me a fixture of his biennial International Seminar on Caribbean Studies held at the University of Cartagena, and the engagement has drawn me closer to the work and the human caliber of novelist Luis Rafael Sánchez and sociologist Angel "Chuco" Quintero Rivera, among other key figures of Caribbean literature and thought. I appreciate the gesture of Ninna Nyberg Sørensen at the Danish Institute for International Studies in Denmark in making me part of a select team of guest scholars that went in early December 2001 to Roskilde University to participate in a Ph.D. seminar on diasporas and transnational dynamics. The vibrant conversation with nearly two-dozen enthusiastic doctoral candidates invigorated my thinking about origin and destination as they pertain to Caribbean populations. The thinking provoked by the reactions to my work at Roskilde subsequently fueled the topic of my talk in February 2003 at the University of Edinburgh, upon the kind invitation of the geographer David Howard and the sponsorship of the English Department. Later that year, in September, my colleagues at the University of Antwerp Rita De Maeseneer and Kathleen Gyssels with the assistance of the Postcolonial Literature Study Group mounted an imposing Caribbean literature conference, and the speaking role they gave me enabled me to rehearse the autobiographical mode that would eventually find its way into chapter 1 of this book. The Antwerp conference also allowed me to exchange ideas with younger Caribbeanists, such as the Dominican literary scholar Nestor Rodríguez of the University of Toronto and the Haitian-American writer Myriam J. A. Chancy, who at the time edited the journal *Meridian*. An invitation to participate in a week-long program of Caribbean culture at the University of Antioquia in Medellín, Colombia, in early November 2003, provided the occasion to acquaint myself with the work of Dominican-born literary scholar Elissa Lister, at the time transitioning from the University of Antioquia to Medellín's Universidad Nacional, and to witness at close range the respect that the black Colombian writer Manuel Zapata Olivella, who would die at the age of 84 less than two weeks later (November 19), commanded among the compatriots who knew about his life-long dedication to unearthing the African heritage in Colombian society. Since my rank in the industry has not yet soared so high—making my time so dear that I must restrict my presence in learned parlors to the delivery of my words to others—in the encounters listed here I have invariably gained invaluable insight by staying and listening to others, and I therefore thank the conveners who involved me in them.

I cannot close without expressing my gratitude to Licia Fiol-Matta and José Quiroga, editors of the series New Directions in Latino American Cultures, for their interest in adding this book to their already impressive list of titles. Since our first conversation at the LASA Congress in Houston, Spring 2003, I have enjoyed my communication with Gabriella Pearce, my editor at Palgrave who contracted the book, and that includes her tender promptings to try to keep me close to schedule. My appreciation goes also to Yasmin Mathew, the first production editor, to Elizabeth Sabo, who subsequently filled that role, and to Maran Elancheran in the production team, for their labor in ensuring that the book saw the light with no more blemishes than the reader can be expected to forgive. As a crucial deadline approached, I found myself in urgent need of assistance by able typists, and two angels came to deliver me: Sandra Smith from the staff of the Office of Curriculum, Instruction and Programs at Syracuse University's College of Arts and Sciences, and Silvia Olivo, the Office Manager in the Business Center of Hotel Santo Domingo, where I stayed in late April 2005 when I attended to several commitments related to the VIII Santo Domingo International Book Fair. I am enormously grateful to them for their material intervention to make this book possible.

Finally, I need to acknowledge several publishers for their permission to reuse portions of this volume that have previously appeared in print in modified form. The pertinent pieces are: "Caliban's Betrayal: A New Inquiry into the Caribbean." *For the Geography of A Soul: Emerging Perspectives on Kamau Brathwaite*. Ed. Timothy J. Reiss. Trenton and Asmara: Africa World Press, 2001. 221–243; "Colonial Migration and Theoric Awakening: An Antillean's Voyage of Discovery." *Beyond Home and Exile: Making Sense of Life on the Move*. Occasional Paper No. 23. Ed. Bodil Folke Frederiksen and Ninna Nyberg Sørensen. Roskilde: International Development Studies, Roskilde University, 2002. 190–231; "El Caribe frente al discurso occidental." *El artista caribeño como guerrero de lo imaginario*. Ed. Rita De Maeseneer and An Van Hecke. Madrid and Frankfurt am Main: Iberoamericana/ Vervuert, 2004. 181–197; and "Caribbean Dirges: Rising Rhythms, Precarious Prospects." *Music, Writing, and Cultural Unity in the Caribbean*. Ed. Timothy J. Reiss. Trenton and Asmara: Africa World Press, 2005. 367–389.

PREFACE

An Intellectual History of the Caribbean starts from the certitude that the
world is a very large place, and that the sum of the phenomena transpiring in
it is best fathomed by breaking it down into discernible parts. The world
consists of culture areas and distinct regions whose interconnectedness does
not preclude their discreteness. As a chronicle of Caribbean thought, this
work enacts a postulation of the need to subdivide the intellectual history of
humanity into manageable chunks, namely, countries, regions, culture areas,
and the like. I find a grave problem with scholarly pronouncements that
couch themselves in epistemologically hoarding terms such as Immanuel
Wallerstein's *The End of the World as We Know It* (1999). I believe the audacity of their planetary pretensions should at least cause one to pause. Oddly, in
the preface to his bound volume of conference addresses, the distinguished
social scientist takes care to gloss the word "know" in his all-embracing title,
while leaving unexplained the more troubling word "we." He foregrounds
the "double sense" of the word "know" by reference to its two principal
equivalents in Latin, namely *scio-scire*, which points to an active acquisition of
information, and *cognosco-cognoscere*, which tends to identify the awareness
and familiarity obtained through contact with people, surroundings, and
things (ix). Yet, given its expressive daring, the word "we" would seem more
urgently to demand glossing.

Left without annotation, Wallerstein's use of the first-person plural
pronoun invites us to understand it as inclusive of everyone who might look
at the book, which can potentially encompass the entire species. Such an
understanding assumes that people across the planet know the same world
and know it the same way. No doubt sharing such a view would have to
require a leap of faith. One can hardly deem it self-evident that the world as
perceived from the field of view afforded by a Tibetan temple or an
Amerindian village in Brazil matches point by point the world perceived by
aspiring human scientists at the Sorbonne or seasoned policy-makers in
Washington, DC. As these percipients do not share a vantage point or a viewing stand from which to look at, experience, or apprehend the world, we can
hardly suppose them to share their knowledge of it, either in the content of
their cognition or in their manner of absorbing it. Nor can all the possible
readers of Wallerstein's book fancy ourselves members of a homogenous
community informed by a unified perception of the world we live in. For one
thing, due to the cognitive force of cultural specificities, the distinctness of
disparate regions, the delimiting impact of national or communal histories,

and the uneven balance of power among societies around the planet, one must concede the multitudes that inhabit the "we" while acknowledging the variety of worlds that the multitudinous "we" inhabits.

The Caribbean whose intellectual history this book intends to trace is a comparatively young cluster of societies, their genesis dating back to no earlier than the colonial transaction that the 1492 arrival of Columbus unleashed. Young societies understandably abhor formulations that announce the epilogue to the narrative of human advancement, as Francis Fukuyama famously did in *The End of History*, which argued that societies could go no further than they had gone in Western liberal democracies, their inequities at home and their abuses abroad notwithstanding (Fukuyama 1992:xi). Naturally, young societies would have even less sympathy for terminal claims that apocalyptically herald "the end of the world as we know it." Most likely they would find it unfair that just as they have begun to assume their rightful place in the community of nations, having only recently stepped out of formal colonial domination, the same world powers responsible for their former condition should now espouse discourses that declare the game of history over. Their disappointing perplexity would perhaps match the predicament of Rutherford Calhoun, the roguish black narrator of Charles Johnson's comic novel *Middle Passage*, at a point in the story when his familiar reality may cease to exist:

> History, as we knew it, would *end*, for there would be no barriers between the secular and the sacred. I was starting to scare myself now and figured I'd better stop. Gods only appeared, Reverend Chandler had said, on Judgement Day. For my part, I wanted to live a little longer. I was only twenty-three years old. The Apocalypse would definitely put a crimp on my career plans. I needed the world as I knew it, as evil and flawed as it was, to *be* there for a while. (Johnson 1990:103)

The pages that follow will insist in saying that Caribbean thought has a history of its own, coterminous with the differentiated history of people in the region, irrespective of the web of mutuality that might interlace their lives with societies in many other parts of the globe. This book thus calls for chronicles of the story of human culture, specifically literary utterances and intellectual discourse, to itemize the contents of the planetary "we" and to address the variety of worlds that the multitudinous "we" inhabits. The rise of area studies in universities of Europe and the United States at least from the mid-nineteenth century onward and the development of ethnic studies initiatives in those academic sites over a century later, entailed the recognition, no matter how grudging, that knowing the world required discrete attention to its constituent parts. The imperial imagination may have polluted the outcome of certain area studies projects, leading, for instance, to the emergence of "Orientalism," to recall Edward W. Said's appraisal of Western study of the East. Ethnic studies undertakings may also have, at their worst, yielded superficial modes of multiculturalism. But a justifiable dissatisfaction with the particular product of determinate area or ethnic studies projects will hardly suffice to negate the crucial importance of examining specificities and differences in any assessment that purports to learn and speak holistically about human society.

The desire to have difference and specificities recognized would seem fairly uncontroversial. The ecological imperatives, belief systems, social organizations, natural resources, and historical circumstances that shape the lives, the knowledge, and the outlooks of peoples in their respective portions of the globe would seem to argue reasonably for it. But it becomes particularly urgent for people thinking critically about human society in places like Malaysia, in Southeast Asia, or Curaçao, in the Netherlands Antilles, which have suffered a long record of exclusion from consideration in meganarratives of humanity and the condition of the world. Nor will it escape these critical thinkers that their very location in Malaysia and Curaçao places serious limits on their authority to speak holistically about the species, the ability to comment on the whole of humanity being a privilege retained by the group of nations occupying the upper crust of the global system spawned by the colonial transaction. The voices most empowered to pronounce judgments of planetary dimension on the present and the future of humanity come from the cluster of societies that holds the greatest share of economic, military, and political power internationally.

That the powerful and the disempowered do not belong in the world in the same way comes up with moving pathos in *El mundo es ancho y ajeno* (Broad and Alien is the World, 1941) by the classic Chilean novelist Ciro Alegría. The novel tells the story of the life, crisis, and destruction of Rumi, an indigenous community at the mercy of the Andean landowners and anti-Indian dominant groups in Peruvian society. Toward the end of the story, it becomes painfully clear that the villagers have lost the land they live and work on, the courts having favored a claim on them by the rich planter Alvaro Amenabar. The young mestizo Benito Castro, realizing that Almenabar's ploy to possess the land seeks primarily to disenfranchise the laborers so that they will have to work for him planting coca in the malaria-infested Ocros River valley, raises his voice in protest. Addressing the villagers and committing himself to join an armed struggle in defense of the community, Castro says:

> The law gives out land, and then pays no attention to what happens to the people on those lands. The law does not protect them. Those who are in charge of things justify themselves, saying, "Go somewhere else. This is a big world." Yes it is big. But, villagers, I know the big world in which we poor people have to live. And I tell you that for us, the poor, it is big but it is not ours. (Alegría 1973:425)

Since the international market of ideas in the human sciences, as we enter the twenty-first century, is dominated by the intellectual industry of the West—as are also space navigation, digital technology, and nuclear weaponry—Malaysian, Tibetan, Amerindian, and Curaçaoan thinkers must come to the bitter realization that they exist intellectually in a world which, as with the Rumi villagers in the Alegría novel, is simply not theirs. They exist in a world wherein a Fellow of Trinity Hall, Cambridge, a journal editor, and distinguished Lecturer in Drama and Poetry at the University of Cambridge, can compile an anthology of "theorists writing on theorists"—16 texts by Western authors, almost all French and German—and call it *Modern Critical Thought* (Milne 2003), without any gentilitial specification. Devoid of ethnic or national delimitation, the words on the title seem to denote the critical thinking that the human mind has produced in modern times, which for the editor corresponds to a period spanning from Karl Marx in the second half of the nineteenth century through the work of Slavoj Žižek in the present. His introductory essay notes "the importance given to French thought, and the neglect of the German sources of such thought" as a peculiarity of "theory" in the English-speaking world (Milne 2003:3). Displeased with such a state of affairs, he seeks with his compilation to suggest "some of the dialogues between German and French thought" as well as to represent work that draws from the interbreeding of those two national and linguistic spaces, pointing to a fusion of speculative traditions "in the new hybrid spaces of theory" (3). But his recognition of the specific national origins of the intellectual products his anthology gathers together does not automatically lead to his considering the insertion of a delimiting marker in the title, be it "Franco-German," "European," or even "Western." He feels confident in calling it "modern critical thought," thus asserting the power of the two Western nations involved to represent the thinking done by the whole of humanity.

One can hardly avoid the implications for speculative utterances produced outside the West, say, in Malaysia, Amerindian Brazil, Curaçao, or Tibet. Do they lack the unqualified valence of their Western counterparts to capture the concerns of the learned portion of the species? Do they lack the flair or the texture necessary to earn the rank of "modern," of "critical," or perhaps even of "thought"? These implications, of course, would worry any thinking member of the non-Western societies named here. They would worry especially those Tibetan, Amerindian, Malaysian, or Curaçaoan thinkers unwilling to perpetrate unto themselves the "act of amputation" implicit in their refusal "to acknowledge" where they "come from," to borrow the language of Margaret Atwood (1973:48). You "may become free floating, a citizen of the world . . . but only at the cost of arms, legs, or heart" (48). Self-mutilating non-Western thinkers, aware of the dismal cultural capital of the legacy of thought native to their ancestral heritages in the world market of ideas, may seek to circumvent their hurdle by distancing themselves intellectually from their roots—autochthonous bodies of knowledge and modes of thought—to apply themselves zealously to the mastery of Western intellectual production, ways of saying, and hierarchies of authority. They would thus diminish their risk of calling attention to the distinctness of their historical selves and become indistinguishable from the Western speaking subjects who can brandish the audacity to enunciate a planetary "we." The Surinamese novelist Astrid Roemer explains the predicament as it applies to writers like her who, coming from an Antillean vernacular setting, ought to come to terms with the demands that Dutch society places on them when they seek to practice their art in the metropolis:

> To strive for success means a Western style of emotion, thinking and acting. But if persons remain more or less loyal to their own inheritance and want to identify themselves because of their political engagement with subcultures which contain their historical roots and, at the same time, want to be successful in the Netherlands, they feel a split in loyalties in all facets of their life and must more or less consciously create models of compromise. (Roemer 1996:39)

An Intellectual History of the Caribbean opposes self-mutilation and speaks emphatically in favor of telling the story of human culture by paying close attention to each of the discernible branches of the human tree without assuming any particular branch to have the versatility to be itself while representing all others or to hold a monopoly over the gift of explanation. The book contends that the cluster of societies that formed in the Caribbean in the course of the colonial transaction has actively thought about itself and the rest of the world for over five centuries and that the expression of that record of thought yields a rich and vast social field for scholars and students in the intellectual history of humans around the globe. The book posits that Caribbean intellectual history is not implicitly expressed in Western chronicles of the movement of ideas even when Western thinkers may have influenced particular cadres of Caribbean intellectuals. I argue that, as a distinct culture area, a region with ecological imperatives of its own, the site of particular kinds of interaction among populations originating in multiple points of the globe, and the arena of economic experiments, imperial clashes, and violent and circumstantial interculturation unequaled elsewhere, the Caribbean constitutes a world apart. The words of Juan Carlos Altamirano, one of the key characters in the novel *The Sign of Jonah* by the Curaçaoan fiction writer Boeli van Leeuwen, seem to argue compellingly for the study of the parts when, glancing at the sea, he muses thus:

> When I think of the dark depths along the coasts of my country, where the sperm whale fights gigantic squids, and of our mysterious, heavily breathing sea that breaks on black rocks and desert beaches; and when I compare the white beaches of the Caribbean islands to them, with their bays like swimming pools, or the choppy, gray waves of Northern Europe, or the Polar sea smooth like a mirror where whales feed on krill, I realize that not even the sea is one entity, but that it is composed of many realities. (Leeuwen 1995:61)

What that world has thought about itself and what forces internal and external have prompted its thinking—as can be surmised from the venues of its expressive culture—requires a discrete account.

Studies of this kind may perhaps contribute to a widening of the "we" that Western thinkers deploy when weaving hoarding formulations about the species. Particularly, they may be able to sensitize students of human culture about the history of injustices responsible for the epistemological inequality that allows some clusters of societies and not others to market discourses of planetary dimension. Studies of this kind may perhaps also help to reassure critical thinkers from such places as Amerindian Brazil, Tibet, Curaçao, and Malaysia that despite the pressure of the international intellectual industry that would have them trade the distinctness of their speculative traditions for the lingua franca of Western histories of ideas, the world—the one that is large and inhabited by a multitudinously diverse "we"—is still in dire need of the autochthonous wisdom and bodies of knowledge that they might contribute to a necessary conversation about the best ways to imagine a future for endangered humanity.

Zoologists L. C. Dunn and Theodosius Dobzhansky closed their 1946 study of heredity, race, and society with musings that remain powerfully evocative over a half century later:

> In the realm of culture there is enough room to accommodate the diversified contributions not only of different individuals but also of every nation and race. It is a waste of time to discuss which particular contributions are superior or inferior. There is no common measure applicable to the works of a poet, an artist, a philosopher, a scientist, and the simple kindness of heart of a plain man. Humanity needs them all. (Dunn and Dobzhansky 1946:115)

While acknowledging, with Said, that, because of the pervasively global impact of colonialism, "we cannot discuss the non-Western world as disjunct from developments in the West," and that, since imperial movements "consolidated the mixture of cultures and identities" on a planet-wide scale, we today cannot presume to be "purely one thing," this study asserts the entitlement of the Caribbean to be taken as a place of knowledge that requires a discrete examination (Said 1993:325, 336). It challenges the prevailing geopolitics of ideas that renders the less economically powerful peoples of the earth ineligible to represent the complexity of the human experience, and it advocates a view of humanity that is sensitive to the vision that informs Roemer's writing of her "multi-ethnic diaspora novels," namely, the "recognition of Differences, the understanding of Differences, the acceptation of Differences, the integration of Differences" (Roemer 1996:43).

With the foregoing considerations in mind, and building on the line of inquiry I developed in *Caribbean Poetics* (1997), I have conceived *An Intellectual History of the Caribbean* as a contribution to intellectual diversity in the academic study of culture, literature, and society by foregrounding Caribbean utterances and experiences in the contemporary discussion of the formation and structure of the modern world. I thus hope to counteract the prevailing geopolitics of ideas that pervades the scholarly community, which gives credence to a scenario wherein the lives, thoughts, and words of certain nations or culture areas brandish the authority to embody the human condition in the whole planet whereas those coming from other regions can elucidate themselves only.

The book comprises an intellectual history of the Antillean archipelago and its continental rimlands by reckoning the writings penned by natives of the region as well as a body of texts interpretive of the region produced by Western authors. Stressing the experiential and cultural particularity of the Antillean world, the study considers four major questions that people from the region can hardly fail to pose to others and to themselves: What literature and thought can come from a civilization that is aware of its catastrophic beginning? What makes the conceptual paradigms fashioned by the Western intellectual industry capable of illuminating the distinct experience of Antilleans but not vice versa? Do Antilleans lack the conceptual resources required for the interpretation of culture, theirs as well as others'? Why cannot the specificity of Caribbean humanity accroach the paradigmatic flair to exemplify the drama of the entire species?

With the foregoing questions at the core, *An Intellectual History of the Caribbean* attempts an account of thought production that is unaffiliated to the chronicles of ideas that ascribe a Hegelian structure to the movement of the mind. Instead, I pursue here an archeology of the ideas to which events that have happened in the region have given rise from the conquest in 1492 to the contemporary moment. The ideas that come to the fore in this book occur in the wake of a human chronicle that opens with the conquest and the colonial transaction, going through successive stages of domination, insurrection, resistance, adaptation, and nation building. Similarly, the narrative of subject positions that this book ventures to offer is framed by a sociohistorical sequence wherein social actors appear enmeshed in processes marked by succeeding engagements with Empire and foreign domination. These go from anticolonial rebellion, negotiation with prevailing regimes in the native land as well as the pertinent metropolis, advocacy for independence or semiautonomous governance, national replication of former colonial structures, to culminate in the present stage of pervasive economic decline, with the attendant diasporic uprooting that has increasingly widened the contours of the Antillean world through the rise of enclaves in urban centers of Europe and the United States.

Among the topics that invariably surface in this interpretive history of thought and events, I set out to explore questions of national or regional identity, cultural self-assertiveness, the problematic legacy of the mulatto ruling elite, the angst caused by the region's asymmetrical exchange with the global capitalist order to which it is linked, the failure of national development projects, the persistence of liberatory ideals, the growing economic and political dependence on Western powers, the unabated brain drain that expels human capital to foreign shores, and the enduring desire to imagine a promissory future. On the whole, one can read *An Intellectual History of the Caribbean* as an effort to articulate a new "theory" of Caribbean history, culture, and destiny. However, this book endeavors to probe the very notion of "theory" on account of the problematic rapport the theoretical has had with the Caribbean region and its people.

The book begins with an "Introduction" whose first section defines the Caribbean geographically, historically, and culturally, showing the region's unity in ecosystems, in geology, and in shared legacies of domination. The Caribbean, center of the modern world, witnessed the clash of the imperial ambitions of Western colonial powers and the cruelty of slavery and other coerced labor, but, that bitter history notwithstanding, therein emerged a cluster of societies that, though holding a marginal place in the structure of power in the world, exhibit all the greatness and the pettiness of humanity. Assessing the contemporary moment, the second section of the "Introduction" examines the widespread tendency among cultural critics to celebrate the Caribbean musical achievements, inviting reflection on the implications of that emphasis and the possibility that it might reflect a loss of faith in the region's ability to come out of its present political and economic cul-de-sac.

The remainder of the book consists of three major parts and an "Epilogue." Chapter 1, "Colonial Migration and Theoric Awakening," artic- ulates the author's approach to the study of the region by upholding the claim that Caribbean intellects cannot help but speak for themselves when analyzing their world. It advocates a stance of intellectual self-affirmation for the Antillean person, and, by drawing largely from intellectual and sociopo- litical autobiography, it announces the "theoretical" approach that dominates the rest of the book. Chapter 2, "The Endless History: the Caribbean versus Western Discourse," surveys representations of the Caribbean and its people from Columbus in 1492 to the French encyclopedists to postcolonial critics at the end of the twentieth century, showing the devalued otherness to which Western authors have subjected the region's inhabitants. This part of the book highlights the extent to which Caribbean discourse can be understood as a compilation of the varied responses that writers and thinkers from the region have articulated in response to the discursive denormalization and defamation perpetrated by the West, not excluding, of course, the number of authors of Caribbean origin (Naipaul et al.) or from whom Antilleans might expect a natural allegiance (Frederick Douglass et al.) who have echoed Western deprecation in their appraisals of the region. An evocation of the region's catastrophic history and the indigenous efforts to understand the logic of the human experience there is also included, along with an evaluation of the uncritical application of "postcolonial" paradigms to Caribbean life.

Chapter 3, "Caliban's Dilemma: Disabling Memory and Possible Hope," travels through the region's literature and historical events to find the failure of Caribbean leaders (from aboriginal warrior Enriquillo in the early sixteenth century, to black Maroons in the eighteenth and nineteenth centuries to late twentieth-century statesmen) and the people's continued adherence to the sanitized memory of heroes. Using the figure of Caliban as a cultural and political metaphor, this part of the book tells the story of the hero's miscon- duct and concludes by proposing ways in which the historical imagination in the region, aided by new approaches to the past and the lessons of several generations of emigrants, can reinvent itself and thereby contribute to the rehabilitation of Caliban. Finally, the closing pages, "Epilogue: A Century of Caribbean Diaspora," maps the location of the Caribbean diaspora in North America, England, Holland, France, and Spain, considering the ways in which émigré communities may have championed a refashioning of the relationship between the Caribbean and the West at the cultural and political level. It considers the ambiguous position of U.S.- and European-bred Antilleans who can now wield the power to redraw the image of the Caribbean from the very center of the West. It looks at the works and the interventions of several such figures to construe a hypothesis regarding what to expect as the new century progresses.

Introduction: Caribbean Unity
in Nature, History, and Prospects

I
The Name and the Mystery

The narrator of Agatha Christie's thriller *A Caribbean Mystery* refers to the West Indian setting of the story as somewhere where everything stayed "the same every day—never anything *happening*" (1964:12). The remark, said in passing, presupposes the existence of a body of opinion about the region that the author assumes will resonate with her audience. The sense of that locale, where Miss Marple has gone on vacation to recover from a bout of pneumonia, as a peculiar spot where reality has an odd texture of its own contributes, no doubt, to the dramatic tension of the plot as the octogenarian detective investigates the murder of Major Palgrave.

At the end of 1936, intrigued by the zoological peculiarity of the Caribbean, zoologist Ivan T. Sanderson went to investigate the region's fauna, concentrating on Trinidad, Curaçao, Haiti, and Surinam. An altogether favorable observer of the area, enthralled by all the shapes life took there, Sanderson narrated his excursion for the benefit of readers in the outside world with utmost enthusiasm, beginning with an evocation of the Trinidadian hunter who served as his guide: "Vernon Dixon Capriata, whose ancestry included English, French, Spanish, Negro and, I am sure, some Carib stock. I can safely say that his personality radiated the better qualities of each" (Sanderson 1965:14). As he recounts his perusal of the richness and variety of nature's creatures in the region, Sanderson evinces an awareness of speaking about a world of mystery. Relating the *historia animalium* of this world of mystery, the author does not assume his reader's certainty even about the region's geographical name. He therefore explains:

> The word "Caribbean" is fraught with as much difficulty as the word "jungle." It has many different meanings among various people. Caribbean lands are properly the countries of the Carib Indians, whose original home was the Guianas, whence they spread to Trinidad and over most of the islands of the West Indies. Nowadays, the Caribbean has become synonymous with the West Indies; among which neither the Guianas nor even Trinidad rightly belongs though both are included in the West Indian political provinces of the English, Dutch, and French. (17–18)

He predicates his explanation on subjective perception as he indicates that the "Caribbean" seemed to him the only appropriate word to describe the lands of his journey, further stressing his predilection by noting the "considerable beauty and significance" of the word (18). A British visitor writing for Western readers, Sanderson, his genuine affection for the Caribbean notwithstanding, contributed to the aura of mystery attributed to the region by construing its name as a matter of preference rather than as a mere cartographical fact that one simply looks up the way one would the Balkans or the Carpathians.

But the Caribbean, which in this book we also refer to interchangeably as Antilles and West Indies, does have a determinate geography. It consists of an archipelago shooting out of the Gulf of Mexico plus the coastal regions of South America, "from Colombia to the Guyanas and the riverine zones of Central America, in so far as those parts of the mainland were the homes of people engaged from time to time in activities which linked their lives with those of the people of the islands" as defined by Federico Mayor, former director-general of UNESCO (Mayor 2003:vi). While encompassing a larger geography, Mayor's way of mapping the region resembles the "third" of the definitions outlined by Andrés Serbin in its emphasis on region, common ethno-historical elements, and shared aspirations although it need not accept the formulation of what Serbin dismisses as a "persistent Afro-Caribbean bias" (Serbin 1990:7–8). The Caribbean consists of numerous insular and continental territories that are ecologically, geologically, and historically interlinked.

THE PHYSICAL ENVIRONMENT

Examining the complex flora and fauna that greeted the first settlers in the Caribbean, Puerto Rican geographer Francisco Watlington adduces paleographic and archeological evidence to provide a panoramic vista of the physical environment in the region's prehistory. Though focusing on the Greater Antilles as the core of his inquiry, his work reveals the Caribbean region as the hub of diverse geographical "teleconnections between the surrounding islands and mainlands, and with other regions near and far" (Watlington 2003:30). Noting the region's "botanical linkages," the author observes that "the original pre-human flora of the Greater Antilles accrued over many millennia from adventitious seeds and other propagules translocated by birds, bats, winds, and ocean currents. Most plants came from tropical South and Central America, but a good number arrived from Africa and North America," and he speculates that "the translocation of maize mosaic virus and its vector insect from the Greater Antilles by a hurricane" may have been "a major reason for the collapse of Classic Maya civilization" (Watlinton 71–72, 84). Showing that the Caribbean, like the rest of the planet, underwent drastic physical transformation, as "glacially-driven climatic cycles mediated an ever-changing landscape," he stresses the "highly seasonal climate" that characterized the region during the Pleistocene: "Lowland winters were as cool as in the present United States sunbelt along Latitude 30°N. The central mountain ranges from each island had even cooler temperatures, declining progressively with altitude. Snow fields, glaciers and treeless paramos capped the higher peeks and ridgelands" (Watlinton 72).

The physical environment and the way nature behaves in the Caribbean recur even in social science and humanistic observations of life in the area. Michel Devèze, a historian of French colonization in the Americas, stipulated the specificity of the Caribbean world by saying: "The Caribbean space has lived a life of its own, just as the Caribbean Mediterranean harbors cyclones of its own" (Devèze 1977:9). By the same token, in evoking a sociohistorical background for her reading of texts by Haitian novelist Jacques Stephen Alexis and Cuban fiction writer Alejo Carpentier, literary critic Michaelle Ascencio proposes this formulation:

The history of the Antilles, of Haiti, Cuba, Jamaica, Barbados, and of the majority of the islands, shows how the Antillean people, how the men and women of the Caribbean have had to endure two ills of very different sorts, one natural and the other social, which have caused great ruin, misery and destruction: hurricanes and sugar. (Ascencio 1990:117)

The awareness of a certain intensity to the Caribbean as a material place, with ecological and tellurian manifestations that have an inescapable impact on people's lives, makes it appropriate for a short history of the area by Oruno D. Lara, a native of Guadeloupe, to begin with an account of the substratum space of its oceanography and geodynamics. Lara explains that the general east-west orientation of atmospheric movements in the tropics explains the decisive role played by the Atlantic Ocean, the Mediterranean, and the two continental American masses in the Caribbean climate: "The Atlantic has a pronounced bearing due to its dimension and the temperature of its warm waters (20°C average) on the surface. The winds may then get up speed along a distance of over 6000 kms from the Canaries to the Caribbean" (Lara 2000:23).

A site of atmospheric confluence in the tropical latitudes, the Caribbean becomes every year, from June through November, a runway for the hurricanes associated with the torrid belts of the Equator (24). With winds that have often reached up to 230 miles per hour, a speed they maintain for several minutes, hurricanes originating in the Caribbean devastate the islands, enter the Gulf of Mexico, pick up strength in the Yucatan peninsula, in the Gulf of Campeche, and then head toward the coasts of the United States to extend their paths of destruction (25). On the way back from his first voyage in February 1493 Christopher Columbus felt the violent lashing of the waves in a hurricane. Another hurricane in May 1609, in the vicinity of the Bermudas, caused the shipwreck of George Sommers, a founding settler of the colony of Virginia, and gave William Shakespeare ideas for the plot of his last play, *The Tempest* (1610). Storm tides and millions of tons of water submerged the Tortugas islands in 1757. Setting the ambience of the story of his confederate soldiers who escape on a balloon from Richmond, Virginia, to find themselves in the midst of a storm that hurls them to an island in the Pacific, Jules Verne's *The Mysterious Island*, offers this description of the natural event: "It surpassed in disasters those which so frightfully ravaged Havana and Guadeloupe, one on the 25th of October, 1810, the other on the 26th of July, 1825" (Verne 1965:9). Puerto Rico suffered a similar fortune in 1899 and the cyclone of 1932 destroyed the city of Santa Cruz del Sur in Cuba (Lara 2000:26–27). As these very few examples mean to suggest, cyclonic disasters constitute a pervasive source of stress in the Caribbean region.

The May 8, 1908 volcanic eruption of Mount Pelee, which destroyed the city of Saint Pierre, Martinique, leaving a toll of nearly 3,000 human casualties, stands out for its magnitude. But active and dormant volcanoes proliferate in the region, with those in Grenada, Saint Vincent, Saint Lucia, Martinique, Montserrat, Saint Kitts, Nevis, Saba, and Saint Eustatius showing the most frequent activity (Lara 2000:37). La Soufrière in Basse-Terre, Guadeloupe, had a prolonged phreatic eruption in 1976 with a series of 26 major explosions through the beginning of 1977, causing the evacuation of 7,500 people. The event provided the thematic frame for Daniel Maximin's 1987 novel *Soufrières*, which dramatizes the state of mind of several Guadaloupeans as they await the volcano's eruption. Saint Vincent's volcano has the same name as that of Guadeloupe, and a modified version, Soufriere Hills, is the name of the one in Montserrat. This geological feature is connected to the peculiarity of tectonic activity in the Caribbean plate, which has, since middle Eocene time, "moved generally eastward relative to both North and South America, with active arc volcanism occurring in the Lesser Antilles in response to west-dipping subduction of Atlantic oceanic lithosphere of the North America plate" (Dolan, Mullins, and Wald 1998:2). Geologists studying the region have pointed to a number of notable events, including the collision of the southeast Bahamas banks with "the island of Hispaniola since the late Miocene and the large earthquake shocks that have castigated the Caribbean over the years" (Mullins et al. 1992:205–206). They have also focused on the three major zones of seismicity identified by specialists in the north-central Caribbean (Dolan, Mullins, and Wald 1998:39). They have sought to explain how and why Hispaniola separated from Cuba, moving east, while Cuba remained welded to the North America plate and why Puerto Rico split apart from Hispaniola, opening the Mona Passage as result, in order to understand "the strike slip dismemberment of the Greater Antilles island arc and the present morphology of Cuba, Hispaniola, and Puerto Rico" (56).

The August 4, 1946 earthquake that ruptured a 195-km-long section of the plate boundary beneath northeastern Hispaniola is only a highlight in a seismic history that has often terrified the inhabitants of the Caribbean. On this island alone history records, in a series of devastating earthquakes, the one that destroyed Santiago and La Vega on December 2, 1562, the one on October 18, 1751 that wrought havoc in Azua and damaged parts of Santo Domingo, and the one on May 7, 1842, which devastated Santiago on the Dominican side and Cap Haitien on the Haitian side, leaving a death toll of 5,000 people (Moya Pons 2004:70). The Septentrional fault system, showing activity whose most recent rupture dates back to approximately 800 years ago, "extends from the Windward Passage between Hispaniola and Cuba, through the northern part of Hispaniola and offshore eastward to the north of Puerto Rico" (Dolan, Mullins, and Wald 1998:3). Knowledgeable observers of active tectonics especially of Hispaniola, where the Septentrional fault appears to exceed California's San Andreas fault in imminent danger, have encouraged the authorities to take precautionary measures in preparation for a grave seismic event. In January 1999, 73 researchers from different parts of the world convened in Puerto Plata to assess the risks presented by the Septentrional fault, and after a week of field work they resolved to write an urgent letter to then President Leonel Fernández alerting him to the danger (Ortiz 2001).

As these comments on hurricanes, volcanoes, and earthquakes should suggest, nature occurs in the Caribbean in a particularly compelling way as the morphology of the environment has a direct impact on the material well-being and the daily existence of people. To be safe from indifferent nature in the sanctity of their home in an urban low-income neighborhood or in a rural agricultural village, families need to have houses that can withstand the onslaught of torrential rains, cyclonic winds, and a turbulent ground. And it does not take superior insight to guess that the resources required to ensure one's safety against such powerful forces would most likely be outside the reach of the economically disempowered, who make up the majority of the people inhabiting the Caribbean territories. The victims of the flood that hit the Haitian–Dominican border town of Jimani in the wee hours of morning on May 24, 2004 experienced their disempowerment as a fell blow. Estimates taken 2 days after the flood placed the death toll above 860 people with several hundreds still missing. By day three, the Dominican authorities, who felt they could not wait for the victims to be identified by relatives, proceeded to bury in mass graves the badly decomposed bodies because of the health risks they posed. Some survivors did not have a chance to identify their dead. And some probably wished they had not seen them, as must have been the case with 28-year-old Leonardo Novas, who had to watch helplessly "as his brother and his family were carried away in a crushing torrent of mud" (Prengaman 2004:11). One can thus understand why commentators on the Caribbean, even when approaching the region from the perspectives of the social sciences and the humanities rather than earth sciences, should deem it appropriate to incorporate the physical environment in their reflections.

CONQUEST AND DOMINATION

But, to return to the name of the region, the word Caribbean, which today designates a sea, a cluster of populations, and the region that envelopes them, has its root in the language used by Christopher Columbus, the Admiral of the Ocean Sea, in the logbook wherein he recorded the details of this eventful arrival in the lands that for him constituted a "new world." He makes first mention of the term "Caribes" in the log entry for December 26, 1492 in a passage where he describes a conversation he has had with an aboriginal king he has befriended on the island that he renamed "Española." Seeing that Columbus and his crew had had a rough time at sea, the king offered him protection and compassion: "He, with all the people in his village, wept a great deal. They are an affectionate people, free from avarice and agreeable to everything. I certify to your highness that in all the world I do not believe there is a better people or a better country" (Columbus 1987:153). After having their energies replenished by plentiful food and cordiality, Columbus and his men learn that the villagers, who neither possess nor have knowledge of arms, have a feared enemy "whom they call the *Caribes*, who come to seize them and who carry bows and arrows without iron tips," at which point the Admiral promises the hospitable king to see about "the destruction of the Caribes" (154).

The arrival of Columbus, armed with weaponry whose power of destruction the native inhabitants of the Caribbean had not seen the like, and the subsequent domination of the aboriginal population, both the docile and the warlike portions of it, radically transformed the nature of life there. Captivity and coerced labor became the order of the day for the natives, whose numbers dwindled rapidly due to the debilitating impact of their extreme exploitation. The indigenous population decimated and the gold and precious substances that had fueled the greed of the invaders already exhausted, the mineral economy that the original Spanish settlers had developed suffered a serious downturn. Then, as the conquerors had ascertained the fertility of the soil, the biodiversity of the environment, and the value of a coerced labor force that still survived, agriculture supplanted mining. Thus emerged the plantation. The farming of coffee, cocoa, and sugar soon became the principal industry of the colonial economy and brought about the importation of enslaved African workers, ushering in a successful slave-based enterprise that for centuries would enrich the colonial powers of the West while it reduced African nations and the native inhabitants of the Americas to a bleak state of helplessness.

The economic success of the Spanish colonial experiment in the Caribbean as well as North and South America soon awakened the entrepreneurial appetites of Holland, France, and England, unleashing a process of fierce inter-imperial competition among the European nations that boasted naval power. Progressively, Spanish hegemony in the newly conquered lands broke down as Spain's imperial competitors asserted their presence. The Caribbean became the stage chosen by the various colonial expansionist projects of Europe to dramatize their head-on confrontations, crafty encroachments, or expedient alliances. To describe that peculiar political location of the region, as an arena of overseas imperial strife, the Dominican writer and statesman Juan Bosch coined the apt phrase "imperial frontier" (Bosch 1970). In mid-April 1655, a British invasion of Santo Domingo led by William Penn, whose son would subsequently spearhead the colonization of Pennsylvania, and Robert Venables proved unsuccessful. The campaign was part of an initiative known as "the Western design" advanced by the government of Oliver Cromwell, Lord Protector of England, who decided to seize the opportunity made evident to him by the assessment of Thomas Gage, a former

Dominican priest whose 1654 book *A New Survey of the West Indies* established that Spain's Caribbean possessions lay defenseless. For want of a formal pretext to wage war against Spanish possessions, the Lord Protector inaugurated the hostilities in a document drafted by the poet John Milton under the title "Scriptum domini protectoris contra hispanos" (Morales Padrón 1952:318–319).

In launching the expedition that would materialize the "Western design," the English set their eyes firmly on Española or Cuba as primary targets, although a minority opinion insisted on Trinidad or the area around the mouth of the Orinoco River (Morales Padrón 1952:320–321). Penn and Venables, commanding a force of nearly 9,000 soldiers, arrived in Santo Domingo, but the defensive put forth by the Spanish govenor, Don Bernardino de Meneses Bracamonte y Zapata, count of Peñalba, proved formidable. After three weeks of suffering losses in battle, coupled by fatigue, hunger, and disease, the expedition's officers, gathered in a "Council of War," voted to desist from the attempt to capture Hispaniola, an outcome that General Venables attributed largely to the "mischief" and "cowardice of our men" (Venables 1900:30). As they resolved to withdraw from the island, they agreed "to attempt Jamaica in the next place," another of Spain's nearby possessions that had been the scene of Columbus's longest residence in the West Indies, in 1503–1504 (Venables 1900:31; Cundall and Pietersz 1919:1). Thus began the English colonization of Jamaica, which in time would become an economic center of the British Empire. Successfully expelling the Spanish and developing the plantation economy to its maximum degree through the intensive use of enslaved African labor, the English domination of Jamaica marked a moment of reconfiguration of the balance of power in the Caribbean.

Soon Spain would see its Caribbean domains diminished, retaining only Cuba, Puerto Rico, and Santo Domingo. France would take hold of Guadeloupe, Guiana, Martinique, and the western third of the island of Hispaniola known by the name of Saint Domingue. Aruba, Bonaire, Curaçao, St. Eustatius, Saba, and Surinam would go into the imperial hands of Holland, in addition to a half of St. Maarten, the other half claimed by France. Great Britain would take hold of by far the largest number of territories, running the alphabetical gamut from Anguilla and Antigua to Turks/Caicos and the Virgin Islands. Divided into distinct spheres of colonial domination, Caribbean societies, "as traditionless and artificial new creations on depopulated land, were the most radical sociotechnical experiment of the age" (Osterhammel 1997:31). The rise of the plantation as the region's dominant industry triggered a remarkable demographic phenomenon and turned the Caribbean into "the historical center of colonialism" from the middle of the seventeenth through the end of the eighteenth centuries (31). By 1700 some 450,000 captive Africans had entered the non-Spanish West Indian territories, and by the end of the eighteenth century the number of enslaved Africans coming to British, French, and Dutch Caribbean territories had soared to some 3,300,000 (31). In the eighteenth century Jamaica stood out as England's most profitable overseas possession, just as Saint Domingue held the same status for the French. By the end of the nineteenth century historian James Anthony Froude would feel moved to reminisce that time when "the West Indian colonies" had earned recognition "as precious jewels, which hundreds of thousands of English lives had been sacrificed to tear from France and Spain. The Caribbean Sea was the cradle of the Naval Empire of Great Britain" (Froude 1888:9). He refers to the time when, thanks to the wealth and power exacted from its Caribbean operations, Britain, through the notorious East India Company, succeeded in redefining its relationship with India. The British in India had pursued "no plans to conquer and certainly no plans to prosel-tyze," limiting themselves to conducting trade from port cities through local political heads (the Nabob or regional prince of Bengal), but by 1755, faced with the reticence of indigenous authority, Company boss Robert Clive could feel confident enough to declare "We must become the Nabobs our-selves," announcing a shift to a new policy of colonial subjugation that would last until the mid-twentieth century (Osterhammel 1997:32).

The Caribbean, as these details show, matters enormously to an under-standing of the modern world, the global outcome of the colonial transac-tion. At the same time, the complex processes and the intricate dynamics that have partaken historically in the formation of societies there have rendered the understanding of the Caribbean itself a challenging task. Split into several distinct colonial domains—with the same territory at times changing colonial hands more than once—the region has housed all the races, religions, cul-tures, and desires of the globe. The colonial transaction broke this part of the world into imperial blocs and caused the various societies there to look in the direction of different metropolises abroad. Linguistically and politically the Caribbean comes from a history of fragmentation. Most societies in the region today exist as independent nations, but some territories remain colo-nially attached to foreign polities. Nor does it appear that the sovereign Caribbean states have succeeded in securing the material well-being of their populations to the point of making the ideal of national independence particularly appealing to the societies that have yet to achieve sovereignty. A collection of essays on the "non-independent Caribbean" edited by Puerto Rican scholars Aaron Gamaliel Ramos and Angel Israel Rivera (2001) provides a substantial exploration of this political predicament.

The Cultural Geography

The Caribbean is a geography, a differentiated culture area, and a scenario wherein the human experience has displayed distinct characteristics. Geographically speaking, the term encompasses the islands of the Antillean archipelago, including the Bermudas, as Lara would posit (Lara 2000:24)—the continental territories of Belize, Guyana, Guiana, and Suriname, and the Atlantic coastal areas of such Central and South American nations as Honduras, Nicaragua, Panama, Colombia, and Venezuela. Some of the continental countries in the region herein mapped are linked to the cultural geography of the Caribbean not only through the nexus between their Atlantic coastal lands and the sociohistorical events that shaped the structure of life in the area but also through the mobility of migrants from the islands to the continent. Labor migration from Jamaica, Barbados, and other British West Indian islands at the turn of the twentieth century, for instance, accounts for an ethnically differentiated settlement that emerged in the Costa Rican province of Limón (Harpelle 2001:184). Ronald D. Harpelle has studied their origins, development, and vicissitudes in *The West Indians of Costa Rica* (2001). Similarly, focusing on Costa Rican fiction writer Quince Duncan as well as on Panamanian authors Carlos "Cubena" Guillermo Wilson and Gerardo Maloney, literary scholar Ian Smart has usefully outlined the growing body of Spanish-language Central American writings that show unmistakable linkages to the literature of the English-speaking islands, an affinity evidently stemming from the history of West Indian migration to the continent (Smart 1984).

Colombia comes particularly to mind as a useful example to illustrate a country where the sociocultural texture of its Caribbean portion stands out for its marked contrast to the modalities of its Pacific and Andean areas. The latter not only predominate in the country's overall geography, but they have conventionally provided the cultural and social models for conceptual constructions of the Colombian nation. The historian Alfonso Múnera Cavadía's *El fracaso de la nación* (1998) has engagingly examined the ideological stumbling block that the sociocultural difference of Colombia's Caribbean coast posed to the discourse of the patricians who in the nineteenth century set out to define the nation. That the linkages of Colombia with the Caribbean transcends even the country's own Atlantic coast is suggested by the commerce of the Cauca and the Chocó regions with Jamaica and Cuba, apart from Cartagena, as we gather from *María*, the 1867 novel by Jorge Isaacs. Set in the first half of the nineteenth century, the story of this classic Latin American novel links Colombia's non coastal region with the Caribbean not only through the sugar plantation network and the traffic of African slaves but also through the Jamaican birth of María, the beautiful daughter of Jewish parents whose life, evoked by the first-person narrator, forms the core of the text (Isaacs 2001:18, 165).* As to the Colombian territories actually located on the Atlantic coast, such as Cartagena and Barranquilla, cultural life there and the declaration of local authorities exhibit an adamant self-assertion of Caribbean identity unequaled by the cultural discourses coming out of some of the most central islands of the Caribbean archipelago.

Perhaps even more remarkable, the State of Quintana Roo, on the Yucatan Peninsula region of Mexico, at the start of the twenty-first century, during the administration of Governor Joaquín E. Hendricks Díaz, moved to

---

* I owe this point to my privileged access to Alfonso Múnera Cavadía's unpublished work on the Caribbean background to the story of María in the novel by Isaacs.

emphasize the region's Caribbeanness by organizing an impressive yearly competition called "Prizes of Caribbean Thought" to "promote knowledge and research on the politics, economy, history, culture, environment, and anthropology" of the region, contending that, as the language of the promotional brochure says, "Caribbean nations share the same sea, which, in good measure, has determined our economic, commercial, and cultural development," and declaring the need for "the countries forming part of this region" to search jointly "for new means of integration, in order to find common solutions to the problems they share." The competition invited essay submissions in six areas of knowledge, awarded the winners in each category the generous sum of $20,000 dollars, and published the winning manuscripts in attractive editions issued by Siglo XX Editores. That such a purposeful initiative of Caribbean self-affirmation should come from an area of Yucatan where Maya heritage abounds in the phenotype of the native population, the ancient architecture and the survival of the Mayan language can perhaps be justified best by pointing to the ecosystemic affinity of the Peninsula with the physical environment of the islands shooting out of the Gulf of Mexico. Nor does the area lack historical ties to the more central Caribbean societies. Suffice it to mention the thousands upon thousands of enslaved Maya Indians who were sold to work on Cuban and other Caribbean plantations alongside their African counterparts.

Naturally, the preceding pages have stressed an understanding of the Caribbean as a region concretely located in a distinct geography, but we must also consider the human bridges that interminably stretch the expanse of the region. Miami, a city on the southern United States, lies at a distance of only 90 miles away from Cuba, close enough to share its tropical ecology. Compounding that geographical fact, the difficult rapport of U.S.–Cuban relations since the triumph of the Revolution in 1959 has led to a migratory flow, occurring in several stages, which has made Cubans the dominant ethnic presence in that city. As a result, at the beginning of the twenty-first century it is more that just metaphorically that one can speak of Miami as a Cuban city. Similarly, the city of New York houses so many millions of Jamaicans, Dominicans, Haitians, and Puerto Ricans, for instance, that one can conceivably think of it as the largest of all Caribbean cities. Consistent with the numerous emigration waves that have afflicted the region from colonial days to the contemporary moment, West Indian people have established settlements in various cities of Spain, England, Holland, France, and other European societies as well as in the United States and several countries of Latin America.

When speaking of the geography of the Caribbean experience, we can hardly afford to circumscribe our diction to the literal denotation of the term or to limit the scope of our utterance to the strictly tellurian geography. The myriad flights of population that have characterized the Caribbean experience have culminated in the cultural and existential expansion of the sending world over several centuries. West Indians made up a substantial portion of the black community that emerged from 1730 onward in Liverpool, where today some black Liverpudlians can trace their roots in that city "for as many as ten generations" (Costello 2001:8). Elsewhere in England and much later in time, namely London in the mid-twentieth century, people from the British Caribbean made up an ethnic enclave so aware of its cultural apartness that Samuel Selvon could venture to imagine them as part of an insulated urban cosmos in *The Lonely Londoners* (1956). In short, a vast and growing diaspora has widened the cultural geography of the Caribbean to encompass key sites in Europe, the United States, and Latin America. To fathom the Caribbean, then, one has to train one's eyes on three primary spaces: the insular, the continental, and the diasporic, and none today can be dispensed with in a serious attempt to understand holistically the cluster of societies involved.

Forging the Modern World Imperially

As the foregoing ought to suggest, the study of the Caribbean world constitutes a challenging task. Knowledge of a region with such a vast, fractious, checkered history can hardly come easily. The subject at hand includes the distinct national or societal stories of the numerous sites from Anguilla to the Virgin Islands with their intricate internal episodes and their inescapable interlacing with other societies in the region. Every society there, in turn, has dealt in complex ways with two or more Western colonial powers. Knowing the region, then, will of necessity require an understanding of the decisive impact it may have had on events that other parts of the world experienced as crucial. The English colonies of the West Indies, as the Trinidadian statesman and historian Eric Williams argued, played a key role in bringing about the economic advantage that enabled Britain to lead the Industrial Revolution. Before that, as Froude would reminisce, "the golden stream" that flowed from the region "into the exchequer at Madrid" had furnished the Spanish monarch Philip "with the means to carry on his war with the Reformation" (Froude 1888:10). Similarly, the French Empire would most likely not have had to cede the fertile lands of Louisiana to the burgeoning power of the United States in 1803, had Napoleon's government not needed to concentrate enormous military resources in seeking to quell the resolute insurrection of the slaves of Saint Domingue on the western part of Hispaniola. The 40,000 French soldiers that General Leclerc, the consul's brother-in-law, led into the island had little precedent in overseas military expeditions. When Leclerc's army failed to reduce the insurgents despite the ploy that led to Toussaint's capture, Napoleon lost heart and resorted to cutting his "Caribbean losses" by selling Louisiana to President Thomas Jefferson (Wills 2003:114). A curiously interlaced Caribbean story recalled by Alejo Carpentier is that Josephine de Beauharnais, the wife of Napoleon, was born in Martinique and may have been conceived in Guadeloupe (Carpentier 1999:152–153).

The case of Saint Domingue illustrates also the extent to which the West Indies have influenced the texture of the relationship amongst the world powers themselves. The region has through the centuries been rhyzomatically interlinked with worlds elsewhere. To understand it one must attempt to pin down those linkages. When in the eighteenth century, for instance, the Dutch asserted themselves in New Amsterdam, the city that would subsequently become New York when the British wrest the baton from them, they owed the solidity of their imperial might to the successful outcomes of their Antillean possessions. Witness the prominence of Pieter Stuyvesant in the government of Holland's enterprises in North America as well as the Caribbean. Similarly, one could see that fluctuations of power relations among the European colonial nations in the Caribbean were mediated by the clashes, conflicts, and collaborations marking their interactions in Europe. For example, the treaty of Ryswick of 1697 signed among several European powers to resolve conflicts on the continent made no mention of the island of Hispaniola, but people there appealed to the terms of the accord to settle their own border disputes in what by then had become a shared colonial domain, with the Spanish retaining Santo Domingo in the east and the French holding Saint Domingue in the west. The partition of the island into two distinct colonies actually dates back to the early 1600s when Dutch traders, spurred by Prince Maurits, developed a thriving illicit commerce with the people of Santo Domingo, to the dismay of the Spanish authorities whose repeated attempts to thwart the resident's trade with Spain's political and religious enemies proved ineffective, causing them to resort to the drastic measure of forcibly evacuating the people living in the northern coastal area and burning down their cities. In 1605, when Spain depopulated western Hispaniola, Prince Maurits ordered a fleet of 16 ships to offer assistance to the residents of the affected lands in exchange for their "abjuration of the King of Spain and the renunciation of their Roman Catholic faith" (Klooster 1997:8).

The nations that directed the colonial transaction remained invariably alert concerning the actions, initiatives, successes, and failures of their imperial competitors in the Caribbean. The corsair and English Renaissance poet Walter Raleigh wrote in 1595 to Queen Elizabeth I to request authorization for the conquest of Guyana, emphatically urging her to see herself in the mirror that the king of Spain presented. The Spanish monarch, he argued, went from being a nobody to parading himself as the greatest prince of Europe simply because he had wisely taken advantage of the riches of these Indies. Such opportunities, Raleigh insisted, now presented themselves to her majesty the Queen. Privateers and slave-traders John Hawkins and his cousin Francis Drake had preceded Raleigh in spearheading the project to plunder Spanish possessions, and in so doing "had opened up broad prospects for England in the Caribbean" (Churchill, II, 1990:164). Since Elizabethan days, the memorable Winston Churchill tells us, the English

had tried to get a foothold in the Spanish West Indies. In 1623, on his way back from his fruitless expedition to Guiana, a Suffolk gentleman named Thomas Warner explored one of the less inhabited West Indian islands. He deposited a few colonists on St. Christopher, and hurried home to get a royal patent for a more extensive enterprise. This achieved, he returned to the Caribbean, and though much harassed by Spanish raids, he established the English in the disputed sea. By the 1640s Barbados, St. Christopher, Nevis, Montserrat, and Antigua were in English hands and several thousands arrived. Sugar assured their prosperity, and the Spanish grip on the West Indies was shaken. (Churchill, II 1990:176)

Examples abound of the clashes and tensions among Western nations and their convergence in the Caribbean. England, Spain, and France all had a stake in the events that culminated in the Haitian Revolution and the emergence of Haiti as a sovereign republic in 1804. During the second half of the nineteenth century, France, England, and Spain competed with the United States for control of Samana Bay in the Dominican Republic. Holland and France wrestled fiercely for hegemony over the diminutive territory of Saint Martin, ultimately settling for a partition of the island into two colonial halves, Dutch Sint Maarten and French Saint Martin. The Caribbean served as the principal arena for the Spanish–American War of 1898 in so far as the conflict revolved around Cuba, with Puerto Rico coming in as a welcome war booty. The outcome ushered in a refashioned world order that would give the United States a leading role in the affairs of the planet. During the 1930s, American historian Charles M. Andrews integrated the Caribbean in his study of the mainland North American colonies that subsequently became the United States on the grounds that from the seventeenth century onward we cannot understand "the constitutional and commercial developments of the English colonies in America" apart from the history of Barbados, the Leeward Islands, and Jamaica since those settlements "formed part of a single Atlantic world" (Andrews 1934–1938 II: 271, cited in Brereton 1999: 315). The agreement on October 30th, 1946 to establish the Caribbean Commission by the governments of France, the Kingdom of the Netherlands, the United Kingdom, and the United States was signed in Washington D.C., and U.S. leadership in the whole accord seemed easily discerned. A consultative and advisory body created to promote the well-being of the territories of the countries associated with the member governments and concerning itself with matters of common interest in the area, the Caribbean Commission came about as an expansion of the Anglo-American Caribbean Commission created on March 9, 1942 to mediate the interests of the two world powers at a time when U.S. influence had penetrated even British West Indian colonies. In mid-twentieth century, with Soviet-supported socialist Cuba at one end and the U.S.-ruled Free Associated State of Puerto Rico serving as its counterbalance, the Caribbean again occupied the proscenium of history during the period known as the Cold War. One could muse that when Soviet Prime Minister Nikita Krushev ordered the withdrawal of missiles from Cuba in 1961, giving in to U.S. pressure, his action prefigured the fall of the Berlin Wall, announcing the subsequent decline of the Soviet bloc and the rise of the United States as the political champion of the global society.

The Languages and Cultures

From the foregoing discussion stressing the interconnection of the Caribbean with other nations of the planet, it follows that studying the region to some extent involves also examining the other parts of the globe with which it is geopolitically linked. Therein lies a primary difficulty of knowing the Caribbean world, a difficulty made less manageable by the numerous languages spoken there. Indigenous languages survive in Belize, where a portion of the population speaks Maya or Yucatec, another speaks Kekchi, also of Mayan family, and a third speaks Black Carib, a language of the Arawakan family. Maya and Black Carib remain vital in Guatemala, and Maya boasts nearly a million speakers in Mexico's Yucatan Peninsula. Some 100,000 natives of the Guajira Peninsula on the Caribbean coast of Colombia speak Goajiro, a language of the Arawakan family. Some 75,000 natives speak Black Carib while over 10,000 speak Miskito in Honduras, and some 200,000 speak Guaymi and Cuna in Panamá. Carib, Guajiro, Warao, and Piaroa survive with nearly 150,000 speakers in Venezuela. Small communities of Carib and Arawak speakers thrive in Surinam, and the aboriginal culture of Arawak-speaking natives of Guyana has marked the worldview of Guyanese novelist Wilson Harris, one of the few prominent literary figures from the Caribbean who has overtly drawn from the language and the thought of the indigenous population.

The Caribbean population also speaks the languages of the major European nations that controlled portions of the region during the colonial transaction, namely Spanish, Dutch, French, and English. The linguistic legacy of the Swedes, who owned St. Bartholomew from 1784 through 1878, and that of the Danes, who controlled St. Thomas, St. John, and St. Croix, until December 12, 1916 when under new ownership they became the U.S. Virgin Islands, seem to have left a less perceptible trace. Countries such as Belize, where a Spanish-speaking minority coexists with a majority that speaks English, the official language; Honduras, a Spanish-speaking country that harbors an Anglophone community on the Bay Islands on the Caribbean coast; and Puerto Rico, where people supplement their native Spanish with officially sanctioned instruction in English as a second language, reflect linguistically a staggered history of colonial domination. One may also deduce such a legacy of alternating European control of societies in the region from the formation of several Caribbean creole languages. Typically a West Indian creole draws largely on the language brought by the European nation that maintained political hegemony in the particular sphere of influence corresponding to a given society. For instance, people in Barbados speak an English-based creole known as Bajan and in French Guiana they speak a French-based creole. But Papiamento, the creole of the Netherlands Antilles draws more from Spanish than it does from Dutch, the official language of the islands. Similarly, the two creoles of Suriname—Sranan Tongo or Taki-Taki, spoken by a majority of the population, and Saramaccan, spoken by the Bush Negroes of the interior—draw their base from English rather that Dutch, the country's official language. The population of Dominica officially speaks English, but in everyday speech the people generally revert to a French-based creole, and the same holds true for the people of Saint Vincent as well as for differentiated communities in Trinidad and Tobago (Katzner 2002: 339–368).

In addition to aboriginal, European, and creole languages spoken in the region we ought to make meaningful reference to the Hindi and Tamil speakers of Guyana, Trinidad and Tobago, and Surinam, where a small population of about 50,000 Javanese speakers can also be found. These communities descend from the people who came to staff Caribbean plantations from India as indentured laborers following the abolition of slavery in the British West Indian colonies in 1838. As many as 416,000 Indians came as indentured workers to Guyana, Trinidad, Jamaica, St. Lucia, Grenada, St. Vincent, and St. Kitts between 1844 and 1917 (Claypole and Rabottom 1989:24). Around the same time came 142,000 indentured Chinese workers to Cuba and hundreds of Portuguese Madeiran cane workers to Guyana and Trinidad, where a small Chinese presence had existed since 1807. For the most part, these indentured immigrants retained their ancestral language after several generations (Claypole and Robottom 1989:20, 40). Today, as a result of the presence of the numerous populations from across the globe who found their way to the region, the Caribbean displays a rich, varied, and complex tapestry of the word. While English there has gained as much currency as in the rest of the world—being the language of international business, politics, diplomacy, computers, the Internet, and in a word, "the language of globalization"— one language alone will not provide the means necessary to achieve an appropriate understanding of the texture of Caribbean life (*Economist* 2001:65).

Except for those from the Hispanophone countries, where distinct creoles did not emerge, Caribbean writers have a choice when deciding the tongue in which to cast their works. Attempts to put Haitian creole to literary and intellectual uses precede the founding of the Republic in 1804, and over 100 years later such foundational figures of Haitian letters as Oswald Durand and Georges Sylvain remained committed to exploring the expressive possibilities of the language of the people (Bajeux 1999:iii). Major twentieth-century Haitian writers such as Félix Morisseau-Leroy, author of a vast *oeuvre* in creole, beginning with the poetry chapbook *Dyakout* (1951), and Frankétienne, author of the ground-breaking novel *Dezafi* (1975), written originally in creole and subsequently reissued in French as *Les Affres d'un défi* (1979), have produced an impressive corpus of writing in the country's vernacular. The very useful *Mosochwazi Pawòl Ki Ekri An Kreyól Ayisyen / Anthologie de la littérature créole haïtienne* (1999) compiled by Jean-Claude Bajeux affords a convenient look at the longevity of writing in Haitian creole. Similarly, *Open Gate: An Anthology of Haitian Creole Poetry* (2001), a collection of creole original verse with English translations edited by Paul Laraque and Jack Hirschman, the English renditions done by Hirschman and Boadiba, by gathering texts spanning from the pioneers through poets born in the mid-1970s, attests to this vernacular's continued vitality. The literary careers of Antillean authors Diana Lebacs and Frank Martinus Arion, who throughout their productive lives have alternated between Papiamentu and Dutch, exemplify the linguistic scenario of the Caribbean territories that have been colonially linked to Holland. A useful compilation of creole texts from eighteenth-century Surinam put together by Jacques Arends and Matthias Perl (1995) provide a privileged glimpse at the evolution of Sranan and Saramaccan. The Anglophone Caribbean has already produced a whole branch of literature that has a long history of speaking confidently in the vernacular, with writers of the prominence of the venerable dialect poet Louise Bennett and the London-based Linton Kwesi Johnson, both of whom have produced the entirety of their works in Jamaican creole.

To know the thinking of a multilingual culture area requires the skills of the polyglot. Yet students of the Caribbean, including some who have attained scholarly prestige, too often satisfy themselves with knowledge of only one linguistic bloc of the region even while purporting to make holistic claims. Even key interventions in the realm of Caribbean literature and thought such as Edouard Glissant's *Discours antillais* (1981) and Antonio Benítez-Rojo's *La isla que se repite* (1989) represent looks at the region's cultural history that depend for their data primarily on each author's knowledge of his own Francophone or Spanish-speaking bloc. The question of language demands serious attention since it contributes to sustaining the region's historical fragmentation more effectively than any other factor. Sometimes approaching a single country, say, Surinam, which harbors ethnic groups and religions galore, presents difficulty if one has mastery of one language only. The novelist, poet, and playwright Astrid Roemer has called attention to the importance of Winti, an "Afro-Surinamese religion" that she prefers to call "a survival strategy with a militant, political-revolutionary value," but in tracing that "breath/spiritual force" to the interior of the country, "where the so-called 'bush-negroes' live," she at the same time would seem to identify it with a setting that does not rely on Dutch for its means of verbal communication (Roemer 1996:42–43). Similarly, the cosmology of vodou is more likely to express itself via Haitian creole than in standard French, and the same holds true for the relationship between kumina or obeah with Jamaican creole. To know only one of the languages of a bilingual or multilingual society is to have one's access to the knowledge of the overall national reality partly blocked. In that respect, language remains as the ultimate border. When it comes to mediating the rapport between Caribbean societies, linguistic difference, more than any other obstacle, has the power to encourage and preserve the otherness of neighbors, preventing the harmonious identification that might otherwise naturally ensue. Language has to a large extent kept open the tellurian wound that sets the territory of Haitians apart from that of Dominicans on the island of Hispaniola that they share. Language probably also has conferred vitality and depth to the borderline that separates the tiny island of Saint Martin, splitting its 30,000 inhabitants into two disparate polities, Dutch on one side and French on the other.

An awareness of the challenge that language presents to the student of the Caribbean must include a recognition of the creoleness that underlies the region's tongue even when the words deployed morphologically match the familiar Western words brought to the region from Spain, Holland, England, or France. The works of fiction writers Luis Rafael Sánchez and Ana Lydia Vega lend themselves most suitably to an exploration of the distinct expressiveness that the Spanish language acquires in the lips of Puerto Ricans. A well-known study by critic Efraín Barradas on the writings of Sánchez delves expertly into this question of the nativization of Spanish (Barradas 1981:70–79). The celebrated experimental novel *Tres tristes tigres* (1967) by the Cuban fiction writer Guillermo Cabrera Infante and the award-winning text *Sólo cenizas hallarás* (1980) by the Dominican novelist Pedro Vergés dramatize the peculiar sound and sense with which Cubans and Dominicans have stamped the language brought to them from Castile. Writers from the Hispanic Antilles draw amply from "their dialectal environment," having learned to recognize the language "spoken in the streets," as a "cultural legacy" that they can put to use in evoking "an authentic Antillean world" (López Morales 1994:21). An assessment of the linguistic diversity of the Caribbean population must therefore take into account, in addition to the myriad tongues in which the region speaks, the meaningful difference contained in the interior of perfectly standard European words, a subtle difference that stems from the overall creolization of expressive forms in the course of five centuries of an intense human experience in this discrete part of the world.

On Knowing the Caribbean

It behooves students of the Caribbean, therefore, to start from a recognition of the complexity of their subject. Carpentier, who had "the immense fortune of visiting most, if not all Caribbean islands, can attest to something absolutely marvelous, something which at this moment tourists from all over the world are discovering, namely the diversity, uniqueness and originality of the Caribbean world" (Carpentier 1999:152). They must approach their inquiry armed with an attitude of humility in light of the daunting challenge that the task of learning the Caribbean world represents. As illustration of the magnitude of the enterprise, suffice it to mention two ground-breaking scholarly instruments that have set out to organize the state of knowledge about the Caribbean in the fields of literature and history. The first, *A History of Literature in the Caribbean*, a three-volume compendium edited by A. James Arnold, took 15 years to complete, from a first editorial colloquium at the University of Virginia in 1986 to the issuing of the last of the volumes by John Benjamins Publishing Company in 2001. An unprecedented scholarly feat, this first-rate collection of studies brought together the skills of specialists in all the literary forms practiced across the region, all languages included. Nor would the project have come to fruition without the perseverance, erudition, and scholarly leadership of Arnold and his team of subeditors (Arnold 2001:ix). Equally ambitious in its scope, the other scholarly instrument, the six-volume *General History of the Caribbean* sponsored by UNESCO, began publication in 1997 with most volumes appearing by

2003. Nearly two decades in the making from planning through publication and drawing on the expertise of several teams of historians under the guidance of UNESCO's Advisory Scientific Committee, the *General History of the Caribbean*, with each volume edited by a leading specialist in the period or theme therein covered, constitutes the most comprehensive history of the region ever published. A look at these two remarkable compilations of Caribbean knowledge, apart from stressing the intellectual vastness of any project that earnestly undertakes to know the region, evinces the fact that the story of the human experience in this particular part of the globe admits of no simplification.

We can structure the events that people in Caribbean societies have lived since the colonial transaction to the present neither as the story of a triumph nor as that of a defeat. The Caribbean experience does not lend itself to treatment as a lineal narrative. It would seem better advised to approach this subject by focusing on the survival and resilience of the Antillean person, the way she has emerged from a checkered history of glory, disappointment, aggression, hope, betrayal, and joy since 1492 when heavily armed invaders came in their ships to disembowel Tainos, rape Tainas, burn religious temples, and generally trample upon the human dignity of the native population. Political utopias and creeds of equality, justice, and social transformation having failed to keep their declared promises, positions that in the beginning of the twenty-first century articulate the possibility of a better world often meet with skepticism, disdain, or disbelief. The Caribbean, of course, partakes of the widespread crisis of political faith, and although the region gave to the world some of the earliest instances of struggle for freedom and human rights, liberatory projects and discourses here seem to awaken increasingly less enthusiasm as the lives of people appear to revolve primarily around the business of material survival in dependent and declining economies that offer the Antillean person no social guarantee. Against that background, it seems fitting to delve into the ways the lives of people here have evolved to understand the Antillean person's recurring impetus to affirm herself, particularly in the realm of ideas, which is the concern of the present study.

At a time when the law of the jungle appears to dominate international relations, the Caribbean mind may have a useful lesson or two to share with the rest of humanity. The Caribbean person's familiarity with diversity, hybridity, ethnoracial pluralism, and cultural difference, as connatural ingredients of the way human relations have developed in the region, may have a thing or two to say to a world seduced and taunted by the might of homogenizing forces. The Caribbean person knows one thing for certain—having had to learn it the hard way—that there isn't only one model of humanity, and that, even should the single model force itself into existence, it can never do so without leaving a trail of blood and a heavy toll of human suffering since it can only gain ascendancy through an incalculable dose of violence. We have no concrete grounds for assuming that the events that have shaped Caribbean societies had to take place at all or exactly the way they did. As a prominent narrator of the American past would say, "there is nothing inevitable about history" (McCullough 1992:214). "Because the outcome of great events becomes so well established in our minds, there is a tendency to think things had to go as they did," says David McCullough, but "things need not have happened as they did. Life in other times past was never on a track, any more than it is now or ever will be. The past after all is only another name for someone else's present. How would things turn out? They knew no better than we know how things will turn out for us" (McCullough 214, xiv).

Europeans could conceivably not have arrived on Antillean shores when they did or they could have traveled there as visitors interested in trade and cultural exchange rather than in plunder and domination. They could have leaned toward an appreciation of the humanity of the aborigines, the way the Venetian Marco Polo, over two centuries before the fateful trip by Columbus, experienced curiosity and eagerness to learn about the peoples of the various provinces he visited in China, as with his coming upon the Tartars, about whom he learned that they believed "in a deity whose nature is Sublime and Heavenly" and among whom the wealthy "dress in cloth and gold and silks, with skins of the sable, the ermine, and other animals, all in the richest fashion" (Polo 1930:92). By the same token, the plantation could not have emerged the way it did, as a sort of economic boa constrictor that in its voracious appetite for accumulation of wealth swallowed the lives of massive populations. One could speculate that, had the plantation not become a major industry that created an exorbitant demand for labor power in the Caribbean, the depopulation and pauperization of Africa through the massive enslavement and exportation of its population would not have occurred. The impact of sugar production, introduced by the Arabs upon conquering the Mediterranean basin (Sicily, Cyprus, Malta, Rhodes, Maghrib, and Spain) beginning in 711 and spreading by 996 had unleashed less traumatic dynamics there. While the sugar plantation wrought its havoc on the lives of the natives of Spain and Portugal's Atlantic islands (Madeira, the Canaries, and Sâo Tome) from the 1450s onward, only when it reached the Caribbean did it become a force that fueled world wars, mobilized millions of people across vast oceans, and reconfigured the balance of power on the planet (Mintz 1986:23–24). Things no doubt could have turned out differently. But they did not. We have before us a history of catastrophe, of survival, of contradiction, of endurance, and we can do nothing to erase the irremediable fact that all the beauty, the wisdom, the ugliness, the sadness, and the joy of Caribbean life and the distinct cultural characteristics of the Antillean person, what makes her unique as a member of the human family, was cast in the cauldron of that history.

II

THE MUSICAL TURN

A recurring theme in contemporary interventions that purport to interpret the Caribbean addresses itself to performance art in general and music in particular. A salient branch in Caribbean studies publications, especially in Great Britain and the United States, identifies popular songs, rhythms, dance routines, and the work of musicians as a social field wherein they profess to find conceptual ground for making statements about Antillean worldviews and the spiritual resources brandished by people in the region to cope with the demands of a challenging present in impoverished societies. This emphasis may have to do with the international success that Caribbean musical artists have enjoyed since the second half of the twentieth century, when such figures as Harry Belafonte, Bob Marley, Celia Cruz, Tito Puente, Gloria Estefan, Ricky Martin, Shaggy, Sean Paul, and Lauren Hill helped to make the sounds of calypso, reggae, dancehall, salsa, soca, guaracha, merengue, and other Caribbean rhythms familiar to the ears of audiences worldwide. Also, when looking at the region from the outside, many people often equate Caribbean culture with music. The text on the Caribbean section in the website of "Moving Here: 200 Years of Migration to England," a publicly funded database supported by Britain's National Archives that offers access to digitized materials on the immigrant experience of the country's distinct ethnic groups, states plainly that "most people associate" music "with Caribbean culture" (www.movinghere.org/uk/galleries/histories/Caribbeanculture/culture.htm). No less important, Caribbean scholarship has received the influence of British cultural studies with its concern for popular music "as a creative expression and articulation of personal and group identity" (Edgar and Sedgwick 1999:287). Probably reacting to such formulations as Theodor W. Adorno's 1941 essay "On Popular Music," which rendered that expressive form collusive with the forces of social domestication in capitalist society, some of the initial disseminators of British cultural studies argued for granting a measure of agency to audiences, contending that through their involvement with that form of entertainment rather than the more "elevated" cultural forms consumers can exert their resistance of status quo, a case made with particular emphasis when applied to subordinate or minority groups who through popular music seem to fend off the values and attitudes of the dominant culture (Hall and Whannel 1964; Hall and Jefferson 1976). Probably as a result of these various factors combined, popular music currently holds a favorite spot in Caribbean scholarship. The recent bibliography abounds in titles that run the gamut from a specialized exploration of music in the construction of the Puerto Rican, Cuban, and Dominican nations by Juan Otero Garabís (2000) to an edited volume on *Music, Writing and Cultural Unity in the Caribbean* compiled by Timothy J. Reiss (2005).

Given the importance that popular music has acquired as a field of inquiry with aspirations to shed light on and elicit meaning from the examination of Caribbean life, it seems appropriate to devote Section II of this "Introduction" to an attempt to locate this musical turn of the scholars in the larger spectrum of Caribbean intellectual history. Perhaps one might usefully proceed by recalling the "One Love Peace Concert" on April 22, 1978, when Bob Marley, playing against a backdrop of increasingly violent political conflict, summoned to the stage Prime Minister Michael Manley, leader of the

People's National Party (PNP), and his foe Edward Seaga, head of the Jamaican Labour Party (JLP). Marley had the two contenders shake hands, and eyewitnesses recall that peace reigned in the land over the next few days. The moral power displayed by this reggae legend for a crucial instant in Jamaican life would seem to encourage the emphasis of several ethnomusicologists and cultural studies scholars who stress the transformative and ultimately liberatory role music plays in the Caribbean. In this respect, Jocelyne Guilbault embraces Peter Manuel's view that "music functions not merely as a passive reflection of broader sociocultural phenomena but also as an active contributor to the processes of cultural change," arguing further that "music participates in the process of production in a society in multifaceted ways" (Guilbault 1993:xvii). Speaking specifically of zouk, the one Caribbean musical form her study considers, Guilbault finds that, "as an economic sociopolitical, and cultural force in the Lesser Antilles, [it] has been inextricably linked with significant changes in these areas and practices" (xvii).

That ethnomusicologists and other scholars are not alone in declaring the sociopolitical power of music in the Caribbean is evident in current assessments of cadence-lypso or cadence, the rhythm that in the 1970s became established as the national music of the island of Dominica. According to Gregory Rabess, a journalist, grassroots organizer, poet, critic, and cadence-lypso performer, this music afforded an outlet for youths, permitting them to enjoy, while at the same time arming them with a tool of social protest that "pointed them toward their *kwéyol* roots and identity" (Rabess 1993:104). Some lines from the lyrics of his "Cadence Music," a text by Rabess that sets out to trace the genealogy and trajectory of the form, offer a political teleology:

> Its distant progenitor
> created in Africa
> survived the Middle Passage
> cocooned in the souls of our forefathers
> marooned in the Caribbean,
> it rose its head throughout Slavery and after
> mutated to Jing-ping
> Lapo Kabwilt, Bele
> Calypso and Cadence
> and now Cadence-Lypso
> a true progeny
> containing all features
> worthy of its ancestors . . .
> a veritable hallmark.
> And now,
> unleashed
> its force, its dynamism,
> its melody, its rhythm,
> imbibes us
> with added strength

hope, courage, vigor
to battle on,
to struggle on,
to freedom.
    (Rabess 1993: 91)

Similarly, U.S. drummer and ethnomusicology professor Gage Averill, who has done extensive research on Haitian Konpa, the subject of several of his scholarly articles, concludes his short social history of the form affirming that studying "the evolution of popular music" involves not just an examination of changes in sound, nor is it strictly a case of representations about music, attributions of styles, or claims to ownership. Analysis of popular music really needs to plot relations between musical sound and its social construction to demonstrate how it is affected by—and how it in turn affects—social forces" (Averill 1993:88). As this quote suggests, Averill does not think it necessary for the student of popular music to ask *whether* it affects "social forces." However, except in very literal moments such as that of the bipartisan handshake conjured by Marley in April 1978, the precise ways in which music affects the concrete social reality of people in the Caribbean may not be easily discernible to the lay observer. As a result, scholars often take pains to stress that the role of the region's musical sounds decidedly transcends the realms of entertainment and the festive. For instance, while acknowledging "festivity" as "the most immediate and tangible dimension of steelband symbolism in that pan almost always evokes a spirit of revelry or well-being," Stephen Stuempfle argues in his study of popular music in Trinidad and Tobago that "festivity" has to do with "much more than license and exuberance." He explains that "[a]t festive moments Trinidadians and Tobagonians imaginatively explore their experience and various visions of themselves. The pan, as an indigenous instrument of festivity, is one vital means by which the nation creates, contemplates, and celebrates itself" (Stuempfle 1995:235–236).

Trinidad is also home to chutney, a musical form born of the experience of the island's Indian Caribbean community that has become increasingly popular since the 1980s. Tracing the roots of chutney, Tina K. Ramnarine places its genesis in a clipper ship built in Glasgow that sailed in March 1877 with goods for trade to Calcutta, whence it subsequently came to the Caribbean with "bound coolies" (145). Today chutney has carved for itself a new performance space in carnival, together with calypso, soca, and steelband, as well as in centers of the Caribbean diaspora outside of Trinidad, in the world music scene (1). Chutney also follows the rule enunciated by Ramnarine to the effect that "Music in Trinidad is deeply implicated with political processes" (145). Specifically, the scholar explains that "dialogues in chutney reveal how music can operate as a medium for reconceptualization of what constitutes contemporary Trinidadian society, the contestation of identities within the postcolonial state and interactions which do not result from simply conceived ideas of division (colonizer/colonized) or between different ethnic groupings" (Ramnarine 2001:145).

At times, Caribbean writers and thinkers have proclaimed the region's musical heritage as an indispensable aid to the survival of its inhabitants. "Jamaica: fragment of bomb blast, catastrophe of geological history . . . has somehow miraculously—some say triumphantly—survived," says Kamau Brathwaite, adding, emphatically, thus: "How we did it is still a mystery and perhaps it should remain so. But at least, we can say this: that the secret and expression of that survival lies glittering and vibrating in our music" (cited in López de Jesús 2003:88). That same fundamental confidence in the decisive vitality of musical expression as an existential tool capable of ensuring that the community will endure informs Brenda F. Berrian's study of Martinican and Guadeloupean popular songs. Berrian starts with an embrace of the view on art articulated by African American thinker Bell Hooks: "The arts remain one of the most powerful, if not the most powerful realms of cultural resistance, a space for awakening folks to critical consciousness and new vision" (Berrian 2000:1). Informed by that conviction, she approaches her assessment of Guadeloupean and Martinican song lyrics from 1970 to 1996 by focusing on the "space of empowerment and identity" carved by vocalists, songwriters, and musicians (7). She thus arrives at the close of her study confident that the music and lyrical messages spread at home and abroad by performers from the Francophone Antilles fulfill the "natural requirements for the understanding of the Self" (238). In so doing, they guarantee the vitality of "the French Caribbean musical village," which, inseparable as it is from "its communal and popular cultural contexts," corresponds to the very survival of the community since, as the author posits through a quote from J. H. Kwabena Nketia: "A village that has no organized music or neglects community singing, drumming, or dancing is said to be dead" (238).

None of the scholars, writers, or performers thus far cited, however, would venture to specify with precision in exactly what way musical expression intervenes in society to deploy its liberatory, empowering, resistive, and revolutionary potential for the discernible benefit of the people of the Caribbean. Save for very rare moments such as that when Manley and Seaga were lured by reggae rhythms to shake hands on stage and forge consequently a brief moment of peace in Jamaica, few proponents of the socially and politically transformative function of music would venture to make a case that relies on history rather than on lyrical flare. Nor would they attempt to materialize their contention by illustrating their assertions with documentable examples. One cannot take lightly this apparent incongruity between the power that writers and cultural critics ascribe to Caribbean music and the power that the rhythms and their performers have actually exhibited in the modern history of the region. I explore this question by outlining the disappointing decline of restorative political and economic options in Caribbean societies simultaneously with the insertion of rhythms from the region into the market corridors of the world music scene, punctuating the resulting scenario with a discussion of the diminished relevance of Caribbean literature and thought production in the wake of the postcolonial cultural studies industry.

THE LAST RESORT OF CULTURE

Caribbean history in one of its possible readings consists of a series of unkept promises and failed leaderships (Torres-Saillant 2001). The legacy of the maroons, otherwise noble and exalted, can also be one of betrayal. Guarocuya, better known as Enriquillo, the Taino chief who led his people in war against the Spanish colonial regime in Santo Domingo starting in 1519, ended up signing a peace treaty that thenceforward made him and his insurgent troops members of the colonial regime's military structure, with duties that included the persecution and capture of other Taino and black maroons (Mir 1969:156). Over 200 years later on the island of Jamaica an equally opprobrious deal was sealed by the heroic maroon rebels that Cudjoe led against the British colonial forces. Under the terms of the March 1, 1739 treaty signed at the peace cave in the town now known as Accompong, the insurgents agreed to help sustain the colonial regime by accepting the task of capturing other runaway slaves (Campbell 1988:131, 258; Robinson 1994:91). Guarocuya and Cudjoe epitomize a long history of moral disappointment in a region that for long yearned for the anticolonialist Spartacus that the Abbé Raynal once announced. In his memorable *The Black Jacobins*, C. L. R. James speculates that Pierre Dominique Toussaint Louverture, the great leader of the Saint Domingue insurgents in the 1790s, found in Raynal's prophecy an allusion to himself as the predestined individual to whom history had entrusted the formidable mission of liberating his community (James 1963:25, 82, 171, 250). But political leaders in the Caribbean have rarely lived up to the expectations of their people.

The Wine of Astonishment, the penetrating novel by Trinidadian author Earl Lovelace, explores the bitter reality of Caribbean people's frustrated hope and unrewarded faith at the hands of morally feeble leaders. It evokes the existential adventure of a community of black Spiritual Baptists in the village of Bonasse who struggle to maintain their moral integrity by preserving their religious faith against the animosity and the censorship of mainstream society, which demands their conversion to Catholicism or Anglicanism. People in the Bonasse community have pinned their hopes on the rise of one their own to the policy-making positions in local government. The whole village, as we learn from Eva, the wise and loquacious peasant woman who narrates the story, has fixed its eyes on young Ivan Morton, a lucky and intelligent lad who promises to go far. Since his childhood the community has showered him with prayers so he would do well in school and fulfill his dead mother's dream that he would "qualify himself and rise to take up the greater burden to lead his people out of the hands of Pharaoh" (Lovelace 1986:40). On the very first opportunity that Morton gets, when he comes back as a professional with a degree from a British university and has secured a key bench in the echelons of public service, he relinquishes the house he inherited from his parents "right here with his own people" to move up in an "old mansion of brick and stone that stand up on the top of Bonasse hill looking over the sea and the whole village" (8). Symbolizing the pinnacle of the social structure, the big house on the hill belonged formerly to the Richardsons, the family that for generations, through the end of the colonial regime, directed the lives of Bonasse residents. To the disillusionment of Eva's husband Bee, the most optimistic of the community members, the police surround their quarters, search their facilities, and lock up their church, declaring their worship illegal. Sitting powerfully in the Legislative Council, Morton moves not one finger to alleviate their plight. When Bee appears before Morton with the grievance, instead of getting support he hears a sermon in which the young lawyer urges him to desist from his pagan faith. We hear the details of Morton's patronizing counsel as Bee reports them to Eva: "Tell me he not against the principle of the freedom of worship but what worrying him is that I, we should still be in the dark ages in these modern times when we could settle down and be civilize" (13). After the rise to power of a black leadership, life for the residents of Bonasse shows no improvement. The authorities outlaw the religion of Spiritual Baptists, and those who protest have to face Corporal Prince, a black policeman whose brutality has no limit when dealing with his people, while Morton looks the other way.

Only Bolo, a revered stickfight champion, manages to rebel against the oppression that afflicts the people of Bonasse. But his resistance degenerates into a personal grudge. Obsessed with his own individual dignity, he becomes indiscriminately wrathful, his indignation turned against his own people: "he was a full terror in the village. . . . It look as if he despise Bonasse people, as if every time he see a man, he want to cuff him down or kick him" (102). In their varied forms of moral deformation, Morton and Bolo exemplify the corruption that has led Caribbean leaders to fail to keep the promise that is implicit in their rise to leadership. Both reveal their kinship with a nefarious legacy that one can trace back to Enriquillo. Both harm the community, which suffers irreparable damages in the process. Even when, after numerous tribulations, the Spiritual Baptists succeed in reopening their church and worshipping freely, they realize they have lost something important as they fail to reproduce their former spiritual momentum. They try to intone their sacred hymns, but the songs that come from their lips produce an Anglican or a Catholic resonance, "and it wasn't like old times at all" (144). Besides, the community has lost the moral strength to repudiate collectively the mendacity of Morton, who has mastered the logic of political clientelism and electoral demagoguery, making sure to repair a road or two or find jobs for a couple of residents when the time of new elections draws near (135). As the novel closes, we are left with the impression that Morton will thrive for long. His lack of scruples will keep him in power, as will also the invaluable assistance of associates like Mitchell, an opportunistic organizer who has learned to take advantage of collective hopelessness by exploiting racial and interethnic tensions. He pragmatically reasons that Morton might not be ideal, but the alternatives promise to be no better. At least, "he is still our own and if we don't support him, de Gannes or the Indian will come in" (138). In his logic, race should disqualify the opposition of de Gannes, a light-skinned mulatto lawyer, and the Indian Ramsumir, a physician who only recently returned from England. Convinced that his listeners share his racialist logic, it is only rhetorically that he asks, "You want the Indian to rule you?" (138).

For Eva, the only source of consolation lies in the vitality of popular culture. As she walks through the village, she comes upon a group of young fellows playing the pans in a steelband tent, accompanied by two girls dancing to the music. The sounds and the performance fill her with joy, and she feels a great emotion of the kind she used to experience during worship: "The music that those boys playing on the steelband have in it that same Spirit that we miss in our church: The same Spirit; and listening to them, my heart swell and it is like resurrection morning" (146). She says nothing to Bee who walks beside her, but she senses that he shares her feeling. Their mutual nod suggests to her their common sentiment that they have experienced "something holy." Through this reconnection with the spiritual energy that Eva and Bee thought they had lost, despite any metamorphosis it may have undergone, Lovelace's novel dramatizes the triumph of popular music as a venue and a mechanism of moral survival. Music here serves as a manifestation of the indomitability of a certain will that refuses to bend or give in to pessimism despite the abundance of contrary evidence that the region's history persists in constantly bringing forth. Since Eva shares with Bee the recourse to music as a vehicle of self-affirmation, the source of the "ambivalent" answer that Lovelace's novel offers may lie in more than just its "gender ideology" in light of "the imprisonment of the male subjectivity" (Shetty 1994:65).

The Wine of Astonishment allows us to read the plot's outcome as an evocation of the resistive spirit of ordinary Caribbean people who would grab on to any resource within their reach to sustain their basic humanity and to fend off the forces that seem vigorously bent on effectuating their moral annihilation. Music no doubt has often afforded them a handy resource enabling them to assert themselves culturally and to vindicate their humanity in the field of symbolic politics, the realm where metaphor rules. In a region like the Caribbean, most of whose population descends from slaves and indentured workers, instrumental sounds and the lyrics uttered by the poets of the oral tradition often served as the principal venue for the public dissemination of the values and yearnings of the community. The rise of scribal and print culture would have to wait until the mid-twentieth century in the majority of Caribbean societies, with efforts to massify formal education starting in most cases in the 1960s when many of them gained independence. That background gives substance to the observation by sociologist Ángel G. Quintero Rivera that: "In the Caribbean, before the word, in the beginning it was the drum, rhythm, and movement. In complex conditions of 'encounters' among 'migrants' speaking diverse languages, music and dance preceded the first 'discourses'. The construction of socio-cultural identities for Caribbean peoples has been inextricably linked to our sonic forms of expression and communication" (Quintero Rivera 1998:14).

Besides the relevance of musical expression as a result of the non-scribal demands of oral societies, an area of relevance, with implications for resistance and political self-assertion, has to do with the history of prohibitions in colonial times. Suffice it to mention that the very first Act of the Tobago Assembly, which was promulgated in 1768 to ensure the good government and supervision of slaves for the productivity and safety of the colony, forbids musical performance by the enslaved population. Clause 19 of the Act bars planters, overseers, and other plantation authorities from "allowing any slave or slaves to beat any drum or drums, empty casks, boxes, great gourds, or to blow horns, shells or other loud instruments upon such plantation or allow slaves belonging to other persons or plantations to assemble and mix with their own, for that or any other bad purpose, such person shall forfeit the sum of ten pounds" (Nardin 1969:315). Against a background of prohibition of musical expression, one can understand the compulsion that survives into the present to construe performance as inherently resistive and subversive. But prohibition was not the only policy affecting music on the plantation. The prominence of work songs coming from the slavery period suggests that plantations also allowed, and may even have encouraged, music making on the job. For one thing, as Lara Ivette López de Jesús suggests, since singing helped slaves release the tension caused by their thankless tasks, "it was good for the master to have them sing" (López de Jesús 2003:42).

The Rhythms of Success

A lapse into autobiography can perhaps help locate conceptually my pause concerning too hurried a discursive move to construe Caribbean music as inherently liberatory. Consumers of popular entertainment forms too often assume that in their mere affirmation of "our culture" they are doing their share to assist in the collective undertaking of enhancing the moral and material well-being of "our people." As a young member of the English Department at Hostos Community College, a bilingual campus of the City University of New York located in the South Bronx, I was often sought to serve as faculty advisor for Dominican and other Hispanic Caribbean student organizations. In rendering that service I occasionally found myself disagreeing with the activities that the student leaders proposed to organize and for which they needed my signature. They often asked me to bless salsa or merengue concerts featuring well-known bands or dance functions starring dynamic disc jockeys. Frequently their projected plan of work for the one year of their tenure as leaders of their organizations lacked a sufficient number of discussion panels covering the issues that truly impacted their families and their own life chances. I expected activities that would bring to the fore such questions as unemployment, access to health services, housing, immigration, and unfair distribution of public spending among the schools in the city's various ethnic neighborhoods.

I awaited proposals that would bring to campus poetry readings, political fora, or lectures by public intellectuals. I insisted that students coming to

Hostos suffered no dearth of salsa or merengue since these musical expressions were integral to their daily diets in their urban, low-income New York City neighborhoods. Their obligation as student leaders, I argued, was to help their peers sharpen their intellect, critical consciousness, and ideological orientation, and this required their developing the patience to sit through a lecture, engage actively in a panel discussion about a serious social matter, among other interactive, extracurricular forms of learning. Occasionally, students were persuaded by my argument that convening a large crowd to participate in a merengue or salsa performance by a popular band required no leadership quality since that kind of event had its own power of convocation. In my periodic sermons, I contended that to be a real student leader "you would have to get your peers to attend talks, participate in fora, and organize the community, in other words, do things that they would not normally do of their own accord." Experience taught me, however, that there were two major obstacles against my counsel. Elected leaders generally had no faith that their peers would go for the less strident, less entertaining student activities I favored. Also they were absolutely certain that a merengue or salsa event would attract a numerous and enthusiastic audience. Going my way, they would risk failure; going their way, they guaranteed success. Ultimately, I resorted to suggesting hybrid activities that would mix a "thought" component along with a frivolous entertainment part.

My dealings with the student leaders in the South Bronx saddened me because I took their frequent reticence to delve in less popular but necessary events as a defeatist outlook on cultural expression and social change. Had they been acquainted with contemporary cultural studies practices, chances are that they would have refuted my view of their choice by pointing to my own failure to see political value in a dance activity featuring a DJ or a salsa or merengue performance. My plaint should not be taken as a retrograde yearning for the idea of culture favored by the old Western academy that acknowledged only the great books, sculpture, painting, and classical music as valid ingredients. Nor do I limit cultural expression and intellectual engagement to activities among people bearing stern countenances. The joy triggered by good Caribbean popular music no doubt has its place, and it can help ground us firmly in our reality even if our reality happens to be a precarious lot. Quintero Rivera's study of tropical music accepts the challenge of "conceptualizing joy," which for him "involves, necessarily, to speak about sadness, but from the perspective of joy; to meditate on, investigate, and reflect on those processes that obstruct joy, as well as the possible opportunities for its future development" (Quintero Rivera 1998:14).

Given the rapacity of the corporations behind the mass media and entertainment offerings that now form part of the regular diet of people in the Caribbean, it behooves us to think twice before imputing resistive and liberatory content to the work of popular music performers unless we can feel certain that they offer something uncharacteristic of their industry. At the same time, we must remain mindful of the influence on our scholarly endeavors of the market forces currently dictating the logic of the human sciences in the Western academy. Terry Eagleton's critique of the profession's current obsession with culture merits attention in this respect: "in the face of this cultural efflorescence, one sober fact needs to be recalled. The primary problems which we confront in the new millennium—war, famine, poverty, disease, debt, drugs, environmental pollution, the displacement of peoples— are not especially 'cultural' at all. They are not primarily questions of value, symbolism, language, tradition, belonging or identity, least of all the arts. Cultural theorists qua cultural theorists have precious little to contribute to their resolution" (Eagleton 2000:130). The critic decries a strange process whereby the anticolonialist discourse of the 1960s gave way to the postcolonial meditations that visit us at present, and the sociopolitical advocacy of three decades ago was supplanted by the exclusive focus on culture (127). "What placed the topic of culture most immediately on the agenda for our age was no doubt the culture industry—the fact that, in an historic post-war development, culture has now become thoroughly locked into the general process of commodity production" (124). Eagleton regrets the prevailing scenario that absolutizes culture by rendering us all entirely cultural creatures: "In any case, why is everything reducible to culture, rather than to some other thing? And how do we establish this momentous truth? By cultural means, one assumes; but is this not rather like claiming that everything boils down to religion, and that we know that because the law of God tells us so?" (92). He objects to the tenor of the postcolonialist project that would have us talk of "hybridity, ethnicity, and plurality" rather than of "freedom, justice, and emancipation" (85). Ultimately, a problem with looking at Caribbean music from the perspective of cultural studies lies in the propensity of that field, in the words of Francis Mulhern cited by Eagleton, to leave "no room for politics beyond cultural practice or for political solidarities beyond the particularisms of cultural difference" (43).

Since music cannot claim to be exempt from the power of multinational corporations to flatten subversive meaning and to depoliticize forms of communication, a bit of caution would seem warranted when appraising the place of Caribbean music and dance in the world today. Speaking at the Caribbean studies seminar "El Caribe: Un mosáico pluricultural" held in the city of Cancún in May 15–16, 2003, under the auspices of the State Government of Quintana Roo, the surinamese social scientist Glenn Sankatsing noted, not without discernible pride, the considerable recognition that Caribbean music enjoys internationally relative to the small extension of the region and the size of its population. He accentuated his point by urging us to compare the acclaim of Caribbean rhythms in the global market with the lesser renown of musical forms emanating from places with far vaster territories and significantly larger populations such as the former Soviet Union, India, and China. Consistent with Sankatsing's impression, Guilbault has studied the way in which zouk, the popular music of the Creole-speaking Caribbean, has entered the sphere of "world music"—that area of the entertainment market that emerged in the 1980s consisting of popular music from smaller industrially developing countries that are "mass distributed worldwide" (Guilbault

1993:xv). With the rise in New York of such rhythms as merengue, salsa, konpa, soca, and reggae, music can attest, more patently than any other expression, to the phenomenon described by anthropologist Constance Sutton as the "Caribbeanization" of the city (Allen and Wilcken 1998:1–2). What awaits examination at this stage, though, is whether the entrance of rhythms from the region into the global arena of world music corresponds in fact to a betterment of the position of Caribbean societies in relation to the world capitalist system with which they must interact economically and polit- ically. Guilbault at least refrains from too optimistic a diagnose: "Although world music may have triggered a subtle transformation of the power center in the music industry, it remains to be seen whether it will continue to foster the acceptance of world differences without parallel shifts in political and economic systems" (210).

SHRINKING THOUGHT HORIZONS

The rise in visibility of popular music among contemporary Caribbean expressive forms coincides with an ambience of precarious prospects for the region. Over the last two decades, societies in the archipelago and the continental rimlands have experienced a perceptible loss of political self- confidence, a diminished claim to autonomous economic viability, and a crisis of leadership. Viewed against the quincentenary struggle of Caribbean peoples to cast off the trappings of external domination and to assert their human dignity in the eyes of the rest of the world, the ascendancy of their voices and instrumental sounds on the music scene internationally provides understand- able grounds for rejoicing. London, Paris, Berlin, and even Copenhagen, among other European capitals, have become familiar with the sounds of calypso, reggae, and other Caribbean rhythms. As one can gather from the musical themes in Pedro Almodóvar's film *Women on the Verge of a Nervous Breakdown*, Cuban and other Hispanic Antillean sounds have already entered the menu of Madrid's music diet. In the United States, cities like Miami, New York, and Chicago now naturally move to the beat of Dominican merengue and bachata, just as in the Northeast the tempos of Puerto Rican bomba, plena, and salsa predominate.

The foregoing scenario might at first suggest that the Caribbean region, as a culture area, has at long last assumed its rightful place among those branches of the human family enjoying world-class status. Having come up from a past of dehumanizing slavery and colonialism, the region, its artistic competitiveness established, has attained parity with the major societies of the West, one might presume. Rhythms, songs, and dance, along with native cuisine, normally occupy the limelight of Caribbean cultural events. One might therefore suppose that if the music has entered the proscenium of world culture, most other labors of the Caribbean mind must have done so also. Yet, at the beginning of the twenty-first century we witness a shrinking of the space that Caribbean writers and thinkers had gained worldwide in the intellectual arena during the 1950s, 1960s, and 1970s, when books by the likes of C. L. R. James, Wilson Harris, Kamau Brathwaite, Alejo Carpentier, Nicolás Guillén, Marie Viau Chauvet, René Depestre, Samuel Selvon, Jacques Stéphen Alexis, Boeli van Leeuwen, Albert Helman, and Eric Williams would come out from major presses in the West and would frame the ongoing discussion about the colonized. At the time it seemed that the world had come to recognize that the Caribbean mind had much to contribute to the task of imagining a restorative future for our species by helping to moderate the necessary conversation between the West, the Third World, and the socialist bloc.

The Caribbean today no longer enjoys its former rank in the forefront of the intellectual community. That poet Derek Walcott and novelist V. S. Naipaul have both earned the Nobel, the highest distinction given to literary artists, does not alter the scenario herein described. One might actually detect a disquieting correlation between the Western recognition of these luminaries— their superior talent notwithstanding—and their refusal to speak to the world as Caribbeans or for the Caribbean. Walcott has at different points repeated his dismissal of the dogma of those Caribbean writers who fuss too much with their history and has echoed the Joycean desire to awake from the nightmare of history (Walcott 1996:24). Naipaul, for his part, declared quite early in his career his distaste for those West Indian writers who take sides with their people: "To the initiated one whole side of West Indian writing has little to do with literature, and much to do with the race war. The insecure wish to be realistically portrayed. Irony and satire, which might help more, are not acceptable; and no writer wishes to let down his group . . . The gifts required, of subtlety and brutality, can grow only out of a mature literature; and there can be advance towards this only when writers cease to think about letting down their sides" (Naipaul 1981:68–69). Naipaul has shown no interest in asserting his Caribbean identity. His quest, when not pursuing Englishness, is that of the immigrant who "must reinvent the earth beneath his feet," as noted by Salman Rushdie in his review of *The Enigma of Arrival* (Rushdie 1991:149). A 1973 British companion to English and American literature declared Naipaul then as "the greatest of West Indian novelists," and it particularly praised his lack of "time or patience for much of what he sees as the stupidity and worse of Trinidadian life," his "pointing a finger at the pathetic overseriousness of so many West Indians," plus the fact that "he does not seek to reform; he accepts anarchy and laughs at it" (Pollard 1976:112).

The other two West Indian authors who have attained the status of international celebrities, namely Stuart Hall and Paul Gilroy, both Jamaican-born, rank among the obligatory references in academic debates that draw on cultural studies and postcolonial perspectives. They have achieved their distinction, however, on the strength of discursive interventions that privilege global dynamics. They owe their prestige to their having excelled as learners in the British intellectual circles that centered around Raymond Williams. They do not particularly emphasize nor make the Caribbean the subject of their inquiry. They seem to have circumscribed their commitment to the 'milieu of their productive work' and their exilic condition rather than their ancestral homeland, a predicament that Aijaz Ahmed has perceptively described in connection with the thematic emphases of many well-known literary figures from the Third World (Ahmed 1994:129–132). Hall and Gilroy pay little heed to the principle articulated by their fellow emigrant, Trinidadian novelist Samuel Selvon, who posited that the West Indian writer had no greater responsibility than "that of making his country and his people known accurately to the rest of the world" (cited by Dabydeen 2000:64). Ironically, the greatest literary and intellectual prestige on the world market—which is now, more than three decades ago, a fundamentally Western market—has come to those West Indians who have reneged or downplayed their cultural specificity as speakers grounded in the Caribbean experience and who have been less willing to flaunt the great wisdom that the region knows it can contribute to the world. Sadly, this reality may prove too compelling for young Caribbean authors or scholars as they assess their options to chart their own intellectual careers in the near future.

Conversely, a figure like Kamau Brathwaite, who has devoted his life to deciphering the Caribbean and to uncovering native meaning that can shed light on the human experience as a whole, went from publishing some eight volumes with Britain's Oxford University Press between 1967 and 1987 to having difficulty finding publishers in the 1990s despite his numerous awards and a loyal cadre of readers (Savory 1995:219, 221). Indefatigably committed to discovering and formulating the schemes of thought and analytical tools epistemologically pertinent to the catastrophic history of the Caribbean, Brathwaite has posited the existence of uniquely Caribbean ways of knowing and ways of saying. Witness his upholding an alternative periodology, as illustrated in the description of the counter-Renaissance that the region endured contemporaneously with the European Renaissance. The sight of Jamaica reverting to pre-Manley levels of economic dependency, the corruption and frauds that in the twenty-first century continued to make Dominican society institutionally unreliable, occasionally causing ordinary citizens to yearn nostalgically for the former stability provided by the blood-drenched Trujillo dictatorship, and the sad persistence in Haiti, the land where black slaves asserted their humanity against European colonial rule, of near slavery conditions for some 25,000 children, the so-called *restavecs* (Cadet 1998:4), and other equally odd historical developments in the region would seem to confirm Brathwaite's contention that one cannot study Caribbean history following the logic of a Hegelian chronology, a lineal progression, leading to the outcome promised by dialectics. With characteristic vision, Brathwaite shuns liberation projects that ignore cultural specificity, hence his developing the notion of a reformed Caliban, an *alter native* less interested in cursing Prospero than in reconnecting with mother's milk, native tongue, and roots of self. He invests himself laboriously in the task of evincing the experiential implications of "nation" language and the global vision of what he calls "tidalectics," a philosophy of history curtailed to the distinct measure of Caribbean life (Brathwaite 1991:44–45).

The originality and dynamism of Caribbean thought, exemplified by the literary texts and social criticism of Brathwaite and others in the 1960s and 1970s, should command as much attention in the intellectual industry today as the region's rhythms command in world music circles. But something else seems to have happened. A loss of luster of the products of the Caribbean mind has occurred in direct proportion to the globalization of the region's musical forms. We have seen the unseating of Caribbean ideas and conceptual paradigms from the forefront location that they enjoyed decades ago. This came about with the reconfiguration of the academic industry in the West since the late 1980s, especially with the emergence and prodigious growth of "post-colonial cultural studies." The new marketing of Third World knowledge under the globalizing label of "post-colonial theory" came to the academic industry precisely at the moment when the prominence of Caribbean ideas, championed by such figures as Sylvia Wynter, Lamming, Césaire, Carpentier, and Fanon, had begun to command international attention. A mixture of ethnic and area studies modulated conceptually by the paradigms of Western critical theory and informed by the angst characteristic of postmodern thought, the new field removed the Caribbean from its position of relative centrality as producer of autochthonous meaning. The centers that dominated the marketing of the new industry were in major British and American universities and had no particular allegiance to the region. Perhaps sensing that the focus of Third World thought production had shifted away from their region, Caribbeanists gradually came to give in to the new academic world order. Thus marginalized, they began to assert the relevance of their studies by highlighting their link to the larger, grander, and more "theoretical" postcolonial field. The "theoretical" currency of a dynamic thinker like the Martinican Edouard Glissant, whose engaging interventions had earned him distinction for the originality of his concepts as far back as the early 1970s, now gets established through his presumed rapport with postcolonial theory, as we gather in a study of his work by scholar Celia Britton (1999). A specialist on the works of the Martinican writer labors arduously to show the ways in which, through the development of key ideas like Antillanité and Creolization, "Glissant fully enters the arena of post-colonial theory" (Dash 1995:48).

The surrender to the epistemological might of the postcolonists by some Caribbeanists illustrates the erosion of the region's intellectual self-confidence. With the likes of Jacques Roumain, Lydia Cabrera, and Pedro Mir, the Caribbean word had flaunted its pathfinding role in the search for alternatives to the confining legacy of Western discourse. Many thinkers from the region resisted the practices that reduced the human experience in the Caribbean to mere fodder to feed the voracity of Western critical theory, declaring it as a valid and rich source of autochthonous knowing. This happened in the wake of impressive political, literary, and conceptual interventions, along with concomitant social movements from the 1940s onward. But now we can hardly find traces of that former sense of intellectual autonomy, authenticity, and leadership. Nor do the scholars seem to be particularly disturbed by the state of affairs whereby the Caribbean, having once exerted influence as a thought-producing region and cradle of indigenous paradigms, must now be subsumed as a subsection of a global epistemic structure, becoming a recipient rather than a producer of knowledge. The postcolonial project, whose champions owe their authority to their dexterous handling of the teachings of Lacan, Foucault, Deleuze, Derrida, Kristeva, Bourdieu, Lyotard, and the like, reaffirms the epistemological centrality of Western critical theory. Postcolonialists resignify paradigms that the Caribbean had long developed, repackaging them anew and exporting them back to the dependent scholarly economy of the Caribbean. Thus an endemic formulation such as creolization turns into the more costly imported commodity known as hybridity. The Caribbean focus on the people's "little history" and the common attention to communal "resistance" subsides so that we can make space for "subalternity," the preferred product in the scholarly branch of the global economy. Devoid of the former self-confidence attained through decades of cultural self-affirmation and close, thorough, expert scrutiny of the particularity of Caribbean life through the late 1970s, Caribbean scholars now face the temptation to secure their legitimacy by reference to the wisdom of the contemporary pillars of the Western tradition, the same way it used to be prior to the rise of anticolonialist thought in the region. The Caribbean mind may have to endure being relocated to the back of the bus of theory even when conceptualizing Caribbean life itself.

Farewell to the Future

The economic, political, and cultural context that might explain the region's loss of intellectual self-confidence, as illustrated in the diminished authority of thought-production in the Caribbean, perhaps also accounts for a regional decline that at a certain level involves even the music. I would draw attention to *Buena Vista Social Club*, a 1999 documentary telling the story of a group of accomplished Cuban musicians whom avant-garde U.S. musician and entrepreneur Ry Cooder rescues from oblivion. The drama of this case acquires greater force if seen in relation to the ideological purpose and restorative vision of the 1964 Soviet-Cuban film *I Am Cuba*, directed by Mikhail Katalosov and written by the poet Evgeny Yevtushenko. Enacting the asphyxiating political climate, pervasive economic inequality, and the society's prevailing moral decrepitude during the Batista regime, the film makes a poignant case for the urgency of social transformation. The plot traces the roots of current oppression back to the Spanish conquest and the establishment of the plantation by the colonial regime. The rapacious Creole ruling class and their U.S. economic bosses appear as the twentieth-century agents of the colonial transaction. The film opens with scenes that implicitly indict the tourism industry, showing the debauchery of U.S. visitors and the local corruption that ensues. Arranged as a composite of four subplots, each depicting a distinct angle of the disheartening plight of the Cuban population, *I Am Cuba* stresses the courage, selflessness, and overall superior human caliber of the rebels whose triumph brings the film to a close. The film celebrates the dismantling of a U.S.-dominated social structure and the dawn of a revolutionary order. An emphatically happy ending, this document extols the return of moral health and national pride to Cuba, a country wallowing for too long in the mire of its harlotry as a recreational satellite of the United States. Released only four years after the triumph of the Cuban Revolution and only three years since the defeat of the Bay of Pigs invaders, the film draws much of its dramatic zeal, accentuated by a thrilling photography, from the boundless enthusiasm discernible in the country at the moment. Because the counter-revolutionary expedition had received crucial U.S. support, the Cuban government could successfully represent the outcome as a victory over the might of Yankee imperialism, adding powerful symbolism to the revolutionary epic forged by Fidel, Che, and the other angels of anticolonialist transformation. Much had happened in recent Cuban events, indeed, to justify the sense of moral certainty and righteousness evident in *I Am Cuba*.

Released 35 years later, *Buena Vista Social Club* offers images that would seem to raise doubts about the success of the Cuban Revolution and uncertainty about the country's future possibilities. We witness a scenario in which the social order ushered in by the Revolution has failed to sustain the remarkable talent of Ibrahim Ferrer, Omara Portuondo, Compay Segundo, Rubén González, Eliades Ochoa, and the other outstanding singers and musicians whom Cooder discovered and delivered from poverty and meaninglessness when he went to Cuba in the mid-1990s. Photographically, the film displays a denunciatory visual narrative, with images of placards and signboards bearing lapidary captions about the greatness of the Revolution in close proximity to the dilapidated façades of Havana buildings. The film makes us relish the extraordinary skill of the pianists, percussionists, vocalists, and string instrument players, while the camera dwells insistently on the disrepair of automobiles, houses, and public places. Darkness and lack of splendor characterize the interior of the homes of Ferrer and Segundo. The somber urban landscape that surrounds their lives in Havana contrasts glaringly with the radiant glamor bestowed on the musicians in New York, when they come for their 1996 Radio City Music Hall concert. Surveying Times Square and other highlights in the city, they voice their exhilaration, and Ferrer wishes that his wife were with him so that she too "could see all this." At the concert, performing before a large audience in the entertainment capital of the world, the Cuban musicians regain the distinction of their early years when they had their former glory during the Batista era. As the last scene captures the theatrical majesty of the Hall and as a closing image of Ry Cooder fades into black, we can hardly resist our gratification at seeing the genius of those musicians from socialist Cuba finally rewarded, though in the heart of U.S. capitalism.

The State's Cuban film institute, Instituto Cubano de Arte e Industria Cinematografica (ICAIC), which 35 years earlier had partnered with the Soviet organization Mosfilm for the production of *I Am Cuba*, also appeared as an associate of Road Movies, the company that released *Buena Vista Social*

Club in 1999. An official cultural institution of Cuba, perhaps ICAIC feels it must tolerate the condemnatory visual narrative that the film conveys. Perhaps the Cuban authorities have resigned themselves to the bitter realization that, as things now stand, no country in the Caribbean can survive the ardent animosity of the United States, and that they ought to make gestures to appease the mighty neighbor to the North. One way of interpreting the desire to have Washington lift the embargo is as the goal to regain the embrace of the United States to help the country come out of its current economic stagnation. Advancing toward a less inimical rapport with the United States, however, may mean that the society will have to relax the scruples that stand out in *I Am Cuba* regarding the socialist ideal of equality and the marketing of the island and its people in the industries of the pleasure economy. The climate that has allowed tourism, with all its voracious appetite for prostitution, to creep back into Cuba with a vengeance speaks perhaps to a reformed vision of the future there. At any rate, Cuba at present finds itself enmeshed in a peculiar song-and-dance predicament that calls for negotiating the survival of the Revolution's socialist platform in an economic juncture that urges it to pander to capitalist visitors and investors. To cater to foreign commerce and investment, it must cope with the sad reality that capitalist consumer logic will most likely end up imposing itself.

An article on the emergence of supermodels in the island begins thus: "Cuba is a land associated with music, sports, cinema, art, literature, architecture, and, of course, cigars . . . The world may be on the verge of another realization, that Cuba has some of the world's most beautiful women" (Suckling 2003:60). Canadian entrepreneur Dean Bornstein, who represents "75 of the island's hottest models, including a handful who are overseas," has recently opened offices in Havana for his company, The Havana Productions Co., "which is already on the way to becoming the premiere film, television, music and fashion production company on the island" (60–62). "The talent is all here, it is just a question of packaging it and marketing it," says Bornstein, who "hopes to do for Cuba's best models and its fledgling fashion industry what Ry Cooder did for the island's music" (60–62). Bornstein anxiously awaits the moment when Cuban models could work for U.S. firms, moving beyond their current markets that exist mostly in Europe. Some of the models themselves share Bornstein's anticipation, as we gather from the words of Paneca Fernández, who rhetorically boasts: "Why should someone want to go to Miami and use models there when they can have the real thing in Havana" (70). If the supermodels succeed in bridging the geopolitical divide that bars their entrance to U.S. markets, the Cuban authorities stand to gain, since a portion of their earnings would go to the State, "a fact of life for almost all Cubans who gain permission to work overseas" (67).

The year 1999 when the story of the Cuban musicians and Ry Cooder came out in film, marked the eve of the century's end and the waning of the millennium. Many then found in the temporal shift occasion to reflect on the past and the future of the Caribbean. The previous year several academic institutions in the United States had held symposia in connection with the centennial of the war of 1898, the event that put an end to the last remnants of Spain's imperial presence in the hemisphere. That eventful war also established the sociopolitical and economic hegemony of the United States in the Americas, and historians and other human science scholars in 1998 undertook to assess the fortune of the Caribbean over the past centuries, the long while during which it served, in the apt phrase of Juan Bosh, as "imperial frontier," providing the stage for the Western colonial clashes that culminated in the rise of the United States as master of the region. An off-spring of the colonial transaction, historical cradle of its sinful birth, to use words uttered by Arcadio Díaz Quiñones during a talk in the symposium "Caribbean Writing and the Global Culture" held in New York City's The Americas Society on May 8–10, 2003, Caribbean nations would be included by Uruguayan writer Edouardo Galeano among those places and peoples of the earth that have specialized in losing.

MUSICAL CONSOLATION

Perhaps no document evokes the disappointment of the Caribbean experience as painfully as *Portrait of the Caribbean,* a 1992 BBC documentary hosted by Stuart Hall. The evocative lyrics and enthralling music of Bob Marley's "Redemption Song" serve as the soundtrack to each of the documentary's seven parts. The miniseries purports to explore the present, the past, and the future of the region, surveying the European conquest, the colonial transaction, the pervasiveness of slavery, as well as the cultural inheritances and political legacies bequeathed to the region by Africa, Spain, Holland, England, and France. The idea seems to be to help the audience understand how the region acquired its present visage and what potential it has for development in the future. After an overview of five centuries of human experience modulated by colonial relations in the region, the host closes with an exhortation. Hall muses that Caribbean societies have displayed a propensity to fashion themselves after Western societies, and he believes they ought to desist from that tendency and seriously begin to construct an image of themselves patterned after their own likeness. Irrespective of how much substance could be found in that closing formulation, one might worry about Hall's locating the diffi-culties that the Caribbean has faced in the collective imagination of people there. The impulse to explain current Caribbean stagnation in terms of the inability of inhabitants in the region to see themselves through an authentic prism would seem hardly sufficient.

The data and the interviews in *Portrait of the Caribbean* would seem to suggest forces outside of the people's imagination as factors to explain the challenges the Caribbean faces at present. One key interviewee, the revered author of the epic poem *Cahier d'un retour au pays natal,* the pivotal essay *Discours sur le colonialisme,* and the seminal biography *Toussaint Louverture,* the Martinican writer, intellectual, and politician Aimé Césaire gives up on the dream of independence for his country. He declares separation from France as neither feasible nor desirable for Martinique. The country should only aspire to attain increased autonomy within its status as an overseas French department. This renunciation of the ideal of independence can strike a hard blow in the hearts of those who remember Césaire as one of the most compelling anticolonialist voices decades ago, when he launched vigorous critiques that decried colonial oppression, indicted dependency, and pressed for liberation. But the scenario described by Puerto Rican scholars Aaron Gamaliel Ramos and Angel Rivera, which shows the nonindependent societies in the Caribbean region enjoying greater levels of material well-being than their sovereign counterparts, would seem to offer solid economic grounds for contextualizing Césaire's change of heart (Ramos and Rivera 2001:xv, xx).

We owe an equally evocative admission of defeat to the late Michael Manley in an interview he gave for the documentary *Life and Debt*, a moving and insightful film on the Jamaican economy by Stephanie Black released in 2001. Soon after leading the People's National Party (PNP) to a landslide victory in 1972, Manley began nationalizing industries with the aim of reducing the country's legacy of dependence inherited from the colonial past. Speaking for Black's camera, Manley narrates his dealings with the major lending institutions—the International Monetary Fund (IMF) and the Inter-American Development Bank (IADB)—and the stranglehold that they eventually placed on his government. As the need for loans to activate the fledgling Jamaican economy grew, the banks imposed ever more stringent terms that ended up increasing the country's indebtedness, thus exacerbating the very dependency from which his political project sought to liberate the country. As the banks gradually and relentlessly curtailed his alternatives, he found himself having to sign agreements that would eventually harm Jamaica, but he had to swallow his pride and hope unrealistically for the best, while going home at night feeling "like a walking contradiction." The sadness of the Manley story, as well as of the various Jamaican industries that were made to cave in by the banks in order to make room in the economy for foreign imports, is contrapuntally embellished by the beauty of the lyrics and rhythms that provide the themes for *Life and Debt*, just as Bob Marley's stress on "redemption" melodically punctuates every transition in the disheartening narrative of *Portrait of the Caribbean*.

Speaking to graduate students at Syracuse University on April 4, 2001 during the symposium "Caribbean Writers Imagine the Millennium," prominent fiction writer, essayist, and playwright Luis Rafael Sánchez declared that, wanting a redemptive vision of the future for his country, since he saw no way out of the colonial cul-de-sac that his celebrated novel *La guaracha del macho Camacho* dramatized in 1976, his works sought primarily to bear witness to the reality that there is a place on the earth called Puerto Rico and that there live people with loves, obsessions, fears, joys, and sorrows of their own. Readers of Sánchez will have noted that all he has to say about humanity he says through the exploration of the predicaments of highly evocative characters located with precision in a city section of San Juan and a discrete moment of the Puerto Rican experience. The renowned Cuban writer Antonio

Benítez Rojo shared the stage with Sánchez in the conversation with the Syracuse students, and he expressed a similar view of the region's possibilities. For him the emphasis should be on the new cultural forms that emerge as a result of intra-Caribbean interactions and the rapport of the region's people with the rest of the world. He seemed to suggest that by focusing on those forms we can find sufficient reason to feel satisfied about the contemporary outcomes of the region's history. Addressing the same group a week later, Edouard Glissant, who insisted that we should regard his book *Caribbean Discourse* as poetry rather than as historical analysis or sociocultural reflection, also circumscribed the meaning of the Caribbean experience to the concatenation of cultural forms. This consensus among luminaries of Caribbean letters opting for the appraisal of cultural forms as the focus of their intellectual emphasis corresponds to a prevailing climate that seems to favor a concern for expressive forms over proposals for social transformation.

In a climate marked by political skepticism and doubt about the possibility of real social chance, the attention of the learned tends to gravitate toward those social fields that promise some psychological gratification. The rise of Caribbean music in the world market coincides with the region's growing need to export its people abroad and its increased reliance on industries that arrest development, such as free industrial zones and tourism. As indebtedness and economic dependence grow, with the Caribbean word losing its former prominence in view of newly emerged reconfigurations of the academic industry, the scholarly instinct seems to demand comfort zones, hence the turn to music, art, and the performance of expressive culture. These fields, enjoying the power of symbolization, suitable for deploying images, weaving metaphors, and inventing alternative worlds, have proven irresistible for colleagues in the profession. Of course, not every performer who rises to the top is politically a Bob Marley. A good many in fact use their access to the limelight to propagate recalcitrant ideas that work against the goal of inclusion, social justice, and equality for all. We glorify the rise of Caribbean music in large measure because the phenomenon soothes us, enabling us to cope with the anguish of defeat. The beat of those most enticing Caribbean sounds reigning supreme in the global music market offers a sort of consolation prize for the grief endured by people in the region who face the deleterious consequences of their long catastrophic history. We are Eva, with the Spirit of her church destroyed and the village of Bonasse in the grip of an unbeatable opportunist, managing to derive our share of necessary joy from listening to the young play the pans in a steelband tent and feeling "like resurrection morning."

CHAPTER 1

Colonial Migration and
Theoric Awakening

Yo,
    un hijo del Caribe
precisamente antillano.
Producto primitivo de una ingenua
criatura borinqueña
                y un obrero cubano,
nacido justamente, y pobremente,
en suelo quisqueyano.
Recorrido de voces,
lleno de pupilas
que a través de las islas se dilatan,
vengo a hablarle a Walt Whitman,
un cosmos,
            un hijo de Manhattan.

(I,
    a son of the Caribbean
Antillean to be exact.
The raw product of a simple
Puerto Rican girl
        and a Cuban worker,
born precisely, and poor,
on Quisqueyan soil.
Overflowing with voices
full eyes
  wide open throughout the islands,
I have come to speak to Walt Whitman,
  a kosmos,
           of Manhattan the son.)

          Pedro Mir [1993:47]

AN ANTILLEAN'S VOYAGE OF DISCOVERY

The preceding lines, written by the revered Dominican poet Pedro Mir, a native of San Pedro de Macorís, a city known for its baseball players and rhapsodic wordsmiths, come from *Countersong to Walt Whitman*, a 1952 poem that converses intertextually with *Song of Myself* by the towering American poet. There, the Antillean voice, rooted in its unbelievable archipelago of sugar and alcohol, aware of the long regional history of infamy that renders the nations of the hemisphere subservient to the powerful colossus to the north, launches a reformulation of Whitman's personal "I" as a collective "us" that encompasses the peoples of the Americas. As the foregoing proemium would suggest, Mir only proceeds to assemble his cultural and historical vision after locating accurately his point of departure, his origin, the specified site of his particular human experience. Similarly, we in the human sciences can, I believe, identify the theoretical orientations that inform our scholarship in terms of a recognition of the precise place of our provenance. The procedence of an Antillean person inescapably will bear the mark of a colonial condition, a legacy of migration to the imperial metropolis, and the precarious organization of knowledge born of an unequal rapport with the centers of power in the world system. Confident in the utility of the self-identification practiced by the speaker in Mir's poem, I undertake to describe my intellectual engagement with Caribbean culture by first narrating the episodes of my theoric awakening, which must start with an account of my point of departure.

When I was a child I thought like a neocolonial child about human culture. As I became a man, a particular sort of confluence of lived experience, awareness of past events, personal circumstances, social condition, and complex schooling prompted a reexamination of my childish ways. I chanced upon the realization that I brought something to the table when interacting with the so-called human sciences. That is, I had a baggage that I had better own to, lest I deceive others and confuse myself. Therefore, in proposing the outline of Caribbean intellectual history that this book has undertaken, I have thought it necessary to unpack the contents of my baggage. The next two large sections that follow this meditation will attempt to document the difficult interaction between thought production in the Caribbean region and the master discourses of the Western intellectual tradition. A chronicle of that interaction will illustrate the friction between marginal Antillean intellects and their dominant Western counterparts. The chronology herein considered goes from the 1492 incursion by Christopher Columbus into what Aphra Behn would later term "the other world" (the dark realm where her narrator meets the royal slave Oroonoko) to the currency of "postcolonial" emphases on the globalized Other in the U.S. and European academy (Behn 1994:5). Persuaded that in discussing cultural phenomena one can no more achieve the impartiality of a disinterested speaker than one would in immigrant or abortion rights debates, I have opted to devote this section to placing my cards on the table by tracing the roots of my "subject position," hence its autobiographical texture.

This opening section intends to convey the belief that we all have a story that explains us and that "where we come from" marks how we read traditions and what sort of learning we derive from them. Where we come from includes class origins, ethnoracial procedence, sociopolitical upbringing, sheer remembrance of things past, and the discrete chronological fraction of our life span. Conceivably, one can digest erudition without allowing the specificity of one's background to inform the scholarly experience. At times, a non-white scholar functioning in the Western academy might feel compelled to achieve such a feat. Colleagues from "the other world" might wish to establish their intellectual equality vis-à-vis their Western counterparts by becoming indistinguishable from them as regards the bodies of knowledge they master, the schemes of thought they embrace, and the discursive practices they deploy. As I have gotten older, though, I have become fiercely averse to that course of action, which I have come to regard as epistemological self-annihilation. Thus, I start precisely with where I come from, giving an existential geneology to my utterances, to my choice of concerns among the problems that occupy my peers in the profession, and to the kinds of interventions that strike me as compelling. Narrating the story of my background will enable me also to contextualize what one could call my "commitment to theory." The autobiographical narrative potentially will support the contention that in the human sciences the "theoretical" itself has a geopolitical and a cultural history, which it behooves us to keep in mind as we consume the products that the intellectual market offers to us as "theory." The way we choose to deal with the constituent factors of our background may determine how we experience the formulations we are offered and the credulity with which we consume theoretical products.

A Theoric Preamble

I use the adjective "theoric" in the title to this section to mean the same as "theoretical," a value it frequently had in older parlance. I intend with this reminiscent usage to stress the word's association with "public access" so as to render less self-evident, etymologically at least, the widespread acceptance of an equation between turgid density of expression and speculative depth. I find it significant that the ancient Greek word *theoria*, while conveying the idea of contemplation as a mental engagement, invariably denotes the act of looking at reality concretely with one's own physical eyes. The term theoric most often referred to the viewing of public spectacles, including religious functions and solemn embassies. Derived from the neuter *theoricon* and its plural *theorica*, the word came to name specifically an Athenian fund "raised by tax on the people" for the purpose of defraying "the expenses of theatrical representations" and other events. A law promulgated by Eubulus, as chief commissioner of the fund, prohibited the application of the theoric money toward any other use, including war. The theoric fund, established by Pericles in 450 BC, was thought worthy of an entry in the 1728 *Cyclopedia, or Universal Dictionary of Arts and Sciences* by British encyclopedist Epraim Chambers. One might add that this *Cyclopedia* not only earned its author a seat in the Royal Society, but it also became foundational as a reference source for the more famous *Encyclopédie* launched later by French *philosophes* Denis Diderot and Jean D'Alembert.

At any rate, the theoric fund covered admission costs for all citizens who could not afford to pay the price of seats at the theater and public performances (Wilson and Goldfarb 1983:25; *Webster's New Universal* 1983:1893). A contemporary approximation of the Athenian politics of access to cultural and artistic products could be Bertolt Brecht's Berliner Ensemble whose performances the working class could afford to see because of substantial subsidy by the East Germany government. I find the interpenetration of speculative thought and democratic access to the matter to look at, which is so explosively submerged in the story of the theoricon, deeply illuminating as I ponder on the intellectual market today, and, more relevantly still, on my own conceptual and linguistic demeanor as I try to speak my way into the available pigeonholes of that market. I draw from this a simple lesson: that intellectual height should never ignore the social ground beneath the feet of the intellectual worker involved. In the end, irrespective of the altitudes to which we might wish our ideas to soar, the fact remains that somebody ultimately will have to pay the tab. The totally ethereal might achieve prestige while at the same time risking to yellow into banality.

I identify wholeheartedly with Edward W. Said's plaint about the current professionalizing turn of literary and cultural discourse: "As for intellectuals whose charge includes values and principles—literary, philosophical, historical specialists—the American university, with its munificence, utopian sanctuary, and remarkable diversity, has defanged them. Jargons of an almost unimaginable rebarbativeness dominate their style . . . an astonishing sense of weightlessness with regard to the gravity of history and individual responsibility fritters away attention to public matters, and to public discourse" (Said 1993:303). I have come to terms with my unwillingness to entertain or admire ideas unless I can see how they matter in the world. I approach learning, thus, as an effort to make sense of the world and to establish how best to locate my position with respect to the other members of the species within the social realm. I have lost patience for reading works whose sole justification for existing would seem to be that they "make a contribution to the field" by "further problematizing" an already encumbered and not particularly earth-shaking contention propounded by one of the thinkers that the market recognizes as theorists. The autobiographical rendition of my background in this part of the book attempts, therefore, to narrate the story of how I reached the state of mind that presently informs my participation in the academy. This account of my "theoric awakening" provides also a justification not only for my discursive behavior but also the liberty I grant myself of citing the bibliographical references often judged obligatory by colleagues in the profession only when and if they truly can shed light on the particular problem I am tackling, namely exploring the difficult rapport between Caribbean discourse and the Western human sciences.

Knowledge in My Father's House

Early education in subordinate, neocolonial Caribbean society taught youngsters to locate real humanity in a world existing away from home. As a student in Third Standard in Trinidad, Cynthia, the main character in Merle Hodge's compelling novel *Crick Crack, Monkey* copes with this experience by creating a double whom she names Helen, a better version of herself, one that matched more closely the idea of humanity she extracted from books. "Books transported you always into the familiar solidity of chimneys and apple trees, the enviable normality of real Girls and Boys who went a-sleighing and built snowmen . . . Books transported you always into Reality and Rightness, which were to be found Abroad" (Hodge 1981:61). Thus she invented Helen, her double: "No, she couldn't be called my double. She was the Proper Me. And me, I was her shadow hovering about in incompleteness" (62). Maturing in that context meant primarily for learners to develop the mental prowess necessary to place themselves in the midst of humanity by reconfiguring the world in a manner that contained their home. Kamau Brathwaite has referred to his maturing as a "de-education," a process that for him entailed a period of "self-education," which led gradually to a "whole sense of being Barbadian, Caribbean" (1992). Growing up intellectually for me meant unlearning the lessons that had taught me to view book learning innocently. My father had instilled in me the sense that intellectual cultivation mattered for its own sake while at the same time it helped you rise above those around you. "Read for two hours everyday," he would dare me, "and in two years you will not be able to stand the company of the loafers you hang out with on the corner." I never heard my father brag in haughty pride about anything but scholarly possessions: his command of the Spanish language, historical erudition, and world sapience.

During frequent rounds of drunken wakefulness, Silvio Sr. would quote Shakespeare, recite the Lake Poets, and recall moments illustrative of the wisdom of the ancients. He would call to mind that Sophocles once lamented to a fellow playwright that for three days he had failed to come up with the right hexameter line for a tragedy then in progress. Instead of sympathy, his plaint elicited this swagger: "But Sophocles, in three days I can write three whole plays," to which our sage retorted, "yes, I know, and then they last but three days." In his youth my father had shown above average aptitude in baseball, the American sport that had become the national pastime following the years of U.S. military rule of the Dominican Republic from 1916 through 1924, and he remained a passionate fan all his life. When I once teased him about his coincident taste for an entertainment of the uncultured masses, he pulled out from his mental knapsack a literary legitimation. He pointed out to me that a good deal of the Homeric epithets actually name sports activities: the archer or he who strikes from afar, for Apollo, or the javalin or discuss thrower for this or that Achaean warrior, and so on. After linking his sports interest with erudite textuality, he felt he need say no more.

Coming from a family in which Greek and Roman first names abounded (Sixto, Cástor, Augusto, Silvio, César, Porfirio, and the like), my father spoke about ancient Hebrew history with a particularly telling sense of connection. He would evoke Saul's sensitivity to music, explaining how a harpist's Lydian melody would swing the king's mood in one direction while a Lybian tune would reverse the effect. He judged David a great ruler and castigated

Salomon for ruinously mishandling the glorious kingdom that his father had left him. As a result of the frequency with which our father would plunge into learned narrative, the names of philosophers, statesmen, sanctified Western authors, as well as past and present rulers in the most central parts of the globe triggered a familiar resonance in our ears. My sisters and I did not need to wait until we entered school to become acquainted with difficult-to-pronounce multisyllabic names such as Aristophanes or Thucydides. We went to see Federico Fellini's *Satyricon* when the film arrived at the Teatro Colón in Santiago, and the recognition seemed comforting especially when it came to the episode featuring the widow from Ephesus, a story we had heard recounted by our father, an ardent reader of Petronius. We knew before leaving home what people went to do in school. This pre-empted awareness was enhanced by our mother Aida, who took it upon herself to teach us how to read before we began the first grade. Aida's operatic name was a reminder of the urban middle-class aspirations of Chea, her own mom. Overpowered by the seductive thrill from the city's siren's song, Chea had left her rural home-town of Guayubín in La Guajaca, in the country's Northwest, for the din of the capital city of Santo Domingo, forsaking husband, children, and all.

We, Aida's children, did not have enough contact with Chea to develop the affection that grandmothers proverbially evoke. We called her Mama Chea but the name entailed no endearment. Perhaps we intuited that some of the dreams that Aida could not pursue had to do with her mom's choice to pursue hers, however indefinable those may have been. Aida married Silvio Sr. when she was only 17, arresting her education though she evidently had the brains for it, and desisting from the idea of becoming an operatic singer though the voice she lulled us with seemed worthy of the finest stage. Despite her uncaring mother, an inconsiderate and often abusive spouse, the burden of seven children, and lacking a formal education, Aida not only forged ahead, but in all matters of consequence she was the primary parent. That included, oddly enough, matters of schooling. Her insufficient learning did not diminish her desire to help us learn. Silvio Sr. may have influenced us through his customary display of erudition within hearing range of us, but it fell upon our largely unschooled peasant mother to materialize the necessary logistics such as getting us admitted into the public school or teaching us our first letters. A devout Christian, she found solace from the harshness of ordinary life in her reading of the Bible, which she often brandished as a weapon against our father, whose assiduous drinking, ineptitude as a provider, and frequent disparagement she credited to the "iniquity" of his spirit.

The sight of my mother quoting the holy scriptures to fend off the aggression of her "iniquitous" spouse powerfully reinforced the idea that book knowledge had weight, a message I habitually received from my father. The message, on the whole, hinged on a sharply differentiated idea of knowledge, one that left little room for diversity of heritages. Cultivation of the intellect meant merely the pursuit of familiarity with the cultures that make up the narrative of the Western tradition, namely Hebrew, Greek, Roman, and the achievements of Christian Europe. Neither my father's phenotypical blackness nor his ancestral link to Haiti, the Caribbean country with some of the most unadulterated expressions of African cultural survival in the region, had any mitigating effect on his radically Eurocentric understanding of human culture. His paternal grandfather had in the nineteenth century crossed over to the Dominican side of the island of Hispaniola, where he settled, formed a Dominican family, and contributed to intellectual life in the City of Santiago as one of the founding members of Alianza Cibaeña, then the only local public library. Not atypically for his generation, my father evinced a neglectful regard for the implications of his uncritical embrace of the view that equated humanity with the West. He thus overlooked the extent to which the narration of humanity based on such an equation inevitably nullified him as a black Haitian-descended Dominican in the midst of a specifically Caribbean occurrence of the human experience.

Invasion and Two-Way Mobility

In 2001 I came across a photograph of my father in which, he, a teenager, appears sitting at a table playing dominoes with two of his older brothers. Sitting in the middle, facing the camera, is Pedro Augusto, a stout young man whom the family would later distinguish for his irascible character and his sportsmanship. He would later become an ace first base for the Santiago baseball team Las Aguilas Cibaeñas. To Pedro's right—camera left—is Luis Tomás, the eldest, who would in adult life become important in local government, serving at one point as the Mayor of Santiago. Across from Luis Tomás sits my father, dominoes in hand, looking askance to his left in the direction of the camera, showing an adolescent's face not older than 14 years of age. This estimate of my father's age in the picture would place the scene in 1924, the year when the marines left after eight years of direct U.S. military rule in the country. The picture captures a daytime scene and one assumes the three boys' father, Don Pedro Saillant, the civil court judge, to be at work. Their mother, Doña Delfina Fernández de Saillant, a respected *couturière*, might be similarly occupied. But depending on the exact dates, Don Pedro and Doña Delfina, the paternal grandparents I never met, may be an ocean away. U.S. immigration records show them both entering through Ellis Island on August 29, 1923 as visitors. They came to see their wayward son Delfín, who had arrived in the United States as far back as 1919 via Cuba and who would remain here for the rest of his life (AFIHC 2002). The presence of my paternal grandparents in the United States in 1923 speaks of their relative economic well-being since they could afford to travel abroad. They would later send their only daughter María Amparo to a private high school in Philadelphia. But their presence also speaks of the bilateral mobility that colonial domination forges. When an imperial nation holds a dependent one in its mighty grip—whether the tool of conquest involves an army or the banks—channels of communication between the two countries ordinarily open. Their asymmetry notwithstanding, the connectedness that links the director and the directed societies moves people inevitably in both directions.

This bidirectional mobility dates at least from before the founding in 1844 of the Dominican Republic, the second so-called independent State in the Caribbean. Prior to becoming a founding father, the ideological architect of the Dominican nation Juan Pablo Duarte spent time in New York (Duarte 1994:40). William L. Cazneau, a veteran of the Texas and the Mexican wars, had himself appointed envoy to Santo Domingo in 1853. Once there, he and his partner Joseph W. Fabens gave vent to their entrepreneurial impulses, acquiring generous plots of land from the Dominican government to build a colony for U.S. citizens who wished to relocate to the Dominican Republic. They operated the American West India Company, which, among other things, sought to promote interest in the Dominican soil among people in the United States. Concomitant with their enterprise, several books appeared that depicted the small Caribbean country as a "new Eldorado," luring American readers with descriptions of the "vast mineral, agricultural, manufacturing and commercial resources" of the land, and further stressing the "scarcely credible" fact "that such vast wealth, and especially mineral wealth, should have lain there so easily attainable, for so many years and almost within the suburbs of our great commercial cities, without exciting at least the cupidity, if not the enterprise of the Yankee" (Courtney 1860:9). Fabens and Cazneau's transnational real estate project did not yield the fruit they had desired, nor did their picturesque scheme to import camels to the Dominican Republic with the purpose of improving transportation options in the country, but the two crafty adventurers continued to deploy their business and political maneuvers until mid-1871 when they finally "removed themselves from the Dominican scene" (Welles 1966:400–401).

A pivotal year, 1871 marks the end of the U.S. government's formal attempt to annex the Dominican land. The interest in adding the Dominican side of the island of Hispaniola to the U.S. territory had gained momentum during the James K. Polk administration and continued intermittently to surge and wane until after the Civil War, when President Ulysses S. Grant took it up with obstinate passion. The formidable opposition he encountered both in the U.S. Congress and in the most intransigent faction of the Dominican nationalist movement thwarted Grant's annexationist plan, but while it seemed feasible a good many U.S. politicians and entrepreneurs traveled to peruse the country and ascertain its ripeness for annexation. In the last resort, Grant secured congressional approval to send a commission of inquiry to the country to gather the necessary data to help him make his case. Made up of Senator Benjamin B. Wade, Senator Samuel G. Howe, and Senator Andrew D. White, who would subsequently go on to serve as founding president of Cornell University, with the ex-slave and now prominent abolitionist Frederick Douglass as secretary, the commission arrived in Santo Domingo on January 16, 1871. Though their findings established "the physical, mental, and moral condition of the inhabitants of Santo Domingo" to have been "more advanced than had been anticipated," they did not help Grant promote his case before congressional opposition (*Report* 1871:13). Speaking before Congress on April 5, 1871, not without longing, he invoked the report to support his unwavering belief that "the interests of our country and of Santo Domingo alike invite the annexation of the Republic" (Welles 1966:400–401).

That the annexation did not take place does not mean that U.S. interests failed to shape Dominican society, which fell progressively deeper into the sphere of influence of the director society to the North. Nor did the bipolar flow of people diminish. That explains the presence in New York on February 19, 1901 of Pedro Henríquez Ureña upon completing his high school in the capital city of Santo Domingo. In time he would become an internationally renowned philologist, a first-rate scholar of Hispanic literatures, deserving of such honors as an invitation to occupy the prestigious Charles Elliot Norton Visiting Professorship at Harvard University during academic year 1940–1941. The lectures he gave as part of that engagement became a book that Harvard University Press published under the title *Literary Currents of Hispanic America* (1945). The inside flap of the book cover carried a biographical error in referring to the "real milestone" of "these lectures by a South American scholar." I can't help musing that the oversight of calling Henríquez Ureña "South American" stemmed from the inability of Harvard folks at the time to imagine Dominicans as literary beings, familiar though they found them as political subordinates (Torres-Saillant 2000:263).

When Henríquez Ureña first came to this country at the dawn of the twentieth century, he found a considerable number of his compatriots living here already. In recalling that first visit, his diary describes "the hotels and houses that lodged the Dominicans who came to New York for their summer vacation, whose number increased every year" (cited by Roggiano 1961: xxviii). He describes the Manhattan neighborhood where he and his brothers lived as one that "teemed with Dominican exiles who now increasingly headed for New York" (xxxi). Around 1918 Pedro and his sister Camila both pursued graduate studies in Spanish literature at the University of Minnesota in Minneapolis. He had completed a master's degree and now worked on his doctorate while she was finishing her M.A. As their father had been serving as interim president at the time of the U.S. military takeover of their country two years before, they must have had to cope with embarrassing moments. A suggestive passage in the novel *In the Name of Salomé* by Julia Alvarez evokes "the difficulties Pedro encountered because of his color and accent" and the irony—not overlooked by a student newspaper on campus—that he and Camila seemed to condone the occupied status of their homeland by coming to an American university to advance their scholarly pursuits (2000:234–235).

Colonial bipolarity did not bring to the U.S. territory only Dominicans who had scholarly inclinations. It also brought the likes of Francis Rebajes, an entrepreneurial adventurer turned coppersmith and costume jeweler. As lucky, resourceful, and audacious as a Horatio Algers hero, Rebajes was born in the city of Puerto Plata on February 6, 1906. His father had sent him to secondary school in Barcelona, Spain, but he could put up neither with the scholastic routine nor the effeminate uniform. Appalled at what he regarded as merely "a male finishing school," which required him to dress up "like a sissy," he dropped out and returned to Puerto Plata, where he read the adventure stories of Emilio Salgari and pursued odd jobs (Alig 1953:8). After some time of working and saving his monthly salary, he decided to seek his fortune in the United States. With the support of his father who paid his passage, gave him 300 dollars, and "presented him with his first long-trouser suit, a ceremony that held for Rebajes all the significance of a bullfighter's permit to wear the pigtail," he boarded a ship headed for New York in 1923 (8).

Living in Harlem, he roamed the streets with a gang of penniless intellectuals who valued him as one of their "main sources of food" given his dynamic employment record as a busboy in small cafes, big cafeterias, and the Automat. At a Greenwich Village party during the depression he met his wife Pauline Schwartz. Her parents did not think highly of him, but in retrospect he would say he could hardly blame them since he "lived like a bum" at the time. When the couple married, they didn't have a place to live and had to rely on a Peruvian friend to take them in (Alig 1953:43). Rebajes failed to get a steady job for months. Wandering the streets he "picked up tin cans, and, for want of something to do, cut them, pounded them, and modeled them" with his friend's tools (43). In so doing, he discovered his talent for using the hammer and anvil to make images of various sorts. As his creations multiplied so did his clientele, beginning with Village intellectuals "who appreciated the value of a well-made object with originality and imagination" (43). In 1934 he opened his first store at 184 West Fourth Street in the Village, began using copper, acquired a collection of hammers and specialized tools, and soon could buy another store, hire staff, and install machines. Writing in 1953, Wallace B. Alig credited Rebajes with "centering the metal craft industry along Fourth Street today" (44).

By the time of Alig's feature on Rebajes, the shrewd Dominican had exhibited his work at the Metropolitan Museum of Art, had earned a medal of honor awarded in 1937 by the French International Exposition, and had designed six illuminated metal murals in 1940 for the theater in the New York World Fair's U.S. Government Building (Alig 1953:6). His business had also expanded so rapidly that in the early 1940s he moved to 377 Fifth Avenue, an establishment "designed by Puerto Rican architect José Fernández," added dozens of employees to his operation, and had outlets all over the country. In 1953 Pauline and Frank Rebajes lived happily with their cat Tabby and their turtle Tortuga in a Malverne, Long Island home that Frank designed and built himself with the help of a Puerto Rican named Luis Ramos. To relax from the pressures of their large and growing commercial enterprise, they got away to beaches in the West Indies every winter. The totally rosy texture of their story gave Alig reason to construe the Rebajes adventure as "proof that the much-touted American dream can come true" (45). In 1958 Rebajes sold his factory operation and original designs to his foreman Otto Bade and later moved to Torremolinos, Spain, where he continued to craft handwrought pieces (Greenbaum 1996:72). Enrique Castaños Alés, who interviewed the dynamic jeweler for a profile that appeared in the Malaga newspaper *Sur* on August 20, 1989, described the aesthetic and esoteric interests that occupied the artist during his years in Spain (Castaños Alés 1996). Rebajes died on June 8, 1990, in Boston, Massachusetts (Greenbaum 1996:70).

I can only venture a wild guess about the chances that my grandparents could have had of attaining any material success comparable to that of the talented and shrewd Rebajes had they chosen to stay in the United States. His special gift as a craftsman notwithstanding, Rebajes also came to the United States armed with reflexes, attitudes, and an ideological outlook that probably did not abound among the Dominicans of his generation and which must have eased his passage into mainstream American business. Coming to the metropolis as the scion of an occupied country, Rebajes displayed a political sentiment that did not interfere with his embracing of the American economic ethos. Although when he first arrived in New York he went to live with "a group of friends from home" who had met him at the pier and though Hispanics came to his aid at key moments in his life, he characterized it as "a mistake of Latin Americans" to "settle in quarters only among themselves, neglecting to get to know the real native-born Americans" (Alig 1953:743).

Disdainful about ethnic loyalties, he also had casual views about the meaning of blood ties: "One's family is an imposition while friends are people of one's choosing. I don't associate with members of my family simply because they are my family" (7). One could conjecture that such lack of a sense of community and his rather noncommittal attitude toward family, in the midst of the ethnically stratified society that he came to in the 1920s, must have freed Rebajes to apply himself devoutly to the cult of individual economic achievement that informed the American dream ideology. That both his parents came to the Dominican Republic from Mallorca, Spain, can permit the supposition that his Mediterranean features did not severely clash with the racial predilections then prevailing in New York. Had he landed in the Southwest, where the existing racial logic drew a clear line between Hispanics and Anglos, perhaps his mobility would have faced hurdles.

Culturally too Rebajes leaned toward things American, representing the new, as compared with older worlds. Visiting Europe and North Africa in 1952, he sampled the art galleries only to conclude that The National Gallery in Washington, DC was "the most perfect I have seen." He found El Prado in Madrid "too squeaky and dilapidated" while the Louvre in Paris left him with the impression that "the massive plaster ceiling was too oppressive" (Alig 1953:45). Equipped with the right instinct for capitalist accumulation, he thought objects of art should have an exchange value just as any other commodity does, and that "Real artists are interested in money" (Alig 6). He harbored no Benjaminian qualm about the aura that the artwork would lose in the process of its mechanical reproduction (Benjamin 1999:283). Devoid of any interest in the context that rendered a work of art unique, its ritual function in the fabric of tradition, Rebajes confidently dismissed what Alig termed "commercial snob appeal." Preferring to make "a good design available to everyone," he sought first and foremost to sell a product that he considered beautiful to as many people as possible. Once you make the "original piece," he asked rhetorically, "What's the difference if we make a million copies" (Alig 1953:6). Rebajes had already moved to Spain in the 1960s, when a great Dominican exodus began that would lead to the formation in New York of a large ethnic enclave made of people from his country of birth. For those compatriots, it would become more difficult to ignore the 1965 U.S. military invasion that prompted their uprooting, to move about as ethnically unencumbered individuals, to find ample economic opportunities in profitable markets, and to wholeheartedly embrace the American dream ideology.

Foreign Domination, Native Identity

The United States invaded the Dominican Republic in 1916, when my father was only six, which means that the formative years of his public socialization from childhood through adolescence occurred under foreign domination. When the Americans left in 1924, having disarmed the civilian population and conferred upon the Guardia Nacional they had created a monopoly over violence, Dominicans had learned to see U.S.-style institutions as indispensable. American consumer products dominated their market, American baseball had replaced cockfighting as their national pastime, and the population's taste buds had been weaned into U.S. flavors. A character in the novel *Cuando amaban las tierras comuneras* by the late Pedro Mir explains the meaning of the phenomenon to a child by drawing a parallel between the occupation and the shift from going about barefoot to first wearing shoes. Before, your feet could cope with the roughness of the uneven, harsh, and bumpy ground, but once you learn to walk in the protection that shoes offer, your feet grow tender, delicate, easily hurt, and you have to wear the protection forever (Mir 1978).

Raised in a society where the logic dictated by the U.S. occupation reigned supreme, my father probably lacked the analytical distance required for discerning how stridently his own national experience discredited the supposition of the Western heritage as a paragon of human value. The most rabidly Western of all nations in the Christian-capitalist world system, the United States came to the Dominican Republic to civilize an underdeveloped people. At the very start of the twentieth century, in a speech that became known as expressive of a "corollary" to the Monroe Doctrine, President Theodore Roosevelt asserted the right of the United States to intervene in the internal political and economic life of any country in the hemisphere deemed insufficiently proficient in managing its affairs to the satisfaction of the international community (Munro 1964:77). My father did not seem to have grasped the sad irony of thinking highly of a civilization that held him in very low esteem in so far as it viewed his nation as inept.

In a letter to Joseph Bucklin Bishop on February 23, 1904 Teddy Roosevelt, faced with the prospects of intervening in the country, claimed to have "been hoping and praying that the Santo Domingans would behave so that

I would not have to act in this way. I want to do nothing but what a policeman has to do in Santo Domingo" (Bishop 1926:494). Nearly a year later, in a special message to Congress submitting a treaty that would authorize the U.S. takeover of Dominican finances, Roosevelt called "attention to the urgent need of prompt action on this matter," stressing that the "protocol" proposed offered "a great opportunity to secure peace and stability in the island" while affording "a practical test of the efficiency of the United States Government in maintaining the Monroe Doctrine" (Bishop 1926: 495–496). Later, in his *Autobiography* (1913) Roosevelt would recall with some resentment the attitude of those legislators who, though agreeing that Dominicans "of course must be protected and must be made to behave," had at the time opposed his manner of accomplishing the feat (1925:580).

The entry on the Dominican Republic appearing in the eleventh edition of the *Encyclopaedia Britannica*, published the year of my father's birth, gives an idea of what the West saw when it looked in the direction of his Caribbean homeland. The entry, entitled "Santo Domingo" in keeping with colonial usage, speaks of "a state in the West Indies," occupying two-thirds of Hispaniola, that has "the finest lands." It praises the country's fertility by saying that there: "tobacco and cacao flourish; the mountain regions are specially suited to the culture of coffee, and tropical fruits will grow any-where with a minimum of attention." The article recalls the gold and silver that the Spanish extracted from the land annually during the early years of the colonial conquest. Describing present resources, the article points to the riches that remain: "Platinum, manganese, iron, copper, tin, antimony, opals, and chalcedony are also found. In the Neyba valley there are two remarkable hills, composed of pure rock salt. Only an influx of capital and an energetic population are needed to develop these resources." The encyclopedia makes it clear that the "energetic population" necessary "to develop" the country's natural resources did not live there. The energy had to come from elsewhere. The disparaging tone of the following characterization would seem to suggest that the encyclopedia did not even conceive of the natives as possibly able to read the entry written on them: "The people are mainly mulattoes of Spanish descent, but there are a considerable number of negroes and whites of both Creole and European origin. Politically the whites have the predominating influence. People on the whole are quiet, lazy, and shiftless, but subject at times to great political excitement" ("Santo Domingo" 1910:194–195).

The *Britannica* entry mentions in passing the receivership that put Dominican fiscal life, the collection of customs and other revenues, in the hands of U.S. agents, the native population of the country having apparently proved untrustworthy in the handling of its own financial affairs. First, "an American company," meaning a private firm that managed the securance of bonds until 1899, "defaulted in the payment of interest," at which point the U.S. government took direct control: "In 1905, to forestall foreign inter-vention [by European creditors] for securing payment of the State debt, President Roosevelt made an agreement with Santo Domingo, under which the United States undertook to adjust the republic's foreign obligation, and to assume charge of the customs houses. A treaty was ratified by the United States Senate in 1907, and an American citizen is temporarily receiver of customs" (194). Perhaps one should not fault the *Britannica* author's lack of prescience for failing to intuit that American hands would not loosen their grip on Dominican fiscal affairs until 1940, when the depraved dictator Rafael Leónidas Trujillo declared the country's "economic independence." Nor perhaps did the writer have a way of foreseeing that a U.S. military invasion would become necessary after all, the mere receivership having apparently proved insufficient for Washington to accomplish its civilizing goal in the country.

Washington's decision to relinquish the collection of Dominican customs into the hands of Trujillo in the tyrant's tenth year of continuous hold of ruthless political power points to a partnership between the U.S. democracy and the Dominican dictatorship that further framed my father's life span socially, politically, and existentially. By 1924, the putative year of the afore-mentioned photograph and the American military disoccupation, Trujillo had risen to visibility on the political arena. Empowered with key American contacts, having excelled as the highest achieving of the officers trained in the U.S.-formed Guardia Nacional, it would take him no more than six years to get himself elected president of the Republic (Vega 1992). He used to advantage his rank as chief of the armed forces, which, with the success of civilian disarmament, now enjoyed exclusively the power to intimidate. Incarceration, murder, and psychological terror made Trujillo *presidenciable*, especially after masterminding the overthrow of his protector President Horacio Vásquez, who had to resign and go into exile.

In 1930, the year when Trujillo's 30-year-long reign of terror began, my father was a 20-year-old man with a poetic gift and a flair for crisp journalistic prose. I cannot tell whether my father had occasion to formulate in his mind a clear position on the cultural policies of the dictatorship, but he never verbalized it. The Trujillo regime's obstinate and well-funded promotion of a notoriously Eurocentric view of Dominicanness looked to the Spanish conquerors and colonial settlers to find the ethnoracial foundation of the nation while prophylactically excising any cultural form evidently associated with the African heritage (Torres-Saillant 1995:128–129). I have no memory of my father's articulating, in my presence, any position of black self-affirmation other than his occasionally recalling, with detectable satisfaction, the comment an acquaintance of his had made about his family: "The Saillants are the only blacks in this country who don't suffer from a complex of inferiority." Nor do I remember his ever attaching any significance to his Haitian ancestry other than to mock the silly class yearnings of his nephew Luigi. During a conversation with longtime friends of the family, Luigi heard that the Haitian progenitor who had started the Saillant lineage on Dominican soil several generations back was a blood relation of King Henry Christophe, and the detail heaved his chest with enthusiasm. Too impatient to wait until the morning, he came pantingly to awake his learned uncle in the middle of the night to verify if it was true that "we are royalty."

But my father displayed no insecurity about his own worth. Though we always lived in poor neighborhoods and meals occasionally skipped our table, he undertook to convince us that we were not nobodies. Poverty did not reduce us to the level of those whose condition we shared. We were "the children of Silvio Saillant," a rank that even to this day one or two of my siblings would feel comfortable pulling. He despised Trujillo because of the morbid pleasure the dictator derived from his humiliation of people. Trujillo, who liked to be called "El Jefe" (The Chief), once summoned my paternal grandfather, then a civil court judge, to reprimand him for something or other, and my father never forgave him. When he became a columnist for the newspaper *La Nación*, he swore never to put Trujillo's name in print, and he didn't, not, of course, without repercussions. In a country where the capital city bore the name of Ciudad Trujillo, where people learned to add "and Trujillo" when thanking God for any small blessing that came their way, and where sycophant praise of the ruler occupied the energies of all media, the absence of any reference to Trujillo in my father's articles glared too brightly in the eyes of the regime's commissars. He ended up in the notorious Nigua Prison. Mario Vargas Llosa's novelization of the Dominican dictator's last years in power gives a credible portrayal of the horror of Trujillo's prisons (Vargas Llosa 2000). When my father luckily came out of prison, he no longer had a career in journalism. Nor was his literary calling so compelling that he could compensate by seeking refuge in his poetry as did so many in his generation who carved a niche of concealment in the obscure beauty of metaphors. The primary goal of their words was to avoid friction with the awful density pervading the political climate.

When the dictator finally bit the dust on May 30, 1961, a flurry of assassins' bullets having reached their up to that point unimaginable destination, my father had reached his fifties, which made him practically an old man by Caribbean standards of that period. His time had passed: for poetry, for journalism, for meaningful life in the public sphere. Ironically, the members of his generation who had mustered the necessary resourcefulness to navigate the regime's voracity for servility seemed to have aged considerably less than he. He withdrew into himself, cultivated his garden of private honor, suffered privation rather than genuflect, and drank himself into oblivion. Still, one could scan in him the sparks of a resistive spirit even if the outer man as sociopolitical animal was crushed. He may not have asserted his African heritage nor otherwise protested the incongruence of the prevailing Western cultural discourse with the ethnoracial and cultural reality of his country. But he named his first child Melania, a word whose Greek etymology (μελας, μέλαν = black) evinces an approving recognition of her very dark skin. A machista fellow, the predictable product of a phallocratic social order, he nonetheless encouraged my three sisters to value themselves highly, become self-sufficient, and avoid dependency on their spouses. He even insisted that they should learn to hold their liquor so as not to be at a disadvantage vis-à-vis their male counterparts when they went partying.

The regimes that crushed my father's possibilities did not manage to flatten his human complexity. What he salvaged from the rubble of his sociopolitical annulment I regard as the most valued inheritance he bequeathed to his children. Concomitantly, from my mother, who came from lowly, peasant origins, I treasure the example of hard work and her stomach for coping with adversity. My father never once gave the impression that he thought one should bow to people with power or authority. Though we always lived in marginal *barrios*, our house would always stand out in the neighborhood because of the occasional visit of notable personages, intellectuals, and politicians who were friends from his childhood or youth. The crafty Joaquín Balaguer, Trujillo's heir in the autocratic control of the Dominican State, came to the house when I was a child. Juan Bosh, the democratically elected president who was deposed by a U.S.-backed military coup in 1963, also came to the house for a chat. All of his children were already settled raising families and building lives in New York when the news reached us in 1983 that President Salvador Jorge Blanco had made a stop at our father's house during a trip to Santiago. These presidential visits to a sociopolitically defunct old friend who lived in dismal conditions speaks to the kind of *cadre* my father had belonged to in his youth. I particularly cherish the recollection I have of my father's demeanor during the visits of those powerful acquaintances. He displayed no excessive gratitude for their deigning to enter his humble abode, no overflow of reverential admiration for their accomplishments, no abject prostration—simply courteous cordiality. He had them sit on the mahogany chair that he assigned to visitors, located directly across from his. He did not give up his seat, which was invariably the best kept piece of furniture in the living room. Though they ruled the whole country outside the door, he left little room for doubting who retained authority in the private sovereignty of his house.

My father believed in God, but he eyed the Catholic clergy with utmost suspicion. He did not instill in his children a submissive, unquestioning respect for the institutional mandates of the church nor for the sanctity of the prelacy. We did not keep up with the timely observance of the sacraments. I was already in my teens when I had the holy waters of baptism poured over my head. In fact, my mother, fearing the ultimate consequences of letting her children continue to live out of the grace of God, made the unconventional but practical move of assembling and dragging us all to church for a collective baptism, with her brother Pompo standing as *padrino* and his mother-in-law Filleya as *madrina*. It was also she who ensured that at least some of us had our first communion. But, on the whole, my father felt no particular compulsion to comply with the steps dictated by the church for the salvation of our souls. Although he never renounced Catholicism, the default religion of any person born in the Dominican Republic since the country defines itself officially as Catholic, my father displayed greater sympathy and tolerance— perhaps even appreciation—toward non-Catholic Christians who would come to our door offering the "word of the Lord," and voicing the good tidings that the kingdom was "at hand." He would at times lend a courteous ear to the spiritual lobbying of Jehovah's Witnesses or Seventh Day Adventists. I believe he respected in them their conversion, their conviction that the

Lord had revealed Himself to them, in short, their sense of a personal engagement with the faith they professed. The institutional ranks of bishops, archbishops, and cardinals did not impress him, but he did not easily disdain an individual who, scriptures in hand, came to him as an impassioned believer.

CHILD LABOR, INVASION, MIGRATION

I was in the third grade when my mother apprenticed me to the shoemaking sweatshop owned and operated by her brother Pompo, much to the chagrin of my father who probably resented what my initiation into child labor might tell others—and most importantly him—about his inability to provide consistently for the family. However, in due time he not only grew to accept the idea that I would be a worker, but as years passed he came to appreciate the fact that having a job, being able to support myself, grounded me in a much firmer reality than that of the other youngsters with whom I would otherwise hang out on the corner. He himself pointed this out to me one day when he saw me greet a distant cousin named Lucas, a man then some 15 years my senior, by asking first about his family and then about his job. The serious substance of my brief exchange with Lucas truly impressed my father. Though he did not expand on the matter, what he regarded as psychological growth must have made up in his mind for any loss I may have suffered as a result of my premature entrance into the adult arena of the workforce. My sisters have often said, not without a measure of pity, that I had no childhood, and I have invariably shrugged off their lamentation by retorting that they subscribe to too bourgeois a model of what childhood should be.

I did have a childhood, but one of a certain kind. As an apprentice to a master leather cutter in the sweatshop, I quickly became an adept assistant whose services mattered to the overall operation. It soon became necessary for me to put in longer daytime hours on the job, meaning that I had to switch to night school, the educational structure designed to address the learning needs of grown-ups. The first half of the academic year in the third grade, whose second half I completed at night, would be my last daytime classroom experience until my final semesters an ocean away at Brooklyn College, New York, many years later. This meant in fact that for the rest of my childhood and through adolescence I spent my days at work and my nights at school interacting mostly with adults. I recall with amusement an older army man who would buy me candy in exchange for help with his homework. Perhaps I ought not to have missed my chances of playing hookie or running off to the river in pursuit of mischievous delight in keeping with a given desirable form of roguish childhood. But I may also have garnered abundant recompense in that I did not have to undergo the mental regimentation that went on in the schoolyard to instill in the young an uncritical acceptance of the ideological and cultural biases of the State. I did not have to join my peers in the daily incantation of the national anthem or in the routine worship of the flag. Night school students were presumed adults and as such were spared the rituals that the State devices to instill obedient patriotism in its future soldiers, voters, parishioners, and consumers. I have the suspicion that the lack of such socialization makes it easier for people to become genuine citizens—the kind for whom love of country never precludes demanding that the country adhere to norms of equality, social justice, and human dignity.

I remember being at work on the morning of April 28th, 1965 when, thanks to the political parley of grown-up shoemakers around me, I learned that an American military occupation had occurred. An 11-year-old, I was 5 years older than my father had been when he lived his U.S. invasion 49 years earlier. The Lyndon B. Johnson administration resorted to a military intervention in order to prevent "another Cuba," which meant, in effect, that U.S. soldiers came to fight the *constitucionalistas*, the liberal movement that had taken up arms four days earlier seeking to restore the constitutional order. A year and a half before, democratically elected President Juan Bosch, the winner of the cleanest elections the country had witnessed in the century, was overthrown by a right-wing faction of the military that frowned on the democratizing policies implemented by the new government. A military junta took over and the revered liberal president went into exile. Seven months of a democratic experiment had proven too suffocating for the ruling elites that followed Trujillo in the control of the State. The corporate leadership, the Catholic prelacy, and the military officers that had served as the dictatorship's praetorian guard orchestrated the coup, with CIA support, on the justificatory grounds of Bosch's presumed leftist leanings.

A triumvirate followed the military junta, and the new government dealt harshly with political dissidence. A small guerrilla movement that rose in protest against the unconstitutional ruling structure suffered a grievous defeat, with the armed forces killing the rebels even after they had surrendered. The state of social upheaval continued intermittently until April 24th, 1965, when a liberal faction of the military declared itself in favor of a return to the Constitution, rallying massive support in the civilian population. A civil war broke out with clearly delineated flanks: the government forces and the conservative military who defended the status quo created by the *coup d'état*, on the one hand; and the liberal constituencies (civilian and military) committed to bringing back the deposed president and the democratic order, on the other. After three days of battle, the *constitucionalistas* had practically defeated the coup leaders, and just as they began to prepare a declaration of victory as prelude to restoring the interrupted Bosch government, U.S. soldiers came, sided with the coup leaders, the oligarchy that the Trujillo dictatorship had spawned, and reversed the outcome.

The *constitucionalistas* obviously lost. Since the occupying forces were no fans of Bosch, rather than restoring the deposed president, they merely set out to promote new elections in which they had a favorite whom they called in from his exile in New York. They brought in Joaquín Balaguer, who had served as Trujillo's puppet president until he had to escape the people's indignation in 1962, and put the resources of the State at his disposal for use in his campaign. They then allowed Bosch to return as a mere participant in the election but offered him no protection from the State-funded right-wing aggression that the Balaguer camp launched against him. Vowing to shoot Bosch wherever they chanced upon him, the military murdered hundreds of Bosch supporters without earning even a reprimand from the U.S. forces that ruled the country. Bosch had to campaign without leaving his home (Moya Pons 1995:390). Predictably Bosch lost, and the highest achieving of Trujillo's henchmen became president of the Republic, now in a system that called itself democratic because undeniably an election had taken place. The country in safe, right-wing, Trujillista hands, U.S. marines could now disoccupy it again.

Ironically, thousands of Dominicans too began to disoccupy their homeland mostly because of a shortage of matter of which to dream. After 30 horrendous years of bloodletting and humiliation under the Trujillo dictatorship, they had dared to indulge in democratic aspirations. They took to the streets enthusiastically to cast votes for a president who promised them a climate of human decency, and a military coup thwarted their yearning for social change. Then they took up arms, obstinately believing democracy to be a thing worth dying for, but the mightiest military and economic power on earth would turn against them and side with their foes. They had to give up their dreams of determining their own political future. Back in the National Palace, Balaguer would prolong his presidency to 12 consecutive years by resorting to graft, intimidation, police brutality, personal use of State resources, incarceration, electoral fraud, murder, and other unorthodox means that *The New York Times* acknowledged but still found morally palatable enough to regard him as a "prudent" leader in a 1970 feature article on his successful rule ("Prudent Dominican" 1970). Hardly any doubt exists that with the consolidation of the antipopular regime, the people's hope received a deadly blow. The poet Pedro Mir's sequence "Concerto of Hope for the Left Hand" opens with lines that interpret with poignant pathos the prevailing atmosphere of defeat: "The rollers fell on the cobblestones. And / dawn as she danced became a cloud of dust. / Oh, everything was left reduced to dust: Dust" (Mir 1993:141).

Hopelessness fueled the instinct to escape. Emigration began in unprecedented numbers, reaching unforeseen proportions. Balaguer's economic restructuring, which curtailed employment options for the masses, closed doors at home. The new immigration law passed by the U.S. Congress in 1965 opened them abroad. The migratory flow that started would remain unabated for the next four decades (Hernandez and Torres-Saillant 1996:3). Bereft of the will to put up a fight with the forces of adversity, my father became a passive witness to history. He watched from the viewing stand of his powerlessness how young antigovernment activists would appear on sidewalks, their mouths full of flies, murdered by paramilitary death squads. Sometimes police officers or army soldiers themselves would barge into the house of a marked revolutionary and shoot him right there in the presence of mother, spouse, siblings, or offspring. Silvio Sr. did not harbor oppositional feelings against the Balaguer regime perhaps because he remembered the president as a childhood friend. He failed to see the regime systemically, stemming naturally from the dictatorship that had rendered him irrelevant. Perhaps too, the product of a conservative social order, he genuinely felt no sympathy for the plight of leftists.

My father passively witnessed, as my mother, suffocated by his lack of economic resourcefulness in the face of the pressing basic needs of seven children, was dragged by the migratory flow to the United States in search of material survival. After settling in a Brooklyn apartment, cruising the garment factories, and peddling Avon products to Hispanic customers, she sent for the children in two stages. I arrived with the first shipment on April 3, 1973, at the age of 17, a sociopolitical offspring of the 1965 U.S. invasion and the right-wing Balaguer regime that followed, just as my father had been socialized by the 1916 U.S. military occupation and the devastating dictatorship that ensued. I believe I owe it to my early induction into the ways of grown-up life as well as to my having a specialized skill to sell to the job market that I made the crossing to a relatively productive existence without grave, discernible trauma. Because of my working experience in the shoemaking trade and my uninterrupted interest in academic pursuits, my dual occupation as an aspiring scholar and an income-producing worker helped me continue a relatively familiar life. Throughout the 1970s I sold my services to some of the shoe factories that had not yet vanished from New York in the transformation that eroded the city's former industrial economy to make way for the dominion of the service sector. I also held on to my routine of going to school at night, and when I graduated from Brooklyn College in June 1979, I could earnestly say, with greater veracity than that of Richard Nixon in the "Checker's" speech, that "I worked my way through college."

Power, Authority, and the Resistive Spirit

I should probably ascribe to my father's drunken séances of thunderous erudition the cultural lure of Greco-Roman antiquity that inclined me toward the study of Latin and Ancient Greek. Indeed, I most likely owe to his ardorous embrace of literary cultivation—which continued through sobriety—my overall interest in pursuing languages and literatures. But if I trace these influences to him in such a straightforward manner of inheritance, following a rather conventional understanding of how parents transmit values to their children, I should perhaps also consider a less easily fathomable legacy of which I am a fortunate beneficiary: his reticence to genuflect and his sober rapport with authority. I found it telling in this respect that though he probably admired Balaguer, as one might gather from his not expressing disapproval of the statesman's thuggish public record, he did not become unduly enthusiastic when I told him I had met the old man. I met Balaguer in New York City in 1984 shortly after my return from a 25-day sojourn in Moscow and Leningrad as a guest of the Maxim Gorky Institute of World Literature. It had fallen upon me to introduce Balaguer at the Milbank Chapel in the Columbia University campus during the launching of two books that he had published since 1978, the year when he relinquished power, his effort to remain as president despite adverse election results having failed thanks to national and international pressure.

The book-launching was organized by New York–based devout members of Balaguer's Reformista Party. My sister Melania, now called Marina as a result of the proverbial metamorphoses that immigrant names underwent in the hands of immigration officers, talked me into doing the introduction to help a close Reformista friend of hers who had a key role in coordinating the event and who depended on the event's success to raise his standing in the party's echelons. I seem to have accomplished the task to the satisfaction of my sister's friend, and several days later, I received a letter of appreciation from Balaguer himself, a man whose political career many thought to have ended in 1978, but whose return to the presidency once more for a ten-year rule in 1986 would prove otherwise. The letter praised my gift for literary analysis and described me as a worthy son of my father, his old friend, with whom he said he spent good time together when they were classmates at Escuela Paraguay in Santiago. When I showed the letter to my father during a trip to Santiago later that year, he completely ignored the fluffy flattery, training his eyes immediately on the inaccurate reference to the school in question, and said, casting the letter disdainfully aside, "What a liar! We were never at Escuela Paraguay together."

Somehow I feel I had already learned, from having spent an entire childhood with him, the obscure teaching that the letter incident would seem to embody. Indeed when I shook hands with Balaguer at Columbia University, I experienced none of the petrification that acquaintances had reported when in the presence of personages of historic stature. I noted rather the unmanly, gummy shake of the old man's cold, boneless hand. As I looked him in the face I noticed the crusty secretion on the corners of his eyes, then the oddly combed hair, and finally the silvery dandruffs glistening loudly against the shoulders of his somber black suit. I noticed in the legend the unsightly disrepair of the man. I later learned from the novelist Viriato Sención, author of *They Forged the Signature of God* (1996), that a devotee sitting in the audience had wept uncontrollable tears of veneration when Balaguer appeared on stage.

My father's nonchalance toward figures with power or fame had already instilled in me a sense of emotional wakefulness and psychological alertness in dealing with big names. As a result, when I have subsequently shaken hands with a mayor, including the capricious, adulterous, and mean-spirited autocrat whom *Time* magazine would proclaim "Mayor of the World" after September 11, 2001, no particular tremor has gone through my veins. I do not recall receiving a transfusion of thrill during the times when the governor of New York has given me a proclamation, the president of the United States has waved a hand in my direction, the late John Cardinal O'Connor made eye contact with me, a Nobel Prize–winning author entertained my comment or question or a highly paid public intellectual or scholar sat at the same table or partook of the same panel with me. This awareness I feel I inherit from my father, and that inheritance has proven enormously valuable to me as I, a son of the Caribbean, now *devenu* "New American" after having lived the "American experience" in situ for three decades, have roamed the corridors of the U.S. academy and have sought to locate my place within the scholarly community.

My father's sober interaction with awe-inspiring names has prepared me for better absorbing the lessons of my own contact with that class of people. My own association with the anointed has taught me that physical proximity to power, authority, or fame can afford us the opportunity to see through it, to see what it's made of and how it is maintained. While such awareness will in no way exonerate you from your vulnerability in relation to their might, you get a glimpse of the posing, the scheming, the strategizing, and the dandruffs of those socially, politically, and intellectually above you. You find, for instance, academics and thinkers busily, continuously, and tactically at work in the primary accumulation of prestige no less than their corporate counterparts occupy themselves furiously in the amassing of capital. This by no means excludes those who owe their highly paid standing to their adamant critique of capitalism. Later on, after some essays of mine involved me in what became a serious intellectual altercation featuring pens from the left and the right, I chanced upon the shocking realization that dissidents too stand guard over a private turf that they would fight to the death to protect from other dissidents (Torres-Saillant 1999:402–403). It became clear to me that for a new voice on the block to have its say it may not suffice that you advance positions whose lineaments accord with the ideology professed by the members of the intelligentsia controlling the arena wherein you wish to speak. They may require obeisance. You may have to subordinate your diction to the texture of the prevailing discursive order. You may have to prove worthy of admittance into the corridors of their court by quoting the appropriate texts and procuring the consent of given overseers.

I now accept that in academic pursuits no less than in statecraft or business matters one cannot reasonably expect anyone with power to risk parting with it without resistance. That sharing power inevitably entails the possibility of losing it, I believe, can be accepted as a fairly uncontroversial assertion. The power of academics or public intellectuals who have successfully marketed a particular interpretation of society and culture, have earned recognition as spokespersons for particular schools of thought, have appropriated or coined particular terminologies, or have established their seniority in particular sectors of the realm of thought production, is no exception. The intellectual who achieves market success in the profession of ideas enjoys a status comparable to the ancient diviner—haruspex or auspex. This interpreter of the present and contextualizer of the future—rendered prophet by default without facing the danger of Laocoon's liability—has authority at times to guide the kinds of questions that scholars in the field will judge meaningful. Sacvan Bercovitch has spoken of the "special genius of liberal symbology in staging interpretation as a means of coopting dissent" (Bercovitch 1988:12). If we applied a comparable notion to dissidents, it could easily translate into preserving the state of affairs that has conferred upon them the rank of high priests within the sphere of dissidence. One could conjecture that they have good reason to wish for conditions to stay the same since, were the existing state of affairs to suffer an alteration, they could lose their place as other voices might conceivably end up in charge of the rank of head-interpreters or directors of protestation.

Until after graduate school in the Comparative Literature Department at New York University I did not have occasion to develop a language with which to articulate my sense of pause vis-à-vis intellectual power brokerage. But the diffuse teachings of my father's mixed signals, the awareness that his desire to instill erudite leanings in me fructified only because my unschooled peasant mother fought against enormous odds to secure her children's material survival, and the eminently terrestrial outlook that working for a living from primary school onward seems to have fostered in me—all combined to make me, I recall, less uncritical of the whole institution of scholarship and knowledge production than my graduate school peers. When I took my first European history, classics, and art history courses at Brooklyn College, I thought of humanistic knowledge and the words that are used to transmit it as totally impartial endeavors. Like the Native American writer Betty Louise Bell, I regarded words as "neutral, without political or personal affiliations, as equalizing in their availability as death" (Bell 2000:32). But soon some of the words of the great minds of the West began to reveal themselves with a degree of offense whose virulence I only wished my father had warned me about when he regaled us with his Eurocentric erudition at home in Santiago decades earlier.

On the Partiality of Book Learning

When I found Georg Wilhelm Friedrich Hegel in the *Lectures on the Philosophy of History* expounding on the subhuman identity of blacks, it became clear to me that I could not limit my engagement with that author to a strictly scholarly enterprise. As I myself was the subject of the offense he hurled, I had to take it personally. Nor could I accept the response by an acquaintance, then a philosophy doctoral candidate at a university in Boston, who explained the notorious chapter away by asserting that one cannot read Hegel through the details of his arguments but that one has to focus on what matters, namely the system of thought that the arguments comprise. I simply could not see how I would so selflessly give the benefit of the doubt to such an unkind document and allow a factually erroneous text to educate me. On the contrary I should distrust any system whose structure rested on scandalously inaccurate details. And I am in no position to allow anyone to make me doubt that I, black as night, am as human as Elizabeth I, Robespierre, Rosa Luxembourg, or Al Capone.

Discerning the rabid negrophobia of many of the giants of Western discourse, I became acquainted with the clumsy juggling that an intellect afflicted with racism can display. Hegel, for instance, set out to deny blacks a space in the narrative of humankind, for which he had to portray them as devoid of a sense of honor, lacking an idea of God, and wanting any notion of courage. Concerning, for example, the business of courage, he had to account for the existing reports that marveled at the defiant boldness with which black Africans met the guns of their white aggressors during the wars of conquest. Hegel granted that blacks often resisted the military advance of the white colonizer, allowing themselves to be shot down by thousands in war with Europeans, but instead of recognizing therein any trace of authentic courage and heroic immolation to the cause of freedom, the great German philosopher went on to interpret their bravery negatively as expressive of "contempt for humanity" and "want of regard for life" (Hegel 1956:96). One thinks of a comparable passage in the *Notes on the State of Virginia* (1784) in which Thomas Jefferson relies on counterintuitive reasoning to avoid the possibility that blacks may possess the virtue of courage. In describing their valor, he found them "at least as brave" as and a bit "more adventuresome" than whites, but he deployed an interpretation that turned the apparent virtue into a grave flaw, insofar as the boldness of blacks "may perhaps proceed from a want of forethought, which prevents their seeing a danger till it be present" (Jefferson 1944:257).

As a person who embodied the problem of blackness that had for so long triggered the antipathy of Western discourse, I at one point realized that the so-called great books did not for the most part speak amicably when addressing me. Some in effect were scandalous in their degree of bad manners. I came upon passages galore containing rabid hostility in the works of Immanual Kant, David Hume, Jules Roman, James Anthony Froude, Anthony Trollope, Ernest Renan, John Emerich Edward Dalberg Acton (a.k.a. Lord Acton), Sir Richard Burton, David Livingston, and Thomas Carlyle, to name only a few of the most blatantly aggressive. As one moved further into modern times, and the postulates of such towering figures as Karl Marx, Friedrich Nietzsche, and Sigmund Freud gained center stage in the major Western universities, their influence may have helped to tone down overt racial animosity in utterances about non-whites. They, however, did not actually set out to demolish the racialist paradigms that had cohered in the definition of humanity they had inherited from their predecessors. The defamation of non-whites in Western discourse neither began with Enlightenment rationality nor ended with subsequent subversions of it. André Breton, the father of Surrealism, praised Aimè Césaire's handling of the French language by pointing to the Martinican poet's blackness, and Robert Graves spoke comparably when applauding the black St. Lucian poet Derek Walcott's mastery of the English tongue (Breton 1983:80; Graves, cited by Dawes 1977:5). They both presented the juxtaposition of blackness and linguistic dexterity as an extraordinary phenomenon.

The anthropologist Lewis Henry Morgan, the author of *Ancient Society or Researches in the Lines of Human Progress from Savagery Through Barbarism to Civilization* (1877), was no Gobineau in the militance of his white supremacist pronouncements. But he concurred with other anthropologists that whites represented "the pinnacle of human development," hence his belief that intermarriage with whites would lead to the biological advancement of American Indians. He found evidence of this on a visit to Kansas and Nebraska, where he noted that "The color of the Indian women is quite uniform and is light. It shows that white blood infused into them in the East has been well diffused throughout. The next cross will make a pretty white child" (cited by Hilden 1995:149–150). The offspring of those mixed marriages would themselves "intermarry respectably with our white people and thus the children will become respectable and, if educated, in the second and third generation will become beautiful and attractive" (150). Patricia Penn Hilden reminds us of the influence that Morgan's ideas had on Karl Marx and Fredrich Engels. She notes that Engels's seminal work *The Origins of the Family, Private Property, and the State*, "a text much quoted by socialist-feminists of his era as well as those of the contemporary movement," draws amply on Morgan's *Ancient Society* (242).

Given such affiliation and the Hegelian outlook that Marx and Engels never totally distanced themselves from, the fundamentally Eurocentric texture of historical materialism should come as no surprise. The definition of humanity that informed their theory of social change partly explains Marx's unenthusiastic appraisal of the independence movement in Latin America and his spirited justification of the takeover of the North American Southwest territories by "the energetic Yankees," who yanked the lands in question from "the lazy Mexicans who could not do anything with them" (Marx 1977:365–366). The inexorability of the teleological progression that Marx and Engels envisioned required Europeans or North American Anglos to occupy the driver's seat in the locomotive of human history. European intellectuals, from those in the Frankfurt School to those who excelled in the structuralist movement that dominated French thought beginning in the 1960s, vigorously reassessed the presuppositions of Enlightenment thinkers and creatively revamped Western ideas about language, but the core of their inquiry remained the Western subject. Non-Western intellects could partake of those developments only through a leap of faith inducing them to engage in cultural adjustment and ethnoracial adaptation to fit themselves into the received accounts. But a recognition of the endurance of the racial imagination suggested to me that if you are a non-white who has traveled to the republic of Western letters as a colonial migrant, especially if you belong to one of the ethnic or racial groups that Western discourse has assiduously undertaken to inferiorize, you cannot uncritically inherit Western intellectual developments irrespective of how enticingly progressive they might feel. I now more than ever think it dangerously unwise to cease asking the question: In exactly what way does this particular Western notion—which was not conceived with me in mind—have to do with me?

INEQUITY IN THE MARKET OF IDEAS

After reading Roland Barthes at NYU in the early 1980s I discovered to my amazement the privilege that Western academics had when it came to substantiating their claims about history, knowledge, truth, or the human condition. They could forgivably restrict their scholarly references and literary illustrations to authors from their own country. Their provincialism did not diminish the global authority of their postulates. Similarly, I have often wondered about the extent to which one could write Michel Foucault's *History of Sexuality* in such a way that it spoke about the species inclusively instead of limiting the genealogy to the evolution of sexual conduct and sexual discourse to France, Greek antiquity, and some Latin and Hellenic authors of the first and second century AD. Conceivably Foucault's reading (in *Histoire* III) of the section on dreams involving sexual intercourse in the second century AD manual *Oneirocritica* by Artemidorus Daldianus might elicit a different discussion of sexuality and dreams if the author sought comparable material from Aztec, Ethiopian, and Polynesian societies of the same period (Daldianus 1975:58–65; Foucault 1988). This conjecture should at least give us some pause before our rushing to accept that the findings that Foucault's ambitious project purports to unearth regarding the chronology of self-awareness of sexual subjectivity ought to apply automatically to indigenous and mestizo cultures of the Americas, African societies, Asian peoples, and Caribbean communities.

The discovery that Western narratives of humanity could afford to ignore the historical experience of people from backgrounds similar to mine made me suspicious of their accuracy. I remember distinctly that this thought cohered in my mind in the Fall of 1982 when, after a brief conversation with the instructor, I made a decision to drop a course for which I had just registered. It was a genre course entitled "The Historical Novel," and the reading list included the likes of Victor Hugo, Sir Walter Scott, George Eliot, Benito Pérez Galdós, Honoré de Balzac, Giuseppe di Lampedusa, and Leo Tolstoi. Since I had already read what Georg Lukacs had to say on the subject and the authors listed tickled my appetite, I signed up enthusiastically, thinking also that the course would offer me the opportunity to write a research paper that looked at two Dominican historical novels, *Enriquillo* (1880) by Manuel de Jesús Galván and *La sangre* (1912) by Tulio Manuel Cestero, with the hope of determining how these Caribbean specimens of the form compared with the European ones on the reading list as well as to ascertain how they measured up to the generalizations about the genre put forth by Lukacs. When the professor categorically informed me that he would accept only papers dealing with the novels on the list, I immediately extinguished my enthusiasm for the course. I had already understood that any look at any aspect of human culture that advertises itself as having panoramic pretensions ("the historical novel") but chooses its evidence in a culturally narrow way is annoyingly deceptive.

I cannot help sensing a sort of connection between the foregoing incident and another that took place at the start of my first semester in graduate school in the Fall of 1979. I had to go to a classroom on the fourth floor of the Main Building, located on Waverly Place right across from Washington Square Park, for the first of a two-part seminar on literary theory and criticism. We had begun with Plato and would continue through Dryden. The following semester the excursion would take us from Alexander Pope through to the post-structuralists. At any rate, on this particular evening, as I was approaching the classroom door, a white, corpulent security guard stopped me to ask what I was doing on that floor. When I explained my business there he sternly demanded that I show identification. His incredulity addressed, he let me go on my way. Until that moment I had not seen nor would I see anytime thereafter a guard verifying the identity of another student on the floor. Symbolically, a parallel has insinuated itself into my mind between the professor who didn't allow my Dominican novels into his classroom and the security guard who didn't see an NYU graduate student when beholding me.

Subsequently I taught the Humanities core course as an adjunct for NYU's General Studies Program, covering Homer to Italian opera in one semester and Milton through Picasso in the other. It must have taken at least eight months before the staff at the entrance door of Bobst Library became familiar enough with my face to be able to stop squinting their eyes to look more closely at my ID card every time I presented it, the uncertainty most likely caused by the apparent discrepancy between my racial visage and the faculty status that my card displayed. I believe these incidents stem from the same predicament. My physical presence, my body did not seem to belong in the role of a graduate student strolling spryly on the fourth floor of the Main Building anymore than it did in the elevated status of the NYU faculty. The presence there of folks who looked like me defied the norm that was familiar to the staff just as for my professor permitting the entrance into his classroom of my two Dominican novels would have meant having to step outside the realm of the familiar. The bodies of people and the bodies of knowledge they produce often suffer a common antipathy when they hold the losing end of the colonial rope.

Circumstances in graduate school conspired to keep me reminded of my difference, and I came to regard that self-awareness of alterity as a good thing. I owned to my ontological self-recognition as a worker and a colonial migrant in the way I read books and interacted with the systems of significance they promoted or embodied. I discovered I had a perspective. In that discovery, I differed radically from my father who never reached a point of ethnoracial and cultural self-awareness enabling him to require that, to be valid, definitions of human culture had to include him or he had to fight those definitions should they exclude him. My perspective sentisitized me to the possible horror of succumbing to suicidal reasoning, a thought process whereby colonial peoples deny themselves epistemological self-sufficiency. Suicidal reasoning is fostered by the imperial imagination, whose spell causes us to see the citizens of the colonial powers as the only producers of valid meaning.

A healthier, more self-loving stance would seem to encourage the colonial migrant to affirm the opposite, to affirm, for instance, that Antillean people harbor all of humanity's complexity no less than the French, the Chinese, or the Iroquois. Their experience has what it takes to illuminate the drama of the whole species. They contain the stuff of the universal as well as any other branch of the human family. Self-protective reasoning rejects outright the logic that construes its notion of humanity on the basis of preferred powerful nations, against whom the rest of the world's population is expected to measure itself, relegating everybody else, that is, to a secondary ontology. Owning to my colonial difference enabled me to resist the impulses of the imperial imagination, distancing myself from other minority scholars who have allowed themselves to be coerced into self-effacement, losing, therefore, the moral ascendancy to marshal any cause on behalf of the disempowered.

WESTERN EDUCATION AND COLONIAL ALTERITY

The novelist Sención says that luck is a historical category, and I count myself lucky for the circumstances of my colonial mobility. I came to the Western academy not as a foreign student from the colony whom the Metropolis picked for special treatment. I came to the United States as a labor migrant. I had occasion to recognize myself as an ethnic minority and gradually developed a deep sense of kinship with constituencies whose conditions of social marginality I shared. I had my mother's legacy of endurance and my father's rare sense of self-worth as beacons to mark my path in the struggle for survival. When I arrived at the university I was certainly glad I had made it there, but I also knew the dues I had paid for it on the labor arena. The bank loans I had taken announced that my regimen of payment would continue for quite a while longer. That constant awareness of the material cost of my intellectual advancement probably kept me from experiencing graduate school as admission into a realm of privilege that entailed the unspoken agreement to sever my ties with my origins. I also had the good fortune in 1983 of ending up in a Hispanic Caribbean literature course with the late Hydee Vitali, a Puerto Rican professor at NYU who taught her linguistic bloc of the Antilles with a deep sensitivity toward the other languages and bodies of knowledge that coexisted in the region. I treasured her cultural self-confidence, her unequivocal understanding that the Caribbean's lesser prestige on the global intellectual market did in no way equal a lesser value as a culture area. To her conviction that in the world academic economy marginal regions need devoted advocates, I owe my discovery of the Caribbean as a main research interest, marking my shift in intellectual zeal from the faraway archipelago in Mediterranean Hellas to the familiar island-cluster of the nearby Antilles. My spending eight weeks in the summer of 1986 in a Comparative Poetics seminar led at Princeton University by Earl Miner, a literary scholar who, after establishing himself as a major Dryden scholar, went on to master Chinese and Japanese literatures, further solidified the epistemological ground on which I would tread. A rare individual, Miner's academic praxis reflects the belief that different culture-specific literary systems are truly equal, and my contact with him at the time proved invaluable. Vitali and Miner, joined by A. James Arnold, of the French Department at the University of Virginia, Charlottesville, and Timothy Reis, then chair of the NYU Comparative Literature Department, formed the core of my doctoral dissertation committee. Arnold, a Paul Valery scholar early in his career, had become a major Caribbeanist by the time I met him. After an indispensable book on Césaire, he would go on to assemble the monumental three-volume compilation *A History of Literature in the Caribbean*. For his part Reiss, who had achieved distinction writing on European figures and moments of the early modern period, had started a foray into the Caribbean and would in the years to follow add several Caribbean collections to his output. These mentors had the special gift of viewing the Caribbean as a thought-producing region with intellectual traditions worth studying.

Probably as a fortunate result of the state of mind I came to graduate school with, I may have been spared the symptoms of the "scholarship boy," whose psycopathology Richard Hoggart pinned down in *The Uses of Literary* nearly five decades ago. Emotionally uprooted from his class, "He has moved away from his 'lower' origins, and may move farther. If so, he is likely to be nagged underneath by a sense of how far he has to come, by the fear and shame of a possible falling back" (Hoggart 1966:245). The scholarship boy feels "ashamed of his origins; he has learned to 'turn up his nose,' to be a bit superior about much in working-class manners. He is often not at ease about his own physical appearance which speaks too clearly of his birth; he feels uncertain or angry inside when he realizes that that, and a hundred habits of speech and manners, can 'give him away' daily" (246). Self-effacement functions in the mind of the scholarship boy as a prerequisite to intellectual upliftment: "He would like to be a citizen of that well-polished, prosperous, cool, book-lined and magazine-discussing world of the successful intelligent middle-class which he glimpses through doorways or feels awkward among on short visits, aware of his grubby finger-nails" (247).

When the Mexican-American essayist Richard Rodríguez "traveled to London to write a dissertation on English Renaissance literature" at the British Museum, having risen above the lowly station of his peers in a Sacramento, California, immigrant community, he felt "finally confident of membership in a community of scholars" (Rodríguez 1983:69). There he chanced upon Hoggart's book, and when he found the description of the scholarship boy in chapter 10, he was struck with a profound sense of identification: "For the first time I realized that there were students like me, and so I was able to frame the meaning of my academic success, its consequent price—the loss," and he recognized therein an apt representation of his own conflict as he straddled environments, "his home and the classroom, which are at cultural extremes, opposed" (46). Accepting it as an inexorable fact that intellectual cultivation must estrange students from their humble origins—communal, family, and ethnic loyalties included—, Rodríguez came back home to earn notoriety as an eloquent spokesperson against bilingual education and affirmative action, two social programs that had come into effect in the United States to address the inequities that ethnically differentiated communities such as his had suffered for ages.

I had occasion to think about the British quandary of young Richard Rodríguez when a one-semester teaching assignment caused me to live in London in the Spring of 2003. The thought came to me specifically on the day when I went to see the exquisite art and grounds of Kenwood House, a delightful eighteenth-century neoclassical villa in North London's Hampstead Heath. I went to the charming museum attracted by its connection to the Honorable William Murray, Lord Chief Justice of England, Lord Mansfield for short, the eminent judge who on June 22nd, 1772 pronounced a pivotal ruling in the case of the black slave James Sommersett. Brought to England with his master's entourage, Sommersett had absconded, was subsequently caught, and, as punishment, his owner determined to sell him to a plantation in the sugar islands of the Caribbean. When the case came before Lord Mansfield through the diligent offices of abolitionist Granville Sharp, Sommersett, confined in irons, awaited his fate on board the *Ann and Mary*, the ship lying in the Thames that would carry him to Jamaica. On the grounds that slavery in the country did not exist, Murray ruled that Sommersett's master had no ownership claim that "could be allowed or approved by the law of England. And, therefore, the black must be discharged" (Heward 1979:144–146).

The ruling proved a crucial landmark on the road to abolition, and it brought freedom to many blacks who lived in the metropolis as slaves. Murray's household had taken in an infant girl, the daughter of a slave woman whom a nephew had rescued from a Spanish vessel in the 1750s. The family named the girl Dido, after the deserted Carthaginian queen in the *Aeneid* of Virgil, and she served as constant companion of Lady Elizabeth Mary Murray, a niece of Lord Mansfield's who lived in the house. The two posed for their portrait together in the garden at Kenwood, and when Dido grew up the family entrusted her with managing the farm adjacent to the house. "That a black should be so trusted surprised visitors," particularly, Massachusetts Governor Thomas Hutchinson who put in writing his disapproval of such crossracial familiarity (Usherwood 1981:41). Needless to say, Murray granted Dido her freedom prior to the Sommersett case, as a man of his humanitarian fiber probably needed to avoid the contradiction of owning a member of the family. During my visit to Kenwood House I harbored the hope, instigated by Catherine Smith, the colleague who first awakened my interest in Murray, of gazing at the Dido and Elizabeth painting done by Johann Zoffany.

It turned out that the Kenwood House collection did not include the portrait of the two young women and that the piece is with family heirs in Murray's native Scotland. However, my interest quickly found a replacement as I zeroed in on the black male figure accompanying Princess Henrietta of Lorraine in a large portrait by Sir Anthony van Dick (1599–1641). The generationally mongrelized conception of the figure—manly face and upper body, childish demeanor, and smaller frame from the waist down, but showing no intent to represent a dwarf—brought to mind the plight of black males in Britain during the seventeenth and eighteenth centuries. Cute, exotic beings from Aphra Behn's "other world," often brought as enviable gifts to ladies of high station and made part of the intimate space of English womanhood, they inevitably grew up and their sexual potential became discernible. Their ornamentality as pets eclipsed by their evinced manliness, they were often put out on the street and left to fend for themselves. As we learn from the pioneering research of Edward Scobie, a native of Dominica, in his *Black Britannia* (1972), many became resourceful beggars, notorious thieves, or they simply perished in their disempowered insignificance. Some did manage to live well and a few even became celebrated Afro-Britons, including Ignatius Sancho, who, brought from Cartagena on the Caribbean coast of Colombia to England in 1731 as a gift to three maiden sisters in Greenwich, grew up to become quite a respectable citizen who enjoyed the friendship of notables in literature and the arts, and Julius Soubise, brought at the age of ten in 1764 from St. Kitts to England, where he gained the favor of Catherine, duchess of Queensbury, who in her own words "sent him to school, supported him genteely and provided him with an education," a privilege that he ill used, becoming a womanizer, gambler, and sybaritic rogue (Scobie 1972:95, 89; Gerzina 1995:54–67). But, on the whole, the passage from child to man for a black male in the entourage of an aristocratic British lady was fraught with uncertainty, and the generational indecision in van Dick's black page to Princess Henrietta struck me as evocative of that perilous predicament.

Van Dick's black figure triggered musings regarding my own location and my inestimable luck not to have been born then and to have come to the United Kingdom under rather auspicious circumstances. In the seventeenth or eighteenth century, a male of African descent coming from the Caribbean, I would most likely have faced a harsh lot. Having come to England as a politically aware educator rather than as a grateful scholarship boy, I also had ideological advantages over young Richard Rodríguez. I wondered whether, had I come to England at the age he did, I would have considered a compelling link between me and the black in van Dick's painting, or if instead I might have merely gaped with admiration at the comeliness of Princess Henrietta. I might not have visited Kenwood House in the state of mind I did. As I came loaded with a sense of history, I could not help but draw connections between the glory of Britain and the misery of the conquered peoples whose lands and labor built that glory. I became cognizant that the triangular trade and the path charted by the East India Company formed the structure of the world that brought me into being.

In England I wished to see with my own eyes the city of Liverpool, birthplace of the Beatles in the twentieth century and leading center of the transatlantic slavery industry in the eighteenth century. Another painting by Johann Zoffany entitled, "The Family of Sir William Young" exhibited at the Walker Art Gallery in Liverpool depicts the household members of Young, governor of Dominica and owner of several West Indian sugar plantations. The richly dressed black slave who steadies one of the children on a horse in the picture reminds one of the coerced labor and the peculiar overseas forms of commerce that financed such ornate elegance as the family attires so lusciously display. I also wished to see Bristol, a city with its feet steeped in the mire of slavery and transatlantic plunder, especially to visit the British Empire and Commonwealth Museum, a new cultural undertaking that graphically chronicles the dramatic 500-year history of the biggest imperial enterprise the world has ever known. It pleased me to see that, unlike London, Bristol is not committed to concealing its opprobrious history. London conceals its involvement in the transatlantic slave trade and the plunder of the Orient through the East India Company as fervently as it promotes the monumental past of the royal family. Nick Robins, a proponent of the view that history ought to "rescue the memory of those cast aside by the powerful," contends that the East India Company's "escape from reckoning enables the people of Britain to pass over the source of much of their current affluence and allows India's continuing poverty to be viewed as a product of its culture and climate, rather that as something manufactured in pursuit of external profit" (Robins 2002:16).

An Antillean in London, the awareness of my own colonial history placing an irksome cultural chip on my shoulder, I occasionally resented having to pay to take a peek at the props of official English historical memory: the honored dead at Westminster Abbey, the royal dresses at Kensington Palace, the lugubrious incarcerations at the Tower of London. Caribbean societies generally do not charge visitors for glancing at local history. Had they a fraction of the self-importance of the English, they would abound in spots and props for a glimpse at which a fee could be charged: this is where Columbus disembarked, and the course of humanity was radically changed; this mountain teemed with runaway slaves committed to imagining life outside the logic of the plantation; this is where Taino women first poisoned themselves with their children rather than accept enslavement by the invading European hordes; this is where your ancestors made the money that enriched your world and impoverished ours; this is the sun, the landscape, the sand that appears in tourism brochures, in the new industry that was built upon the ruins of the plantation economy; and so on, ad infinitum.

Because of my age and sense of history, I did not, like young Richard, come to Britain, in awe of the glorious intellectual tradition, to pay my worshipful respects to the idols lodged in the temple of English letters. I came, rather, armed with revisionist memory, much like the speaker in the Merle Collins poem "Visiting Yorkshire—Again," who says: "Yorkshire was not really as I remembered it / But then, the last time I visited / the Brontes had created for me a world / . . . of indeterminate shades / of art / that had no colours / of pleasure that existed / for its artistic self" (Collins 1992:17). Visiting as an adult, the black woman "walking the cobbled streets" is less entranced by "the mystic moors": "After the Brontes, / I decided not to visit with Keats / and Wordsworth / Discovered that art / in England / comes in Black and White / in rich and poor / that an art called Black / exists / for England / in some region called the Fringe" (18). The poem's calling attention to a racialized England invites recollection of the enslaved Africans who, when brought to the metropolis and given an education, seized the opportunity to speak against the injustice to which England had subjected their people. Quobna Ottobah Cugoano, a Fantee kidnapped as a boy and taken to Grenada before receiving his freedom and being brought to England, authored his *Thoughts and Sentiments on the Evil and Wicked Traffic of Slavery and Commerce of the Human Species* (1787), the first of the slave narratives and the one displaying the fiercest indictment of slaveholders. Unlike the moderate plaints of many who would follow after him, Cugoano rebuked his culprits severely, blatantly labeling them "brutish," "base," and "wicked" thieves. He even ventured to implicate in the "evil" of the slave economy every citizen "in all Great-Britain and her colonies that knoweth anything" unless thy openly oppose "such notorious wickedness" (Cugoano 1999:12, 79). Nor did Sancho's propriety and polite discourse prevent him from raising his tone in condemnation of the oppressors "of almost all of our unfortunate colour," as he, in an October 11, 1772 admonitory letter to Soubise, urges him to: "see slavery, and the contempt of those very wretches who roll in affluence from our labours . . . hear the ill-bred and heart-racking abuse of the foolish vulgar" (Sancho 1998:46).

My index finger stiff with historical indignation, I held a retrospective grudge for the payloads of exceptional literary talent that white English writers have often invested in advancing agendas of ethnic hatred and racial phobias. Imagine the stylistic dexterity of Anthony Trollope's vigorous prose going to the crafting of a book such as *The West Indies and the Spanish Main* (1860), in which the renowned novelist expostulated on the racial inferiority of non-whites, the impossibility of mulatto upliftment, and the unearned misfortune of white planters brought low by the emancipation of West Indian slaves, which regretfully deprived them of their once abundant labor force. The genial pen that gave us the Bersetshire novels, a series that presents a fascinating tapestry of Victorian society, also wrought the tempered cadence of these sentences: "I do not think that education has as yet done much for the black man in the Western world. He can always observe, and often read; but he can seldom reason. I do not mean to assert that he is absolutely without mental power, as a calf is. He does draw conclusions, but he carries them only a short way. I think that he seldom understands the purpose of industry, the object of truth, or the results of honesty. He is not always idle, perhaps not always false, certainly not always a thief; but his motives are the fear of immediate punishment, or hopes of immediate reward. He fears and hopes that only" (Trollope 1999:56–57). A Trollope fan writing on the author's life and works comments in passing about such Negrophobia as the above passage illustrates saying: "Trollope is critical of the blacks, considering them feckless, unstable, childish and lazy. He realizes that this will lay him open to attack, but, with that plain common sense and realism that always characterized him, he claims that 'It will avail nothing to humanity to call a man a civilized Christian if the name be not deserved'" (Pollard 1978:84). Though writing over a century after *The West Indies and the Spanish Main* came out, this commentator seems intent on getting his readers to side with Trollope against blacks, almost as if unable to imagine the possibility of blacks figuring among his readers.

No comment about the nineteenth-century British man of letters and his latter-day ally seems necessary except perhaps to say en passant that the problems an African descendant Antillean reader faces when approaching Trollope's antipathy did not disappear with the passing of the Victorian era or the advent of self-rule following independence. Witness the tortuous ordeal of Anglo-Caribbean poet Fred D'Aguiar who, in authoring a preface to a recent edition of *The West Indies and the Spanish Main*, must wrestle with the task of rebuking Trollope's ideological aggression against his people while celebrating the stylistic virtues of this "readable, maddening, and ultimately triumphant book," thus endeavoring to achieve a measure of intellectual balance and analytical objectivity (D'Aguiar 1999:v–viii). Undue showing of moral passion or giving vent to ethnic indignation can invariably call into question the rigor and the acumen of a Third World speaker, so D'Aguiar's restraint turns inexorably into praise. In *An Autobiography*, which appeared posthumously in 1883, Trollope praises his own achievement in the writing of *The West Indies and the Spanish Main*. Similarly, though conceding that the book contained some "inaccurately" stated facts, that "many opinions were crude," and that he possibly "failed to understand much which I attempted to explain," he remained pleased to have produced, "these faults" aside, "a thoroughly honest book" that engaged him in "unflagging labour for a period of fifteen months" (Trollope 1996:220–221).

Reissuings of Trollope's Caribbean chronicle continue unabated into the present. The book still receives the glorification of admirers, as we gather from a 1999 edition that carries a laudatory blurb by prolific travel writer Paul Theroux hailing it unabashedly as "One of the Ten Essential Travel Books." Nor can one do anything about the possibility that many Western readers might still get their learning about Caribbean humanity from the stylistically accomplished bigotry of Trollope's prose. Looking perhaps for a sense of epistemological balance, I employed part of my stay in England in acquainting myself with voices committed to less inimical representations of the offspring of "the other world," namely the practitioners of the other English art to which the Collins poem alludes. I thus came upon a wealth of writers ancestrally connected to Africa, Asia, and the Caribbean, some of whom figure in the collections *Empire Windrush*, compiled by Onyekachi Wambu (1999), and *Voices of the Crossing*, coedited by Ferdinand Dennis and Naseem Khan (2000). These writers, fitting in the chronology started by the Windrush generation, greatly widen the human visage of England by drawing attention to contemporary manifestations in the great metropolis of the legacies of racism, ethnocentric bias, religious narrow-mindedness, and other features of Western modernity. These concerns occupied my thoughts during a fair portion of my sojourn in England, and whether they would have come to mind if I had visited the metropolis as a scholarship boy will have to remain a matter of pure speculation.

READING WITH AN ATTITUDE

I neither went to England as a scholarship boy, nor was I unaware of my colonial alterity when I entered the halls of Western academia. As a result, access to erudition did not alienate me from family and community, as it did young Richard, according to his own account in *Hunger of Memory* (1983). I lived in the Dominican enclave of Washington Heights, in Northern Manhattan, during my NYU graduate school years. While I could perhaps complain that the neighborhood did not provide me with erudite interlocutors with whom I might discuss my interest in Ariosto's *Orlando furioso* during a seminar on the Italian Renaissance, my meticulous line-by-line examination of the ancient Greek original of the *Philoctetes* for a Sophocles course, or my master's degree thesis on the French, German, Spanish, Italian, and English contributions to the Arthurian Romance, I experienced no severance of communal ties. The topics of my small talk changed when I took the train from Washington Square up to Washington Heights, but the neighborhood did not lack material to engage me in conversation. Once the community identified me as a scion who was into books and learning, who was pursuing the intellectual accreditation of a doctoral degree, it made me responsible for contributing to neighborhood advancement projects, cultural events, and political causes. I became a desirable invitee to membership in committees of various sorts. Community organizations would often call on me to deliver lectures on myriad topics without regard for the specificity of my field of expertise. They overestimated what I could do because they needed me, and I had to respond accordingly by often going to the library for a few days to give myself a crash course on the subject of my commission in hurried preparation for the upcoming lecture. In short, I received enough clues to understand that my graduate school training did not matter only to me. Two separate receptions coordinated by community organizations to celebrate the completion of my Ph.D. degree further accentuated that understanding.

Instead of becoming estranged, therefore, my ties to the community grew stronger. As I possessed the high literacy that so many in my community could never hope of acquiring, I had the feeling that the people in the community had entrusted in me the portion of their struggle that corresponded to the academic trenches. While other community activists advanced the cause of the collective in areas dealing with issues such as housing, employment, voter's registration, and health, it seemed to fall on the likes of me to attend to the areas of symbolic politics, epistemological recognition, and fair cultural representation. Thus far my published writings have screamed against "world literature overviews" that omit most of the Third World, have argued that the Caribbean has produced metadiscourses of its own to speak about its own complexities, have protested the exclusions that Dominicans have perennially suffered in the United States as well as in the Latin American academy, and have promoted the insertion of the U.S. Hispanic experience in national constructions of Americanness. I have found my place in the academy in the realm of epistemological warfare, as a strategically cantankerous advocate fending off exclusionary narratives of humanity, of nation, of citizenship.

I realized it behooved me to read as an ethnic if I wished to circumvent suicidal reasoning. Reading as an ethnic meant one had to stay alert about the tendency of Western discourse to leave large portions of the planet's population out when speaking about the species. One had to remain vigilant about one's exclusion from the account in question, so as to, when necessary, validate one's experience as ground to contest the said account. Reading as an ethnic meant one refrains from uncritical acceptance of any paradigm, worldview, or critical lexicon coming from England, Germany, and France as marking a stage of knowledge that supersedes preceding ones and automatically applies to our condition though we are not Brits, Germans, or French. It means you invariably ask yourself whether you may already have autochthonous concepts that provide explanation for the problem at hand, that is, whether native intellects had already given names to the issues in question or had provided perspectives to deal with the given human complexity under perusal, thus making the adoption of the Western input less urgent.

The ethnic reader that I envisioned and wished to emulate is an emancipated intellect who recognizes her colonial upbringing, the preponderance of Western notions in his own formation, but who does not buy into the epistemological monopoly of Eurocentric formulations. She has not given up on the potential of alternative knowledges coming from precolonial systems of significance—if she is Amerindian, African, or Indian—or syncretic thought born of the cultural fusion of the colonial transaction—if she is Antillean. The ethnic reader, therefore, has the power to overcome the compulsion to update his or her critical vocabulary regularly in order to incorporate every new usage that the industry makes current especially if the matter under study remains more or less the same: society, culture, equity. The language that the ethnic reader uses to speak about his or her community does not change with every neologism or lexical innovation contained in the latest critical theory book that comes on the market.

Reading as an ethnic, I find it insufficiently compelling to incorporate the term "habitus" in my critical lexicon, all due respect to the late Pierre Bourdieu notwithstanding. But I find nothing denoted by the term that we did not already recognize in existing terminology prior to the French sociologist's decision to make use of his knowledge of Latin. I am mindful of Cervantes's exposing of scholarly postures to lend intellectual respectability to one's words. In the "Prologue" to his *Don Quixote* (1605), the author refers to the advice he received from a friend to help him raise the level of authority of his writing. Among other strategies, the friend recommends this: "you have to make use of those scraps of Latin that you know by heart or can look up without too much bother" (Cervantes 1949:13). The word "simulacrum" comes into the language of many colleagues through a particular contact with Jean Baudrillard's discussion of the contemporary moment as dominated by a hyperreal society of simulation (Baudrillard 1994). But for a Spanish speaker who has grown up hearing the word "simulacro" in ordinary speech the term would not automatically trigger an engagement with French critical theory. In my case, the term evokes memories of the song "Teatro" by the remarkable diasporic Cuban singer La Lupe played often by radio stations in my childhood. The song opens with these lines: "Teatro, lo tuyo es puro teatro / falsedad bien ensayada / estudiado simulacro." I am told by German speakers that the same can be said of a perfectly ordinary word like "cathect," which has now become loaded with postmodern intertextuality. The question of what words or whose words one chooses to convey one's meaning matters enormously.

The intellectual industry of the West has the capability of appropriating, resignifying, and giving currency to or withholding it from words in a very asymmetrical fashion. The Caribbean critical term "creolization" cannot hope of achieving the global dissemination that a comparable term accepted into the Western critical lexicon such as "hybridity" has attained. The recognition of that asymmetry can cause the ethnic minority scholar to suppress autochthonous terminology and replace it with the language that the Western academy will more easily recognize. Speaking at Syracuse University on April 4, 2001, Antonio Benítez-Rojo gave a brief account of the authors through whom he came upon chaos theory for use in his analysis of Caribbean culture in his celebrated book *The Repeating Island*. When Puerto Rican fiction writer Mayra Santos Febres questioned his need to rely on those authors, given the availability of similar paradigms in the cosmology of Santería in his own native Cuban culture, he immediately agreed with her and proceeded to explain his choice in terms of what he thought would be preferred in the U.S. academy.

The famous conversation between Alice and Humpty Dumpty comes to mind here, specifically the passage in which she questions his use of the word "glory," to which he scornfully replies: "When I use a word, it means just what I choose it to mean—neither more nor less" (Carrol 1923:246). Not easily dismissed, the feisty Alice retorts, "The question is whether you can make words mean so many different things," to which her egg-shaped interlocutor replies: "The question is which is to be master—that's all" (246). The lesson I draw from Lewis Carrol here is that it all comes down to who has the power to impose a given denotation for a word. From Columbus's naming of the "Indians" when he came to the Caribbean in 1492, to Livingstone's naming of Victoria Falls in the Zambezi region in the nineteenth century, to contemporary critical theory's naming of the Other, the West has invariably reserved for itself and systematically deployed its formidable power to denote by renaming peoples, realities, and sites even if they already bore names of their own. "Thus I renamed them all," brags the Admiral of the Ocean sea, when detailing in a letter to his monarchs and to posterity the impressive record of his exploration, domination, and resignification of lands and peoples in the Caribbean (Columbus 1988:115). In light of that background it seems incumbent upon emancipated intellects from the Antilles and elsewhere in the Third World to assert their authority and their right to endow words with nuances of their own.

COMMITMENT TO THEORY AND ETHNIC PREDICAMENT

To avoid the risk of epistemological obliteration that suicidal reasoning fosters, the ethnic scholar must overcome the temptation of living intellectually in constant pursuit of an elusive cutting edge whose lead remains the exclusive province of Western academics in England, Germany, and France. A self-protective stance would encourage the ethnic minority scholar to remember at all times that Western academics too read as ethnics, except that they can afford to assume that their findings apply equally well to all other ethnics. Conversely, inquiries into the human experience of Africans, Latin Americans, Asians, or Antilleans by native scholars are never assumed to contain the cross-cultural explanatory power necessary to account for the Western portion of humanity. The unequal status of Third World knowledges vis-à-vis their Western counterparts spawns an arrangement whereby English, French, and German thinkers, even when they have made their name by launching a radical and revolutionary critique of Euro-North American imperialism, become automatically the intellectual masters of non-Western thinkers. As no self-respecting ethnic minority voice can feel satisfied with that subservient status, which is sustained by unequal relations of force between a center and its margins, the rapport of the non-Western intellect with the a priori epistemological authority of the West should be one of suspicion and distrust.

Reading as an ethnic, then, means for me to recognize my obligation to subvert the a priori authority of my theoretical masters. I do not mean here to incur the "damaging and self-defeating assumption that theory is necessarily the elite language of the socially and culturally privileged," an error brought to our attention by Homi K. Bhabha, who refutes the contention that "the place of the academic critic is inevitably within the Eurocentric archives of an imperialist or neo-classical West" (1994:19). Bhabha, more rhetorically than inquisitively, asks the following: "Are the interests of 'Western' theory necessarily collusive with the hegemonic role of the West as a power bloc? Is the language of theory merely another power play of the culturally privileged Western elite to produce a discourse of the Other that reinforces its own power-knowledge equation?" (20–21). Whatever one might say in response, it seems, in light of the foregoing discussion, that the answer is less unproblematically negative than this distinguished colleague would wish us to think. But even if we simply chose not to accept the terms of his questions in order to avoid binarisms and to show that polemics does not require polarization, one might still wish to consider whether the tools for codifying "that Third Space of enunciation" that Bhabha says he has "made the precondition for the articulation of cultural difference" could not possibly hinge on the authority of some Caribbean, African, or Indian truth-claim rather than on Western critical knowing (38). In other words, one could wonder about exactly why it is that the codification itself, the actual theory—not just an illustration of the idea in a passage from the fiction of Naipaul or a particular tributary insight from an essay by Wilson Harris—could not come from a non-Western intellect. I, for instance, feel unattended in my curiosity regarding whether Bhabha definitely had to have recourse to Jacques Lacan to develop his notion of "mimicry" and that there was nothing in the vast history of thought production in his native India that could provide a comparable clue to the concept (Bhabha 1994:85). Benítez-Rojo, one might recall, admitted that he could have found in Cuban Santeria the conceptual resources afforded to him by chaos theory had he chosen to make use of them. I wonder about the wisdom, ancient and vibrant, of the *Rg Veda*. I wonder, for example, about the Creation myth that educes a time prior to the beginning when "not even nothing existed," when there was "neither deathlessness nor decay." There the speaker considers the birth of the gods as subsequent to the beginning of the world and raises doubt as to whether the divine Lord has any knowledge about how all got started. The closing lines, in V. V. Raman's English translation from the Sanskrit, read thus: "Who really knows, and who can swear, / How creation came, when or where! / Even gods came after creation's day, / Who really knows, who can truly say / When and how did creation start? / Did He do it? Or did He not? / Only He, up there, knows, maybe; / Or perhaps, not even He" (*Rg Veda* X. 129). If people in India could since millennia ago entertain such notions, it seems reasonable for one to trust they must have conceived of the kind of behavior referred to as "mimicry" and other conceptual formulations that have become trademarks of the French academic industry. An essay by poet and translator A. K. Ramanujan about Indian ways of thinking and the inexorability of their "contextual sensitiveness" would seem to suggest no less, as he upholds the existence of distinct Indian ways of looking at the body, space, and time, and he challenges the representation of such a conceptual and cultural difference as somehow connected to any historical (lack of a Newtonian revolution), social, or intellectual backwardness (Ramanujan 1990:52).

Nor does it seem to me sustainable for an Indian or Antillean scholar to construe the category of thought production called theory as one devoid of its own cultural specificity. The Western academic market uses the term theory to refer to a certain kind of discursive intervention, which constitutes a peculiar way of organizing knowledge. In the humanities and the social sciences the word theory does not designate, as it does in physics or biology, a systematic ideational scheme of broad scope based on empirical observation or relying on experimentation, regularity of findings, and testing of a working hypothesis to arrive at sound explanations of phenomena. Literary scholars, cultural critics, and sociologists are not committed to the task of constructing "a complete unified theory of everything in the universe," which Stephen W. Hawking tells us is a fixation with physicists who long for a scheme that would make possible "the unification of physics" (Hawking 1988:154). Subject to revision or replacement if they fail to hold in light of pertinent data known to be true, theories enable scientists to make predictions. When their theories prove to have no use for that purpose, they normally discard them (Hesse 405–408). Witness the example of American physicist Ephraim Fischbach whose 1985 findings seemed to suggest that in a vacuum lighter objects fall faster than heavier ones, leading to numerous experiments internationally by other scientists who wished to test the validity of his claim, with the result that by 1992 the overwhelming evidence to the contrary had rendered Fischbach's "discovery" untenable (Cuevas and Lamb 1994:12). No comparable system of verification or revocation exists in the human sciences.

In the republic of letters, theory normally refers to a particular reading of society, humanity, or given texts and its currency does not depend on confirmation or explanatory value but on its appeal to consumers on the intellectual market. Similarly, its waning seldom comes as a result of a vigorous refutation that proves it false, but rather through the loss of luster that comes with overuse, especially as another more exciting "theoretical" intervention, offering a more dynamic array of expressive possibilities, gradually wins the favor of the scholarly market. The hoax played by Alan Sokal on the cultural studies journal *Social Text* (46–47 [Spring/Summer 1996]:217–252) would seem to suggest that merely emulating a particular diction and quoting the right people—those recognized as theorists by a particular coterie—can give an intervention the required "theoretical" bent and earn admission into the pertinent fora (Sokal and Bricmont 1998:269). Colleagues in their monographs and their conference presentation use the word theorize as a transitive verb, meaning often no more than "expand on." You leave a point "undertheorized" if you fail to flesh it out. The prevailing assumption, of course, is that a formulation's theoretical value lies in its general applicability, which presupposes a level of abstraction that transcends the explanation of the specific phenomenon on which it was deployed.

I could, for instance, analyze the Dominican Revolution of 1965 in a manner that highlights principles that operate in the genus of events that the episode represents, revealing coordinates that others might wish to apply in their examinations of revolutions elsewhere. But recognition of theory does not occur in a geopolitical vacuum. It requires a context and normally entails an act of faith. Readers recognize the element of theory in a text when they can identify its author as an intellect who possesses the status of theorist. Theory, then, consists of the utterances of a theorist. Given the scenario of epistemological asymmetry described earlier and the unequal relations of force that sustain it, we cannot in the academic industry boast of having an intellectually leveled field. Historical events affecting the lives of people in the Dominican Republic, for instance, cannot muster the weight of symbolic irradiation necessary for readers to regard any lesson therein contained as useful for shedding light on the European occurrence of the human experience. Since in the prevailing academic imaginary the West represents humanity while places like the Caribbean yield meaning of merely local significance, the content of Dominican events remains trapped in the status of "cases," commanding solely illustrative value. The content of events in France, on the other hand, can easily acquire a paradigmatic worth.

A truth-claim voiced by Dominican speakers about the 1965 events will therefore appear inherently to have less theoretical value irrespective of the modicum of abstraction they may have thrust into their formulation. The marginality of their subject matter in the context of the academic market internationally will render their interventions less desirable for citation. Quoting them will not provide anxious young scholars the security of intellectual legitimation. At this point, only by translating their autochthonous bodies of knowledge and ways of knowing into the axes of analysis and terminologies of the Western academy can Antillean or Indian scholars hope to earn induction into the fellowship of the theoretical ring. Rajogopalan Radhakrishnan has ventured to affirm that human science scholars from "the other world," who "tend to internalize more deeply the cultural and symbolic ideologies of the colonizer" than engineers, doctors, or scientists, often let the England of Dickens or the moors of the Bronte sisters have a greater hold of their imagination than their native habitat: "The problem here is not the Western influence per se, but the gratuitous dominance of the influence" (Radhakrishnan 1996:xvi).

Non-Western voices must contend with a scenario wherein the paradigm of modernity as a development ideal "and the language of the colonizer situate themselves in a position of pedagogical authority with respect to indigenous knowledges and languages" (xviii). As the geopolitics of academic work currently stands, non-Western speculative inquiry has no easy walk to attaining the rank of theory. Even so, the need patently exists for Third World intellectuals to launch their "indigenous critique," namely, the sort of "critique that will not pit belonging and progress as adversarial terms," so that the fund of critical knowledge emanating from "within [the] lived worlds" of Hindus, Muslims, Igbos, and Yorubas can effectually surface (xix). Radhakrishnan glosses the implication of the situation of an Indian woman who contemplates "her son's separation from her by way of progress and knowledge" in this poignant way: "Her concern is more profound [than a mere clinging to tradition]: How is it that my son, who is so passionately committed to matters epistemological and critical, is able to dismiss his own traditional resources in such active ignorance" (xix).

Nor should we underestimate the most obvious reason for the widespread association between theory and Western discourse, namely that the intellectual histories of culture areas such as Latin America and the Caribbean do not have a spot of authority and prestige reserved for authors who trade primarily in the deployment of paradigms. The most cursory glance at thought production in these regions will show that the greatest intellectuals there have invariably achieved their prominence on the basis of the articulateness of their analyses of situations in their respective societies. They advance knowledge and provide engaging interpretations of differentiated social realities. The most important intellectual interventions in the regions involved, including José Marti's "Nuestra América," Jean Price-Mars's *Ainsi parla L'Oncle*, Anton de Kom's *Wij slaven van Suriname*, Frantz Fanon's *Peau noires, masques blancs*, Aimé Cesaire's *Discours sur le colonialisme*, Pedro Mir's *Tres leyendas de colores*, Jose Luis González' *El país de cuatro pisos*, Paulo Freire's *Pedagogia do oprimido*, Roberto Fernández Retamar's *Calibán*, Eduardo Galeano's *Las venas abiertas de América Latina*, and George Lamming's *The Pleasures of Exile*, to cite only a few, came into the republic of letters as finite discussions of specific historical, social, cultural, political, and existential problems. At no point do the schemes of thought employed by these authors attain ontological autonomy or rise above the worth of the content of their inquiries. They achieve their eloquence in the intimacy they show with the concrete reality under perusal. They write as insightful commentators on and hermeneuts of their societies, histories, and cultures, addressing identifiable problems and hoping to contribute to effectuating change. They do not restrict their address to their peers in the scholarly community. Nor do they limit their ambition to making a contribution in the republic of letters by moving the implications of a particular truth-claim a few steps further than where a previous discursive intervention left it. They normally aspire to achieve more than merely to go conceptually beyond the confines reached by the preceding theorist.

Lacking a sense of themselves as theorists, primarily authors who view their paradigms as their main subject, the Latin American and Caribbean writers cited earlier exhibit no expertise in the linguistic mannerisms and rhetorical trademarks of the scholar who's intent on cultivating a theoretical garden. They do not stress unduly the coinage of terms so as to stave a particular social field with their own verbal insignias. They do not make their signification dependent on the reader's erudite expertise in the family of texts in which they wish to place their own. They, for instance, would most likely not publish a sentence as intertextually overburdened as this: "If we contest the 'grand narratives,' then what alternative temporalities do we create to articulate the differential (Jameson), contrapuntal (Said), interruptive (Spivak) historicities of race, gender, class, nation within a growing transnational culture?" (Bhabha 1994:174). Nor do they insist on alerting the reader as to their paternity of terminology or particular perspectives on issues by means of such mnemonically self-referential phrases as: "This is what I have called . . . ." The short 1949 article by Jacques Lacan on the "Mirror Stage" often included in literary theory anthologies richly illustrates the practice of self-attribution, assertion of ownership, and discursive staking that characterizes the verbal demeanor of authors who become established as theorists. ["The conception of the mirror stage that I introduced . . . thirteen years ago; . . . this activity retains the meaning I have given it . . .; I have myself shown in the social dialectic . . .; the objective notion of . . . and the presence of . . . confirm the view I have formulated . . .; . . . a form of its totality that I shall call orthopaedic . . .; . . . fragmented body—which term I have also introduced into our system of theoretical references," etc.] (Lacan 1998:178, 180–181). The zeal of Lacan's desire to stake a claim on words and ideas would strike an odd cord among Antillean thinkers while addressing their natural audience. They would generally fail to display the rhetorical demeanor and verbal strategizing whereby Western authors tend to promote the theoretical status of their speculation. As such, they make fewer gestures to enable the reader to recognize their utterances as theory.

A Latin American or Caribbean scholar, of course, can undeniably have the possibility of attaining the status of theorist should he or she abide by the Western rules of the game. Demonstrating dexterity in the application of Western critical innovations to Third World texts and social realities, even if one took the liberty of slightly subverting the director texts by noting implications not articulated by their authors, one certainly can, ceteris paribus, penetrate the circle of prestige of the theorists. But if that procedure should too closely resemble the practice of giving in to suicidal reasoning, one might wish to undertake to explore alternative ways of upholding one's "commitment to theory." For me, an Antillean native whom the bipolarity of colonial migration has brought to the corridors of the U.S. academy, theoretical expertise becomes first and foremost a matter of professional necessity.

I need to become conversant in what the academy calls critical theory in order to make communication with my peers possible. Learning it enables me to understand their references and follow their meaning. I might even be called upon to teach a theory course, and my training should enable me to comply. But I do not necessarily and immediately become an adept convert, a devout believer whose worldview gets updated by every new publication "in the field" that draws me closer to the cutting edge. In that respect, reading the works of authors like Jacques Derrida and Jean François-Lyotard becomes primarily an important effort of cultural literacy that contributes to my professional development and enables me to show competence on the job, but that competence does not in-and-of-itself satisfy the urgency of my search for truth and intellectual self-protection. I still feel obligated to uphold a "commitment to theory" that does not outright disqualify non-Western voices that are informed by their autochthonous bodies of knowledge, cultural systems, and forms of knowing. The idea ultimately is to resist the formidable monopoly of the Eurocentric imaginary in the definitions of humanity promoted by the intellectual industry in the West and to seek to restore the epistemological validity that non-Western thought production has been denied in the academy.

ETHNICITY AT SIEGE IN THE GLOBAL SOCIETY

At present the effort to affirm the intellectual legacies of non-white ethnic minorities faces a particularly grievous challenge given the advent in U.S. and British universities of influential trends in the organization of literary and cultural knowledge that favor a movement away from the ethnic, the national, the local, stressing rather the cross-cultural, the transnational, the global. Again influenced by developments in Western critical theory, chiefly postmodernist perspectives, and specifically the British cultural studies movement that began at the Birmingham Centre, critics variously associated with subaltern and postcolonial studies, including some prominent figures who are phenotypically non-white, have embraced the latest advances in the profession and have advocated expansive understandings of the field. Paul Gilroy's *The Black Atlantic* (1993) would seem to disavow even the formulation of the otherwise familiar notion of African American literature, insinuating that such a manner of tabulating the cultural products of U.S. blacks fails to account for the rhizomatic ties that link those artifacts to African, European intellectual history, and the Caribbean, ultimately fomenting nationalist approaches to the study of literature and culture. Instead, Gilroy prefers the social field he calls "the black Atlantic," a designation that emphasizes diasporic mobility, cultural formations that have connected the black experience to all three sites of the triangular trade, and black culture as an integral part of Western modernity. The "image of the ships in motion across the spaces between Europe, America, Africa, and the Caribbean" serve for him as an organizing principle of the "rhizomorphic, fractal structure of the transcultural, international formation" he calls "the black Atlantic," which transcends "both the structures of the nation state and the constraints of ethnicity and national particularity" (1993:4, 19).

Given the success of Gilroy's intervention, as is witnessed in that some U.S. universities and cultural institutions have already incorporated Black Atlantic Studies among their bona fide fields of inquiry, one may have reason to fear the deleterious effect that the highly appealing desire to liberate the study of blacks from "the constraints of ethnicity and national particularity" may have on the survival of ethnic studies initiatives, which in the U.S. academy came into being as a result of a social and political struggle. The creation of these academic initiatives sought to remedy centuries of exclusion of the human experience of non-white ethnic minorities from the standard narrative of the American nation and to rectify the model of humanity upon which the narrative was built. It might therefore become necessary to justify their existence once again by declaring that the national specificity of the word "American" in the compound gentilitial designations African American, Asian American, or Native American to describe bodies of writing does not necessarily entail an espousal of extreme nationalist ideas of literature, and it does not subscribe the programs in question to the idea of American literature propounded by the architects of the national canon prior to the 1960s. The Civil Rights, Women's Rights, and other social movements over the last five decades have had a transformative impact on what we do in the classroom, especially in the human sciences. Those events—far more than any development in French or British critical theory—have brought about a rethinking of traditional notions of citizenship, national belonging, and Americanness. It seems at this juncture necessary to remind ourselves of the enduring significance of various sorts of borders that make justifiable and indispensable the continued existence of national literary studies and of ethnically inflected analyses despite our aspiration to transcend them in the future.

I see no direct connection between our use of the gentilitial designation "African American" or Asian American or U.S. Hispanic for a given ethnic corpus and the deployment of "narrow nationalist perspectives" incurably committed to "the spurious invocation of ethnic particularity," to use Gilroy's dismissive characterization of the unnamed ideologues whose positions his book sets out to prove wrong (Gilroy 1993:29). This is not the place to pass judgment on the validity of Gilroy's proposed metaphor, the degree of academic rigor evinced by his argument, the source of his extreme faith in the explanatory power of his phraseology, or the ideological atmosphere that explains the celebrity of his book precisely within the national confines of the United States. But even the evidence that he himself adduces in his discussion of nineteenth-century black American thinkers (i.e., his insistence on the European paternity of their ideas) could serve to dispel the fear that the specificity implicit in "African American" might irremediably foster the examination of black culture without regard for the world outside the geography of the United States. I actually do not see how, in studying the black cultural and literary experience in North America, one could remain oblivious to the subject's rhizomatic links to Africa, the Caribbean, Europe, Latin America, American Indian societies, and the various differentiated segments of the U.S. population across the land's multiplicity of histories, knowledges, and cultural forms.

During a visit to the Schomburg—a branch of the New York Public Library named significantly after a black Puerto Rican who distinguished himself as a historian of the African heritage and who excelled among the luminaries of the Harlem Renaissance—I purchased a book of photographs of African American men and women of letters. The book's cover, which featured the face of novelist and short-fiction writer Edwidge Danticat, gave me some food for thought. Dandicat came to the United States from Haiti, knowing no English, when she was a young girl. Her gracing that cover as a bona fide member of the community of authors therein assembled indicates to me that the designation African American is not devoid of its measure of elasticity. Even a compilation as recognizably mainstream as *The Norton Anthology of African American Literature*, edited by Henry Louis Gates, Jr., could suffice to illustrate the inexorably cross-cultural, interlingual, and transnational complexity of the body of utterances known collectively as African American literature.

By including Equiano's slave narrative, for instance, the *Norton* transgresses geographical boundaries since the author, a native of North Africa, lived his "American" experience largely in the West Indies, before ending up in England. The inclusion of slave narratives itself is significant. The anthology does it without demoting the genre to the realm of the "non literary world," as Cleanth Brooks, R. W. B. Lewis, and Robert Penn Warren do with the work of Frederick Douglass and other "informal" writings in their "American literature" compendium (1973:1016–1017). One cannot accuse the compilation by Gates et al. of upholding traditional (purist) ideas of literariness. The same goes for the selection of Negro spirituals, blues lyrics, and samples of black oratory. But to return to the "dogmatism" that so horrifies Gilroy's fancy, the serious study of the black American experience makes it very hard for literary scholars to commit the sin of narrow nationalism.

The writings of such authors as Victor Séjour, Eric Walrond, and Paule Marshall, all anthologized in the *Norton*, would simply not allow it. The text by Sejour is an English translation of a French original, French being the literary language of many African-descended Louisiana Creoles in the nineteenth century, which alerts us to the linguistic complexity in the literature of the United States. Walrond's book *Tropic Death* (1926), which was published in New York City in the wake of the Harlem Renaissance, draws on the author's experience as a black British subject who was born in 1898 in Georgetown, Guyana, spent his childhood in Barbados, and went to school in the Panamanian city of Colón, in the Canal Zone, prior to arriving in the United States on June 30, 1918, where he would play an active role in the black cultural life of New York City. Finally, the inclusion of Paule Marshall, whose writings are fueled mostly by Caribbean history and West Indian immigrant life in New York City, implicitly recognizes the ample breadth of the very idea of African American literature. The works of Marshall, along with those of Toni Morrison and Gayl Jones, have received attention precisely with a focus on their "inter-American links" in the book *Bridging the Americas* (1995) by Stelamaris Coser.

I have no intention of pastoralizing the open-mindedness of Gates and the other colleagues who compiled the *Norton*. I merely wish to stress that the appellation African American literature and culture names a field of study that is inherently traversed by an experience that is black diasporic, which renders it naturally amiable to cross-cultural, transnational, and multilingual examinations. One must remember that this area of inquiry, consistent with the other domains of knowledge within the larger field of ethnic studies, came into existence precisely in response to exclusionary formulations and homogenizing articulations of national culture in the United States. As such, it is intellectually poised to challenge rather than promote "narrow" nationalisms. The emergence of ethnic studies perspectives has contributed to our widening the lens as we consider the cultural forms and bodies of writing that merit inclusion in the field of American literature. They have almost invariably endeavored to subvert the paradigms deployed by those seeking vigilantly to patrol the borders of the canon.

A similar case can be made to show that Latino literature, while existing within the confines of the United States, has little patience for confining definitions of the country's culture. For instance, one needs to know Spanish and English to read the writings of María Amparo Ruiz de Burton, a native of California who in 1885 published *The Squatter and the Don*, a novel dealing with the political and sociocultural effects of the Anglo occupation of the Southwest. Tomás Rivera, a Texan born in Crystal City, wrote his first novel in Spanish, and the South Texas poet and cultural icon Gloria Anzaldúa combines Spanish and English in her texts. The rapport of Spanish and English—complicated at times by the use of words and phrases from the indigenous Native American languages of the Southwest—is a constant feature of Latino literature, one that contributes to the opening of the American mind by foregrounding the too long neglected fact that the country's literature speaks many different languages. One could invoke the Yiddish and other non-Anglophone survivals to make plain that the literary use of languages other than English has occurred among whites as well.

Perhaps Gilroy's extreme confidence in the explanatory power of his black Atlantic metaphor over the paradigms coming from African American studies hinges on a mind-set that regards any configuration of cultural experience within a national framework as retrograde and inadequate. This militant antinationalism has problems of its own. The evangelists of transnational dynamics and the heralds of the global society speak as if they in fact believed that we as a species have already left the nation-state behind. They see the world presently going through a stage of historical evolution characterized by a state of affairs in which world systems now serve the functions formerly served by particular polities, differentiated cultures, or individual societies in shaping people's worldviews and immediate realities. They quickly dismiss social movements that do not articulate their cause in planetary terms as efforts that are stymied by the quagmire of filiopietistic affiliations to imagined communities. Our national or tribal identity having become obsolete, we are urged to think of ourselves as global beings. A problem the evangelists of the global society would need to address, though, is the strange coincidence between their views and the arguments of the agencies of world capitalism such as the IMF that seek to persuade Third World rulers and business leaders to desist from the idea of developing national industries and achieving economic self-sufficiency. The imperial mega-banks would advice that at this stage of the game the thing to do for the sake of local populations is to remove economic barriers to foreign investors so that international capital can move unencumbered. The documentary film *Life and Debt* (2001) by Stephanie Black beautifully and painfully illustrates this predicament as it relates to Jamaica's dependent economy. I do not know of one country where loss of economic autonomy in the name of participating in the global society has brought about enhanced material well-being, justice, and equality for the population.

Capital always knew how to transcend national boundaries. Decades ago the institutional vehicles through which capital pursued the business of accumulation globally were called multinational corporations. From the conquest of America, to the scramble for Africa, to the contemporary spread of Free Trade Zones throughout the Third World, Western capitalism has yearned to transcend boundaries, cross over cultures, erase distances, and remove all the impediments that might obstruct or slow down the process of planetary domination and global accumulation. Border crossing is a primary occupation of empires. As such, Western empires have competed fiercely among themselves for hegemony over the process of redistricting the globe. Learned observers of the transformations that follow from imperial mobility have at various junctures proclaimed the advent of a new world. The European war of 1914–1918 produced considerable cartographic shifts. Isaiah Bowman's 1922 book *The New World*, surveying the outcome of post-war restructuring, asked several questions, including these: "How much of the old world is left? What kind of people compose the new states? Will the new democracies survive,—in Poland and Yugoslavia and Austria, for example,—or are some of the experiments in self-government likely to fail? . . . Will the strong states administer their colonies and protectorates in the interest of the natives? . . . Has the day of deliverance come for the oppressed minorities of the earth . . .? . . . Will strong nations continue to struggle for trade privileges, raw materials, and economic zones, with the prospect of war between them . . .?" (cited by Short 1998:5–6).

When George Bush père in the 1980s announced the arrival of a new dawn in human history, calling it "a new world order," his speech echoed a long tradition in the rhetoric of empire. But perhaps we need to emphasize here that the newness in question, the historical freshness enunciated in the pronouncements of imperial town criers, seldom matches the perception of those whose condition remains as bad as they had known it prior to the proclaimed rearrangements. The politically and economically disinherited throughout the world do not have their reality transformed necessarily by every stylistic change in the form of international domination. I find it comforting that Habermas's musings on "the post-national" in a book of his on the subject center specifically around the member countries of the European Union, which he calls "societies of well-being" (Habermas 2000:98). That is as it should be. Still too many communities on this planet inhabit a world that for them has remained too much like it was for their parents, grandparents, and great-grandparents. The indigenous population of Brazil still does not enjoy the status of citizenship under the law. The children of Haitian immigrants in the Dominican Republic are not recognized as Dominicans, despite the principle of *jus solis* embraced by the country's constitution, which means that they do not receive the birth certificate that would qualify them to enter school, benefit from standard social services, and fend off deportation. Similarly, Palestinians still yearn for a place that they can call their own, where they can, in the words of Edward Said, "recreate our national identity as a people" (Said, 2001a). In other words, partaking of the succor that a fair nation-state might offer still remains a goal to aspire to for too many people around the world.

Rey Chow reminds us that for "those who lived as colonized subjects, globalization—in particular, cultural globalization—has always meant the experience of exclusion: adopt Western ways and evacuate your own . . . To globalize has meant one thing: to subordinate, derogate, or extinguish one's native language, culture, history, in order to accommodate those of the West" (Chow 2001:69). She further prompts us to recognize "the asymmetry of power relations that persists with the global circulation of certain cultural stereotypes" (73). During the XXIII International Congress of the Latin American Studies Association, which met in Washington, DC in September 6–9, 2001, I shared a panel on the Caribbean diaspora and the redefinition of national literature with Ambrosio Fornet, one of the most prominent literary scholars from the Republic of Cuba. Fornet's paper reaffirmed a position he has held since he began writing about Cuban American literature in 1992, namely that the works of American authors of Cuban descent such as Oscar Hijüelos and Cristina García are "not Cuban in the proper sense of the term because they are not written in the mother language of 99.9% of Cubans." Regarding his unmitigated espousal of the sphere of the national for the consideration of literary texts, Fornet stated plainly that the national remained valid in literature insofar as it still mattered outside of it. "The nation-state still has some tasks left that it needs to accomplish especially for the underdeveloped countries," he added.

THE ENDURING SIGNIFICANCE OF BORDERS

For ethnically differentiated minorities in the United States and elsewhere, especially those that have endured duress on account of their difference vis-à-vis a cultural and political center of power, the nation-state still has some promises to keep and miles to go before one can permit it restfully to retire. That's one way of putting it. Another is that the disempowered have nothing but the nation as a structure within which to fight for material improvement, equality, and justice. Only the nation at this point provides them with a political forum—sustained by constitutions, the law, and the occasional influence of "the international community" to demand respect and assert their rights, including the right to redefine the nation. So-called communities of color in the United States have for many decades now fought in various ways to attain full citizenship. Their effort has yielded considerable fruit. Witness the fact that lynchings and Jim Crow prohibitions no longer figure in the menu of sorrows that blacks have to endure. We cannot deny the areas of tangible progress before us. The nation has indubitably come closer to living up to the true meaning of its creed. We still have serious challenges that cry for urgent redressing: alarming numbers of black males in the state penitentiaries; overrepresentation of black children among the unschooled, the unfed, the hopeless; and severe underrepresentation of black adults in the faculty of universities throughout the country, to name only a few of them.

There is no planetary, post-national, post-ethnic, and cross-cultural tribunal where U.S. blacks can go to file a complaint and seek to correct these social ills in their community. Like Latinos, Asian Americans, and even—albeit problematically—Native Americans, African Americans need the nation-state to confer a logic and a logistics to their struggle for human dignity. They need to assert themselves as Americans, and in so doing they do not incur in the myopia of narrow nationalism. Rather they help to free Americanness from, on the one hand, the rigidity of Eurocentric ontologies and, on the other, the spatial confinement that border patrols specialize in securing. Whether one has been brought into the Union by the social death of slavery (blacks), by territorial dispossession (Native Americans), by conquest and regional domination (Latinos), or by imperial bridging of vast distances (Asian Americans), the major non-white ethnic minorities in the United States share an experience of common diasporic uprooting and a hypermnesic sense of the presence of the dyad *elsewhere/yoretime*. I see that hypermnesic sense as a deterrent against narrowly conceived ideas of nation. The works of some major Latina writers like Julia Alvarez could be read as continuous exercises in counting the multiple valid ways of asserting Americanness without the encasement of narrow nationalism. Alvarez, for instance, constructs her American identity by constantly deambulating within the polarities of Hispanic and Anglo symbols, values, and forms.

For reasons that one might wish to term dialectical, people at the margins often precede their mainstream counterparts in recognizing the pitfalls of rigid formulations of citizenship and nation. Speaking in 1906, a time when Italians had not yet ascended to whiteness in the United States, the secretary of the Society for the Protection of Italian Immigrants Gino Speranza argued for an "international citizenship" to rescue us from the ambivalence fostered by the situation that "makes a man an American while here, and an Italian while in Italy" (cited by Foner 2000:169). Speranza sought to draw attention to the complex political location of a large part of the U.S. population that felt a dual allegiance to here and there: "We may have to bring ourselves to the point of recognizing foreign 'colonies' in our midst, on our own soil, as entitled to partake in the parliamentary life of their mother country" (169). These transnational dilemmas are inescapable for people who have a history of diasporic uprooting that their present disempowerment causes them to remember. Ethnically differentiated and racialized communities in the United States did not begin to think about the porosity of borders, liminality, margins, interstices, in-betweenness, displacement, periphery, hybridity, and crossings when prompted by critical theory. They did not have to wait until the Western intelligentsia, managing to reassert its epistemological predominance through such successful projects as cultural studies and post-colonialism, made these terms part of its nomenclatural arsenal. The experiential sites, situations, and positions that those terms connote correspond tangibly to the stressful ways in which those communities have lived their history.

When the writers, the literary scholars, and the cultural critics from racialized ethnic minorities in the United States think of American literature they tend at once to display two dissimilar but not mutually exclusive intents: to assert their rightful place in the national corpus that the designation names and to challenge the sociocultural framework that first went into its naming. Suffice it to glance at the project of "re-writing American literary history" evinced by the authors included in *Criticism in the Borderlands: Studies in Chicano Literature, Culture, and Ideology* (1991) edited by Hector Calderón and José David Saldívar, to name only one such intervention. The work of Toni Morrison, for instance, is heavily invested in scrutinizing the remnants of an African cultural survival that accounts for the distinct diction of her ethnic community, but that intercontinental exchange coexists in the author's mind with the desire to assert the neglected centrality of the black experience to the national American literature and culture. She observes in her 1992 essay *Playing in the Dark* that "American means white, and Africanist people struggle to make the term applicable to themselves with ethnicity and hyphen after hyphen after hyphen" (Morrison 1993:47). By the same token, the young American writer of Dominican descent Angie Cruz, author of the novel *Soledad*, which evokes life in the New York City neighborhood of Washington Heights, is very much rooted in this country. She knows there can be no material home for her in the Caribbean homeland of her parents, but as an *elsewhere/yoretime* it inevitably informs her cultural world in the United States. When I interviewed her at the Public Theater in New York City on July 13, 2001, I posed this question: "Do you remember consciously deciding at one point that your characters would be Dominican?" to which she quickly and unhesitantly responded: "No, I just never thought they would not be." And her work is no less American than Mark Twain's.

In sum, since from the perspective of ethnic studies the national context presupposes neither a rigid understanding of Americanness nor a narrow conception of the nation, it would seem appropriate to grant that promoting African American literature as a body of writings that occurs in the United States specifically does not automatically place us into disquieting complicity with any retardatory intellectual projects that we might wish to distance ourselves from. At the very least, we will not incur a more grievous fault than we would if, in the name of a presumed theoretical currency, we wholeheartedly embraced the approach and vocabulary dictated by an Afro-Saxon scholar speaking about the correct way of studying the U.S. black experience from the intellectual authority of the British academy. Siding with proponents of the black Atlantic could bring us into a perhaps much deeper folly since we might help to perpetuate the practice of telling racialized minorities that there is an external "we" in privileged possession of a more reliable discernment of the logic of their history than they could possibly learn via their entrenched native perspectives. Would this not entail our persisting in "the assumption that 'we' can survey the world, redraw the boundaries, give sanction to (or withhold it from) *some* histories, languages, voices, experiences," as Said would wonder? (Said 2001b:67).

Nobody in his or her right mind would obstinately oppose current critical challenges to the employment of "traditional frameworks" in the study of literature. Contemporary literary theory has raised very incisive questions regarding the validity of the idea that literary artifacts exist within a national sphere or of the assumption that works of literary art exist in some sort of stable form that makes their identity unarguably distinct from other manifestations of verbal expression. But our recognition of the value of the questions raised does not immediately endow us with indisputably correct answers. We live in a very complex world, and an awareness of that reality has made me weary of thinkers who seem overconfident of the paradigms they deploy or the metaphors they devise to pronounce the last word on the structure of life, culture, history, and society throughout the entire globe. As a result, I have come to apportion my intellectual respect mostly to humble luminaries, folks, for instance, like the late Edward W. Said, who believed unwaveringly in the existence of "an autonomous aesthetic realm," yet, despite his vast erudition, had the wisdom to admit ignorance concerning exactly "how it exists in relation to history, politics, social structures, and the like" (Said 2001b:64).

The bodies of knowledge produced, gathered, unearthed, and disseminated by ethnic studies ventures in the U.S. academy have spawned paradigms, emphases, and analytical perspectives formerly unfamiliar to our industry. Shelley Eversley of the University of Washington notes that African American literary scholars "offer our criticism as a means to explore the terms and implications of race, not just blackness, but race and its imposition on the various aspects of art, identity, narrative form, culture and, yes, history" (Eversley 2001:21). This and other legacies indeed provide us with the wherewithal to cultivate the study of African American literature and culture as well as American literature generally in a way that would not replicate older exclusionary nationalist paradigms. Said asked whether one could at this point formulate "a theory of connection between part and whole that denies neither the specificity of the individual experience nor the validity of a projected, putative, or imputed whole" (2001b:68). I would respond, definitely, yes. We can. And that is so, in the American case, because of the intellectual groundwork that generations of ethnic studies scholars have laid, which has transformed the state of knowledge in the human sciences. Because of its ties to agendas involving the demand for full citizenship by racialized minorities existing within discrete polities, the ethnic studies perspective shows acute awareness of the importance, as Said insisted in reminding us, not always of "synthesis or the transcendence of opposites but of the role of geographic knowledge in keeping one grounded, literally, in the often tragic structure of social, historical, and epistemological contests over territory—this includes nationalism, identity, narrative, and ethnicity—so much of which informs the literature, thought, and culture of our time" (2001b:68).

Needless to say, the deployment of ethnic differentiation within a national framework in the study of literature and culture can boast no inherent virtue, having merely a predicamental value. When all segments of the population have achieved full citizenship, and the cultural field has been leveled, and the racial imagination has totally lost its power to confer or deny worth to intellectual achievements, such a differentiation will become superfluous. That will happen when literary curricula are automatically inclusive, that is, accurately representative of the diversity of talent in the entire population without the teacher having to make a conscious effort to achieve fairness, and when a third year English major in my class will not say of Amy Tan that her work is not American literature because "she's Asian" (I say, "well, ethnically, but she was born in California, and her books cover strictly American experiences," and she insists, "yeah, but she's Asian!"). I envision then no longer having to spend time demonstrating that Latinos have been a part of the United States for ages, meaning, that there is nothing foreign about a novelist named Américo Paredes whose characters have Spanish surnames. At that time U.S. publishers will not wonder whether there are enough readers in a particular racialized community before accepting a manuscript by one of its authors, the book industry having already stepped out of the schemes of thought responsible for persuading them that the sorrows of Twain's young Huck Finn (the "human" experience) speak to all of us, whereas the conflicts of Sandra Cisneros's Esmeralda (the "ethnic" experience) matter only to readers in the author's particular group. That day a dear friend of Toni Morrison and brilliant white American writer will no longer introduce her by saying, in a spirit of highest praise, that he doesn't think of her "as a black writer or a woman writer, but simply as a writer" ("you mean, a white male writer?" she gorgeously retorted, as she recalls during a 1990 interview with Bill Moyers for the PBS series "World of Ideas"). These futuristic evocations describe the advent of an era when social equality and justice have reached such plenitude that ethnic minorities will not suffer any consequences whatsoever on account of their difference. The ethnic and national differentiation evident in the designation African American will lose then all meaning except as a neutral descriptor. At present, however, disdain for that designation would seem premature. Things being what they are rather than what we hope they will become, it behooves us for now to take advantage of the worlds of knowledge, symbols, and forms in the vast field of African American literature and culture, which rhizomatically connects regions and traditions, experiences and times.

Intellectual Self-Defense in Caribbean Thought

The epistemological disadvantage of U.S. ethnic minorities in relation to the mainstream cultural discourse in the United States compares meaningfully, I believe, with the plight of Caribbean peoples vis-à-vis the Western thought production industry. As a native of the Dominican Republic brought by colonial migration to the corridors of the U.S. academy, having, of course, passed the existential probation that stems from exilic uprooting, I happen to belong in the ethnic compartment apportioned in this country to Latinos as well as in the cultural platform of the Antillean who must, for the sake of intellectual self-respect, recognize his contradistinction to the West. The Antillean's rapport with the Western tradition cannot strip itself of the formidable complexities that lie at the core of the colonial experience. We can hardly refute the claim by Puerto Rican sociologist Angel (Chuco) Quintero Rivera at a panel in the "Gran Cuenca del Caribe" bookfair in Barranquilla on May 9, 2002 that "we too are the West" just as we partake of African and Amerindian heritages. Indeed, syncretic cultural formations do not have the option of excising any of their constituent elements.

To de-Westernize radically seems neither feasible nor desirable for the Antillean person. Despite how much one might still grieve over the cruelty of the colonial transaction, the bloodshed and the dehumanization perpetrated by the Western encroacher, the fact remains that we are civilizational mixed-bloods, the cultural offspring of the conquerors and the vanquished. We are stuck with the parents history gave us. The insistence here on closely scrutinizing the implications of passively receiving the successive stages of Western discourse—whether it involves postmodernist thought or its dark-skinned, postcolonial manifestation—cannot rest on a yearning for lost origins. There is no longer an available point to which one might wish to return. In the Caribbean, the language of instruction in the schools, the organization of society, and the forms of development espoused by the ruling elites all have Western parentage. The Antillean is an heir to the Western tradition. But at least one must recognize oneself as an ambivalent heir, one who accepts the inexorable kinship without ignoring the repository of harm lodged in that inheritance. Unlike normal heirs to the tradition, Antilleans have the delicate task of imagining the story of human culture in a manner that promises to safeguard their creativity from the encroaching might of the West, to which they nonetheless are bound by blood ties. In other words, the need to proclaim the source of their originality, which, stemming from a history of creolization, lies precisely in its propensity to avoid containment within the cultural or intellectual border of any single tradition. "The only thing pure in the Caribbean is our impurity," says Luis Rafael Sánchez (2003:52).

The West is both internal and external to the Caribbean. Western discourse construed the Caribbean as a site of lesser humanity, as a location outside the confines of history proper. It stigmatized the feeling and the thinking of the Caribbean mind. As such, an Antillean cannot embrace intellectual development in the Western tradition without at least showing self-awareness of a difficult relationship with it. One might praise a Caribbean intellectual achievement by highlighting the region's thinkers' adaptive dexterity, their promptness at catching up with advances in the Western academy. One might, for instance, praise Edouard Glissant's "vision of global creolization" contending that it conceives the Caribbean "as a sea exploding outwards, not concentrating inwards," so as to report that the Martinican thinker thereby achieves the lofty status of postcolonialism (Dash 1995:148). But one might also, perhaps more self-respectingly, consider Caribbean intellects as providers, rather than recipients, of the paradigms that the Western academy has marketed as "postcolonial theory." Roman de la Campa has aptly observed that "Mapping of Caribbean culture has always conjured images of hybridity, mimicry, syncretism, and transculturalization," reminding us that Antillean writing "gave meaning to such categories" long before the advent of "postmodern troping" (De La Campa 1997:87).

Caribbean discourse, if it is realistically to aspire to cultural authenticity, must remind itself that it does not belong in the same chronology that Western critical theory assumes. Contemporary Western discourse exists in a post-Fordist, postindustrial era, but one easily infers that the actual places that serve as unspoken referents for those terms are Euro–North American technocratic societies. Clearly, industrial capitalism does not really disappear when it seems to vanish from the metropolitan sight of the Western percipient. The factory, the sweatshop, the assembly line, the abusive foreman, and the meek, disempowered workers may have become rare in New York, London, Paris, or Berlin, but in the Caribbean they continue to be part and parcel of the ordinary human drama. Sometimes a factory leaves New York precisely because it knows it can find more auspicious capitalist conditions to continue to exist in the free industrial zones of, say, an economically dependent nation like the Dominican Republic. Antillean intellects must beware of inadvertently subsuming the narrative of their peoples and places under a temporality that is forged by the experience of somebody else elsewhere. They must insist on building chronologies by looking at their own historical clocks.

Ultimately the challenge for Antillean intellects is to pursue the task of identifying and affirming autochthonous meaning by asserting the creolity of their knowing. This will often entail a perhaps inevitable loss of scholarly glow since one may have to speak outside the realm of the existing debates in the profession. To the question "who are you in conversation with?" which aims to locate each scholar's theoretical positionality within the dialogues that the academy recognizes as valid, one may have to summon the temerity to say "nobody," and perhaps express resentment at the expectation that everybody should participate in conversations whose terms leave out so much of the world. At a conference on Brathwaite in the Mona campus of the University of the West Indies on January 11, 2002, the scholar Oyèrónké Oyěwùmí spoke emphatically about her conviction that Brathwaite's concept of "nation language" can help elucidate cultural, social, and linguistic realities in Africa. She thus evinced a refreshing understanding of the utility of a Caribbean paradigm to speak meaningfully about humanity in other parts of the globe. Her intervention reassures me that the knowledge spawned by the human experience in the Caribbean can conceivably muster explanatory power sufficient to shed light on the drama of the species within and beyond the archipelago and its rimlands. The legacy of Brathwaite and others points to the necessary search for native meaning, autochthonous metadiscourses, and indigenous systems of significance to save Caribbean minds and bodies from being reduced to mere fodder to feed the theoretical voracity of contemporary Western discourse. Such legacy exalts the leadership that Antillean intellects can exert, by asserting their creolity, to disobey the Western dictate that would confine them to the back of the bus of theory. It promotes a decolonizing approach to our reading of human culture. It offers me a lesson about knowledge and book learning that my father, erudite as he was, lacked the ideological wherewithal to teach me, namely, the need for intellectual self-defense.

CHAPTER 2

The Endless History: The Caribbean
versus Western Discourse

A ZONE OF ALTERITY

Volume II of the legendary *Encyclopédie*, edited by Denis Diderot and Jean le Rond d'Alembert carries a quarter-page entry entitled "Caräibes, ou Cannibales." The brief article, devoted to inform the reader about the "island savages of America, overlords of a part of the Antilles," powerfully conjures the promptness of the West to imagine the Caribbean as a zone dominated by the uncanny. The caribs, the text explains, "use no swathing clothes for their new born," who, "from the age of four months walk on four," achieving such agility in that practice that, when they grow up, they move "as swiftly that way as a European moving on two legs" (*Encyclopédie* II:669). The tendency to crawl that the *encyclopédistes* imputed to the Caribs does not fail to amaze. When students of the evolutionary development of the human creature trace today the stages that the species has gone through, they normally concur that to reach to the Cro-Magnon level, becoming *sapiens*, having previously been confirmed as *habilis*, the *homo* to whom we trace our origin first needed to establish credentials as *erectus*. It cannot fail to fascinate, then, that the *encyclopédistes* seem by implication to attribute to the Carib population a biological descent outside the genealogical tree of that humanity that from time immemorial burned with the desire to stand up and walk.

"When one of them dies," the *Encyclopédie* continues, "his negro is killed so he will continue to serve him in the next world" (II:669). The language of this passing observation on the burial customs of aboriginal Antilleans suggests that by 1751, the publication date of volume II of the memorable compendium—that major milestone in the knowledge produced by the European movement scholars have called the Enlightenment—already the inexorability of slavery as a natural condition for black people had become rooted in the consciousness of Western thinkers. Apparently by then one could easily use the noun "negro" as a synonym for "slave" or "servant." It falls outside the purview of the present discussion to determine whether Diderot and d'Alembert actually believed that the Antilleans described in the article actually possessed enslaved Africans or if their usage rather had to do with a conceptual fusion between blackness and servitude to the point that any servant, irrespective of ethnic or racial procedence, could generically fit the classification of "negro." Either of the two possibilities would equally well suit the purposes of this book.

Among the other characteristics attributed by the encyclopedia entry to the Caribs, I would like to dwell only on two. The first refers to the assertion that "they eat their prisoners roasted," activity that they share festively "sending morsels to their friends." This observation matters, above all, because, as we will see later, anthropophagy—whether literal or metaphorical—forms an integral part of the conceptual arsenal deployed by the West against the Caribbean in its sustained effort to represent the region as a zone living outside the contours of history and civilization. The other characteristic matters less for its direct denotation than for what it suggests about the process followed by the *encyclopédistes* in the acquisition and dissemination of knowledge. The entry in question informs that the Caribs "have many wives who do not quarrel among themselves," which "Montaigne views as a miracle in his chapter about these people" (II:669). Through this direct reference the article makes evident what could otherwise be ascertained by intertextual reading, namely, that the entry relies heavily on Montaigne's well-known essay "On Cannibals," published a good century and a half prior to the volume II of the *Encyclopédie*. Curiously, in utilizing it as documentation the *encyclopédistes* appear not to have detected the playful and ironic intent of Montaigne's text in the *Essais* (1580). Montaigne wished primarily to use the "savages" in his essay as an instrument whereby he could satirize a certain kind of European barbarism. The French sage therein declares that "there is nothing barbarous in that nation, from what I have been told, except that each man calls barbarism whatever is not his own practice," and he spends a great deal of the body of his essay denying the "barbarity" of the Amerindian nation he is describing while stressing the patent savagery of certain political and social practices in Christian Europe (Montaigne 1957:152). Given the scientific intent of the *Encyclopédie*, whose subtitle reads "Annotated Dictionary of the Sciences, the Arts, and other Matters," its attachment to a literary piece of imaginative prose as a source of historical data, cannot help but invite irony, especially given Montaigne's own disclaimer regarding inappropriately assumed intellectual authority: "I would like everyone to write what he knows, and as much as he knows, not only in this, but in all other subjects" (152). The gullibility that makes the *encyclopédistes* overlook the satirical element of the essay stems probably from the European imaginary's deeply rooted idea of the Antillean world as a bizarre space. The title of the encyclopedia entry, "Caräibes, ou Cannibales" suggests also that by then a seamless fusion had occurred in Western discourse between cannibalism and the Antillean world, a process that started in the pages of Columbus's *Diario* and that in time would envelop the lands, the sea, the people, and the cultures of the region (Hurbon 1999:141).

This section takes as a point of departure the *Encyclopédie's* sloppy handling of the representation of the indigenous population of the Antilles to develop the idea that the devalued alterity to which the West relegated the Caribbean—in a process of discursive aggression that preceded Diderot and d'Alembert—has maintained its currency from the start of the colonial transaction through our day. Concomitantly, I plan to advance the claim that one can trace the development of Caribbean intellectual history by narrating the continued desire of the literary artists, thinkers, and scholars of the region to articulate compelling ways of challenging the legacy of inimical representation bequeathed by Western discourse. I feel no urgency here to confirm or deny the formulation by Jameson that would attribute to Caribbean writing—by virtue of its location in the "Third World"—the necessary function of "national allegory" (Jameson 2000:319). I will simply content myself with the task of tracing the trajectory of Antillean thought in its long and fractious relationship with the Western intellectual tradition at those junctures when it has trained its gaze on the Caribbean. This inquiry will consequently encompass an effort to appraise the advent of "postcolonial cultural studies" as the latest iteration of that fractious relationship.

My visit to Cartagena de Indias as a speaker in the V International Seminar on Caribbean Studies toward the end of July 2001, the year of the sesquicentenary of the abolition of slavery in Colombia, helped to clarify the scope of this reflection. Located on the Atlantic coast of Colombia, Cartagena, described by historian Alfonso Múnera Cavadia, as "symbolic center of the Caribbean" during the sixteenth and seventeenth centuries, served as the main slave factory of the Spanish Empire. Until the end of the eighteenth century, says Múnera, knowledge flowed to Cartagena from the insular Caribbean (Guerra 2001:5A). Inextricably linked to the slave trade, though no formal plantations existed there, Cartagena must have experienced the end of slavery in a very special way. For those whom the colonial transaction had deprived of freedom escaping the social death of their captivity opened the possibility of aspiring to the protection of citizenship. Since the colonial order had inferiorized them racially, they now faced the challenge of affirming their human identity by asserting their place within the contours of history. This entailed the effort to affirm their status as people with the capacity to carve a niche in the pugnatious arena of the public sphere. Black Colombians thus exited the condition of mere property whose value was measured in terms of their ability to sweat for the purpose of increasing or sustaining the wealth of their owners. They then entered the status of free people who were weakened by the legacy of their past of captivity and from then onward had to contend with the challenge of survival in the social injustice of an uneven playing field.

The plight of the African-descended Colombian population in light of the new possibilities opened by their emancipation suggests to me a parallel with the predicament of Antillean thought. Since it emerged as a differentiated culture area, spawned by the colonial transaction that ensued from the conquest, the Caribbean has had to cope with an arsenal of utterances forged by the logic of the imperial imagination that, in placing the region on the outskirts of history proper, would seem to remove it from the expanse of human society. Like the freed blacks of Colombia, Caribbean intellects in the modern period have been presented with the difficult task of demonstrating the rightful place of their people within the confines of history and among the branches of the human family. What Edouard Glissant has called "Caribbean discourse" has as its most immediate catalyst the urgency to articulate or elucidate the process whereby the region's cultural forms and ways of saying came into being and how they attained self-differentiation vis-à-vis those of Europe, Africa, and the other branches of the human family. Caribbean culture broadly conceived came into being in the extent to which the bodies of knowledge and the expressive forms imported to the region by the multiple branches of the human family that stumbled upon one another there, mediated by the Amerindian context they found, gradually distanced themselves from their originating sources while simultaneously growing attached to their environment to the point of recognizing themselves in their achieved distinctness.

The present intervention, then, aspires to give vent to an intellectual will that has for ages insisted on affirming the Caribbean as a differentiated stage of the history of humanity and as a culture area with a specificity of its own. I have elsewhere sustained the cultural autonomy of the Antillean world illustrating the aesthetic cohesion shared by the texts that make up the literary corpus of the region, whose commonality stands but across the writings in English, French, Spanish, Dutch, and the other tongues in which the literature speaks (Torres-Saillant 1997). Here I am concerned with what could be described as a "defense and illustration" (à la Joachim Du Bellay) of Caribbean thought. This undertaking in its advocacy for a region has a distant parallel in the mood of the Creole intelligentsia that in the eighteenth century undertook to refute the widely spread views that posited the inferiority of the lands of the Western hemisphere. The defamation of the Americas, aimed at its flora, fauna, and populations, gained momentum following the pronouncements of two influential Enlightenment figures who espoused the degeneracy thesis, the French naturalist Georges-Louis, Comte de Buffon, and the Prussia-based Dutch physiognomist Cornelius de Pauw. The latter authored a study entitled *Recherches philosophiques sur les Américains ou Mémories interessants pour servir à l'histoire de l'espéce humaine* (1768) in which he characterizes the Western hemisphere as a zone so pervasively ill-treated by nature that everything there had become monstrous or debased (Gerbi 1973:58).

The ensuing debates that involved detractors and advocates of the Americas became collectively known as "la querelle d' Amérique," and the Italian scholar Antonello Gerbi dedicated a seminal study to it. Gerbi does not mention Hispaniola's participation in the debate, his attention dominated largely by the continental colonial sites that had become important, but one of the most articulate champions of the defense of America was the

Santo Domingo presbyter Antonio Sánchez Valverde, the author of the impassioned essay *La América vindicada de la calumnia de haber sido madre del mal venéreo* (1785). Absolving the region of the charge that it had been the birthplace of venereal diseases echoed by European authors from Gonzalo Fernández de Oviedo to De Pauw, Sánchez Valverde argued that, by 1492, when Columbus first stepped on American soil "and before the return from his first voyage in 1493" bubous and syphilis "had already wrought their shameful havoc throughout Europe" (Sánchez Valverde 1988:364). Interestingly, a study of the life and works of Sánchez Valverde indicates that, at least in part, the urgency to refute European vilifications of the Americas had to do with its implication for assessing the quality of Creole intellects. Sánchez Valverde, thus, stressed the potential of the Americas to produce "intellectual work that equaled and even surpassed those anywhere in Europe" (Rossi 1994:153).

Sánchez Valverde's "defense" of the Americas did not lead automatically to a radical articulation of anything resembling what could be called a declaration of cultural intellectual or ideological independence from the European metropolis. Rather he exhibited the desire to gain acceptance and legitimation from Europe, thus displaying an outlook that the learned Creoles of his and subsequent generations typically shared. Focusing on the ideas of Colombian writer, Francisco José de Caldas (1770–1816), Alfonso Múnera has examined the revealing discursive process whereby the learned Creoles vigorously refuted the charges launched against the region by the likes of De Pauw without distancing themselves from a fundamentally "Eurocentric conception of the world in their definition of the identity of the nation" (Múnera 1998:37–38). Caldas upheld Buffon's ethnoecological conception of the inferiority of life in the warm regions, which he applied to Colombia by forging an image of the nation that privileged the geography of the "Andean center" and its inhabitants but reviled the "Caribbean coast." Subsequently, salient Colombian intellectual figures such as Miguel Samper, José Ignacio de Pombo, and even Rafael Núñez, a writer and statesman born on the coast, would echo the views of Caldas (Múnera 39, 46, 48). Múnera concludes his evocation of the "negative images imputed to the coastal areas" in the country's intellectual discourse by stressing the resilience of those formulations, which "continue to have a distressing influence on the destinies of the nation's culture" (49).

The study of the verbal aggression that the Antillean world has endured, a lingering legacy of colonial violence, becomes especially relevant in light of the state of Caribbean knowledge in the European and North American academic industry since the advent of what has come to be called "postcolonial theory." As we shall see later, such a context exerts grave pressure on the discursive practices that the Caribbean might deploy to speak about itself. To a large extent the intellectual history of the Antillean world can be traced by chronicling the rapport of the region's thinkers and writers with the various representations of their societies found in European and North American bodies of writing. According to Laënnec Hurbon, one could say something similar even about the study of the region's history: "any attempt to define the individuality of the history of the Caribbean would necessarily entail an ongoing examination of the region's relationship with the Western world—whether it was characterized by regionality and refusal, or integration and internationalization of the values and symbols of the West" (Hurbon 1999:138). Before proceeding with the chronicle, however, a clarification is in order regarding what this study will not do. This study will not subscribe to the Hegelian model that weaves a narrative of the origin and development of ideas along a quasi-evolutionary path in which great ideas beget even greater ones in succession until we reach the ultimate plane where the Absolute awaits us. This is the model dexterously employed by Arthur O. Lovejoy in his memorable *The Great Chain of Being: A Study in the History of an Idea* (1936) and, to a meaningful extent by Erich Auerbach in his thoughtful *Mimesis: The Representation of Reality in Western Literature* (1953). Conversely, this study subscribes to a notion of intellectual history that does not recognize a separate realm for ideas to evolve other than through a direct connection to circumstances and events in the arena of concrete history. Rather than a history of ideas, then, we are concerned here with an archeology of thought understood as the product of occurrences dramatized in the region from the conquest through our times. Some "of the leading ideas of the modern world especially relevant to Third World problems" to which Gordon K. Lewis assigned Caribbean paternity, namely "négritude, black power, black nationalism, Creole Marxism, Cuban socialism, and the rest" emerged in direct correspondence with the tangible force of historical events (Lewis 1983:329). Antilleanism, transnationalism of the earlier kind, marronage, creolization, Rastafarianism, also sociopolitical and cultural paradigms spawned by the historical experience of Caribbean people, emerged as a direct response to tangible realities with a discernible impact on the daily lives of the inhabitants of societies in the region. The chronology of ideas traced here is not to be found in an autonomous realm of speculation but in the temporality of the developments that shaped the lives of people materially speaking. Such a chronology would start with the conquest that initiated the colonial transaction and would continue with the successive stages of domination, resistance, insurrection, transformation, and adaptation. The social actors involved in the latter stages of the chronology would appear immersed in a sequence of processes that include anticolonial rebellion, negotiation with the regimes in power both in the local setting and in the imperial metropolis, and post-independence nation-building projects, to reach the current stage of diasporic uprooting that has expanded the geographical contours of the Antillean world. At present, as the Barbadian novelist and essayist George Lamming has so aptly noted, the Caribbean encompasses spaces far beyond the region's tellurian geography: "There is a Caribbean world that exists, in a very decisive kind of way, in many metropolitan centres, whether in North America or Europe. There is a Caribbean in Amsterdam, Paris, London, and Birmingham; in New York and other parts of North America . . . . an external frontier with a very decisive role to play in the future cultural and political development of the Caribbean" (Lamming 1996:9).

With the foregoing panorama in mind, this study sets out to explore some of the questions raised by contemporary inquiry into Caribbean cultural identity, the problematic legacy of the elite mulatto leadership, the asymmetrical exchange caused by the globalizing bent of today's capitalism, the persistence of the creed of national or regional liberation, the growing economic and political dependency of Antillean societies as a result of failed national development schemes, the devastating and unabated brain drain that affects the whole region, and the possibility of imagining a promissory future for the Caribbean in light of the mournful scenario that presently pervades it. As a corollary to that multifarious exploration, we will have occasion to reflect on the tribulations of the bodies of knowledge produced by marginal societies in view of the oppressive influence that the paradigms brandished by the Western academy exert on them irrespective of the race or ethnic origins of the thinkers through whom the West chooses to address its margins. To implement the aspirations of this inquiry we will isolate a series of texts and moments as the core of our evidence. The texts will come from creative writing as well as from expository prose dealing with the region's socioeconomic, political, or cultural processes. The moments, on the other hand, will be furnished by select instances of the lived experience of the Antillean person from the start of the colonial transaction to the present.

On Negative Ontology

Caribbean discourse begins its career by confronting the conceptual legacy that conventionally sought to exclude the human experience that the region has witnessed from the narrative of world history as conceived by the imperial scribes in the colonial period and espoused by their descendants, often including voices from the mulatto intelligentsia in the contemporary era. The words of British historian James Anthony Froude, though quoted too often, retain their illustrative value in succinctly expressing a widespread nineteenth-century European view of the region: "There has been no saint in the West Indies since Las Casas, no hero unless philonegro enthusiasm can make one out of Toussaint. There are no people there in the true sense of the word, with a character and purpose of their own" (Froude 1888:34). This outright denial of the Antillean person's potential for greatness in a sense made it incumbent upon native intellects to seek to prove the falsity of the accusation. Both C. L. R. James's powerful evocation of the human dignity of the insurgent slaves of Saint Domingue in *The Black Jacobins* (1939), which he had put out as a play first staged in London in 1936 with the venerable Paul Robeson playing the role of Toussaint, and the compelling 1960 study *Toussaint Louverture* by Aimé Césaire, seemed bent on demonstrating the caliber of Toussaint as a hero whose greatness did not depend on "philonegro enthusiasm." Césaire closes his study by stressing that, shattering the false universalism that had reduced the meaning of "the rights of man" to the European population, Toussaint came to fulfill the larger promise of the "Déclaration" in that he fought "for the transformation of formal rights into real rights, for the *recognition* of humanity, and that's why he inscribed himself, and inscribed the revolt of the black slaves of Saint Domingue, in the universal history of civilization" (1961:309–310). But beyond the figure of Toussaint and other easily recognizable extraordinary individuals, most Caribbean societies applied themselves to the task of unearthing heroes as soon as they became independent or semi-independent. Apart from the monuments erected to glorify those who accomplished great feats by struggling for independence from within the existing social system, numerous effigies also memorialize leaders who made their mark by delinking from the existing order. The system of national heroes established by Jamaica after emancipation, for instance, has foregrounded the memorable exploits of Maroon leaders Cudjoe and Nanny. Haiti's statue "Le Marron de Saint Dominigue," evoking an unknown rebel, Guyana's "1763" monument, and the structure called "Slave in Revolt" all illustrate the region's commitment to celebrating the greatness of even the least known heroes (Higman 1999c:706–707). Readers of the novel *Double Play* by the Curaçaoan fiction writer and poet Frank Martinus Arion will remember that the game of dominoes that forms the core of the plot takes place in a house located at the intersection of the Tula and Carpata Roads, two urban arteries in Willemstad named after the salient leaders of the 1795 slave insurrections (Arion 1998a:3).

The yearning to falsify the charges of those detractors who, like Froude, reduced the Antillean world to subhuman and unhistorical insignificance palpitates in *Documents of West Indian History* (1963), a collection assembled by Eric Williams, which he offered "as the intellectual cement of the edifice of Caribbean collaboration, which has no future whatsoever unless it is the work of West Indian architects, and these are blind men if their past continues to be inaccessible to them. It is the answer to those philistines who, inside and outside the West Indies, deny that the West Indies have a history" (cited in Brereton 1999:327). Williams had good reason to include philistines "from inside" among the detractors meriting refutation. As prime minister of Trinidad, he suggested to the novelist V. S. Naipaul, who had gone to Trinidad on a three-month government scholarship in September 1960, that he should write "a non-fiction book about the Caribbean. I hesitated . . . The novelist works toward conclusions of which he is often unaware . . . However; I decided to take the challenge" (Naipaul 1981:"Foreword"). What resulted was the 1962 travelogue *The Middle Passage*, a book in which Naipaul borrows the gaze of Froude, whom he quotes generously throughout, even quoting the above passage in which the British historian damns the Antillean person, as the frontispiece to his text.

Had Naipaul wished to, he could have mitigated the spell the British historian's views had on him by consulting his compatriot John Jacob Thomas, a Trinidadian scholar, contemporary of Froude, who took it upon himself to respond to his defamatory depiction of the Caribbean by challenging the validity of the judgments and the accuracy of the data contained in *The English in the West Indies, or the Bow of Ulysses*. One year after the publication of Froude's book, Thomas gave to the press the forceful and urbane polemic essay *Froudacity: West Indian Fables Explained* (1889), which successfully demonstrates the lack of scholarly rigor and the sloppy data collection that went into the vilifying volume of an English writer who at the time—as Regius Professor of Modern History at Oxford, a famous historian of Tudor England, a successful biographer, and a fine prose stylist—enjoyed considerable intellectual prestige. Aware of the status of his opponent, Thomas concentrated on exposing the factual and conceptual problems exhibited by Froude's diatribe. He shows, for instance, that, though Froude set out to expostulate on the living conditions of blacks, never once did he "visit the abode of any Negro" whether an affluent or an impoverished one (Thomas 1969:73). Thomas questions the method of data gathering, restricted to "drives about the town and neighborhood," whereby, by his own admission, Froude set out "to learn" what people in Trinidad "were doing, how there were living, and what they were thinking about" (Thomas 94).

After leaving Barbados, the English man of letters chose not to stop in St. Vincent to assess life there, judging that, in his own words as quoted by Thomas, "the time was short, and as a beautiful picture the island was best seen from the deck. The characteristics of the people are the same in all the Antilles, and could be studied elsewhere" (cited in Thomas 1969:74). With these examples of disregard for precision of observation, illustrated also in the visitor's assessment of Grenada "à vol d'oiseau," Froude is shown as an intellectual charlatan, lacking in scholarly seriousness and critical acumen. In thus dismantling Froude's stance of epistemological superiority, Thomas demonstrated the extent to which Western deprecation of the Antillean person need not even attempt to obey the demands of scholarship. Ironically, little did Thomas know that, despite his effective debunking of Froude's book, his compatriot Naipaul nearly three quarters of a century later would quote *The English in the West Indies* as an authority while omitting mention of *Froudacity*. Naipaul also relies on Anthony Trollope's gloomy picture of the possibility for advancement of the black race in the region without distancing himself ideologically from the British novelist's deprecation of the Caribbean population (Naipaul 1981:66). With this alignment with the views of Trollope and Froude, it seems not in the least surprising that he should see the Caribbean experience as reducible to futility: "The history of the islands can never be satisfactorily told. Brutality is not the only difficulty. History is built around achievement and creation; and nothing was created in the West Indies" (Naipaul 1981:29).

Ironically, the more acerbic the indictment of the Caribbean by Naipaul, the greater the admiration he garnered with European readers. A British commentator who celebrated Naipaul in 1973 stressing the "Dickensian proportions and vitality of the Trinidadian novelist's *A House for Mr. Biswas* (1961), highlighted precisely his scorn for the Caribbean (Pollard 1976:111). The critic applauded precisely that

> Biswas himself is a personification of tragicomedy, and Naipaul often seems to
> be pointing a finger at the pathetic overseriousness of so many West Indians.
> (Pollard 1976:111–112).

Written some three decades prior to Naipaul's receipt of the Nobel Prize, the tenor of the critic's appraisal raises questions about the extent to which the West might favor those Third World voices that speak ill of their people or might show a propensity to bolstering those native intellects whose apparent gifts can further confirm the greatness of the West itself. The "Dickensian" virtues of the novel by Naipaul offer an example. The tendency of Western cultural and intellectual self-celebration, the instinct to praise in the other those characteristics that favorably mirror the West, has a long history. Suffice it to mention Aphra Behn's *Oroonoko or The Royal Slave* (1688), a tale that takes place in Cormantine, on the West coast of Africa, and in the Caribbean colony of Surinam. Behn tells the story of the sorrows of a gallant African prince who must cope with the lot of ending his days as a devalued slave on an Antillean plantation. The narrator, who was in Surinam when the royal slave arrived from Africa, speaks from first-hand knowledge, having met him and admired him deeply for his intellectual brilliance and nobility of spirit. However, the narrator does not fail to find it "amazing to imagine where it was he learned so much humanity; or to give his accomplishments a juster name, where 'twas he got that real greatness of soul, those refined notions of true honor" (Behn 1992:79). But she quickly resolves the query by attributing the young man's moral and intellectual refinement to "a Frenchman of wit and learning" who had tutored him, apart from his frequent contact with "all the English gentlemen who traded thither," enabling him to learn their language as well as that of the Spaniards (80). Interestingly, Behn makes no effort to resolve the contradiction that Oroonoko should have acquired his virtues from his contact with Europeans even though the Europeans we meet in the story seem hardly worthy of admiration, displaying instead the baseness and deceit whereby the captain beguiles him into captivity (102).

At any rate, Behn operates on the presumption of a specified geography of knowledge and moral virtue that circumscribes to the Christian West those excellencies of social deportment and intellectual endowments. That such a presumption would persevere may be gathered from Victor Hugo's, *Bug-Jargal*, a novel written "in its most primitive form" in 1818, published in 1820, and then reissued in a revised version in 1826 (Frey 1999:37–38). Set in the context of the Saint Domingue slave rebellion of 1791, the plot revolves around the circumstances facing the French Captain Leopold d'Auverney and the enslaved African prince Pierrot (Bug-Jargal). They both love the same woman (Marie) and, though separated by their contrasting social conditions, display identical degrees of greatness, compassion, and selflessness. In rendering the nobility of his black protagonist in spite of the bestialization inherent to his condition as a devalued slave on the plantation, Hugo had at his disposal the "literary model of the *bon nègre* that had taken form in 18th-century Europe" (Aráujo 1998:99). The appeal of the *bon nègre* for Hugo may be associated with the thematic predilections of the Romantic period. But the mind-set that imagines an inexorably European genealogy to the young man's intelligence and goodness transcends the chronology of literary movements and periods:

> My father was the King of Kakongo. Each day he sat at the door of his hut and dispensed justice among his subjects . . . We were happy and powerful. But the Europeans came to our country; it was from them that I learned the accomplishments which you appeared to be surprised at my possessing. (Hugo 1900?:286)

Nearly a century before Behn's tale, the poem *Elegías de varones ilustres de Indias* (1589) by Juan de Castellanos provided arguably the clearest formulation of the gradation of human worth evident in the story of Oroonoko as well as of Pierrot. The longest poem written in the Spanish language, the *Elegías* matters less for its artistic achievement than for its richness as a historical document that, in addition to mapping the spread of the Spanish Empire in the sixteenth century, reveals the philosophy of history that informed the colonial regime and the view of humanity that served as justification to the plunder and the domination of the conquest (García López 1972:200). Early in the first Canto, Castellanos offers a view of the structure of the world after the flood.

> But the dark earth given
> to brute beasts and men
> was since the flood split
> into two almost equal parts:
> One never known nor seen
> except by its own natives.
> > (*Elegia* I, Canto i)

The half of the globe that lay hidden needed to be brought to the field of vision of his majesty the king of Spain since its native percipients did not really count as we gather from this passage;

> So that our world could have in hand
> a world so far and so concealed,
> and so that our Maker could be known
> whither He still remained unknown
> God lifted up a man, who would give it
> to a King who had it fully earned,
> and thus the two halves with their distant dwellers
> came to be relatives and kindreds.
> > (Castellanos 1944:6)

The thought pattern reflected in these verses allow no room for considering the opinion that the inhabitants of the lands deemed "hidden" might have about their world or about the idea that their world might be granted to a foreign monarch irrespective of whether or not he "had it fully earned." The thinking herein illustrated exemplifies the logic governing the prism of the imperial imagination, which tends to assign significance to the "Other" primarily as a source of well being for "us," or construes the world of the vanquished as merely a negative image of the positive world of the conqueror. Similarly, the imperial "we" arrogates the authority to set the terms for defining humanity. The colonial transaction that spawns the imperial imagination imposes a fixed model of humanity of irremediably Western design. Once conquered, dominated, colonized, the Other loses the option to uphold the accoutrements of their humanity other than through the mediating Westernization of their being. The conqueror controls also the portal that renders accessible the sphere of the recognizably historical. Michel-Rolph Trouillot, exposing the omission of Haitian struggles for liberation from standard accounts of the human experience, notes that the West assigns historical value to other culture areas in terms of their contact with it. In other words, the European "discovery" regulates the entrance of the Other to the realm of the human (Trouillot 1995:144). Naturally, since that entrance into the sphere of humanity is effectuated by Western anxiety over the greater or lesser ontological eligibility of the Other, it remains perpetually tentative, the West retaining the prerogative of haggling over it.

Certainly the partition of the world into two opposing laminae, the negative Other versus the positive "us," concerns a greater portion of the human population than can inhabit the Antillean world. It concerns Africa, Asia, other regions in the Americas, and any other of the culture areas that endured the onslaught of the arms, the troops, and the words of colonialism. But our focus here is the particular challenges that the Caribbean community has had to wrestle with to cope with its dehumanizing past, a past characterized by cruelty and violence rendered acceptable by the republic of letters. Among the numerous documentary riches included in the second and enlarged edition of *The Principal Navigations, Voyages, Traffiques and Discoveries of the English Nation* (1598–1600) compiled by the Elizabethan scholar, diplomat, and cleric Richard Hakluyt, the 1595 narrative "Discovery of Guiana" by the English poet and corsair Sir Walter Raleigh comes in handy in this discussion. Raleigh addresses none other than her majesty, Elizabeth I, with the intention of garnering her support for the immediate conquest and colonization of territories on the Atlantic coast of South America. At the time the English had not yet fully launched their foray into the lucrative business of "civilizing" the lands and peoples of the Americas. They had not yet moved beyond the stage of piratical plunder and exploratory survey of the promising sites of wealth. Witness the state of mind discernible in the ventures of "the Right Honorable, George, Earle of Cumberland" during his Antillean voyages in 1596. During his sack of Puerto Rico, Cumberland's attention is drawn to the island's famed rivers of gold: "This certainly is true, and I have seene the experience, that some of the gravell of one of these Rivers being brought to his Lordship because it looked rich, when triall was made, only by washing away the sand and gravell, there was cornes of very good gold found in it, and that for the quantity and proportion in great measure" (Purchas 1906:87). The East India Company, which would

embolden the English to attempt the institutionalization of overseas settlements globally, had yet to come into existence, receiving its imprimatur by
the queen only on December 31, 1600 (Wild 1999:10–11).

Raleigh, therefore, had some convincing to do, hence his resorting to
inciting Elisabeth's jealousy and envy for the greater wealth enjoyed by Spain,
England's main imperial foe, from its colonies in the Americas. He seeks to
pique her sense of rivalry by stressing the great fortune extracted from Peru
by the Spanish king, who "vexeth all the princes of Europe, and is become, in
a few years, from a poor King of Castile, the greatest monarch of this part of
the world" (Raleigh 1972:390). Raleigh then proceeds to assure the queen
that, after only two years of having conquered the territory in question,
"I doubt not but to see in London a Contractation House of more receipt for
Guiana, than there is now in Seville for the West Indies" (410). The arguments deployed by Raleigh to beseech the queen's support of his colonizing
enterprise make evident the strictly economic nature of England's encroachment into the Caribbean. Suffice it to note the total absence of moral conflict
regarding the plight of the native population upon the despoilment of their
lands. The concern for humanity and for the dignity of the individual one
might find in Raleigh's verse, as a poet who presumably embodied the spiritual
values of the English Renaissance, evidently did not extend to the women,
children, and men of the coveted land of Guiana. The Antillean person elic-
its in him not a whit of the tenderness provoked by his imagining the lifeless
form of Laura, "The Fairy Queen, at whose approach the soul of Petrarch
wept," or, following a reading of Edmund Spenser's *The Fairie Queen*, the
funeral carriage that made the heart of Homer "tremble all for grief"
(Raleigh 1891:8).

Apart from his want of regard for Antillean humanity, two other details
merit observation in Raleigh's account of Guiana: his self-presentation as
discoverer and his characterization of the natives. Throughout his narrative,
Raleigh identifies several of the people, Spaniards as well as aborigines, who
knew the location of Guiana and shared their knowledge with him to help
him find it. Yet, the fact that others have guided him does not seem to
discourage his viewing his trek into the land as "our purposed discovery"
(Raleigh 1972:388). We probably have here an instance of the cognitive
politics of the conqueror that recognizes the existence of knowledge only
when he possesses it. Only what the winner knows constitutes knowledge.
Knowledge acquires cognitive reality only when it inhabits the consciousness
of the conquering "us." In the extent to which the colonial project he
proposes to Elizabeth requires his viewing the Indians and the Spaniards in
Guiana as expendable, the English poet and corsair, in keeping with the logic
of the imperial imagination, can dismiss their prior knowledge and ascribe to
himself the "discovery" of the land in question. As to his characterization of
the aborigines, he undertakes to knock off their quantum of human caliber
by highlighting their insufficient family attachments and their cannibalism.
The Spanish traders, he claims, "buy women and children from the cannibals,
which are of that barbarous nature, as they will for three or four hatchets sell

the sons and daughters of their own brethren and sisters, and for somewhat more, even their own daughters" (Raleigh 1972:390). This lack of loyalty for kin that Raleigh imputes to the natives adds to the conceptual menu that the denormalizing discourse of the colonial project would draw from. It contributes to diagnosing their moral alterity: their selling their relatives evinces their barbarity. By 1860, when Trollope's Caribbean voyage yielded his notorious travelogue *The West Indies and the Spanish Main*, the appeal to familial ties to posit the inferiority of the Other, in this case Jamaican blacks, still remained ideologically useful:

> They love their offspring, but in their rage will use then fearfully. They are proud of them when they are praised, but will sell their daughter's virtue for a dollar . . . I do not deny their family attachments; but it is the attachment of a dog. We have all had dogs whom we have well used, and have prided ourselves on their fidelity. (Trollope 1999:59–60)

The reference to cannibalistic practices has already been identified as a constant in the discourse of colonization. Irrespective of its existence at one point or another in the rituals of this or that aboriginal society of Africa or the Americas, cannibalism had already emerged as a Western obsession prior to 1492. Peter Hulme inquires into the European desire to find confirmation of anthropophagy in the conquered lands and proposes that perhaps in such a practice they thought they could identify the trait "that characterized those parts of the world into which the torch of civilization had not yet shown" (Hulme 1998:7). The association with cannibalism placed the so-called savage in a plane external to the human family in the eyes of the West while giving European nations a handy moral pretext to unleash the carnage and the depravity of the colonial transaction. As the metaphysical poet John Donne would affirm with conviction and crisp clarity in his Easter Day 1627 sermon, what could otherwise be deemed reprehensible as cruelty and theft becomes wholly justified when applied to our moral, religious, and civilizational Others. He said, "The infidel hath no pretence upon the next world, none at all; Nor so clear a title to anything in this world," epitomizing the argument that authorizes Christians "to despoil [the infidel] even of their possession" by means of this formula: "All things are God's, God hath put all things under Christ's feet. And he under ours, as we are Christians" (Donne 1990:378). The background of physical and discursive violence herein described created the conceptual conditions that regulated the entry of the Antillean world into the Western imaginary. Thus, the West enveloped the region in a denormalizing veneer, placing it on an ahistorical zone where the human identity of the population was subject to unending verification. Similarly, the Antillean cosmos, by virtue of its oddity, offered the Western person a site of darkness, mystery, and frenzy ideally suited as an arena for loosening the passions or searching into the most guarded recesses of the soul.

During the Spring of 2001 the U.S. television network FOX found in Belize the appropriate setting for a new "reality show" entitled *Temptation*

Island, whose plot consisted primarily in testing the capacity of participants to contain carnal desire. The cast featured various couples who maintained stable relationships, and once in the sensuality of the tropical landscape, the men and the women were separated for the duration of their stay on the "island." In their perspective isolated spots both would then be subjected to intense efforts of seduction involving stunningly attractive male and female counterparts. The suggestive forestry, beaches, music, and social isolation offered by the setting presumably intensified the enticement to which the participants were exposed. A country located on the Caribbean coast of Central America, Belize is not an island, but its selection as the location of *Temptation Island* would seem to highlight its Caribbeanness since for many viewers the Antillean would no doubt be synonymous with "the islands" despite the existence of several Caribbean nations that are on the continental coast. But most important, there was nothing in the opening episode of the "reality show" that would give viewers an inkling of Belize as a contemporary society inhabited by regular people wrestling with the challenges posed to them by modern life. The home place of Zee Edgell, the author of the novels *Beka Lamb* (1982), *In Times Like These* (1991), and *The Festival of San Joaquin* (1997), Belize is a modern Caribbean society with a sizable body of literature written in English, Creole, and Spanish, a vibrant culture hewn from the mixture of heritages of the colonial past. Since the latter half of the twentieth century, the country has dealt with the consequences of enormous chances, including a process of independence from Britain that was finalized in 1981, "the sugar boom, demographic shifts, the introduction of satellite television, the growth of tourism, and the emergence of gang violence, to name only a few," as summarized by Michael D. Phillips, the editor of a collection of short fiction by Belizean authors (Phillips 1995:9). But this historical, modern, social character of contemporary Belize remains unimaginable for the viewer whose contact with that country starts with the evocation effectuated in the inaugural episode of *Temptation Island*.

Whether knowingly or not, the choice of the producers of the FOX "reality show" resonated with a long tradition of Caribbean evocations in the West, both in popular culture and in the words of the learned. As the examples abound, the novella *Betrothal in Santo Domingo* by the German Romantic playwright and fiction writer Henrich von Kleist could illustrate the issue as adequately as any other text. Set in Saint Domingue around 1803 toward the final stages of the slave insurrection that would lead to Haitian independence in 1804, the story dramatizes the tragic love of the Swiss young man Gustav von der Ried and a local girl named Toni, a 15-year-old mestiza described as having "high yellow complexion" (Kleist 1985:137). The historical scenario and the severity of racial codes that frame the story provide the main source of its dramatic tension. The troops of black rebel leader Jean Jacques Dessalines have laid siege to the city of Port-au-Prince. Congo Hoango, an "ungrateful" servant born in the Gold Coast of Africa, belonged to the benevolent master Monsieur Guillaume de Villanueve when the insurrection started. The master had, as a gift, given him the elderly mulatto woman Bakekan, the biological mother of Toni. When the uprising starts, Hoango murders his kind master, keeping all his property and turning the house into a trap to capture whites. The whites arrive in the house unaware that danger awaits them. Bakekan's feigned cordiality and Toni's beauty put them at ease, rendering them easy victims for the murderous Hoango.

When Gustav enters the ill-fated lodge, Bakekan offers him her proverbial hospitality, urging him to "fear nothing; a mulatto lives here, and the only other person is my daughter, a mestiza" (138). Lured by his hostess, Gustav lowers his guard. Their conversation reveals that he is Swiss, not French, and that he repudiates the cruelties committed by slave masters, whom he blames for the hatred of the insurgent blacks against whites (144). Once he lays eyes upon Toni, Gustav is stunned by her beauty, "except for the color of her skin" which at first he finds "repellent," and he ends up proposing marriage to her (149). Engaged to Gustav behind her mother's back and having violated the prohibition against any carnal intimacy with any of the white guests, Toni begins to plead for making an exception with Gustav and sparing his life (150–151). When her strange request earns her a reprimand, the young fiancée sets out to save her beloved as well as other relatives of his who remain hidden in a nearby location. Bakekan discovers Toni's plan and alerts Hoango, knowing full well he will put her to death. Her plan nearly thwarted by the sudden arrival of Hoango and his troops, the young woman ventures on the spot a risky ploy which, to her own surprise, proves successful, culminating in the rescue of Gustav's family and the arrest of Hoango's men. Unfortunately, confused by the swiftness of the events that transpired, Gustav misunderstands what has happened and believes that his fiancée has betrayed him. Blinded by the ensuing indignation, he shoots Toni to death. When, through the testimony of his relatives, Gustav realizes that Toni risked everything for him and his family, he kills himself.

Betrothal in Santo Domingo pits racial identity against family loyalty. First, Bakekan knowingly exposes her daughter to death by revealing her plan to the ruthless Hoango, maternal protectiveness of the fruit of her womb not even causing her to hesitate. Similarly, the young Toni opens an all out war against her mother for the sake of a stranger who chances into their house. When confronted by her mother with her betrayal, Toni articulates the racial logic of her justification: "I have not betrayed you; I am white and engaged to marry the young man you hold captive; I belong to those on whom you openly wage war and will know how to answer to God for taking their side" (162). The words that Kleist puts on Toni's lips tell much about the German intelligentsia's ideas about the insurmountability of race as a barrier separating the branches of the human family. But, equally important, they tell much about the insuperable alterity of the Antillean world as a site where "normal" human values, such as family attachments and loyalty to one's kin, fail to obtain. Curiously, the 1837 tale called "Mulatto," written in French by Victor Séjour, an African-descended native of Louisiana, also uses the setting of colonial Saint Domingue to dramatize with reverse outcomes the tension between racial and familial loyalties. The mulatto Georges suffers unspeakable indignity at the hands of his master Alfred. Reaching the tipping point, he resorts to killing the master, but when Alfred's dying breath brings out the crushing revelation that he is Georges's father, the young mulatto cannot live with the thought of having committed parricide and ends up shooting himself (Séjour 1997:299). Evidently, Séjour, who as a native of Louisiana had cultural ties to Saint Domingue, differed from Kleist in the way of representing familial ties in the Antillean world. For in his tale, the main character's sense of the sanctity of familial bonds immediately nullifies in his mind the justice of his action against a man who subjected him to the cruelest brutality and humiliation. By opting for suicide, Georges seems to construe his vengeful killing as wrong, possibly to the chagrin of readers who vicariously may experience a sense of vindication at Alfred's righteous undoing.

Kleist's foray into the Antillean world, among other things, matters because it influenced the work of twentieth-century German writer Anna Seghers, who in turn influenced the German playwright Heiner Müller. Seghers wrote the novella *Die Hochzeit von Haiti* (Marriage in Haiti 1949), a story about the misadventures of members of a Jewish family who decide to expand their jewelry business to Saint Domingue upon the advice of their protector Count Evremont, who owns the largest plantation on the island. The slave rebellion erupts and they leave the colony, except for one son named Michael Nathan, who joins the revolutionary struggle, serves as Toussaint Louverture's secretary, and marries a local black woman. Seeking to stay clear of the kind of representation of the Caribbean found in the text by Kleist, an evocation that she found too much marked by the author's own fantasies and his leaning toward the exotic, Seghers approached the Saint Domingue characters as historical agents, especially Toussaint, in whom she found the embodiment of the individual who can rise from the lowest social stratum to become a force of social transformation (Bangerter 1980:102).

Seghers approached the Antillean world devoid of racial othering instincts and with a keen interest in the historical dynamics dramatized by the various actors in the region. The conflict between the *grand blancs*—in difficult alliance with the *petit blancs*—and the enslaved blacks, provided Seghers with an ideal stage for depicting the class conflicts that for centuries have divided humanity in all of its multicolor diversity. Thus, in Nathan's hesitation at key moments, Seghers wished to represent the moral and political weakness of the middle class, just as, in connecting the failure of the anticolonialist struggle to Toussaint's failure of leadership, she ventured to posit the pitfalls of the individualist vision that caused him to become the center of the movement instead of organizing the revolution around the collectivity of the proletariat, as a scholar on her work has usefully summarized (Bangerter 106–107). A similar reading seems to apply to Segher's *Wiederienfhrung der Sklaverei in Guadeloupe* (The Return of Slavery in Guadeloupe, 1949), another novella set in the Antillean world in which the black population's insufficient commitment to the maintenance of their freedom appears to account for their recoil to their former captivity (Bangerter 108).

Das Licht auf dem Galgem (The Light from the Scaffold, 1959), written by
Seghers nearly a decade after her two other Caribbean stories, deals with the
incidents around a revolutionary mission sent from Paris by the Directorate
to the English colony of Jamaica with the purpose of instigating a slave rebellion. The revolutionary enterprise flounders here also as a result of the conflicting attitudes of the emissaries concerning the nature of their mission. The
noble Debuisson, whose allegiance is primarily to the government that
appointed him, loses all political will when word reaches the island that, as of
18 Brumaire of the year VIII (November 9, 1799), the Directorate that ruled
the metropolis has ceased to exist. Conversely, his comrade Jean Sasportas, a
Sefardic Jew militantly aligned with the Jacobins, refuses to bend to the new
order put in place by the Bonaparte dictatorship. Committed to the cause of
emancipation, he continues his fight to the death. As he valiantly approaches
the gallows, he makes a final appeal to the enslaved blacks who have come to
watch his execution, and he urges them to rise following the example of their
Haitian brethren. Galloudec, the third of the emissaries from the French
revolutionary government, momentarily manages to escape in a boat to
Santiago de Cuba. During his oppressive getaway voyage a light coming from
the scaffold where Sasportas is meeting his death moves him to pity, explaining the title of the novella. While the Caribbean writings of Seghers do not
offend the Antillean person by dehistoricizing the region and denormalizing
its people, she seems merely to borrow their world for what it can offer as a
pliable space suitable for her own European explorations. We are told that she
wrote *Das Licht auf dem Galgem* as a response to the 1956 Hungarian
revolution (Fehervary 2001:41). To a large extent the Guadeloupean and
Haitian settings in the two novellas published in 1949 serve as mere vehicles
for exploring her views on the consequences of insufficient class consciousness in the oppressed masses in the former and the relationship between the
individual and the collective in the latter. In other words, although she did
spend some time in the region as part of her prolonged exile from Nazi
Germany, the Caribbean offered primarily a theater wherein to stage the
drama of characters enacting the laws of history envisioned by Marxism.

Seghers's story about Jamaica became the basis for the plot of the 1979
play *Der Auftrag*, a text by German dramatist Heiner Müller that appeared
in English the following year under the title *The Task* (1980). The play
returns to the trio of Debuisson, Sasportas, and Galloudec, emissaries of the
French revolutionary government who have come to the English colony of
Jamaica charged with "the task" of stirring "a rebellion of the slaves against
the rule of the British Crown in the name of the Republic of France," that
country being "the motherland of the Revolution, the terror of the thrones,
the hope of the poor" (Müller 1984:87). Perhaps not surprisingly, in its representation of the Caribbean, Müller's play, despite its artistic kinship with
advanced forms of postmodern dramaturgy, comes closer to Kleist's than to
Seghers's. While Seghers conceives of the Antillean setting as a proscenium of
history capable of illustrating the contradictions and conflicts characteristic of
human affairs, Müller seems to regard it purely as mise-en-scène. In his play,

Sasportas is black, hence his resolute solidarity with the enslaved population. At one point, the names of Debuisson and Sasportas become interchangeable with those of Danton and Robespierre. The play ultimately investigates the psychopathology of political options and the futility of social change through revolutionary action in the European history that the playwright knows and recognizes. The Antillean world serves as an incidental location, but the historical reality therein scrutinized is predicated on the moral and political imperatives of the West.

While Müller in the late twentieth century could take a Caribbean setting to omit consideration of the Caribbean experience, it might seem curious that Herman Melville in his 1855 novella *Benito Cereno* should have conversely Caribbeanized a story that made no reference to the Antillean world in the source that offered him the plot. Melville found his material in a chapter entitled "Capture of the Spanish Ship *Tryal* at Santa Maria Island, Chile" in the 1817 publication of Captain Amasa Delano's *Narrative of Voyages and Travels in the Northern and Southern Hemispheres.* Delano's chapter chronicles his encounter in February 1805 with a Spanish slave ship commanded by a captain named "Don Bonito Cereno," whose strange demeanor surprised the American. Delano was especially shocked by the familiarity with which enslaved blacks on the deck interacted with the captain and the white sailors. When he boarded the ship, Delano's displeasure was provoked by the insolence of a Negro "who kept constantly at the elbows of Don Bonito and myself," and he explained that although he was disturbed by "this extraordinary liberty, I did not remonstrate against it until it became troublesome to myself" (Delano 1994:49). The American captain eventually learns that all along the Tryal has been in control of the blacks, who successfully rebelled and have forced captain Cereno to fake continued authority. In the end the rebellious slaves are captured and severely punished, many meeting their death, and Delano and his first officer are asked to testify in the case again the blacks before the Spanish colonial authorities in Chile.

Melville sets his story in 1799, a change of date that places the events more centrally in the "age of Revolution," which according to Eric Sundquist, meant to evoke the violent struggle leading up to the Haitian Revolution that caused Jefferson to prophesy woe (Sundquist 1998:831). Melville's narrator stresses the role of Babo, "the black—whose brain, not body, had schemed and led the revolt," who, when captured, refused to speak, meeting in silent dignity his death: "The body was burned to ashes; but for many days, the head, that hive of subtlety, fixed on a pole in the Plaza, met, unabashed, the gaze of the whites" (Melville 1942:105). By stressing the mental ability of the slave, Melville, whether intentionally or not, produced a characterization with the potential of heightening his readers' fears of the potential for successful slave insurrection in mid-nineteenth-century United States, especially in slaveholding Southern states. Captain Cereno's ship in Melville's story is not "The Tryal," as in the original narrative by Delano, but the "San Dominick," which resonated with the name of Saint Domingue, the colony that witnessed the insurrection that had taken the greatest hold of the

American imaginary. When the Saint Domingue captives revolted, the founding fathers of the United States had reason to grieve. President Washington, a plantation owner himself, shortly after commanding a successful revolution against the English, found it "lamentable to see such a spirit of revolution among the blacks" on the island, and Jefferson spoke of the "pity and charity" caused by seeing the plantation owners leaving the Caribbean island: "Never was so deep a tragedy presented to the feelings of man" (cited in Wills 2003:36–37). As Wills poignantly glosses, the "greatest tragedy" in question "was not the plight of slaves but of their owners when dispossessed of them" (Wills 37). The Saint Domingue uprising led to the proclamation of the Republic of Haiti in 1804, but it would take until 1862, with President Lincoln no longer beholden to the Southern states, for the U.S. government to feel it could recognize the Haitian republic as an independent nation. Before then, Haiti was the object of scorn in the United States, and it seems clear that the reason for the animosity was the fear of the Haitian example and the influence it could have on the slaves on U.S. plantations. Writing to Rufus King in 1802, Jefferson lamented, "that the course of things in the neighboring islands of the West Indies appeared to have given a considerable impulse to the minds of slaves in the United States: 'a great disposition to insurgency has manifested itself among them' " (Wills 43).

The Saint Domingue upheaval fueled the fears of Southern plantation society first through the numerous refugee planters who came to the United States when they fled the island, bringing with them shocking tales of terror, which "were reawakened with each newly discovered conspiracy or revolt: Gabriel Prossner, Denmark Vesey, and Nat Turner" (Sandquist 1998:831). The readers of the December 1855 issue of *Putnam's Monthly Magazine* where *Benito Cereno* appeared had reasons galore to catch the allusions and references that connected the story to Haiti. *Uncle Tom's Cabin* (1852), the famed abolitionist novel by Harriet Beecher Stowe, makes reference to Haiti as two characters debate the advantage or disadvantage of treating slaves appropriately in light of the kind of retaliation witnessed in the Hispaniola uprising (Stowe 2001:380–381). By the same token, as the 1850s had seen several rebellions among the U.S. slave population, Melville's readers were particularly sensitive to representations of the Saint Domingue events. A scholar writing on *Benito Cereno* has noted that in having Christopher Columbus appear as the figurehead of the "San Dominick," Melville further insisted on drawing attention to the Saint Domingue connection of the plot since the colony was on the island of Hispaniola, the place where the Admiral started the colonial transaction in 1492 (Richardson 1987:72). That one of the December 1855 issues of *Putnam's Monthly* that serially carried *Benito Cereno* also published an article entitled "About Niggers," in which the author blatantly parodied the Santo Domingo uprising to mock the white masters' reaction to the revolt, suggests that Melville's novella was dealing with a topic that commanded attention (Richardson 217). The period also witnessed the publication of several appraisals that presented the rise of Haiti in a good light such as a life of Toussaint by John R. Beard (1853) and an account by William Wells Brown that came to counterbalance the representation of the black Antillean republic that typically came out of influential organs of Southern interests such as *De Bow's Review*, which portrayed black self-government as an event that arrested the "march of civilization" on the island (Sandquist 1998:835–836).

HAITI IN THE ANTILLEAN WORLD

Western discourse has generally viewed the Caribbean through Haiti and has often invoked Haitian experiences generically to represent the whole region. The metonymy that fuses the Antillean cosmos into Haiti has had its costs given the resentment that Haiti's revolutionary saga incited in the West. Said plainly, the West did not forgive the slave insurgents of Saint Domingue the audacity to dismantle the plantation regime, then the kernel of economic life in Europe and the United States. Their triumph over Napoleon's army, a formidable military force trained by a country that shined at the center of European civilization, also humiliated Western martial prowess. As the society that the formerly enslaved blacks erected did not instantly plummet, its continued existence posed a constant source of stress for a Western world system that needed to regard blacks and Amerindians as mere fuel to ignite its own advancement. To a large extent, the tenacious rise of a nation built by insurgent slaves contradicted and debunked the very logic upon which the international hegemony of the Christian West was predicated. The admiration expressed by the likes of William Wordsworth and Alphonse Lamartine for Toussaint Louverture as an exceptional individual not withstanding, the emergence of the Haitian republic elicited mostly hostility from Western discourse, amounting to a "sustained and deliberate campaign to isolate, destabilize, generally discredit and economically punish the Black Republic" (Márquez 2000:15–16). Roberto Márquez points to the book *Haiti's Bad Press* by Robert Lawless as a useful examination of the unrelenting crusade of inimical propaganda that the Caribbean country has endured.

The body of utterances voiced by the West in the misrepresentation of Haiti and thereby the Caribbean found an echo even in figures who by virtue of their non-European ancestry could be expected to speak well of the Antillean world and its people. One might recall, for instance, the distinguished African American orator, abolitionist, and autobiographer, Frederick Douglass. Though he lived in the flesh the debasement of slavery and struggled daringly to dismantle the "peculiar institution," once free, he did not renege his affiliation as a cultural offspring of European and, more specifically, English civilization. "In Spite of our national [American] independence, a common language, a common literature, a common history, and a common civilization makes us and keeps us still a part of the British nation, if not a part of the British Empire," said Douglass on August 1, 1880, during a speech in a ceremony of commemoration of the emancipation of blacks in the West Indies (Douglass 1962:498). Regarding Americanness as existing within the sphere of Englishness even as it related to blacks, Douglass described England as "still the mother country, and the mother, too, of our abolition movement" (Douglass 498). When celebrating the emancipation of West Indian slaves, rather than the proverbial courage of the captive population that had persistently averred its desire for freedom from the very start of their domination in the region, Douglass chose to extol primarily the magnanimity of "the friends of freedom in England who saw in the Negro a man, a moral and responsible being" (497). He thus emphasized what he regarded as the most cherishable aspect of West Indian emancipation, namely that it came about

> not by the sword, but by the word—not by the brute force of numbers, but by the still voice of truth—not by barricades, bayonets, and bloody revolution, but by peaceful agitation—not by divine interference, but by the exercise of simple, human reason and feeling. (496)

He had in mind, then, the glory of the likes of William Wilberforce, Granville Sharp, Thomas Clarkson, and Lord Henry Brougham, who strived in the arenas of lecture halls and corridors of Parliament, rather than the likes of Cudjoe, Nanny, and Sam Sharpe, who tussled on the ground in the violence of Caribbean plantations.

Douglass's faith in the superior civilization of the Western powers and his perhaps lesser faith in that the Antillean world could spawn viable nations on its own probably lay at the core of his active support of U.S. territorial expansion in the region. Despite his friendship with Senator Charles Sumner who applied himself vigorously to the task of thwarting the scheme by President Ulysses S. Grant to annex the Dominican Republic to the United States, Douglass explained toward the end of his life a discrepancy that distanced him from the revered abolitionist:

> To Mr. Sumner, annexation was a measure to extinguish a colored nation, and to do so by dishonorable means and for selfish motives. To me it meant the alliance of a weak and defenseless people, having none or few of the attributes of a nation, torn and rent by internal feuds and unable to maintain order at home or command respect abroad, to a government which would give it peace, stability, prosperity, and civilization, and make it helpful to both countries. (408)

The debate in Congress over the annexation of the Dominican territory concluded in 1871, after a report by a Senate Commission of Inquiry sent by Grant to the country to assess its readiness to become an integral part of the Union failed to sway the opposition. Douglass had traveled to the country as a recording secretary to Senators Wade, Howe, and White, who led the Commission. Almost two decades later, President Harrison having appointed him minister resident and consul general to the Republic of Haiti in 1889, he devoted himself staunchly to persuading Haiti to cede the Môle St. Nicholas to the United States for use as a naval station. He contended that "the concession asked for was in the line of good neighborhood and advanced civilization, and in every way consistent with the autonomy of Haiti," further stressing the value of the concession as a "source of strength rather than of weakness to the Haitian government—that national isolation was a policy of the past—and that instead of asking in alarm what will happen if a naval station be conceded to the United States, it should ask 'What will happen if such a naval station is not conceded?' " (606–607).

To his chagrin, Douglass did not prevail upon Haitian authorities to relinquish the Môle St. Nicholas to the United States, but he remained convinced until the end that the transaction would have made Haitian society a more viable member of the community of nations. The civilizing function that the United States could presumably serve in the Antillean world had already been posited, though in a more nuanced fashion, by at least two African Americans whose views on the region preceded those of Douglass: the Reverend James Theodore Holly and black emigration advocate J. Dennis Harris. An avowed proponent of black separatism who favored emigration by free blacks to an area where they could exercise their political potential outside the sphere of negrophobic white rule, Holly looked to Haiti as a land that promised a fertile ground for the realization of such a dream. In the pamphlet *A Vindication of the Capacity of the Negro Race for Self Government and Civilized Progress as Demonstrated by Historical Events of the Haytians and Subsequent Acts of that People Since their National Independence* (1857), Holly used Haiti as proof of the courage, might, and statesmanship of blacks in at least equal proportion to those of the best among whites. Holly presented the revolution in Haiti as "one of the noblest, grandest, and most justifiable outbursts against tyrannical oppression" ever "recorded on the pages of the world's history," and he traced the country's political development through its present ruler, Faustin I, to marvel at the astonishing achievement of the Haitian people (Holly 1970: 23, 55). He closed his oration with a plea to his African American compatriots

> to go and identify our destiny with our heroic brethren in that independent isle of the Caribbean Sea, carrying with us such of the arts, sciences and genius of modern civilization, as we may gain from this hardy and enterprising Anglo-American race, in order to add to Haitian advancement. (65)

Holly dreamed of "one powerful and civilized Negro sovereignty . . . developed to the summit of national grandeur in the West Indies, where the keys to the commerce of both hemispheres can be held" (66). Reverent Holly left the United States for Haiti in 1861, becoming consecrated as Episcopal Bishop of Haiti in 1874 and remaining loyal to his Christian mission in his adopted country until the end of his life (Bell 1970:11).

Holly's counterpart, J. Dennis Harris, shared with him a belief in the efficacy of a settlement of free African Americans in the Caribbean area although he seems to have lacked the reverend's lofty ideals. Nor did he regard blacks in the Antillean world with as much admiration as did Holly. In his 1861 travelogue *A Summer on the Borders of the Caribbean Sea*, Harris dwells at length on the acts of cruelty and violence perpetrated by Saint Domingue's insurgent slaves, whom he describes as "troops of Barbarians" while omitting a similar emphasis or comparable epithets when citing the violence committed by the French planters (Harris 1970:130–131). Harris assessed the human experience on the island of Hispaniola holistically by saying: "The history of San Domingo was never completely written, and if it were, would never find a reader" (85). He derided Dominican soldiers by exposing the inadequacy of their military attire: "looking for all the world like a parcel of ragamuffin boys, playing militia" (80). The "ridiculous scene" before his eyes leads to his dismissive view of Dominican authorities: "Dominicana has a government—so poets have empires," and he reports about the overall national atmosphere that the observer will encounter a disappointing scenario: "the non-progressive appearance of everything around him" (80). Interestingly, the folly of Dominicans becomes for Harris the reason for Americans to become involved with them. He decried, for instance, the ignorance of Americans about the Dominican Republic and wondered: "why the country should lie so long a comparative *terra incognita*, producing generations of indolent men and women, excelling only in superstition, idleness, and profound stupidity" (82). Out of his indictment of the character of Dominicans, Harris hews out an incentive for American industry and talent to relocate to the Dominican Republic, a country "ripening for immigration" and offering "by far the most extensive and desirable territory" (Harris 103).

A paradox seems to insinuate itself here. Though differing radically in their degree of respect for the Antillean person, Holly and Harris coincide in their seeing the Caribbean region as a suitable destination for free American blacks who had their access to full citizenship and individual self-realization obstructed by institutionalized racism in the United States. Similarly, though inheriting a legacy of social inferiorization as a result of their history of black oppression in North America, they both shared with Douglass a belief in the superior civilization of whites. As the pupils of a white supremacist Western society, they regarded themselves as beneficiaries of the teachings of the "hardy and enterprising Anglo-American race," which constituted a civilizational asset that they were in a position to bring to the Caribbean. They thus aligned themselves with the Western logic that has tended to dispute the human caliber of the Antillean population and subscribed to the credo that the genius and energy of North Americans—even black ones—could rescue the region from imbecility. Douglass, Holly, and Harris, their enigmatic solidarity with the region notwithstanding, were not devoid of the Western lens that construes Caribbean life as external to civilization and history and marginal to the story of humanity. This peculiar manner of imagining the Antillean world, in addition to facilitating the economic exploitation of the region and its inhabitants through the colonial project to the benefit and prosperity of the conquering nations, has also afforded the Western mind a sort of existential and spiritual laboratory wherein to scrutinize and dissect itself.

One could speculate that the Caribbean as the image of a world of alterity was available to European intellects from as far back as the 1719 publication of *Robinson Crusoe* by Daniel Defoe. Though the real-life adventures of Alexander Selkirk from which he drew the scheme of the castaway hero happened in the Mas a Tierra Island, a part of the Juan Fernández Archipelago near Chile's Pacific Coast, Defoe's descriptions endeavor to evoke the Caribbean archipelago, a stage suitable for the main character to test his mettle as a self-reliant man wrestling with questions of religious faith and the moral quandaries of an emerging English middle class. Similarly, Eugene O'Neill's *Emperor Jones* (1920), over two centuries after Defoe, finds in the Caribbean an equally appealing site for exploring the dark recesses of an individual's soul. The play presents us with Brutus Jones, a black American Pullman porter who breaks jail in the United States where he serves a sentence for two counts of murder. His escape takes him to a West Indian island where he soon holds sway over the benighted natives. Confident of his superiority over the "ign'rent bush niggers" who populate the island, he has little qualm about abusing his power and stealing copiously, convinced that, as he boastfully explains to the Cockney trader Henry Smithers: "For de little stealin' dey gits you in jail soon or late. For de big stealin' dey makes you Emperor and puts you in the Hall o' Fame when you croaks," a lesson that he owes to the "white quality talk" to which he listened during ten years of oral apprenticeship on the Pullman cars (O'Neill 1979:77). The natives eventually rise against him, under the leadership of a rebel named Lem, whom the playwright's stage directions describe as a "heavy-set, ape-faced old savage of the extreme African type" (95).

The natives in *Emperor Jones* appear merely as shadows, psychological props that contribute to effectuating the drama of internal turbulence that ultimately causes the emperor's downfall. Hailed as the "first black tragic hero" on the American stage, Brutus Jones suffers defeat in the fight against himself (Brooks, Lewis, and Penn Warren 1973:2006). Appropriately, then, the manner of utterance that pervades the entire play is the monologue. The ghosts of his pursuers that chase Brutus unremittingly through the dense and dark forest of his troubled mind in the end prove overly taxing to his agonized imagination, causing him to run toward rather than away from the avenging gunfire of his material foes. O'Neill counted heavily on the importance of the geographical setting that he chose to enact the scrutiny of the main character's mental travel. Delving into the recesses of the soul or exploring "the problem of the human heart in conflict with itself," to borrow Faulkner's formulation, involves some scenic requirements (Faulkner 1965: 119). Artistic projects so committed to studying the human psyche often find it most convenient to construe scenarios devoid of the pressures of history, class society, and other equally inexpugnable exterior structures. They tend to show a predilection for sites construed as existing outside the ordinary compulsions of civilization. Thus, the Caribbean where Jones arrives lacks any semblance of social order, polity, or organized religion. A locus of unknowing deflated of any sign of remembrance of things past, the island exists as an ahistorical, timeless, potentially dreadful site awaiting possession and historical ignition by external human agency and intelligence. The social marginality that has marked Brutus, as a working-class member of a despised race in segregated America, seems to weigh less in his potential to reach the pinnacle of power on the island than the relative superiority that his Western socialization as an American has conferred upon him. When *Emperor Jones* reached the theater in 1920, the United States had taken it upon itself to launch several civilizational military missions to the Caribbean. Among a series of incursions, the U.S. marines had occupied Haiti in 1915 and the Dominican Republic in 1916, placing the whole island of Hispaniola under direct U.S. rule, until the soldiers left the Dominican side in 1924 and the Haitian side in 1934. Though O'Neill leaves his "island in the West Indies" unnamed, he inserts several clues to induce us to identify it. Among them, the reverberating ritual drum sounds and the references to the "heathen" religious worship of the natives invite an association with Haitian vodou. Also, the emperor's design to use a silver bullet to kill himself before getting caught by his pursuers recalls the historical figure of Henry Christophe, one of the champions of the Haitian revolution who not only gave himself a royal title, like the Emperor Jones, but chose precisely the same form of death.

O'Neill's play cleanses the Antillean world of historical experience and of local humanity, producing the tabula rasa required for the study of the character's psyche. By calling the place "an island in the West Indies" while imbuing it with Haitian insinuations, the playwright renders literal the metonymical fusion of Haiti and the Caribbean that recurs in Western figurations of the region and its people. Since the Caribbean, through Haiti, has received the weight of the defamatory eloquence of Western discourse, as expressed in the imputation of a negative ontology to the Antillean world that the foregoing discussion has outlined, many of the most prominent documents of Caribbean intellectual history have sought to extol the humanity and the history of the region precisely through the evocation of the Haitian experience. Through a sort of reactive identity postulation, Caribbean intellects have seized on Haiti as the arena par excellence for the region to speak about itself. Haiti occupies center stage in Cuban poet Nicolás Guillén's lyrical formulation of Antillean identity in the collection *West Indies Ltd.* (1934). The title poem speaks holistically about the region omitting mention of nations, except for two lines that specify three sites, beginning with a Haitian one:

> Aquí está lo mejor de Port-au-Prince,
> Lo más puro de Kingston, la high life de la Habana.
> [Here is the best of Port-au-Prince, the purest of
> Kingston, Havana's high life.] (Guillén 1980:147)

The Puerto Rican poet Luis Palés Matos foregrounded Haiti in the groundbreaking volume *Tuntún de pasa y grifería* (1937), which meant to formulate in verse a distinctly Afro-Caribbean cosmology. A key poem in the collection, "Canción festiva para ser llorada" (Festive Song to Be Wept), names many

Antillean countries in its regional evocation, but its refrain highlights three:

> Cuba—ñáñigo y bachata—
> Haití—vodú y calabaza,
> Puerto Rico—burundanga—
> [Cuba—náñigos and good time—
> Haiti—vodou and gourds—
> Puerto Rico—a hodge podge],

In the poem, Haiti absorbs the longest stanza, which, in the English rendition by Julio Marzán, reads as follows:

> Macandal beats his drum
> in Haiti's scary night.
> Glowing marble teeth
> grin in the dark.
> Eerie beastly forms
> creep in the treetops,
> and primal, intricate Haiti
> simmers like a threat.
> It's vodou. The power hour
> of zombies and frogs.
> Over the cane fields
> spirits are at work.
> Ogún Badagrí in shadow
> Hones his black knife . . .
> —Tomorrow good ole Massa
> wears the best of ties—
> Dessalines cries out: *Sang*!
> L'Ouverture roars: *Venganze*!
> while somewhere lurking
> in kinky thicket,
> Macandal beats his drum
> in Haiti's fierce night
> (Palés Matos 2000:29–31)

Two of the best known classic Dominican epic poems, *Yelidá* (1942) by Tomás Hernández Franco and *Compadre Mon* (1943) by Manuel del Cabral, both written under the policing eye of a regime that promoted anti-Haitianism as part of the official creed of national identity, need to have recourse to Haiti to articulate foundational episodes of Dominicanness. Hernández Franco's poem stages a theogony involving two distinct pantheons, Nordic gods on one end and Haitian vodou divinities on the other—reenacted carnally in the mating of the Northern European visitor with a Haitian woman to beget the Dominican mulata Yelidá—perhaps suggesting Haitianness as one of the key elements in the construction of Dominican national subjectivity. The Cabral poem, significantly less ambiguous in its symbolism, describes the Dominican speaker's intervention on behalf of a woman who is being tortured in the course of a vodou ceremony (Cabral

1987:147–148). Though neither poet can overtly extol the Haitian experience given the political circumstances under which each wrote, both concurred in stressing the interdependence of their national identity and that of their neighbors on the island of Hispaniola.

Among Caribbean nonfiction prose writers, political thinkers, and social critics, the Trinidadian C. L. R. James stands out as a towering figure. A Marxist who was, above all, an advocate for the human dignity of Caribbean people, he remains most reverently remembered as the author of the compelling study *The Black Jacobins: Toussaint L'Ouverture and the San Domingo Revolution* (1939). Returning in a 1963 appendix to the protagonists of the Saint Domingue insurrection that culminated in the creation of the Haitian nation, James asserted his conviction that "West Indians first became aware of themselves as a people in the Haitian Revolution," and he saw the 1959 Cuban Revolution as an offspring of that foundational liberating saga of the slaves centuries earlier (James 1963:391). In light of his view of the historic slave uprising as a sort of identitarian genesis for the Antillean person, it seems to follow that James should think of Toussaint, the architect of the revolution, as "the first and the greatest of West Indians" (418). A tribute both to Haiti and to James, the seminal 1960 essay *The Pleasures of Exile* by Barbadian writer George Lamming, introduced in Caribbean thought the use of the Shakespearean characters Prospero and Caliban as cultural synecdoches to explore the structure of power relations emanating from colonial history in the Antillean world. Lamming presented the struggle that began with the slave insurrection of Saint Domingue as setting the tone for resistance against oppression, which would become a paradigm of social action and intellectual production for the region into the modern period. He applauded in *The Black Jacobins* the fact that there James "shows us Caliban as Prospero had never known him: a slave who was a great soldier in Battle, an incomparable administrator in public affairs; full of paradox but never without compassion, a humane leader of men" (Lamming 1992:119). Because of the social significance of his intellectual work, in which Lamming discerned "a heart and desire entirely within the tradition of Toussaint himself," Lamming regarded James as "the greatest of all Caribbean teachers" (150, 211).

The same year of the publication of Lamming's *The Pleasures of Exile* Aimé Césaire's *Toussaint L'Ouverture: La révolution française et le problème colonial* (1960) appeared. While not conversing with the writings produced by his peers in the English-speaking bloc of the region or in any of the other linguistic zones of the Antillean world, Césaire matches in his study the commitment of James to locate Haiti visibly on the proscenium of history by stressing the impact of Toussaint and the black revolt in Saint Domingue in causing Europeans to confront the "false universalism" of the ideals of liberation that informed the "Declaration of the Rights of Man" (Césaire 1961:389). Césaire's appraisal of the larger implication of the Saint Domingue uprising finds confirmation in a study by Susan Buck-Morss that convincingly establishes the use G. W. Friedrich Hegel made of that

Caribbean rebellion in his development of the master and the slave dialect and his meditation on freedom in his *Phenomenology of Spirit* (1807). Buck-Morss shows that the famous German idealist philosopher had the Saint Domingue insurgents firmly in mind during his writing of the book (Buck-Morss 2000:844). That Hegel did not mention Haiti specifically, she explains, accords with his characteristic practice of omitting specific facts, just as he makes no mention of the French Revolution either. Besides, given his removal of black Africans from the history of humanity that he would later articulate in the *Lectures on the Philosophy of History*, he had particularly negrophobic reasons to avoid mention of an insurrection that would contradict the racialist texture of his account of the human experience. Césaire returns to Haitian history again in his 1963 play *La tragédie du roi Christophe*, which depicts the events surrounding the reign and ultimate demise of the insurgent slave who became general and concluded his days as king of Haiti. Complex and nuanced, Césaire's depiction of Christophe achieves a degree of pathos that qualifies that character to join the company of the most memorable figures of the ancient Athenian tragic stage. The St. Lucian poet and dramatist Derek Walcott had already dedicated a theatre piece to this character in *Henri Christophe*, a play "privately printed in 1948" that deals with the struggles of Christophe with General Jean Jacques Dessalines, his comrade in the war of liberation and later his competitor in the rule of the emancipated slave population (Walcott 2002:vii). Haiti would occupy Walcott's craft as a playwright again in writing *Drums and Colours*, a play commissioned to "mark the opening of the first West Indies Federation" and staged on April 25, 1958 (Walcott 111). Featuring Columbus, Sir Walter Raleigh, a governor of Trinidad, and some Jamaican personages, the play locates the Haitian leaders in a longer chronology and a vaster tapestry of Caribbean history. Finally in 1984, commissioned by the government of St. Lucia to commemorate the 150th anniversary of emancipation, Walcott staged *The Haitian Earth*, returning to the discrete cosmos of the insurgent leaders and completing a three-play Saint Domingue cycle that now appears published together under the inclusive title *The Haitian Trilogy* (2002:297).

The last major works in the Caribbean corpus to be mentioned here for their choice of Haiti as the historical arena wherein to explore meanings of regional significance are the 1949 novel *El reino de este mundo* by the Cuban fiction writer Alejo Carpentier and the play *Monsieur Toussaint* (1961) by the Martinican writer Edouard Glissant. Carpentier's novel not only tells the story of the Saint Domingue uprising in a powerfully evocative way—based "on an extremely rigorous documentation that is loyal to the historical truth of the events" and details, including "a meticulous verification of dates and chronologies"—but in his prologue he declares how the contact with Haiti gave him the clue for recognizing "what we could call marvelous realism," a characteristic that is inherent to historical life in the region and which separates it from the Western world (Carpentier 1967:9, 13). Glissant, for his part, undertook the composition of his play considering what he called "a prophetic vision of the past" and convinced that "the elucidation of the past whether recent or distant is a necessity" (Glissant 1986:7). The play stages simultaneously two periods lived sequentially by the hero, the moment of his leading the insurrection on the island and his imprisonment in the Chateaux de Joux at Jura. Toussaint also has frequent conversations with dead interlocutors, among whom are the Maroon MacKandal and Guadeloupean revolutionary commander Louis Degrés. The incorporation into the plot of a leader from elsewhere in the Caribbean accords with Glissant's understanding, expressed years later in his *Discours antillais* (1981), that:

> Until the war of liberation waged by Toussaint L'Ouverture, the peoples of Martinique, Guadeloupe, and Saint Domingue (which then became Haiti) struggled together in solidarity. This applied as much to the colonizers as to the slaves in revolt and the freed men (mostly mulattos) . . . such was the case for Delgrés, of Martinican origin, who fell with his Guadeloupean companions at Fort Matouba in Guadeloupe, and whose example was so dear to the heart of Dessalines, Toussaint's lieutenant. (Cited in Torres-Saillant 1997:40)

As these references suggest, the affirmation of the exploits of the Saint Domingue rebels, even when indictment of particular instances of leadership become inevitable, has provided Antillean intellects with a banner for asserting their people's place in the story of humanity against the deprecatory representation perpetrated by Western voices through the centuries. That emphasis in stressing the historicity of the region and the people in question has in fact given Caribbean thought one of the sources of its distinction. Therein lies to a large extent, the region's manner of utterance. As the forgoing textual references have hopefully illustrated, the literary works, political reflections, and cultural speculations rather frequently reveal the assertive diction of an ontological attestation. One might, thus, generalize that in Caribbean intellectual history thought production has largely taken the form of bearing witness, of documenting the human experience in the Antillean world so as to evince its conjugation with and inseparability from the drama of the whole species. Concomitantly with the reiterative proclamation of Antilleans as full-fledged historical beings and, by extension, as legitimate members of the human family, Caribbean thought has with equal eagerness professed the cultural difference that the Antillean world harbors and its consequent originality and authenticity as a differentiated civilizational zone.

ALTER NATIVE CREOLITY

An observer informed by a progressivist view of the development of literature and thought might fear that the persistence of history, of bearing witness, and attesting to the unimpeachable ontology of the Caribbean and its people could preclude creativity. Andrew Bundy, a critic of the oeuvre of the Guyanese novelist and essayist Wilson Harris, faces precisely that problem when he sets out to appraise the great accomplishments of the author in question by rescuing him from too close an association with intellectual production in the Antillean world. He plainly asserts that "Harris's study of the fabric of the imagination sets his writing apart from the concerns of West Indian writers" (Bundy 1999:7). Bundy, therefore, proposes alternative intellectual and cultural kinships for Harris, including South American and French traditions. Bundy's discomfort with Caribbean engagements with history and the deployment of attitudes about "all that recalls the colonial past" seems justified (Bundy 30). Harry, the character in Michelle Cliff's *No Telephone To Heaven* expresses similar suspicion when he says to Clare:

> But we are of the past here . . . We expect people to live on cornmeal and dried fish, which was the diet of the slaves. We name hotels Plantation Inn and Sans Souci . . . A peculiar past. For we have taken the master's past as our own. That is the danger. (Cliff 1996:127)

Bundy contends that a leadership "whose vision of the future is too handicapped by a past that seems to revulse the individual claim to dignity (and hence future distinction) becomes a victim of history" (22). But such a view itself seems debilitated by the presumption that the Antillean person's engagement with the region's catastrophic history is optional. The discussion we have sustained throughout the preceding sections of this study persuades us otherwise. The assiduous concern for the burden of the colonial past will probably obtain for as long as the dehumanizing effects of that legacy continue to surface. Besides, the necessary argument has not yet been made to disqualify the constant brooding over the possibility of a promissory future against a backdrop of a catastrophic legacy from regularly feeding the imagination and fueling creativity. To defend, illustrate, and attest to the Antillean person's distinct visage—her cultural personhood—while asserting her unquestionable place in the saga of human history remain indispensable. The region's condition of subalternity in relation to influential centers of power has not subsided. The structure of the globe today does not favor the Antillean world. The ills of the past continue to keep millions in the throes of poverty and hopelessness. The "oppressed," as earlier generations of intellectuals called them, continue to cope with the axiom of their helplessness. True, in the wake of the political, economic, and technological developments that the so-called global society has spawned, it now becomes more difficult for the oppressed to identify with precision the agents that tighten the strings of their oppression. But that difficulty only heightens their disempowerment.

Antilleans, then, do not have the option of looking askance at their past because it is simply too much with them. Rather, much of the originality of Caribbean intellectual production stems from the deployment of inventive ways of looking back, including what Glissant has called a "prophetic vision of the past." That originality is also predicated on the unfinished and interminable process of self-definition. Much of Caribbean thought marvels at the intricate reality of the present, the outcome of a grievous colonial transaction, and goes back to the history in search of the roots of the prodigious, if uncomfortable, formation of their current world. Looking at Surinam, for instance, the novelist Gabriel García Márquez, a native of Colombia's Caribbean coast, has the impression of witnessing there, strictly as a result of the movement of history, the magical structure of Caribbean reality. With a geographical extension of merely 163,820 km. and a population of less than a million souls, Surinam harbors a community whose members, in addition to the aboriginal settlements, trace their ancestry to Africa, India, China, Indonesia, and Europe. The Nobel Prize–winning novelist notes there the "lively mix of the country's seven races, six religions, and countless languages" (García Márquez 1996:9, 11). He highlights some of the ordinary social practices, such as black Caribbean women's habit of smoking with the lit end of the cigarette inside their mouth, which contribute to conferring a peculiar character to the region. Cartagena, the setting of his 1985 novel *El amor en los tiempos del cólera* (Love in the Time of Cholera), is by no means Surinam, but, Caribbean portion of Colombia that it is, we see there that the main character Fermina Daza "learns to smoke backwards, with the lit end inside her mouth, the way the men smoked at night during the wars, so that the light from their cigarettes would not give them away" (García Márquez 1999:188). In looking at Surinam, García Márquez finds confirmation for the specificity and endurance of what he calls "our magic world," which he compares in resilience to "the unconquerable plants," using a phrase of the Dominican writer and statesman Juan Bosch (García Márquez 1996:11). The country also offers him the occasion to celebrate the Caribbean region's sociocultural syncretism, the product of the pervasive creolization whose emergence historian and poet Kamau Brathwaite studied expertly in his 1971 monograph *The Development of Creole Society in Jamaica: 1770–1820*.

Today the body of writings that has come to be known as "postcolonial theory" in the Western academy has privileged the analysis of hybridity in the cultural and ethnoracial formations that are presumably reconfiguring the visage of the human family globally. In that scholarly meditation the Antillean world figures as a minor component of a vast empirical terrain. The region therein fails to command attention as a prominent locus of intermixture and syncretism in the factual arena of the historical experience and as a discursive precursor of the reflection on hybridity, a category of analysis better known locally as creolization. Predominantly, academics of Indo-Anglian, Afro-British, and other Third World extractions affiliated with major universities in Britain and the United States, the leading exponents of the postcolonial, given the geography of knowledge imparted in their Western education, may not approach with enthusiasm the products of Antillean thought. Through them, as I will further elaborate later, Western discourse has reaffirmed its dominion over the stratification of knowledge and the definition of humanity. The naming by Western discourse of a large zone of intellectual alterity termed "the postcolonial world" implies a partition of the globe into two distinct realms of ontological development comparable to the planetary binarism of the imperial imagination that led Juan de Castellanos over four centuries before to identify the "hidden" world of the conquered Other as a bequest received as recompense by the conquering "we." The promotion of a set of conceptual paradigms presumably capable of explaining life in the "postcolonial world" displays insufficient regard for the vast geographical, historical, and cultural differences that set the multiple branches of the human family outside the West apart from one another. The Caribbean with its intellectual production naturally becomes a casualty in the new arrangement just as it had experienced disfavor when it first entered the Western imagination at the start of the colonial transaction.

However, seen in its autochthonous chronology outside the geography of knowledge that subsumes it under the larger "postcolonial" designation, the Antillean world can claim an intimate rapport with hybridity from the outset. The novelist Wilson Harris has invoked the folk tradition that says that when the Caribs first arrived in the Antillean region, only males came, and they picked Arawak women for wives, suggesting a process whereby the conquerors voluntarily mixed their blood with that of the vanquished to form hybrid families (Harris 1999:240). Harris thus insinuates a history of miscegenation that precedes the violent arrival of Europeans and the forced migration of Africans to the Antillean world. While capturing the rich ethnic, religious, and linguistic diversity of Guyana, as illustrated in *The Secret Ladder* (1963), a novel populated by characters of English, Chinese, Portuguese, and African origins, apart from the symptomatic Stoll, a light-skinned mulatto, Harris stands out among major Caribbean writers for the attention he has paid to the region's Amerindian cultural heritage. He developed that affinity as a result of his close contact with aboriginal communities beginning in the 1940s when his job as a land surveyor took him to the "rainforests of Guyana, so that I became intimately and profoundly involved with the landscapes, and riverscapes of Guyana" (Harris 1999:40). There, he became acquainted with the cultural forms and the body of beliefs of Amerindians in the Tumatumari region, especially the oneiric symbolism of their language, which has clearly influenced his aesthetic vision and literary philosophy (45).

Contributing to foregrounding the multilayered texture of Caribbean hybridity—or creolity, to use a term more familiar in the region—the U.S. historian and autobiographer Patricia Penn Hilden has looked profitably into the cultural traces left by the numerous Indians from North America during the seventeenth and eighteenth centuries who came to work as slaves on Caribbean plantations, especially in the English colonies. Similarly she tantalizingly invites us to muse about possible explanations for the presence of a North American Plains Indian plaster bust and a "gold dust Indian spray" among the spiritual accessories of Santería altars (Hilden 2001:429). With the region's complex legacy of interlaced heritages, Harris seeks not simply to catalogue the ancestries that have integrated the Antillean world's cultural conglomerate. Rather, he would insist that many of those inheritances, which overstep the identitarian contours of the nationalism that pervades Western discourse, give Caribbean life its own peculiar accent. Coming to terms with Caribbeanness then involves, as he says through a quote from a lecture by Dennis Williams, breaking free of the "filialistic dependence on the cultures of our several racial origins [in order to face] up to the facts of what we uniquely are" (Harris 1999:161–162). The Caribbean for Harris admits of no simplification or trivialization since "the life of situation and person" there "has an inarticulacy one must genuinely suffer with and experience if one is to acquire the capacity for a new relationship and understanding" (147). Out of the poetic disquisitions of Harris, with his advocacy for "a philosophy of history" that "may well be buried in the arts of the imagination," comes with clarity a view of the Caribbean as a site with internal coherence while housing multitudes of difference (156).

One of the earliest documents that reflect the process of creolization that the colonial transaction unleashed in the Caribbean is the 1608 epic poem *Espejo de paciencia* (Mirror of Patience) by Silvestre de Balboa Troya y Quesada. Born on the island of Gran Canaria, Balboa came to Cuba as a humble immigrant. He settled in the province of Camagüey, where he married a local Creole woman named Catalina de Caoba. Balboa's poem, written in octavas reales, the meter corresponding to epic poetry that aspired to the loftiness of Virgil or Homer, narrates the story of the 1604 kidnapping of the Spanish priest Juan de las Cabezas Altamirano, bishop of Cuba, from his see in the Port of Manzanillo, by the French pirate Gilberto Girón and his band. The core of the plot chronicles the actions of the rescue party that ventures out in pursuit of the felons, culminating in the successful deliverance of the priest and the death of the pirate. The characters who make up the liberation crew include whites, blacks, and aborigines, and the role of fighting one-on-one with the dreaded pirate, defeating and killing him, goes to a black man, a character significantly named Salvador.

Strong in its descriptions, *Espejo de paciencia* abounds in lively evocations of the flora, fauna, and topography of the island of Cuba, where deities resembling those of Greek and Latin epic poetry wander about unencumbered. These lines illustrate the pervasive apparitions:

> The nymphs beautiful and lovely
> In their petticoats came down the trees
> With fruits from the macagues and for siguapas
> And fragrant pitajaya plants
> Carrying viriyi and jagua fruits
> Out of the bush emerged four goddesses
> Valorous and sober dryads
> Who brought the pastor great relief. (Balboa 1970: 68)

The poet, as we see here in the reference to Cuban birds, trees, plants, and fruits (macagues, siguapas, pitajaya, viriyi, and jagua) has no timid qualms about showing off the island's tropical environment. The speaker at one point seems assertive in naming the tropical location of the action:

> That today our Troy is Bayamo
> steaming at the force of scorching deceit. (55)

These verses seem to proclaim the setting's difference from that of *The Iliad* or *The Aeneid*. Balboa creolizes the Graeco-Roman deities, placing them in a

tropical habitat. The same applies to the ethnic composition of the contingent that undertakes the heroic mission of rescue. Among them we find:

> Juan Gómez, native, with a fine spear,
> And Rodrigo Martín, Indian:
> Four Ethiopians, the color of sloe. (77, 81)

All of them "as soldiers did their duty," a recognition that would seem to
free the virtues of courage and knightly demeanor from the monopoly of a
single race. Indeed, the speaker reserves for a black hero, the slayer of the
pirate, perhaps the most emotional exaltation in the poem:

> Oh, Salvador, Creole, honest Negro!
> Let your fame return and never die out;
> For, it is well that pen and tongue
> Should never tire of praising as good a soldier. (84)

In creolizing strategies such as these illustrated in the aforementioned
lines Balboa tropicalizes the ancient European epic, ushering the tradition
within which Derek Walcott's *Omeros* (1992) would fit nearly three centuries
later. The poet thus brought to the literary realm a portrait of the creolization that everyday life made evident to him in his Antillean milieu. Toward
the end of the century a French observer of the region, the cleric Jean
Baptiste Labat, would also attest to the process of racial and cultural fusion
that had remained unabated throughout the seventeenth century. A resident
of the region from 1693 to 1705, Labat reported on the measures taken by
the colonial authorities to contain miscegenation. Writing in 1695, Labat
noted that in the French possessions of the Caribbean there would be nothing but mulattos but for the king's imposition of a 2,000 pound of sugar fine
to any Frenchman found guilty of procreating with a black (Labat 1970:42).
But that prohibition, just as the ones intended to prevent illegal commerce—
that is, business transactions that involved traders from countries not authorized by France—suffered from incurable porosity. The failure of the Spanish
authorities to contain economic activity even involving Spain's competitors
had caused Santo Domingo's governor, Antonio Osorio in 1605 to resort to
burning the cities that were implicated in the violation. Labat reports about
a law that forbade French subjects to conduct business with the Spanish
under "no pretext whatsoever," but that this interdiction was "easily evaded,"
as illegal commerce on the coasts of Santo Domingo, Caracas, and Cartagena
became a common practice (Labat 1970:170). Perhaps the resilience of economic, political, and religious border crossers emblematically illustrates the
extent to which the texture of life in the Antillean world has resisted confinement, allowing for the creolization of experience in practically every respect.
    Labat bears witness to a phenomenon that would become a key feature in
modern figurations of the Antillean world by Caribbeans, the tendency to

conceptualize the region as a cultural whole even while recognizing the compelling force of nations, whether independent or not, as suppliers of the contours of citizenship and immediate sociopolitical belonging. Labat, looking panoptically at the region, viewed Caribbean societies as united by a common plight: all "in the same boat sailing the same uncertain sea" (Lewis 1983:93). Perhaps because the conquest begun in 1492 was regional, as was the genocide of the aborigines, the importation of enslaved Africans, the introduction of the indentured servants from "the East" and elsewhere, the emergence of Creole alterity, marronage and the struggle for freedom, the advent of resistance movements, and anticolonial ideals; as are regional the ecological conditions and as has been regional the defamatory representation launched conventionally by Western discourse, conceptual regionalism has prevailed in Caribbean intellectual history. The awareness of region insinuates itself even in the most society-specific works of Caribbean authors. The novel by Luis Rafael Sánchez *La guaracha del macho Camacho*, which piercingly delves into present-day Puerto Rican circumstances, contradictions, and stasis—as reflected in the massive traffic jam that recurs as a leit motif throughout the text—happens strictly in the city of San Juan. But, as soon as the work opens and we encounter a woman sensually sprawled on a seductive sofa, the description of her environs immediately makes us aware of the sordidness of the regional context:

> A restless body, she has a body of oh cut it out, can you see?, a body that she sits down, lays out, and plops into a sofa upholstered with a woolen material that's useful for overcoming polar chills but most unreal for any use in these tristes tropiques: the sun carries out an ungodly vendetta here, it stains the skin, prostitutes the blood, roils the senses: here is Puerto Rico, the successive colony of two empires and an island in the Archipelago of the Antilles. (Sánchez 2001:5)

The sense of region in Caribbean thought often appears interlinked with the idea of nation. The Puerto Rican short-fiction writer Ana Lydia Vega offers a view of Puerto Ricanness that is nurtured by Antilleanness. As a student at the University of Puerto Rico, says she, "amid the clamor of the struggles of the 1960s, I discovered myself as a borinqueña and a socialist . . . . I majored in French . . . My doctoral thesis led me toward the study of French Caribbean literature, an unequivocal return to my roots" (Vega 1992:875). Vega describes her second collection of short fiction, *Encancaranublado* as a "work of Caribbean inspiration . . . and a passionate political commitment to Caribbean unity" (876). The title story of that volume, translated into English by Mark McCaffrey as "Cloud Cover Caribbean," dramatizes the forced unity of the Haitian Antenor, the Dominican Diógenes, and the Cuban Carmelo, who risk their lives on a dinky boat to reach Miami and the possibility of material survival. As their frail embarkation capsizes, and they pray for their lives, an "American boat" rescues them, and they communicate with their benefactor—"the captain, an

Aryan and Apollinian seadog of ruddy complexion"—through their Caribbean mediator, a black Puerto Rican, who alerts them to the price they will have to pay the "gringo" for their rescue (Vega 1995:6).

The vision of regional unity espoused by Vega has numerous precedents in Caribbean discourse especially, starting in the mid-nineteenth century, when, Haiti and the Dominican Republic already independent, the possibility that the region might have a future outside the sphere of European colonial rule began to appear imaginable. The French abolitionist Victor Schoelcher, in an advocacy volume entitled *Les colonies françaises* (1852) offered this musing:

> On examining the position of the islands in the middle of the ocean, in looking at them on the map, where one finds them almost touching one another, one cannot help but think that they could very well, one day, make up together a separate social body in the modern world . . . They would be united confeder-ately by a common interest and would have their own navy, industry, arts, and a literature of their own. (Cited in Guérin 1956:179)

Schoelcher was a contemporary of Puerto Rican thinkers such as Eugenio María de Hostos and Ramón Emeterio Betances, the Cubans José Martí and Antonio Maceo, and the Dominicans Gregorio Luperón and Máximo Gómez, all of whom believed in and sought to advance the Antillean Confederation, a political unit that would bring together Hispaniola, Cuba, and Puerto Rico under one shared governance structure. Hostos first formulated the idea metaphorically in his 1863 novel *La peregrinación de Bayoán*, in which the main characters stand allegorically for the islands of the Greater Antilles. In his straightforward political writings, Hostos often articulated the view that patriots had a role to play in the struggle for liberation beyond their immedi-ate homelands: "anyone in any of the Antilles that is not his native land may be of great significance in the life and future of the other Antilles, provided that this Antillean knows how to use his influence for the good of all" (Hostos 1992:94).

In an 1895 letter to Luperón from Chile, Hostos understood the necessary political steps to be as follows: "first liberating Santo Domingo [from its present dictatorial government] and make Cuba and Puerto Rico independent, second, fighting the annexationist influence, and third, propa-gating the idea of the Antillean Confederation" (Hostos 284). Betances, for his part, began his political life in connection with the War of Restoration (1863–1865), the national liberation crusade in which Dominican patriots fought to expel the invading troops of imperial Spain after a conservative rul-ing elite had relinquished independence and brought the country under Spanish colonial control. Still a Spanish colony, Puerto Rico felt the impact of the events in the neighboring island especially since the military force deployed by Spain included Puerto Rican–born soldiers, and Betances joined the ranks of those condemning the invasion, earning him the banishment from his native land for the rest of his life (Suárez Díaz 1970:14–15). Then, he would devote the remainder of his productive years to advancing the cause of independence in Cuba and Puerto Rico as well as fighting annexationism in Haiti and the Dominican Republic. During the 1870s the two countries on the island of Hispaniola had governments with annexationist leanings, and Betances was instrumental in getting the nationalist factions on both sides of the border to collaborate in mounting a joint offensive (Carreras 1961:104–106). When the annexationist Haitian president, Sylvan Salnave, fell from power and the nationalist Nissage Naget took over, Betances sought out his support for the Dominican cause, convinced as he said in a letter to Luperón, that withholding such support would cause Haiti to "perish in the same abyss" (cited by Rodríguez Objío 1939:322–323). Furthermore, he did not recognize national boundaries when it came to defending the Antilles against Spanish or U.S. imperial domination. As to the rightness of meddling in the affairs of a neighboring country, he simply said: "we have a right to participate in [the independence war] in any of the three islands where it starts first" (Bonafoux 1970:lxxiv).

Betances's Antilleanism, encapsulated in the title of the lecture "Les Antilles pour les fils des Antilles" (The Antilles for Antilleans), delivered in Port-au-Prince on April 24, 1870, formed part of his political creed as a "verdadero patriota" (Bonafoux 115–116; lxxiii–lxxiv). The word "patriota" (patriot) for him denoted a zeal for the well-being of more than just one country. His comrade Gregorio Luperón, who offered protection in Dominican territory to Puerto Rican and Cuban independence advocates, including the famed Antonio Maceo, declared it "senselessness" (insensatez) and "infamy" (infamia) "to be Dominican but not Antillean, to know our destiny and to divorce it from the destiny of the Antilles" (Ferrer Gutiérrez 1940:7). Similarly, the revered Cuban liberator and poet José Martí articulated his vision of Hispaniola, Cuba, and Puerto Rico as "the three Antilles that together are to be saved or together are to perish" (Martí 1963:IV, 405). Martí, therefore, did not hesitate to go to Montecristi, Dominican Republic, and offer Máximo Gómez the military command of the war for Cuban independence from Spain in early 1895 especially in light of the reputation the Dominican warrior had accrued as a leader of the Cuban revolutionary forces against the Spanish colonial regime in the Ten Years War (1868–1878). After agreeing on the terms of their collaboration, Martí and Gómez left the Dominican soil, prepared to enter the field of battle to complete the work of liberation that the 1868 undertaking had left unfinished. In their "Montecristi Manifesto" that they co-signed they speak plainly of their belief in the regional and international implication of their armed campaign:

> The War of Independence in Cuba, the knot that binds the sheaf of islands where shortly the commerce of the continents must pass through, is a far-reaching human event and a timely service that the judicious heroism of the Antilles lends to the stability and just interaction of the American nations and to the still unsteady equilibrium of the world. (Martí 2002:344)

Hostos, Betances, Gómez, Luperón, Maceo, Martí, Nissage Saget, and other influential political leaders and thinkers of the same generation and ideological kinship placed Caribbean intellectual production at the forefront of the conversation about nation, regional identity, and border crossing, a conversation that in the 1990s would become associated with what the Western academy, led by U.S. scholars, has termed "transnationalism." One may argue that history denied the Antillean person the option of being merely national. As a result of the fundamentally transnational nature of colonial exploitation—as illustrated by the transcontinental geography covered by the triangular trade and its interconnection with the East India Company routes—too much of what impacts directly on the Antillean person's everyday life has for ages happened elsewhere. The plantation, which has so indelibly marked the structure of life in the region, was first and foremost a transnational machine. When we reach the nineteenth century, the transnational dynamics unleashed by inter-imperial competition, with the United States encroaching on the spheres of influence of the European colonial powers, Caribbean thinkers and political leaders understood that the matter of their people's future involved variables, factors, and agents that did not inhabit one single national geography. Patriotism, therefore, could not preclude regionalism, internationalism, and even universalism. For instance, as Lewis has aptly summarized, Hostos believed that the cosmopolite

> is not the man who fails in his duty to achieve the ends that his homeland imposes upon him, but rather he who, having struggled to achieve those ends, recognizes himself, beyond that, as the brother of all men and imposes upon himself the truth that he must extend the benefits of his efforts to any man in any space and time. (Lewis 1983:272–273)

To a large extent, behind the project of Antilleanism is a transnationalist view encouraged by the recognition that the territories in the region were at the mercy of the fulminating unifying power of Western empires. Thus, when the non-Cuban comrade of Martí became the chief of the Cuban army of liberation, Hostos could only applaud, understanding that: "Dominican by birth, Cuban by glory, Antillean by aspiration, and American by feeling and connection, Máximo Gómez is a universal man because of the renown he deservedly enjoyed throughout the first war of independence" (Hostos 1992:95).

The connection between the unitarian view of the Caribbean with the yearning for national autonomy from external domination is perhaps most patently accentuated by the frequent annexationist leaning of those politicians and ideologues who have opposed regional visions. An insufficient zeal for national sovereignty seems to go hand in hand with a disregard for ideas of regional unity. One notes, for instance, that nineteenth-century Dominican presidents Pedro Santana and Buenaventura Báez, who made various attempts to mortgage the national territory in whole or in part to foreign powers, namely Spain, France, and the United States, did not share the Antilleanist enthusiasm of Presidents Fernando Arturo de Meriño and Gregorio Luperón, both of whom vigorously opposed annexationist projects. A parallel development will probably be observed throughout the other

Caribbean societies. It certainly does in Puerto Rico, where Aaron Gamaliel Ramos has most usefully chronicled the history of annexationist ideas in the country. Among the documents made available by Ramos, one finds a 1900 letter addressed to "the American people" by José Julio Henna, a notable political and intellectual figure of the era. The letter intended to make Puerto Ricans suitable for membership in the Union to the eyes of the mainland U.S. citizen, hence Henna's description of the island's population as "a million inhabitants, people of white race and Christian faith, with the refinement, culture, and intelligence of an ancient civilization" (Henna 1987:69). Apart from the annexationist advocacy of his letter, what stands out in Henna's pronouncement is that in the racial and religious homogeneity as well as the cultural antiquity that he attributes to Puerto Ricans, he seems bent on stressing their difference from the "mongrelized" visage of the typical Antillean person. But in the 1930s a more categorical dismissal of the unitarian view came from the mulatto intellectual José Celso Barbosa, who denied Puerto Rico the possibility of "founding a nation," among other things, because of the dismal political education in the country and the minute size of the territory (Ramos 1987:29). He, thus, considered Puerto Rican sovereignty untenable and then declared his unwillingness to "delude" himself "with the false advantages of an Antillean confederation," contending that, in spite of the country's shared roots with Cuba and the Dominican Republic, to unite with them would in no way afford Puerto Rico the "compensating advantage" that would come from the association with "a powerful and well organized nation" (Ramos 29–30).

Rather than contemplating oneness or unification with the remainder of the region, Antillean leaders with annexationist ideas preferred to stress the features that make their particular territory exceptional. The ex-governor of Puerto Rico, Luis Muñoz Marín, doyen of the Partido Popular and champion of the development policies that in the 1940s caused the exodus of hundreds of thousands of his compatriots from the island, disdained the idea of independence from the United States, a notion that he claimed held little sway in the population. Speaking with young literatti who went to visit him in the comfort of his retirement in 1978, Muñoz Marín emphatically stated: "I tell you that independence is impossible because Puerto Ricans don't want it . . . What is Puerto Rico? An overpopulated Caribbean island. What can we compare it with? With Cuba and Santo Domingo, which are also Caribbean islands . . .? Are those countries really independent?" (Rodríguez Julia 1981:32). The old caudillo's rhetorical question concerning the economic and political autonomy of Hispaniola and Cuba rang true in a way that *independentistas* would find difficult to challenge. In 1978 Haiti's predatory ruling elite, Jean Claude Duvalier having inherited the presidency from his father, owed its permanence in power to its zealous protection of U.S. economic interest in the country and support of the parent nation's anticommunist policies in the region. The Dominican Republic's Joaquín Balaguer, an heir of the Trujillo dictatorship, was in his twelfth year of continued rule, thanks largely to his collaboration with the U.S. hegemony in the region and his willingness to abide by U.S. design in the country. At a time when the United Stated reduced the sugar import quota, Balaguer went on TV to tell the country and the world that if the reduction meant that President Richard Nixon found him at fault, he was prepared to tender his resignation for the sake of restoring the former quota (Torres-Saillant 1989:12). Nor could *independentistas* deny that in 1978 Cuba's material well-being stemmed largely from the economic protection extended by the Soviet Union, and had Muñoz Marín lived to see the country's material decline following the withdrawal of Soviet subsidy, he may have gloated in the confirmation of his views.

Admittedly, unitarian political projects have not succeeded in the Caribbean. Nor has the continued hegemony of the United States and Western Europe in the economic world system into which the region is trapped allowed individual Caribbean nations to attain real autonomy and to participate as equal partners in the international sphere of commerce and trade. Though passionately imagined in the Hispanophone Caribbean in the latter half of the nineteenth century and still invoked through the 1940s, the Antillean Confederation went no farther than the noble bosom of liberal intellectuals and enlightened political leaders. The West Indies Federation, a mid-twentieth-century rebirth of the same idea in the Anglophone bloc of the region, was dissolved in 1962, when an adverse vote in a national referendum in Jamaica terminated the four-year-old experiment (Senior 2003: 513). In the second half of the twentieth century, Michael Manley's dream of giving Jamaica economic self-reliance and the ability to choose political allies freely in the international community caved in when his government had to abdicate to the design of the global banks. One must perhaps ascribe to the pervasiveness of such failures in the region the change of heart reflected in Aimé Césaire's renunciation of sovereignty for Martinique, as we hear him explain in the 1991 documentary *Portrait of the Caribbean*. But neither the economic miscarriage of national projects in the Antillean world nor the barren outcomes of political visions of regional unity has managed to discourage pan-Caribbean figurations or the distinctness of the Antillean person's reality in light of the region's peculiar history. Unity need not automatically imply felicity. Daniel Guérin, decades ago, spoke of a certain "unité dans la misère" born of common misfortunes that the region suffered at the hands of Western colonial powers and of the resistive instincts that an awareness of such a history ignited in many of the Antillean world's intellects (Guérin 1956:104).

Today the evocation of the Caribbean's oneness and uniqueness—its alterity and difference with respect to each of its ethnoracial origins—continues unabated. As he, at the close of the twentieth century, undertook to envision what would become of the Antillean world as the site of a human conglomerate and a culture, the Cuban fiction writer and essayist Antonio Benítez-Rojo concluded his seductive musings by stressing the features that in his view have always made the Antillean person distinct and reiterating the reasons why the Caribbean ought to continue aspiring to unity. He noted the existential rapport with the sea, whose waters have "always made us look outward," which explains Caribbean generosity toward foreigners as well as the feeling of "cosmic isolation" that often "drives us" to head for other lands with the purpose of reaching the places where "the events of major import happen" (Benítez-Rojo 1999:19–20). Urging Antilleans to resist the compulsion to leave, Benítez-Rojo offered this exhortation:

> in order not to become irretrievable exiles, we must clench to the idea that we belong to a large homeland, that we do not sail unaccompanied; we need the certainty that we each individually have formed part of a great collective history and culture. (20)

This renowned Cuban man of letters said those words in August 1999 at the IV International Seminar on Caribbean Studies held in Cartagena de Indias in Colombia. His host, the historian Alfonso Múnera who heads the Caribbean Studies Institute that organizes the Seminar, used his turn at the podium to share, among other things, a view of the "style of the body"—a certain manner of corporal communication that uses movements and gestures to mark one's individuality in everyday life,—that he could ascertain in Jamaica, in Colombia's Caribbean coast, and in the rest of the region to note another distinguishing characteristic of the Antillean person (Múnera Cavadía 1998:8).

These reflections, made as they were on the eve of the twenty-first century of the Common Era, would seem to foretell that the start of the new millennium would be unlikely to attenuate the compulsion among Caribbean intellects to hoist banners of ontological autonomy and to deploy paradigms of regional oneness predicated perhaps less often on the basis of governance structures and more on the grounds of sociocultural figuration. The compulsion, as the foregoing pages make clear, is unlikely to subside because it is integral to the very texture of Caribbean discourse. The Trinidadian scholar J. Michael Dash casts an insufficiently wide historical net when he dates the revival of what he dismissively terms "the mythology of a Caribbean otherness" to the 1971 publication of the famous essay *Calibán* by the Cuban thinker Roberto Fernández Retamar (Dash 1998:73). Antillean "otherness" or "the need to legitimize difference," which Dash links to "a fierce anti-Americanism," appears here pathologized. But historicizing would seem more conducive to understanding the matter. A historically informed analysis would reveal that the question of Caribbean alterity—"otherness" or "difference"—forms part of a lengthy contrapuntal interplay of inimical ascription by Western discourse and self-assertive assumption by Antillean voices from the start of the colonial transaction to the present moment. "The resurgence of this notion," ventures Dash, "demonstrates the seductiveness of one of the major tropes of Caribbean modernism—the island as primeval ground" (Dash 73). But a study of the question that is interested in native etiology would recognize that the affirmation of Antillean alterity accompanies a persistent desire to place the region in history, in response to a legacy of Western denormalization that recurringly bars the Antillean person's entrance to history and the narrative of the human experience. Nor does it seem judicious to explain the question as merely an expression of "Caribbean modernism" unless one thinks of intellectual developments in the Antillean world as a mere tropical extension of Western periodizing of cultural history. To periodize Caribbean thought production thus amounts to uncritically inserting it in the chronology of a Western history of ideas whose narrative logic cuts the past prophylactically into distinct, successive chunks, each characterized by its own distinguishing ideas, which, in turn, impact directly on concrete reality outside textuality. Applied to the Antillean world, this manner of figuration becomes the intellectual equivalent of the political annexationism espoused by the mulatto José Celso Barbosa and the other foes of unitarian visions of the Caribbean.

Studied outside the rigid inexorability of Western histories of ideas, the development of Caribbean discourse yields its own chronology, one that corresponds to the events that have impacted and shaped the lives of people in the region beginning with the colonial transaction. A historiography of ideas that draws on those events would pay attention to the discernible effect on intellectual utterances of a slave rebellion on a major colonial plantation, a European or U.S. invasion sent to crush a nationalist movement, a raid of armed Maroons against a prosperous colonial city, a workers' riot against local authorities, unemployment and famine due to a Western blockade, intra-Caribbean migration in pursuit of shifting industries in the region, emigration to the United States and Europe in connection with the decline of sugar and tropical produce on the world market, the devastating repercussions of an earthquake or a hurricane, and the failure of a ruling elite to safeguard the best interests of the local population, to name only a few of the countless occurrences that have regularly made themselves available to the consciousness of Antillean thinkers and artists. One should think then that ideological or emotional engagements with the powerful incidents that have shaped their lives ought to creep into the motives of their art and thought production at least to the point of making them less than merely passive recipients of the stimuli instilled in them by their consumption of the latest philosophical, artistic, or literary trend in the Western metropolis. A contention such as the claim by Simon Gikandi that construes "creolization" as a characteristic feature of "modernism" in the Caribbean seems to suggest that the writers he studies came to it through their fractious engagement with European modernist tradition or that they had no earlier access to it (Gikandi 1992:10, 16). However, if one reads outside this type of periodizing one finds creolization fully engaged in texts that go from Balboa's *Espejo de paciencia* in 1608 to the 1827 anonymous tale *Hamel the Obeah Man* to Trefossa's 1957 poetry collection *Trotji*. Though written at a moment that matches the chronology of the European Renaissance, Balboa's poem could be read, in effect, as a text divorced from the sensibility that scholars attribute to Renaissance texts, illustrating perhaps the applicability of Kamau Brathwaite's argument that what the Caribbean had was a "counter-renaissance" (Brathwaite 1984:51–52). Indeed, Antillean writers and thinkers, in different degrees of self-consciousness, have persistently explored the phenomena that frame the contours of the human experience in their region primarily because of their awareness or intuition that the movement of history there does not quite follow the lineaments of the historical experience of the Western societies with which they have been colonially linked. That awareness or intuition explains why the writings that make up the overall Caribbean corpus present the sociohistorical and cultural scrutiny of life in the region as their main subject matter. The Caribbean never ceases to look at itself through its intellectual production. Not surprisingly, Caribbean writing stands out for its hypermnesia, a condition, dramatically opposed to amnesia, that exacerbates the memory of the past, producing a state of compulsive remembering that could be deemed clinical were it not for its inevitability and its salutary function as a mechanism for coping with the devastating events that have taken place in the region since the start of the colonial transaction. Perhaps because of a widespread sense that the Antillean person's rapport with the colonial past remains somehow unresolved, history has invariably provided a key fuel for igniting intellectual production. C. L. R. James had this in mind when he pointed to the existence of "something in the West Indian past, something in the West Indian environment, something in the West Indian historical development, which compels the West Indian intellectual, when he gets involved with subjects of the kind, to deal with them from a fundamental point of view, *to place ourselves in history*" (James 1969:45). Describing Antilleans as "more than any other people constructed by history," James, therefore, posited that any political or social activity aimed at bringing about transformation "has got to begin and constantly bear in mind how we came into being, where we have reached, who we are and what we are" (46).

History as Hieroglyph and the Postcolonial

History figures in Caribbean intellectual production as a constant source of reflection, with particular thinkers busy at searching for principles that might obtain for interpreting the particular manner of configuration that events in the region have taken. Caribbean history is often presented as requiring decipherment like Champollion's decoding of the Rosetta Stone. A sense of the coexistence of the present and the past, advancement and retardation, backwardness and progress creates in many a disquiet as to the precise logic that events in the region follow. Today historians have identified the value of different analytical prisms through which to look at the region. Volume six of the monumental *General History of the Caribbean*, which focuses on questions of historiography and methodology, identifies many of the schools of thought and approaches that have informed the study of the region's past since the advent of the historical discipline there (Higman 1999). These include those that stress nationalism and imperialism, ideology, regionalism, class, race, ethnicity, gender, labor movements, orality, and economics. But history in the Antillean world, as Glissant has observed, is not merely the concern of historians. In 1842 the Cuban novelist Cirilo Villaverde mused about the strange pattern he discerned in his country's history, a sort of "perpetual rotation, at corsi, recorsi, like heavenly bodies in their orbit," in which indecisive movement he found confirmation for the view of history advanced by Giambattista Vico, which he found "pretty accurate" for Cuba even if it seemed "exaggerated and perhaps even mistaken" when applied to "certain European nations" (Villaverde 1961:73). He found thriving on the island certain social relations and lifestyles corresponding to a feudal order coexisting and perhaps even competing with the advent of modernity. Interestingly, as we fasten on Villaverde's equivocal position on the race question, it becomes clear that he himself embodied the inconsistencies that he identified in local history. *Una excursión a Vuelta Abajo* (1842), the account of Villaverde's journey on horseback through his hometown, presents enslaved blacks as practically an inanimate feature of the landscape. The author appears unmoved by the anguish of their captivity. To report on the prosperity enjoyed by an acquaintance named Matías, for instance, Villaverde describes him as "married, and with lands, livestock, house, and slaves in his possession" (Villaverde 1961:90).

Seen in light of Alexander von Humboldt's observation of slavery in Cuba when he visited the island nearly four decades prior to the novelist's return journey to Vuelta Abajo, Villaverde's casual view of racial oppression would seem to require explanation. Looking at the captive population, the German scientist expressed the need for a salutary change in the legislation of the West Indies "and the state of men of colour" lest "a catastrophe" might "ensue" (Humboldt 1853:233). Humboldt evaluated schools in Havana unfavorably on the grounds that: "Intellectual cultivation is almost entirely limited to the white, and is as unequally distributed as the population" (245). That Humboldt, a European visitor, should think of blacks as intellectual beings deprived of an education and decry slavery as "no doubt the greatest evil that afflicts humanity," whereas Villaverde, an Antillean intellect who would get to earn distinction as an abolitionist, should decades after the words of the German visitor still show disregard for people in captivity illustrates part of the complication of the Caribbean past. Villaverde's indifference toward the human condition of enslaved blacks would change in proportion to his involvement in the decades that followed in the island's political struggle, leading to the composition of the novel *Cecilia Valdés* whose definitive edition in 1882 would earn prestige as a key document of Antillean abolitionism. We should note, however, that even in its most radical expression, Villaverde's abolitionism did not break free of the ideological ambiguity of many renowned antislavery nineteenth-century Cuban thinkers, who would passionately embrace the cause of abolition without necessarily abandoning their negrophobic racism (Alonso 1998:70, 73). The first part of Villaverde's novel, dating from 1839, did not convey antislavery sentiments, the author not having yet begun to see the institution as requiring urgent attention "from a Cuban point of view" (Rodríguez Herrera 1953:xxvi). But even the definitive edition of 1882, published in New York, where the author was exiled by the island's colonial regime, cannot garner him the rank of a "champion of Cuban abolitionism" (Rodríguez Herrera 1953:xxvi). The scholar Ivan Schulman has noted that Villaverde "chose to restrict the sociopolitical parameters of his tale" by presenting the racial question "in diluted and neutral ways" and by deploying such essentialisms as when the narrator explains the main character's passionate temperament by attributing it to a characteristic of her race (Schulman 1981:xvii).

Villaverde's enigmatic intellectual and political trajectory represents some of the serious contradictions that students of the region's past often encounter, and just as he looked to Vico's cyclical theory of history—the succession of *corsi* and *recorsi*—as a possible analytical model to explain the logic of events in Cuba, Antillean intellects, especially since the 1930s, have occupied themselves with a similar search. The search for models to help decipher regional realities often becomes interchangeable with the identification of metaphors, patterns, and symbols that suggest language for speaking about the region's identity. During the 1930s writers from the Hispanic Antilles, especially the poets Nicolas Guillén, Luis Palés Matos, Emilio Ballagas, and Manual del Cabral zeroed in on *negrismo*, an artistic and spiritual reconnection with the submerged legacy of the African past. Concomitantly writers from the Francophone bloc of the region, largely inspired by the pioneering work of Haitian scholar Jean Price-Mars, formulated the notion of *négritude*, with Aimé Césaire and Léon-Gontran Damas at the lead with their Senegalese ally Léopold Sédar Senghor. Predicated fundamentally on a creed of racial self-assertiveness and a revalorization of the African heritage, négritude connected with Africans, African Americans, and spokespersons of the black diaspora elsewhere, bringing Antillean intellects into visibility in a nearly global landscape. Contemporaneous with these developments, the rise of Rastafarianism and the teachings of Marcus Garvey gave currency in the Anglophone Caribbean, and chiefly in Jamaica, to a sociopolitical movement of proletarian extraction that combined an African-inspired spiritual dogma with a stance of ethnic self-affirmation. Along with these various stances occurring throughout the Caribbean, a number of compelling thinkers and activists added to the region's visibility through the vigorous embrace of a near orthodox Marxism of internationalist aspirations while they unabashedly upheld their identity as black Caribbeans. Their names include the Surinamese Anton de Kom, the Trinidadians George Padmore and C. L. R. James, the Haitian Jacques Roumain, the Martinican Frantz Fanon, and the Guyanese Walter Rodney, whose range of intellectual and political activities reached well into the second half of the twentieth century. The triumph of the 1959 Cuban Revolution gave many Antillean intellects the impression that a major milestone had been marked in the region's history. Witness the coincidence of three major documents by leading thinkers that use the event in their titles as marker of a historical milestone: "From Toussaint L'ouverture to Fidel Castro," C. L. R. James's appendix to the 1963 edition of his *Black Jacobins*; *De Cristóbal Colón a Fidel Castro*, the ambitious historical analysis of the region published in 1970 by the Dominican writer and politician Juan Bosch; and *From Columbus to Castro*, another overview of Caribbean history published by the Trinidadian scholar and statesman Eric Williams also in 1970.

With the precedent of the Cuban Revolution, the newly acquired sovereignty of various British West Indian colonies that became independent, and the expansion of public education, higher learning included, the 1960s ushered in an era of intense political enthusiasm marked by a sense of possibility throughout the region. The two decades that followed constituted a vibrant period of intellectual production. As the new generation that now had risen to international prominence featured strong women's voices, the questions of gender and sexuality necessarily entered the conversation about figurations of the region or the construction of nation-building projects. Along with the prestige of Edouard Glissant, Luis Rafael Sánchez, Boeli van Leeuwen, Derek Walcott, Wilson Harris, and Kamau Brathwaite, to name only a few, emerged the voices of Thea Doelwijt, Elsa Goveia, Bea Vianen, Sylvia Wynter, Aida Cartagena Portalatín, Lydia Cabrera, and Marie Viau Chauvet, among numerous others. While gender inequity did not disappear, nor did all male intellects buy into the idea of sharing power and authority with women, a gender-sensitive way of looking at the past and imagining the future began gradually to make itself felt. The new awareness gave currency to a reconstituted remembering that began to reconsider the key roles played by women in the liberation struggles of the past. The contribution of pioneering figures such as the Jamaican poet Louise Bennett, who created an audience for verse written in West Indian dialect, and the Surinamese poet Johanna Schouten Elsenhout, who achieved distinction using Sranan Tongo, began to receive serious attention. The social criticism of early Caribbean feminist thinkers such as Puerto Rican Luisa Capetillo and Dominican Camila Henríquez Ureña would be eventually discovered, and the identity positions of women whom an earlier generation of male voices had dismissed such as the Martinican Mayote Capecia and Guadeloupean Suzanne Lacascade, began to demand a careful rereading. By the same token, the troubled positionality of the work of Jean Rhys, a white Creole woman born in Dominica who left the island at age 17 never to return, is now accepted as an inescapable intricacy of the Caribbean corpus.

The insertion of women into the intellectual conversation, to the extent that it has occurred, has added layers of complexity to the search for models that might help shed light on the structure of life in the Caribbean. Perhaps not surprising, the paradigms that have gained the most currency as candidates for speaking holistically about the region since the beginning of the 1980s are those mustering the greater metaphorical weight, namely the rhizomatic network of relations that Glissant concocts out of Deleuze as well as the notions of "detour" and "retour," the seductive idea of organized disorder that Benítez-Rojo composes out of Western chaos theory, the logic of the limbo dance, or of Haitian vodou that Wilson Harris privileges in his advocacy for a mythic imagination, or the dialect of the tides (tidalectics) that Kamau Brathwaite proposes as a plausible basis for a philosophy of history in the region. Their metaphorical evocativeness has inseminated the hermeneutic field for students of the Caribbean, who can also draw on the conceptual resources afforded by the discursive strategies and thematic emphases found in the works of the major women writers of the region. One thinks of the biting humor and assertive Antillean diction in the short fiction of Ana Lydia Vega, the radical hybridity in the prose and poetry of Olive Senior, the enigma of discernible reality in the novels of Maryse Condé, and the uses of the past in the fictionalized histories of Cynthia Mc Leod. Together they represent a composite, multi-pronged inquiry into the birth, life, and future of the Antillean world. Their common effort of interpretation shares the desire for an indigenous historiography and a philosophy of history curtailed to fit the Caribbean cosmos.

The compulsion to interpret and the urgency to shed light on the Caribbean experience constitute compelling evidence of the particularity and the originality of the Antillean world. No force, in effect, has so much motorized intellectual production in the region than the desire to pinpoint the meaning of Caribbeanness. The Martinican writers Jean Bernabé, Patrick Chamoiseau, and Raphäel Confiant speak in their 1989 essay *Eloge de la creolité* of Caribbeanness as something to come rather than as an existing actuality (Torres-Saillant 1997:29–30). Therein lies a fundamental weakness of their intervention, which is compounded by the authors' enunciation of creolity in the Caribbean as if their formulation had no precedent in the intellectual history of the region. Yet, the history we have tried to evoke in these pages consistently shows that attesting to the fact of Caribbeanness and boasting the region's creolity have been at the core of Caribbean discourse since its inception. The actuality of Caribbeanness has not been debatable. It is its decipherment that has presented a challenge. A serious implication of the stance of the *créolistes*, their speaking of Caribbeanness and creolity as if they were starting the conversation on these matters, is that their disregard for the vast corpus of utterances that the region has produced to speak about itself links their attitude to a long tradition of Western discourse that has typically imagined the Antillean world as an intellectually virginal terrain. This attitude dates back to the days when Columbus arrived and proceeded to name valleys, rivers, and landscapes unconcerned about whether or not these already had names. The scholarly negligence displayed by the likes of Trollope and Froude, who did not find it necessary to verify their observations, stemmed from a view of the region as an epistemological void to be filled by meaning brought by the visitor. Since Bernabé, Chamoisseau, and Confiant are Antillean "natives," their construing the region as intellectually virginal insidiously justifies the encroachment of paradigms and metadiscourses that others elsewhere might condescend to prescribe to the Antillean world.

During the 1990s "new" paradigms and metadiscourses indeed came from elsewhere and gained favor as critical tools and perspectives to study the Caribbean past, present, and future, namely the way of organizing knowledge about the human experience that bears the name of postcolonial criticism and theory. Stuart Hall, himself a practitioner of the new field, has attested to its remarkably rapid growth in the academic industry of Europe and the United States. The distinguished Jamaican scholar and poet Edward Baugh, a veteran professor of English at the Mona campus of the University of the West Indies, has noted the growing importance of "postcolonial theory" at his school "thanks in part to a new generation of lecturers, West Indians, who have had significant exposure to Postcolonial Studies in the Canadian Academy," and, drawing on his own classroom experience, he reports that the majority of graduate students now write theses "on Caribbean literature and bring, increasingly, some kind of postcolonialist approach to the literature" (Baugh 2000:16). Shalini Puri, the author of a book that is pan-Caribbean in scope, acknowledges that she came to her topic in 1990 "when cultural hybridity was just emerging as the *epistéme regnant* of Postcolonial Studies" (Puri 2004:xi). Entitled *The Caribbean Postcolonial*, the book treats the region as an instance of postcoloniality even while the author suggests an interrogation of the concept by showing, for instance, the ways in which "the very vision of the Caribbean as a place of historical possibility turns on the question of hybridity" (43). As for the overseas French departments, a scholar has observed that published studies of Francophone Antillean literature and culture as well as of the intellectual production of the vast geopolitical region formerly known as *la francophonie* now increasingly use the term "postcolonial" to designate the region under perusal (Suk 2001:19). Jeannie Suk's study of Césaire, Glissant, and Condé sets out "to articulate converging paradoxes of postcoloniality and Antilleanness through" several thematic emphases brought forth by the works of the Martinican and Guadeloupean authors examined (Suk 2001:23). By the same token, in *Edouard Glissant and Postcolonial Theory*, a book written to bear out the Martinican writer's status as a major contemporary thinker, the author, Celia Britton, sets out to juxtapose "Anglophone postcolonial writing and Glissant's theoretical writing," intending to highlight similarities and differences and ultimately to "show the significant contribution Glissant makes to this body of theory" (Britton 1999:5). That the Hispanic and the Dutch Caribbean have not escaped the impact of the rise of postcolonialism is evident in the Antillean authors and traditions represented in edited volumes dealing with postcolonial perspectives in the Luso- and Spanish-speaking Americas as well as in the creation of such organizations as the Postcolonial Literatures Research Group at Belgian and Dutch universities (Castro-Gómez and Mendieta 1998; Schmidt-Welle 2003).

Neil Lazarus in his useful and sedate overview of postcolonial studies, a field that enjoys today "a position of legitimacy and even relative prestige" though it did not exist before the late 1970s, maps the critical and ideological tendencies currently dominant in "a field currently alive with activity and invention" (Lazarus 2004:1, 16). The advent of postcolonial perspectives has not failed to provoke suspicion in those who see it connected to the rise and "newfound power" of Third World intellectuals who have arrived in First World academe (Dirlik 1997:510). As "the progeny of post modernism, post colonialism arguably expresses the logic" of the current phase of capitalism, and its principal voices exhibit "the condition of the intelligentsia of global capitalism" (Dirlik 1997:517, 523). Postcoloniality, in the succinct and often quoted formulation by Kwame Anthony Appiah, represents the condition of a "comprador intelligentsia: of a small, Western-styled, Western-trained group of writers and thinkers who mediate the trade in cultural commodities of world capitalism at the periphery. In the West they are known for the Africa they offer; [and] through the West they represent to Africa" (Appiah 1997:432). But, apart from the sociopolitical circumstances of the main proponents of the new critical perspective, some would take issue with postcoloniality's true explanatory power. The temporality of the "post" prefix has raised questions, as has the politics of inserting or omitting the hyphen that would normally separate the two parts of the compound word (Cooppan 2000:1). Thus, Patrick Colm Hogan, in a study of the colonial legacy in the Anglophone literatures of India, Africa, and the Caribbean, distances himself from the term "postcolonial" because he finds it misleading since many of the works normally listed under the rubric were written not after but during colonialism. However, since the bodies of writing in question were written after colonization, he believes the label "postcolonization" would more aptly describe them (Hogan 2000:xix).

An encyclopedia entry on "Post-Colonial Theorists" describes the figures therein named as members of a new generation which

> emerged in the Western world after the publication of Edward Said's *Orientalism* (1978), having migrated from the peripheries of the post-colonial world to work in the metropolitan centers. Their work questions constructions of nation and the national, focusing on wide-ranging analyses of hybridity, marginality, mimicry, and subalternity. (Benson and Conolly 1994:1303)

After this the encyclopedia proceeds to provide page-long entries on the individual careers of Homi K. Bhabha, Edward W. Said, and Gayatri Chakravorty Spivak (1303–1306). The editors of the encyclopedia, namely the *Encyclopedia of Post-Colonial Literatures in English*, report that, after completing in 1989 a major compilation dealing with Canadian theater, they set their eyes on "the rich literatures of the British Commonwealth" and sailed forth on the much longer voyage of editorial exploration that culminated in the publication of a sizable two-volume reference work with entries covering the literatures in English of Australia, Bangladesh, Canada, the Caribbean, East Africa, Gibraltar, Hong Kong, India, Malaysia, Malta, New Zealand, Pakistan, the Philippines, Singapore, Sri Lanka, St. Helena, South Africa, South Central Africa, the South Pacific, and West Africa, omitting the writings of England, Scotland, Wales, and Ireland merely because these already appear "well documented in scholarly reference sources" (Benson and Conolly xxv–xxvi). Throughout their long process of compilation and writing, editors Eugene Benson and L. W. Conolly operated under the expectation that their book would bear the label "Commonwealth" on its title, that being the standard designation at the time for the vast transcontinental geography made up of all the territories under the tutelage of the British Empire. Stuart Hall has aptly described "what the Commonwealth was" by terming it "the harnessing of a hundred different histories within one singular history, the history of the Commonwealth" (Hall 1997:185). However, the name Commonwealth had lost currency by 1994, when Benson and Conolly completed their compendium, and they opted to adopt the term "postcolonial" from the Australian scholars Bill Ashcroft, Gareth Griffiths, and Helen Tiffin, whose 1989 manual *The Empire Writes Back: Theory and Practice in Postcolonial Literature* had proven enormously influential.

Put bluntly, in choosing the term "postcolonial" over "commonwealth" the editors of the encyclopedia made a business decision since they chose the appellation that enjoyed the greater appeal in the academic market. They worried about the imprecision of the term "postcolonial" but concluded that the other available options suffered from the same defect. Their decision graphically illustrates the extent to which the packaging and sale of ideas in the academic industry, to a large extent, must often respond to market pressures comparable to those at work in other sectors of our capitalist consumer economy, such as the automobile or the entertainment industry. Each case presents us with a scenario wherein a provider must try to make his or her merchandise as luring as possible to the potential buyer. Today the appeal of the term "postcolonial" has spread widely, moving beyond the territories within the sphere of influence of the British Empire and entering the colonial domains of France, Spain, Denmark, Belgium, Portugal, and the United States, the other Western powers who had claimed pieces of the global colonial pie. The Australian promoters of the concept justified the expansion of the geography involved on the grounds that over "three-quarters of the people living in the world today have had their lives shaped by the experience of colonialism," and the literatures the scholars set out to situate in their manual "emerged in their present form out of the experience of colonization and asserted themselves by foregrounding the tension with the imperial power and by emphasizing their differences from the assumptions of the imperial centre," which, in their view, explains the identity of the literatures in question as "distinctly postcolonial" (Ashcroft, Griffiths, and Tiffin 1989:2). Bhabha's suggestions concerning the extent to which the colonial transaction also transformed the structure of life within the imperial nations could justify yet another expansion of the geography of postcoloniality to include the West itself, thus enveloping practically the entire planet and diluting the explanatory value of the category.

Perhaps it is the implication of the Western presence in the postcolonial that explains the intersection of the writings in question with "recent European movements, such as post modernism and structuralism, and with contemporary Marxist ideological criticism and feminist criticism," leading Ashcroft, Griffiths, and Tiffin to warn against

> the pretence that theory in post-colonial literatures is somehow conceived entirely independently of all coincidents, or that European theories have functioned merely as "contexts" for the recent developments in post-colonial theory. In fact, they clearly function as the conditions of the development of postcolonial theory in its contemporary form, and as the determinants of much of its present nature and content. (155)

They place the emergence of postcolonial reading practices right smack in the middle of developments in Western thought during the second half of the twentieth century. According to Ashcroft, Griffiths, and Tiffin, the influential modern movement that we associate with the careers of such salient men of letters as I. A. Richards, William Empson, F. R. Leavis, Kenneth Burke, Yvor Winters, Cleanth Brooks, W. K. Wimsatt, and others, namely New Criticism, "was itself largely a product of a postcolonial USA intent on establishing the legitimacy of its literary canon against the persistent domination of the English tradition" (160). Subsequent attempts to chronicle the rise and development of postcolonial perspectives, such as the solid overview by Ania Loomba, *Colonialism/Postcolonialism* (1998), invariably locate the new field within the evolution of Western critical theory of the last five decades. As such, these chronicles highlight the successive stages of intellectual kinship of postcolonial critics with the likes of Antonio Gramsci, Louis Althusser, Michel Foucault, Pierre Bourdieu, and other leading figures of contemporary Western thought.

The careers of the authors whom the manuals identify as founding parents of "postcolonial theory" perhaps illustrates the Western provenance of the new critical mode. For instance, Bhabha's work, largely drawing on Foucault and Derrida, has Jacques Lacan as its "main methodological source" (Moore-Gilbert 2005:111). Said first established his credentials in the U.S. academy as "one of the pre-eminent introducers of contemporary European critical theory," supporting Foucault, opposing Derrida, and allying himself with Gramscian Marxism and European philology (Goldie 1993:461; Milz 2005:825). Spivak, for her part, first trained in comparative literature at Cornell University, authored a monograph on William Butler Yeats in 1974, and began to accrue prestige as a cultural critic following the 1976 publication of her English translation of Derrida's 1967 work *De la grammatologie* (Moore-Gilbert 2005:882). Spivak's often cited essay "Can the Subaltern Speak?" opens with the intention of challenging the contemporary Western critique that emerges from the interested desire to preserve the subject of the West, or the West as the subject, but she herself finds it hard to forgo the Western subject until after she has paid sufficient homage to it (Spivak 1994). Only after she has engaged Gilles Deleuze and Foucault, dexterously refuting their understanding of the "sovereign subject" through her erudite handling of the German original of *The Eighteen Brumaire of Louis Bonaparte* (1852) by Karl Marx, does she move her analytical lens to India. One gets the impression that she, an intellect born and raised in India, needs first to display credentials in the realm of Western knowing to attain the authority with which to invoke native knowledge.

The adoption of postcolonial perspectives widely in the study of the Caribbean may worry those Antillean intellects who have hoped to liberate the region from the epistemological hegemony of the West. In the Western provenance and sensibility of the protagonists of the new field—the darker skin of the salient figures notwithstanding—Antillean intellects who have spent much of their energy in repudiating the animosity of Western discourse toward the Antillean person might grieve the current outcome as one in which the West once more manages to have its way. The West again confirms itself as the ultimate source of moral and intellectual authority, monopolizing the power to confer or withhold epistemic value. No one interested in the intellectual emancipation of the Antillean world would find reason to celebrate in the present scenario, especially in light of the meager space that the postcolonial organization of knowledge accords to the region. Suffice it to mention respectable overviews of the field, such as the collection *Mapping Subaltern Studies and the Postcolonial*, which features many of the prominent figures, none of whom makes any mention of the Caribbean (Chaturvedi 2000). Another discomfort would necessarily come from the exacerbated concern of Antillean intellects with geography (place) and history (events in time). Disquiet over the apparent temporality of the prefix "post" would raise Caribbean eyebrows. Many territories in the region have not moved out of the colonial condition, namely Anguilla, British Virgin Islands, Cayman Islands, Montserrat, Turks and Caicos Islands (still under Britain); Martinique, Guadeloupe, and Guyana (the three French overseas departments); Aruba, Curaçao, Bonaire, and the rest of the Netherlands Antilles (Dutch territories); and Puerto Rico and the U.S. Virgin Islands (under U.S. sovereignty). Nor do learned observers see "traditional alternatives in sight for the decoloniza- tion of the territories that remained attached to Great Britain, France, Holland, and the United States" (Ramos and Rivera 2001:xiii). Ironically, the majority of these colonies have at present reached a higher level of devel- opment than their independent counterparts, having benefited from their close ties to the prosperous economies of their respective metropolises. For instance, the combined per capita income of the British colonies in the region is more than three times as large as that of the independent Anglophone West Indian nations, while the per capita income of independent Surinam is less than one-fourth that of Aruba and the Netherlands Antilles (Ramos and Rivera 2001:xv). Given such a scenario, the path toward decolonization looks murky for the nonindependent Caribbean territories.

The Australian promoters of postcolonialism did from the outset address the temporal question that the "post" raises. They explain that their use of it did not "suggest a concern only with the national culture after the departure of the imperial power" as in prior uses of the prefix. Rather they mean for the term "postcolonial" to cover "all the culture affected by the imperial process from the moment of colonization to the present day" (Ashcroft, Griffiths, and Tiffin 1989:2). In conferring to the postcolonial gaze such a vast scope, which chronologically starts before 1492, in light of England's colonial dom- ination of Ireland beginning in the twelfth century, and geographically encompasses all but a few spots in the planet, these critics may be charged with expecting the concept to cover too much. Indeed, the entry on "post- colonial criticism" included in the encyclopedia cited earlier discusses among the features of this perspective, in addition to its engagement with the rapport of the colonial margin with its metropolitan center, a set of reading practices that are informed by a sort of postcolonial awareness or sensibility irrespective of the site to which one might apply them (Benson and Conolly 1994:282). The versatility of signification that these various ascriptions confer to the concept would seem to endow it with virtually unlimited semantic reach. Postcolonial readings of Elizabethan theater now abound, and the compilation of essays entitled *The Postcolonial Middle Ages* (Cohen 2000), with chapters on Dante, Chaucer, and on a romance that evokes the strange adventures of Richard the Lion-Hearted, applies the postcolonial lens to cultural documents that precede by very long the historical moment commonly recognized as starting the colonial transaction.

Antillean intellects, scavenging for paradigms that might prove useful in the interpretation of their world, might justifiably doubt that so elastic a concept—so geographically vast and chronologically extensive—could have anything meaningful to contribute to their search for meaning. The Caribbean has indeed, like Indochina, suffered the assailment of colonialism, but it does not seem to follow that the same set of paradigms will suffice to explain the structure of life in both culture areas. Even within the Antillean world itself, Ramos and Rivera find enough diversity of colonial policy and experience as to think it unfeasible to arrive at "a general theory of Caribbean colonialism, much less about the outcomes" (Ramos and Rivera 2001:xvii). Coloniality does not manifest itself identically, homogeneously, within a cluster of nations and cultures such as the First or the Third World, in a culture area such as Africa or the Caribbean, or even in one single nation. The creole ruling classes in neocolonial societies often act as representatives of an external imperial order that sustains the status quo. The literature produced by the local henchmen of imperial power can hardly embody the "postcolonial condition" in the same way as those who devote their lives to bringing about social transformation and a complete removal of the legacy of colonial oppression. The Dominican Republic housed the late Joaquín Balaguer, a man who as a head of state squandered precious national resources on memorializing a glorified version of the Spanish colonial legacy and as a writer authored acidic tracts that promoted anti-Haitian hatred and preached negrophobic ideas of Dominican identity. If the framework of the new field hinges on the existence of a recognizable—hence classifiable—set of retaliatory attitudes toward the imperial center, as in the "writing back" of Salman Rushdie's now famous quirk, we would need to assign a place to the pro-colonialist within the epistemology of postcolonialism.

Apart from any objection stemming from the recognition that not every class within a country, nor every society within a region, nor every region within the colonized world has lived its coloniality in precisely the same way, Antillean voices would have reason to resist the ontological dilution that would result from their placement within the planet-wide identitarian frame of the postcolonial. Prior to the current organization of knowledge, Antillean thought had already for several generations essayed conceptual paradigms, schemes of thought, and axes of analysis deemed appropriate for explicating the region and its people. Already a body of utterances of compelling immediacy had accumulated in response to Western defamation and as an effort to proclaim the epistemological autonomy of the Antillean person. The Caribbean boasts of a long history of writing back and a rich repository of conceptual resources devised to interpret distinct characteristics of the Caribbean person's view of the world as well as to elucidate the multiple manifestations of the region's creolizing experience. The notions of "choteo" (Cuba), "gancho" and "aguaje" (Dominican Republic), "man-of-words" and "trickster" (Anglophone West Indies) are only a few of the expressions of the technology of existential cleverness that the Antillean person has cultivated to cope with a challenging history. Performative strategies deployed in the ordinary struggle for survival, they correspond to the idea of "mimicry" that Bhabha encounters in Lacan. The admission by Benítez-Rojo to Mayra Santos Febres that he could have drawn from the cosmology of Santería interpretive clues equal to those he found in the literature on "Chaos theory" that the West furnished him with attests to the existence of a rich storehouse of indigenous lines of inquiry and analytical tools. The region's spiritual syncretism, cross-cultural fusion, and constant breaching of ethnoracial lines, against a backdrop of domination and its ensuing resistance, whether concrete or symbolic, cannot but have resulted in people's development of distinct ways of looking at the world and unique ways of speaking about their place in the world.

Through the inclusion of several Caribbean texts, among them three selections from the writings of Brathwaite and one, placed at the very start, from Lamming's *Pleasures of Exile*, in their 86-chapter anthology *The Post-Colonial Studies Reader* (1995) Ashcroft, Griffiths, and Tiffin would seem to acknowledge that Antillean intellects have indeed had a meaningful say regarding the structure of the world that colonialism created. But their edited volume makes no gesture to signal the earned rank of Antilleans as precursors of the discursive stances therein represented. As their editorial project suggests, with the advent of the new organization of knowledge that the postcolonial approach espouses, the Caribbean becomes subsumed under a category that it does not dominate, with the inevitable result that it must relinquish the intellectual leadership it enjoyed three decades ago after centuries of reflection dedicated to refuting Western slander, asserting the humanity of the region's inhabitants, and extolling the creative legacy that the people there can share with the world. Some of the paradigms and emphases that Caribbean intellects pioneered now appear recognized as features of postcolonial discourse, with the inevitable consequence that the Caribbean loses credit since the center of the postcolonial resides elsewhere. The Caribbean may also lose the resources to speak about itself in the extent to which the paradigms devised by Antillean intellects, specifically to explain their world, become resignified as explanation of the postcolonial condition, thus presumably possessing equal aptitude to shed light on José Rizal's Philippines, James Joyce's Ireland, and J. M. Coetzee's South Africa.

Despite the success of the homogenizing of the Third World experience that has come with the advent of postcolonialism, Antillean intellects may remain unconvinced that the new field has something to say specifically about them. The Antillean identity of Dominican culture, for instance, resides in more than just the fact that the colonial transaction touched it. Few if any would venture to deny that Dominican culture differs significantly from the cultures of Argentina, Bangladesh, Equatorial Guinea, or Ireland, societies that colonialism has touched also. One could argue, in fact, that Antillean creativity and originality have to do in large measure with the ways in which people in the region have dealt socially, culturally, and existentially with their colonial experience. Puerto Rican sociologist Angel Quintero Rivera, speaking at a Caribbean conference at the University of Antioquia, Medellin, in November 2003, put it poignantly when he said: "We are not what has been made of us, but rather what we have made out of what has been done to us." Explorations of the uniqueness of the Antillean world by Jacques Stephen Aléxis, Gabriel García Márquez, Wilson Harris, and Aléjo Carpetier's focus on "the magical" yielded cultural products that brought the region's writers and thinkers to international prominence. The prestigious awards garnered by Saint John Perse, Derek Walcott, Edourd Glissant, Patrick Chamoiseau, and V. S. Naipaul came to add luster to the intellectual attention that the likes of Frantz Fanon, C. L. R. James, Juan Bosch, Eric Williams, and Cola Debrot had commanded. Prompted to some extent by the anticolonialist movement in the Third World and the emergence of Caribbean studies in the U.S. academy, either concomitant with black studies or within the Latin American subsection of area studies, the Antillean history of discursive self-assertion began to receive wide dissemination while the proverbial arrogance of Western discourse seemed momentarily to wane. Though written later, the words of García Márquez contextualizing his choice of Símon Bolívar as the character of his novel *El general en su laberinto* (1989) express the enthusiasm that the Antillean world often evoked at the time. "More than the glories of the character, I was interested in the Magdalena River, which I began to know as a child, traveling from the Caribbean coast, where I had the good fortune of being born" (1989:269).

Ironically, precisely at the moment when Caribbean utterances seemed to be on their way to becoming established as a major corpus through which a region spoke about humanity and history via the sustained reflection on its own condition, the academy's redistricting of the geography of knowledge came to arrest that development. Having begun to establish its credentials on the intellectual market as an economy with the ability to export ideas, the Caribbean, as in Baugh's testimony of foreign-trained Antilleans coming to the University of the West Indies armed with postcolonial paradigms, opens itself to becoming again an importer of conceptual commodities for which it must pay dearly even while painfully recognizing in them the traces of its own raw materials. Given the Western provenance of the postcolonial perspectives that now dominate the academic industry, Antillean intellects that have had for generations to safeguard their people from Western vilification may reasonably feel ill at ease in the current global order of knowledge. It will not escape notice among skeptical observers that the rise of postcolonialism, a meganarrative that, like the *Elegías* of Juan de Castellanos, breaks the world in two and applies a single reading mode to three-quarters of the population of the planet, comes at a time when Western thinkers have declared the inadequacy of master narratives. Post-structuralist and postmodernist thinkers have repudiated master narratives for their failure to account for the complexity of the human experience. However, the Western academy has become tolerant with the meganarrative of postcolonialism, almost as if suggesting that while all-encompassing systems of thought will fail to explain the Western subject, they still remain epistemologically satisfactory to account for the inhabitants of the postcolonial world. This practice of exporting to the Third World the conceptual refuse that no longer suits the study of the Western subject perhaps too closely parallels the European and U.S. corporate manufacturers' habit of exporting to Africa or Latin America some of the consumer products banned in the First World due to the threat they pose to personal safety or the environment.

Some have cautioned against the self-confidency of the postcolonial perspective in that often the voices involved equate their formal oppositionality with radicalism, running the risk of confusing "theoretical insight" with real social change (Gugelberber 1994:584). Aijaz Ahmed, for instance, has observed that the term "postcolonial" had a more head-on political value with the authors who used it in earlier generations, prior to the neutralizing resignification deployed by current spokespersons of the postcolonial condition (Ahmed 1995:11, 28). Beyond the question of depoliticized utterance, yet another suspicion emerges in relation to the stage of world capitalism in which the new field was born. I mean by this the current political configuration of the global economy, a moment when the great capitalist powers, having defeated the ideological competition presented by the socialist bloc, have come to wield authority over the planet. From their unchallenged supremacy, they urge states in the Third World to loosen their national borders and remove trade barriers in their local economies so that Western-dominated world capital can flow unencumbered as if in a pastorally transnational terrain. The local economies of the periphery have in that context become increasingly less able to resist the dictates of the countries that make up the Group of Seven, which, through such regulatory arms as the International Monetary Fund and the Inter-American Development Bank, have increasingly exacerbated the dependent conditions of regions like the Caribbean. Antillean societies today have severely reduced their possibility of devising strategies of their own to pursue a sort of development that could at least alter the situation that causes the population to have to go elsewhere in order to secure their material well-being.

In a disquieting parallel manner, the mega gaze sponsored by the post-colonial perspective sets conceptual norms for the national and regional cultures of the Third World to follow, proposing to them a new order of world culture. In that new order the identitarian consequences of having shared a colonial past with nations and peoples in different points of the globe and at disparate moments in history constitutes a decisive force of cohesion that determines and transnationalizes their cultural being. This scheme diminishes the value of the cultural meaning stemming from the specificities that have characterized the human experience in each national or regional locus even with respect to its autochthonous ways of dealing with the colonial transaction. If postmodernism constitutes the cultural logic of late capitalism, in keeping with the formulation by Fredric Jameson, then postcolonialism would certainly merit description as the cultural logic of the current phase of globalization (Jameson 1991). This new order has given currency to a cognitive ambience wherein a college teacher can, without thinking twice about it, design a course whose reading list features a Chilean novelist, a Jamaican poet, an essayist from Hong Kong, an African American short-fiction writer, a social critic from New Zealand, a Filipino scholar, and a couple of authors from different regions of India, all brought together on the same plane of signification by the legitimizing frame offered by the post-colonial perspective. To lend credibility to the preceding observation, suffice it to mention a book of interviews with writers from "the postcolonial world" whose editors, apart from noting the place of Joyce as "a central figure for many of the post-colonial writers," include in their collection conversations with African, Caribbean, Chicano, Indian, Maori, and Pakistani authors (Jussawalla and Dasenbrock 1992:15). This new world order of knowledge does not bode well for the Antillean world. Among various possible adverse consequences, a reduction of possibility for studying, promoting, and dis-seminating information about specifically Caribbean cultural processes may take place. The panoptic glance at the totality of the "postcolonial world" may gain in ascendancy in inverse proportion to the diminished interest in looking closely at the societies and culture areas that make up the planet's hab-itable space. Antillean thought would in such a scenario find it hard to assert itself on the international intellectual market, which is likely to remain in the grip of those postcolonial thinkers who, through their deployment of Western paradigms and their reliance on Western thinkers to shed light on Third World situations, contribute to the continued hegemony of Western discourse. But ultimately the gravest consequence will be a gradual defamiliarization of Antillean thought since, as the history that follows intends to stress, only a concentrated look at the region's specificity can realistically empower the learner to interpret with sobriety the complexity of Caribbean life.

The Enduring Plantation

Caribbean intellectual production has centered around the search for answers to a number of seemingly everlasting questions about the region and its people. To the extent that it has meditated about dynamics on a global scale, it has sought primarily to foreground the region's interconnection with developments elsewhere on the planet, as when Eric Williams studied the rise of industrial capitalism in Britain in relation to British operations in the Caribbean (Williams 1944). The manner in which the colonial transaction, through the interlacing of the transatlantic slave trade and the economic geography of the East India Company route, linked the Antillean world to

Africa, Europe, and Asia would make the implications of the region's interrelation with the rest of the world a practically inescapable object of inquiry. This is so especially in light of the widespread awareness that even today the terms in which Antilleans can soundly imagine a future for their societies were set long ago by the texture of that interrelation. Adams Smith described it insightfully over two centuries ago when he, highlighting the "discovery of America, and that of a passage to the East Indies by the Cape of Good Hope," as the greatest events recorded in human history, succinctly noted the consequences that ensued for each of the populations involved:

> By uniting, in some measure, the most distant parts of the world, by enabling them to relieve one another's wants, to increase one another's enjoyments, and to encourage one another's industry, their general tendency would seem to be beneficial. To the natives, however, both of the East and West Indies, all the commercial benefits which can have resulted from these events have been sunk and lost in the dreadful misfortunes which they have occasioned. (Smith 1994:675–676)

The sense that the past endures, that it remains unresolved, conditions Antillean intellects to search for principles, patterns, and institutions that offer clues to an adequate understanding of the history that explains, in the words of James, "where we have reached, who we are and what we are" (1969:46). James was categorical in stating that the region's history was "governed by two factors, the sugar plantation and Negro slavery" (1963:391). Similarly, in a book published a year after these words by James appeared in print, the Cuban historian Manuel Moreno Fraginals published *El ingenio* (1964), a study in which he hoped, through the scrutiny of certain aspects in a series of "critical periods of our sugar-producing life," to facilitate the removal of "the dark veil that covers Cuban history" (Moreno Fraginals 1964:x; 1976:10). Several decades before, Ramiro Guerra, the dean of twentieth-century Cuban historians, presented distinct manifestations in the development of the sugar industry as key to deciding not only the racial composition of the population but also determining the ruin or prosperity of the society as a whole (Guerra 1964:4–6). A contemporary of Guerra, Fernando Ortiz viewed the sugar plantation, in its contrapuntal rapport with the tobacco industry, as the historical site wherein the process of transculturation that he deemed "indispensable for an understanding of the history of Cuba" reached its final consolidation (1970:103).

The plantation, not only of sugar, has continued in later generations of Antillean thinkers to provide a rich terrain for the examination of the emergence as well as the distinguishing features of society and culture at the national and regional levels. Brathwaite concentrated intensely on a key moment of the Anglophone West Indian plantation and the social dynamics that it spawned to trace the processes that resulted in the formation of Jamaica's "creole society" and to establish that, out of the fusion of the two great traditions of Africa and Europe, came "authentically local institutions, and an Afro-creole 'little' tradition among the slave 'folk,' " and that "despite the imitation, despite the inefficiency, despite the debasements caused by slavery," Jamaica, during the period spanning 1770–1820, "was a viable creative entity" (Brathwaite 1971:307, 309). By the same token, Glissant, Brathwaite's Martinican contemporary, in proposing to liberate his country's historiography from a chronology determined by "the French historical model (centuries, wars, reigns, crises, etc.)," offers a periodization that hinges on the plantation as its central axis:

> The slave trade, settlement.
> The world of the slaves.
> The plantation system.
> The appearance of the elite, urban life.
> The triumph of beet sugar over cane sugar.
> Legitimized-legitimizing assimilation.
> The threat of oblivion. (Glissant 1989:88–89)

Among the Antillean intellects of Glissant's and Brathwaite's generation, Benítez-Rojo, who could easily draw on the rich legacy of conceptual speculation about the sugar industry in his native Cuba, went farthest in postulating the plantation as a paradigm useful for analyzing holistically the structure of life in the Caribbean region. Beyond the appeal that many may find in *The Repeating Island's* deployment of "Chaos" as an analytical category, the book's enduring contribution, punctuated by dexterous readings of Las Casas, Guillén, Fernando Ortiz, Carpentier, Harris, Fanny Buitrago, and Edgardo Rodríguez Julía, is the author's commitment to bring to light the salience of the Antillean world in global affairs throughout modern history:

> the Atlantic is today the Atlantic (the navel of capitalism) because Europe, in its mercantilist laboratory, conceived the prospect of inseminating the Caribbean womb with the blood of Africa; the Atlantic is today the Atlantic (Nato, World Bank, New York Stock Exchange, European Economic Community, etc.) because it was the painfully delivered child of the Caribbean, whose vagina was stretched between continental clamps, between the encomienda of Indians and the slave holding plantation, between the servitude of the coolie and the discrimination toward the *criollo*, between the commercial monopoly and piracy, between the runaway slave's settlement and the governor's palace; all Europe pulling on the forceps to help at the birth of the Atlantic: Columbus, Cabral, de Soto, Hawkins, Drake, Hein, Rodney, Surcouf . . . . (Benítez-Rojo 1992:5)

Central to Benítez-Rojo's formulation of Caribbean salience in world affairs is what he called the "Plantation" machine, "capitalized to indicate not just the presence of plantations but also the type of society that results from their use and abuse," and whose "incredible and dolorous history" includes the mobilization of "no fewer than ten million African slaves and thousands of coolies (from India, China, and Malaysia)," the turning out of "mercantile capitalism, industrial capitalism, . . . African underdevelopment, Caribbean population," while producing "imperialism, wars, colonial blocs, rebellions, repressions, sugar islands, runaway settlements, air and naval bases, revolutions of all sorts, and even a 'free associated state' next to an unfree socialist state" (Benítez-Rojo 1992:9).

Perhaps mindful that the plantation did not occur in the same way in every territory within the Antillean world, historian Alfonso Múnera has reasonably warned against too exclusive a focus on that phenomenon lest "we impoverish Caribbean history" (Múnera 1999:7). Coming from a native of Cartagena, a Caribbean section of Colombia where the plantation system did not exist despite the city's importance as a repository of slaves and marketplace for the sale of enslaved blacks, the warning merits attention (Múnera 1998:64). But for an intellectual history of the region, meaningful attention to the plantation (with or without the word "machine" that Benítez-Rojo adopts from Deleuze), seems indispensable. On the plantation it was that the slave master reached the pinnacle of his depravity, as illustrated by some of the entries in the diary of Thomas Thistlewood, a young Englishman who came to Jamaica in 1750 to work as an estate overseer. The diarist kept a meticulous account of his cruel ingenuity for devising punishment for slaves who trespassed plantation rules, such as disciplining a slave named Derby for "eating canes" by having him "well flogged and pickled, then made Hector shit in his mouth," or whipping "Hector for losing his hoe" and then making "New Negro Joe piss in his eyes and mouth and c," or, after gagging and tying hands and feet of Hazat, for attempted escape, he "rubbed him with molasses and exposed him naked to the flies all day, and to the mosquitoes all night, without fire" (Hall 1999:72–73).

The plantation provided the prism through which the West looked at the Caribbean, as evinced by the epithets "Cane isles" (III.91), "Caribbe's cane isles" (IV. 21–22), and "Cane-land islands" (IV. 242–243) in James Grainger's *The Sugar Cane* (1764), a neoclassical georgic poem that evokes the cultivation and manufacture of sugar against the backdrop of the flora, fauna, and daily plantation life on the island of St. Christopher. Urging planters to "let humanity prevail" and acknowledging that the enslaved workers may in their native lands have themselves possessed "large fertile plains, and slaves, and herds" (IV. 211–213), the poem closes with the speaker's wish for his country's continued control of the

Isles which on Britain for their all depend
And must forever [V. 676–677]. (Grainger 2000)

The plantation turned the Antillean world into a realm of opportunity, a site conducive to the full realization of the economic aspirations of Western individuals such as Mr. Rochester in Charlotte Bronte's *Jane Eyre* (1847) whose material well-being and idiosyncratic lifestyle are owed to his former ventures in the plantation economy of the West Indies, the place whence he brought the mad woman he keeps in the attic. Conversely, with the advent of an era of cultural self-affirmation, the plantation has given Antillean intellects an all-embracing image through which to invoke the region. The speaker in Pedro Mir's 1949 poem *Hay un país en el mundo* locates his Dominican homeland in the midst of an "improbable archipelago of sugar and alcohol" [un inverosímil archipiélago de azúcar y alcohol] (Mir 1993:2–3). The plantation, then, seems inevitable for anyone tracing the intellectual history of the region, and perhaps in addition to resorting to the plantation machine as an analytical category, as does Benítez-Rojo, a minimal attempt would come in handy here to outline for the region some of the intra-Caribbean mobility of the machine in question so as to suggest ways of studying the history that has given it the metaphorical valence it has had at least since Fernando Ortiz. One may attempt a minimal overview of the plantation in the Antillean world by drawing from the materials brought conveniently together by the editors of the *General History of the Caribbean* as well as from a still unpublished history of the region with a focus on the plantation by the historian Frank Moya Pons whose work, once published, will make it more possible for students of the Caribbean to see the region in truly holistic terms.

The plantation flourished in the Antillean world shortly after the beginning of the conquest. By 1527, with 19 ingenios and 6 trapiches operating at full capacity on "Española," the sugar plantation had proven economically successful in Santo Domingo, the first colony settled by the Spaniards (Moya Pons 1999:67–68). The advent of this industry led to the great demographic transformation that the archipelago witnessed, with the massive importation of Africans, the decimation of the aboriginal inhabitants, and the fierce imperial competition that Spain had to face mostly from Holland, England, and France. The industry soon waned in Santo Domingo, having practically disappeared by the late sixteenth century. The following century it reappeared on the island again, but now on the western side over which Spanish authorities had lost colonial control. That piece of the island had fallen into French hands and now went by the name of Saint Domingue. Jean Ducasse, the French governor of Saint Domingue, encouraged the construction of sugar mills at the end of the seventeenth century, a time when 1,500 French colonists there used 1,000 black slaves and 2,000 white indentured servants to cultivate the land. As plantations multiplied, so did the number of enslaved Africans imported to the colony, reaching the figure of 24,146 by 1713, which had become 452,000 by 1789, when the white population had reached a mere 38,825 (Moya Pons). Already by 1776, Adams Smith, as an economically inclined observer, could describe the French colony of Hispaniola as "the most important of the sugar colonies of the West Indies, and its produce is said to be greater than that of all the sugar of English colonies put together" (Smith 1994:616). By then the mulattos controlled one-third of the land, causing whites to seek to thwart their social mobility by enacting discriminatory laws that would reduce them to second-class citizenship. These included an ordinance that barred their employment in health-related professions, a colonial legislation that forbade the marriage of mulatto women to white men, and a prohibition that made it unlawful for mulattos to give themselves the title of monsieur or madame, required them to wear clothes made of inferior fabric as compared to those worn by whites, and forced them to quit their own table at home whenever a white man happened to drop in for lunch or dinner.

The Society of the Friends of Blacks, organized by rich mulattos living in France, came into existence to address these injustices and to demand the recognition of the full rights of mulattos as French citizens. They influenced the French National Assembly but the *grand blancs* in the colony would not budge, leading to the 1791 mulatto armed rebellion headed by Vincent Ogé and Jean Baptiste Chavannes that culminated in the execution of the leaders and their 200 followers. The slaves, left out of all human rights agendas, began a rebellion of their own in August of 1791, facing both the mulattos and the white planters. They forged an alliance with Spain, which saw in the slave rebellion an opportunity to defeat France. Slave rebels Biassou, Jean François, and Toussaint Loverture for a time fought under the Spanish flag as "auxiliaries." The English, for their part, hoping to exert control on the Saint Domingue sugar industry, had joined the war in support of the French *grand blancs* who rose up in arms to oppose the economic measures that the Civil Commission of the revolutionary government had enacted. Commissioner Léger Felicité Sonthonax, fearing defeat by the Spanish and the English, took the shrewd measure of inviting the blacks to the French side in exchange for the abolition of slavery, which was confirmed by a law on August 29, 1793. When Toussaint, at the head of an army of 4,000 blacks, deserted the Spanish flank and came to the side of the French, the Spanish and the English soon had to give up their plan to dominate Saint Domingue.

As governor and commander in chief of the French army in Saint Domingue, Toussaint sought to rebuild the ruined economy of the colony by forcing former slaves to work for a salary on the plantations. The workers received one-quarter of the harvest of each plantation, with another quarter going to the owner, and the remaining half to the colonial government. Toussaint's policy, formulated in an agricultural code issued on October 12, 1800 angered the planters who felt oppressed by the new measures (Moya Pons). The new French government of Napoleon Bonaparte, who had come to power through a coup d'état in November 1799, had no intention of honoring the abolition of slavery promulgated by the previous administration. Pressured by absentee plantation owners living in Paris and other constituencies interested in regaining control of the colony, Napoleon first got Spain to yield Louisiana to France in October 1800 and then sent a fleet of more than 80 ships staffed by 58,000 soldiers to take Saint Domingue out of the hands of the former slaves. With the arrival of the French troops led by General Leclerc on January 29, 1802, the war escalated to unprecedented levels of bloodshed. When Toussaint was captured by the French in June 1802, his lieutenants, former slaves Jean Jacques Dessalines and Henry Christophe increased the intensity of the hostilities, defeating Napolean's army by the end of December 1803. Dessalines proclaimed the Republic of Haiti on January 1, 1804 and the newly founded Haitian State issued a constitution that made it unlawful for whites ever to own land or buildings in the country, putting an end to the colonial regime in the former Saint Domingue.

The Haitian uprising was the largest of several rebellions occurring in the Caribbean concurrently with the French Revolution. In Martinique too the *grand blancs* refused the March 8, 1790 National Assembly edict that ratified the rights of mulattos to vote and run for office. The *grand blancs* of Martinique and Guadeloupe in 1791, hearing about the slave rebellion in Saint Domingue, defied the French revolutionary government and forged an alliance with Britain with the purpose of separating from France. They fought the mulattos, the *petits blancs*, and the Republican authorities, whom they defeated. On March 20, 1794 Republican General Rochambeau surrendered to the British, who held control of the colony until 1802. Through a similar alliance of the *grand blancs* with the British, Guadeloupe also fell out of French control in April 1794. Ironically, Commissioners Victor Hughes and Pierre Chretien arrived in Guadeloupe at the head of 1,100 soldiers, unaware that the French authorities had capitulated, and successfully fought the British who had to abandon the island in December, when a Jacobin regime was installed. Commissioner Hughes respected the February 4, 1794 abolition decree but forced blacks to remain in the plantation as salaried workers. General Antoine Richepanse, leading a fleet sent by Napoleon, came to Guadeloupe to restore the colony to its former state, just as Leclerc did in Saint Domingue. The opposition to the invasion, led mainly by mulatto commander Louis Delgrès and 1,000 rebels, suffered a grievous defeat. On July 16, 1802, the revolutionary movement crushed, slavery returned to Guadeloupe.

The death of Haitian revolutionary leader Dessalines refueled the old conflict between mulattos and blacks. The latter, led by Christophe, captured the North, and the former, led by Alexandre Pétion, controlled the South. Christophe maintained the plantation regime. Pétion distributed the arable land among his supporters, who used them mostly for subsistence crops, causing a severe decline of sugar production and agricultural exports. Pétion died in 1818, leaving the throne to Boyer, who, following the death of Christophe in 1820, unified the country at the end of October. Boyer continued the distribution of land among his supporters, hence the continued decline of sugar exports. Boyer's unification of Hispaniola on February 9, 1822 led to a series of ill-fated policies (confiscation of state property, requirement of property titles, nationalization of Church property, and allotment of parcels to Haitian officers), which eventually earned him serious opposition. The rural code, promulgated on May 1, 1826, sought to reorganize the economy by forcing peasants to work on plantations or endure punishment. The policy did not work on either side of the island. Boyer needed to raise funds to honor Haiti's commitment to compensate the French planters, merchants, and bankers who had lost their assets with the dismantling of the colonial regime. King Charles X had prevailed upon the Haitian authorities to agree to that deal in July 1825 by having a warship on the shore of Port-au-Prince with instructions to bombard the city should they decline the deal. Haiti would pay 150 million francs, and in return France recognized the small country's independence. Haiti's economic difficulties, following a series of failed policies, led to political upheaval and the overthrow of Boyer. Haitian and Dominican liberals collaborated in the movement that deposed Boyer, who fled with his family to Jamaica on March 13, 1843. Boyer's regime may be said to have consolidated the Haitian and Dominican peasantry on both sides of the island.

Contemporaneous with the Haitian Revolution, the British Antilles wrestled with the impact of the abolitionist movement, which had begun in the United States and Britain under the leadership of evangelical Quaker groups. The British Parliament received several petitions to abolish slavery in the late eighteenth century. The Haitian example terrified the British and made the idea of abolition less palatable since England might lose its valuable possessions and reduce its presence on the international market. Also, the decline of Saint Domingue as a sugar production center, gave way to the rise of Jamaica, making slavery there even more important than it had been. With its slave population growing from 226,000 in 1788 to 308,000 in 1802, Jamaica's plantation system enjoyed the protection of the British government, which viewed control of the world sugar market as a priority. Abolitionists, for their part, allied themselves with pro-slavery planters from the older English colonies who feared increased competition resulting from increased sugar production in Trinidad and the other newly acquired possessions. Through their success with the House of Commons and the House of Lords, which by 1805 had approved a legislation that prohibited the further importation of slaves to the British colonies, the planters and merchants of the old colonies sought to cut the labor supply line of their competitors, while extending a courtesy to the abolitionists (Moya Pons).

The governments of Britain and the United States for the first three decades of the nineteenth century involved themselves emphatically in a trade war for access to and control of the European sugar market. As the Americans had the upper hand, the British Caribbean suffered severe price inflation, food shortages, poverty, and hunger, which adversely affected the slave populations whose situation worsened during the Anglo-American war of 1812. The French and Spanish Antilles did not suffer the same fate because of their continued access to American goods, but colonists in Antigua, for instance, lacked even the lumber needed for use in coffins to bury their dead after a devastating hurricane and the colonial authorities of Dominica considered relocating the entire population to Guyana, which was among the only British colonies still thriving in the sugar market. Pressure from planters and sugar merchants caused British authorities to resume free commerce with the United States, leading to an 1830 reciprocal trade agreement that finally settled the disputes. Trinidadian planters managed to increase their sugar production substantially by 1834 due to the introduction of new varieties of cane from Tahiti as well as the modernization of some sugar mills, which began to use steam-powered machines, thus reducing the need for slave labor (Moya Pons).

The Samuel Sharpe rebellion in Jamaica in December 1831 at a time when emancipation supporter, William IV, held the throne of England, met with fierce reaction by planters, who burned 16 Baptist churches and crushed the insurgents. Subsequently with the rise to power in Parliament of a new leadership without connection to the West Indian planters, slavery came to an end in the British colonies starting August 1, 1834. The emancipation proclamation applied to children under six and children born to slave mothers from that date onward. All others would remain as apprentices in the care of their masters until August 1, 1840. Apprenticeship meant that they would only work for their masters five days a week and could use the rest of their time to work for themselves or find gainful employment (Claypole and Robottom 1989:168–169). The British government created a fund of 1 million pounds sterling to support planters and other slave owners in this transition. Antigua planters found it more economically expedient to emancipate their slaves totally on August 1, 1834, skipping the apprenticeship period. Slaves in Saint Kitts and Nevis rebelled against the apprenticeship system, but the planters defeated them using soldiers brought from Antigua. The planters implemented practices aimed at boycotting the productivity of slaves in order to keep them from becoming independent of their master's plantations. Convinced that sugar production would benefit from employing paid labor, the Montserrat assembly and the colonial authorities of Nevis decreed the complete emancipation of all slaves from August 1, 1838. The British government then amended the abolition law to reflect this new turn of events, and, as the assemblies of all the other English colonies concurred, slavery came to an end officially in the West Indies.

With the end of slavery, the formerly captive workers practically deserted the plantations. Whenever possible they preferred to work for themselves in small plots of land that they often managed to acquire. This is the time when Trollope visited the region, commiserated with white planters, and characterized free blacks as lazy, suggesting that their view of "emancipation was and is emancipation from work" (Trollope 1999:90). Whenever possible, also, the planters managed to retain the former slaves attached to their former jobs, promoting laws meant to suppress idleness, loitering, gambling, and illegal meetings. By the same token, the fluctuating salaries on the plantations from one island to another as well as the insufficient amount of land for workers to own in the smaller colonies led to considerable intra-Caribbean labor migration. Many workers from Barbados, Nevis, and Montserrat headed for the plantations of Trinidad and Guyana despite prohibition against emigration by the colonial assemblies of those islands. In general, however, emancipation resulted in a continuous labor shortage for the large-scale sugar industry, causing the importation of workers from abroad. The sentiment expressed by Mr. Mason, Antoinette's father-in-law in *Wide Sargasso Sea* by Jean Rhys, that the decay of the plantation is "enough to break your heart" and the consequent plan to "import labourers" perhaps captures the malaise of the white population at the time, a plight to which the author, as a white creole from Dominica, was particularly sensitive (Rhys

1982:35). Workers came from Sierra Leone, Ireland, Germany, the United States, Canada, Portugal, China, and India. The passage of workers from India to the Caribbean ended only in 1917 when the Indian government terminated their contractual exportation.

A turning point occurred in 1841 when French industrialist Paul Daubrée proposed to the planters of Guadeloupe and Martinique a plan that would separate farm from industrial work. The earthquake of February 8, 1843, which destroyed over 40 sugar mills in Guadeloupe alone, created the conditions for planters to begin building the steam-powered central factory suggested by Daubrée. Four of these factories began operating in 1845, initiating a revamping of the sugar industry in the French colonies, which until then lagged behind their English counterparts. These central factories used slave labor but also required some skilled workers for specialized tasks. As a result the colonial government in 1845 created a fund to subsidize the importation of white workers. On July 18, 1845 the French government created a fund to provide loans to slaves to buy their freedom and acquire small plots of land. Following the liberal revolution that had begun in France in February 1848, which brought the abolitionists to power, the colonial authorities of the French Caribbean immediately realized the wisdom of giving in to the demands of the blacks who called for an end to their bondage. Therefore, when the French government proclaimed the abolition of slavery on April 27, 1848 in Paris, the colonial authorities had already decreed their own emancipation on April 22 in Guadeloupe and April 26 in Martinique. While no system comparable to the British apprenticeship period was put in place to protect the interests of planters, they did get an indemnity of 126 million francs as compensation. On the whole, emancipation led to labor shortage for the plantations of the French Caribbean colonies just as it had in their English counterparts. The colonial authorities also designed repressive measures to force freedmen to work on the plantation (Moya Pons). Thus emerged the "workbook system," which required each former slave to carry at all times a notebook that identified with precision the carrier's contracts, nature of work, and schedule of service on the plantation. Anyone caught without the notebook would go to court, face a charge of vagrancy, and do time working without compensation for his or her former master. The workbook system, having functioned with limited success, ended in 1870. But, like their British peers, the French planters also resorted to importing contracted workers. These came initially from France and Portugal and then from Africa and India between 1854 and 1889.

The sugar industry in Cuba received its first major boost with the English invasion of Havana in August 1762 because the British price per slave was cheaper than what Cuban planters had been paying to their local supplier. To the chagrin of Cuban planters, a year later England returned Cuba to Spain, bending to pressure by British planters who feared a permanent annexation would increase the sugar supply to the detriment of their market. With the demise of the plantation regime in Saint Domingue, many French planters brought their know-how to Cuba. The sugar industry on the island really began to accelerate after 1820 with the advent of mechanization, simulating the growth of the slave population to nearly a million by 1860. As the growth of the slave population did not suffice to address the need for labor on the island, the plantation resorted to importing contracted Chinese workers. By 1874 Cuba had received over 120,000 Chinese laborers, who had to work 84 hours per week—even more during the harvest—and sustained severe corporal punishment to force them to conform to plantation life. The planters constantly enacted regulations to control the mobility of these workers and prevent them from obtaining their freedom prior to concluding the eight-year period stipulated in their contract. However, the Chinese proved difficult to control, often attempting to escape and killing themselves at a higher rate than other groups in the labor pool. Even so, through a combination of black and Chinese labor plus major advances in mechanization, Cuba became in the 1860s the world's main sugar producer.

Puerto Rico's sugar industry received the influx of foreign investors who were attracted by the incentive offered by the 1815 Cédula de Gracias, a decree whereby any white Catholic foreigner from a nation on friendly terms with Spain could settle there for free, enjoying a land grant of up to six acres per family member and up to three per slave (Engerman and Higman 1997:79). As a result, four out of every five planters in Ponce by 1827 had been born elsewhere. When importing slaves directly from Africa ceased to be practical, the plantation economy began to suffer from labor shortages. By 1838, planters convinced the governor to use repressive measures to secure laborers for the plantation. Promulgated in June 1849, the *Reglamento de Jornaleros* (Laborers Bylaw) required peasants with less than four cuerdas of land to work as day laborers. The peasants had to carry a notebook detailing their current status as workers, failing which, they would face a penalty of a minimum of eight days of arduous labor in public works. This practice closely resembled the workbook system implemented by the colonial authorities in the French Caribbean. In June 1850, the colonial assembly took special measures to concentrate share-croppers in towns to make them available to the sugar and coffee plantations as needed. Representing the poorest segment of Puerto Rican society, the share-croppers usually worked for peasant families for room and board, lacking any other support network (Moya Pons). In the sugar-producing areas, the plantation owners managed to keep their laborers perennially in debt so they would never leave. The planters would keep their employees' workbooks until they paid their debt while the company continued to offer them food and merchandise on credit, further increasing their indebtedness. Also, after 1850 Puerto Rico could no longer import even contraband slaves, thus exacerbating the manual labor crisis. Even so, by 1850 the island was second only to Cuba as a sugar producer in the Caribbean.

Abolitionism in nineteenth-century Cuba and Puerto Rico invariably met obstacles posed by the conflicting interests of Spain, the United States, and Great Britain. Several conspiracies involving slaves failed on both islands during the first three decades of the century. Then began a reform movement represented by the likes of José Antonio Saco who worried about the "demo-graphic disparity" created by the continuous importation of slaves. Spain intensified its repressive measures in Cuba and Puerto Rico, declaring a sta-tus of martial law in 1837. Consistent with the existence of a movement that favored annexation to the United States, nearly two-thirds of the clandestine slave trade that supplied the Cuban plantation economy came on American ships. Conspiracies organized by white abolitionists and black organizers continued, leading to the La Escalera conspiracy discovered in January 1844. Fearing another Haiti, at the beginning of 1844, a group of wealthy Cuban planters and traders offered President John Tyler the sum of 100 million dollars to help the United States purchase Cuba from Spain and would later offer 3 million to finance an independence movement led by Narciso López. After an initial failure, López tried a second time around in May 1850, when he arrived in Cardenas accompanied by an army of 600 Americans and 5 Cubans, in a sort of proto "Bay of Pigs" operation. The expedition failed, and Lopez tried again the following year, falling into the hands of Spanish officers, who executed him on September 1, 1851 (Montes-Huidobro 1995:xvii–xviii). The Cuban Junta of New York, catering to the whims of annexationists, asked Mississippi Governor John A. Quitman to organize an invasion of Cuba, which he did in November 1854, suffering a quick defeat. The United States, having acquired Florida from Spain for US$5 million in 1820, sought to purchase Cuba, offering US$130 million in September 1854, but Spain refused to part with the "pearl of the Antilles."

Spain also sought to thwart negotiations whereby the United States intended to acquire the peninsula and the Bay of Samaná in the Dominican Republic for a navy coaling station. A Spanish trade agent arrived in Santo Domingo in November 1854 offering to recognize Dominican independ-ence. He immediately joined the English and French agents who also wished to block the American plans in the country. When the Dominican ruling elite, invoking the threat of a Haitian invasion, asked for Spanish protection, Spanish diplomats suggested the annexation of the Dominican Republic to Spain. The head of the Spanish government, General Leopoldo O'Donnell, a former governor of Cuba, viewed Spanish intervention as an opportunity to rebuild the former Spanish Empire in the Americas as well as to keep both Haitians and Americans at bay, especially after October 1860, when the Dominican navy had to expel American adventurers who had taken over some small Dominican islands that were rich in guano. Then follows the annexation of the Dominican Republic to the Spanish crown and the subse-quent nationalist war that concludes with victory to the Dominican rebels in July 1865.

The war in the Dominican Republic caused trouble to the government of O'Donnell, who stepped down in 1864. The change of government and the polarization of opinion triggered by the Dominican affair in Madrid refueled the reform movement, especially as a new governor, sympathetic to the reformers, had come to Cuba. Soon the independence movement regained momentum. On October 10, 1868, on the sugar plantation of Damajuana in

Yara, the insurgents proclaimed the birth of the Republic of Cuba. Their manifesto made provisions for the gradual abolition of slavery and adequate compensation for slave owners. A pro-independence revolutionary movement had erupted weeks before—early September 1868—in the town of Lares, Puerto Rico, while simultaneously a liberal revolution in Spain, on September 16, 1868, overthrew the conservative regime, forcing the queen to seek refuge in France. The three movements had a common liberal strand, but just as the Spanish liberal abolitionists were not progressive enough to consider granting independence to their Hispanic Antillean colonies, so the Cuban and Puerto Rican liberals lacked the vision to espouse the abolition of slavery pure and simple. The Cuban revolutionary leader Carlos Manuel de Céspedes liberated his slaves to use them as soldiers on October 10, 1868, but he opposed the total abolition promoted by black leader Antonio Maceo and his followers. Céspedes did not allow runaway slaves into the revolutionary army and disapproved of any slaves to leave their plantations unless their owners authorized it. The new Spanish government's decree, which, beginning at the end of September 1868, granted freedom to all children born to slave mothers, by virtue of the so-called free womb law, did not get to be enforced in the colony.

Finally, Spain, figuring that such a measure would lessen the possibility of a U.S. military invasion of Cuba, approved the "Moret Law" on July 1870 (Eltis 1999:125). This law, proposed by Foreign Minister Segismundo Moret, granted freedom to all slaves born after September 17, 1868, to those over 60, those who had fought for the Spanish troops during the war, all slaves owned by the State, and any contraband slaves the colonial government had allocated illegally to planters. Though the Moret Law included an arrangement whereby freed youths would stay working with their masters until age 22, it constituted a far more progressive measure than the Cuban and Puerto Rican independence leaders had considered. Cuban planters blocked the publication of the new law in the colony for months, and its full execution did not begin until 1872. Puerto Rican delegates to the Spanish courts continued to lobby for the immediate abolition of slavery with compensation for the slave owners, especially as many planters had established that the industry would benefit from a switch to salaried workers. Having thus convinced the courts, they received approval for a law that liberated the remaining 29,335 slaves on the island on March 22, 1873. The implementation of the law provided that owners would receive their compensation within six months and that former slaves would continue working for their masters for a period of at least three years.

Meanwhile, the sugar bonanza made Cuban planters firmer in their opposition to abolition. The rebel leaders then convinced Céspedes to attack all plantations as a way to weaken Spain's economic power. Many rebel leaders freed the slaves who had fought in their ranks. Even so, Spain won the war and the revolutionary leaders had to sign a peace treaty called the Zanjón Pact on February 11, 1878. The pact granted freedom to all slaves and Chinese laborers who had fought in the war irrespective of the faction they had joined. The deal did not provide for total abolition nor for Cuban independence, and many rebel leaders remained dissatisfied. Black leader Antonio Maceo did not put down his arms and had to leave the island in 1878 to go to the Dominican Republic under protection of nationalist Gregorio Luperón. Another war broke out, known in Cuba as the "small war," in the summer of 1879, but the colonial forces defeated the insurgents in October 1880. Abolition came to Cuba, as it did throughout the region, when the planters managed to resolve the matter of their compensation and their constant supply of labor.

By the 1870s, Chinese immigration having been prohibited in 1874, Cuban planters had become adept at using a combination of indentured, servile, and salaried labor force that included Canary Islanders, white Creoles, Chinese laborers, as well as enslaved and free blacks. Through their delegates in the Spanish courts, they prevailed upon the authorities to institute the Patronage Law, which replaced the Moret Law on February 13, 1880 (Craton 1997:260). The new law stipulated that slaves would remain with their masters working for a monthly stipend, room and board, and medical care for a period of eight years, following which, as freedmen, they would hire themselves out in a known trade for an additional four years. Those who deviated from the prescribed path would face a charge of vagrancy, which carried a penalty of forced labor. While patronage contemplated the possibility for slaves to buy their freedom in the process, it provided a mechanism that assured planters the continuity of slave labor for as many as 12 years.

By 1881 beet sugar dominated the world market, and this had a serious impact on the Caribbean sugar industry, which had to step up its effort to modernize in order to survive the competition. Modernization in some instances led to a rapid increase in production and in 1884 a global overproduction of sugar caused a great trade crisis resulting in a serious decline in sugar prices. Many producers consequently went out of business, leading to the reduction of sugar mills and the consolidation of land and other assets into ever fewer hands. Peasant ownership of land also became a notable feature of life in the region. Especially in the Spanish and the French colonies the central factories bought up neighboring plantations and greatly increased their holdings. Mechanization transformed the sugar industry in Puerto Rico, which attracted foreign merchants and businessmen as investors. In 1888 the colonial government of Puerto Rico contracted a French firm to build a railroad connecting all the sugar cane districts around the island. Coffee production in Puerto Rico, aided by the *Cedula de Gracias,* had given the island a meaningful place on the world market by the 1820s, but after 1830 the sugar industry eclipsed the world production of coffee. Coffee remained stagnant until 1860 and then regained its vigor momentarily until the U.S. invasion of 1898, which was followed by a devastating hurricane that wrought havoc on coffee estates in 1899.

The Dominican Republic did not export sugar in the nineteenth century, producing only dark pan sugar for the local market as well as raw rum for local consumption and for the Haitian market. The Cuban war of independence had an impact on the Dominican economy, as exiled planters, lured by fertile lands, low salaries, cheap cost of supplies, and a welcoming government, began building sugar mills there in the 1870s. Cuban immigrants and later American businessmen with German, Italian, and French connections to sugar trading companies revived the industry. By 1893, Dominican sugar plantations exported 38,564 tons of sugar mostly to the United States. The growth of the industry transformed the Dominican landscape, as virgin forests began to give way to sugar cane fields. Peasants turned their arable lands into cane farms to supply the central factories, ending food production in many areas and provoking a dramatic increase in food prices. The Dominican sugar industry, however, had to face the constant problem of labor shortage. The government and the planters wooed Canary Islands peasants with enticing offers of free land, cash advances, equipment, and other resources. They then resorted to contracting laborers from the Leeward Islands, which had suffered severe economic depression since abolition.

By 1907, 67 percent of the Dominican land devoted to the cultivation of sugar cane belonged to seven central factories established in San Pedro de Macorís. In Cuba too, the majority of sugar plantations changed ownership between 1873 and 1883, and the banks lost their solvency, many of their assets going to American owners and Spanish firms that consolidated them into gigantic central factories. A reciprocal trade agreement signed between the United States and Spain in 1891 increased the economic involvement of Americans in Cuba. The agreement collapsed in 1894, when a customs duty war broke out between Americans and the Spanish. Another Cuban war of independence broke out in 1895, which caused planters on the island to seek annexation to the United States. When Americans did intervene in 1898 they did not annex the island but established a protectorate as a transition to a Cuban national government. At the end of the transition, however, ownership of the Cuban sugar industry had passed to American corporations.

By 1905 over 60 percent of Cuban rural land belonged to American individuals and corporations, the island again occupying first place on the sugar market. Between 1903 and 1910 the American market absorbed almost all Cuban sugar exports with known American tycoons largely controlling the island's economic life. After 1920, the Cuban economy was completely in the hands of American banks and corporations. Fernando Ortiz would say in his 1940 classic study *Contrapunteo cubano del tabaco y el azúcar*: "Even today's national economy is governed by the sugar industry, which enjoys constant protection even though the centrals are no longer Cuban, in exchange for special tariffs on imports, which are not Cuban either" (Ortiz 1970:6). Similarly, following the occupation of Puerto Rico by American forces in 1898, the transfer of lands to American individuals, corporations, and banks began immediately. As a result, the sugar industry received a new injection of economic energy. By 1929 four main American sugar corporations and their associated cane farmers controlled 72 percent of the lands used in cane cultivation, and by 1934 the island could again boast a thriving plantation economy, producing the record figure of a million tons of sugar.

The majority of the Dominican population was concentrated in the northern Cibao region, while the central factories were located in the South, making work in the sugar plantations less than practical for most laborers given the transportation time and cost involved. Besides, workers had learned to employ themselves farming tobacco, cacao, and coffee, these last two having been introduced to their region as reliable commercial crops in 1880. As a result, the sugar industry had to depend on an external source of labor, first from the Leeward Islands and then from the neighboring Republic of Haiti. By 1905, 11 of the 14 existing factories had American owners, the growth of the industry coinciding with the fiscal reorganization of the country under tutelage by the U.S. government. The country had owed a large national debt by 1899, and when by 1901 the international creditors, namely the governments of Italy, France, Germany, Belgium, and Great Britain threatened to intervene militarily to collect their debts, the U.S. government took on the role of mediator to avoid European intervention in the Caribbean. Prevailing upon the Dominican authorities to accept a virtual protectorate, President Theodore Roosevelt imposed a settlement whereby American government agents would administer Dominican customs with the purpose of distributing its income among the foreign creditors and the Dominican government.

With a single American bank consolidating the Dominican Republic's entire debt, the U.S. government secured a loan on behalf of the Dominican State. As collateral to guarantee the loan, Dominican customs remained in the hands of American officers, who would distribute the income as follows: 50 percent to make payments on the loan, 45 percent to the Dominican government, and 5 percent to cover the administrative costs of the receivership. An agreement called the Dominican-American Convention issued in 1907 formalized a posteriori the control of Dominican fiscal life by the U.S. government. During the protectorate, American sugar companies successfully encouraged legislations that catered to their economic interests. For instance, the Law of Agricultural Franchise promulgated in July 1911 allowed for the tax-free export of sugar cane in keeping with the interests of the Sugar Trust, an American corporation that had bought large tracts of land in eastern Dominican Republic for use in growing sugar cane to supply one of the corporation's central factories in Puerto Rico. By the same token, the Law of Partition of the Communal Lands of 1911 came to regulate the land tenure system, making it easier for sugar companies to expand their landholdings. By the 1920s, American sugar companies controlled most of the best farmland in the country and over 90 percent of the Dominican sugar production (Moya Pons).

The rapid Americanization of the sugar industry during the protectorate in the Dominican Republic caused U.S. involvement in Dominican political affairs to escalate, hence the military occupation of the country from 1916 through 1924. American troops had already occupied neighboring Haiti a year before and would remain there until 1934. The U.S. military government that ruled Dominicans for eight years actively protected American economic interests, which greatly increased the presence of U.S. companies there. The military government invited investors from the United States and offered enticing measures of protection, including legislative reforms that were unambiguous in their intent. A new customs tax law in 1919, for instance, designated 254 specific articles manufactured in the United States to be duty free and greatly reduced the import taxes on over 700 other U.S. articles. The American occupation not only accomplished the subordination of Dominican foreign trade to American commercial interests but it left a pervasive predilection for American manufactured goods and entertainment, including such games as baseball, which came to replace cockfighting in the national imaginary. Given the U.S. military control of Haiti since 1915, American firms flourished there too, including, most significantly, the Haitian American Sugar Company (HASCO), established in Port-au-Prince the same year of the occupation. Legislatively, the U.S. military government of Haiti modified the country's constitution to permit foreign citizens and companies to own land and buildings, removing the prohibition decreed by Dessalines's original constitution. Haiti's abundant population offered an unlimited supply of manual labor, which freed the factory owners from having to pay competitive salaries. By 1930 HASCO employed only about 1,000 workers and paid them the lowest salary in the entire Caribbean region. The availability of laborers in Haiti also permitted the military government to find a solution to the labor shortage encountered by the sugar industry on the Dominican side of the island. While some Haitian workers had already identified the Dominican cane fields and central factories as a source of employment, the continuous and massive flow of migrant workers across the island dates from 1916, the year when the United States assumed complete military, political, and economic control of the lives of both Haitians and Dominicans.

With the decline of the sugar industry in the Lesser Antilles after 1884, worsened by the closing of the American market to sugar from the British Caribbean, unemployment grew alarmingly there. Unable to find work, thousands of workers migrated to the neighboring regions where plantations thrived. When work on the Panama Canal resumed in 1904, thousands of black West Indians flocked to the Isthmus. Workers from Barbados migrated also to Cuba where they competed for jobs on the plantations with Jamaicans and Haitians. Between 1901 and 1904 Bermuda received thousands of migrants from Nevis and St. Kitts. When work on a large shipyard there ran out, many of them headed for Cuba and the Dominican Republic. By 1914, the Dominican Republic had received thousands of workers from the Leeward Islands, Caicos, Virgin Islands, Turks Islands, and Jamaica. Dominican plantation owners offered salaries of more than three times the daily salary offered in the English colonies. Between 1921 and 1925, Cuba received over 90,000 Haitians and Jamaicans, continuing the process of intra-Caribbean migration (Guerra y Sánchez 1964:145). The decline of the sugar plantation almost invariably caused labor mobility to the nearest plantation economy in the archipelago. When the industry declined across the board, workers had no other recourse than to trek vaster distances across the ocean, opting for migration to Europe and the United States.

By the 1960s, the period that frames the story "Isolda en el espejo," which Rosario Ferré published in the same volume with her novel *Maldito amor* (1986), the sugar industry had practically disappeared in Puerto Rico, the industrialization that the United States promoted having displaced the island's agricultural economy (Ferré 1986:206). This period also marks the transition to political independence for many nations in the region, and as sovereignty came for them unaccompanied by economic independence, the Puerto Rican model of development seemed an attractive option. The model, launched in 1947 on the island, consisted in inviting "U.S. corporate investment to create new industries in the Caribbean to replace the moribund plantation system," and it led to the emergence of "whole new sectors" in the region's "economies almost overnight," with investment in mineral, manufacturing, and tourism leading the way (Sunshine 1985:43). The Puerto Rican model, adopted in Trinidad and Jamaica, and having St. Lucia–born economist Sir Arthur Lewis as one of its advocates, raised the expectations of many in the region who believed it would solve the problems of poverty and unemployment, but its failure in Puerto Rico itself by the 1970s foreshadowed the economic decline that would ensue in the following decades (48). While black and brown leaders held the seats of political power as heads of sovereign states, they presided over societies where economic power was maintained by foreign corporations in collusion with local elites, displaying a disquieting parallel to the former colonial structures (49).

The rise of tourism and the proliferation of free-trade zones, industries that come from abroad to use the labor and the landscape without contributing to local development or self-reliance, repeats the pattern whereby the huge profits of the colonial plantation invariably went to the Western metropolises. Jamaican economist Michael Witter added a disturbingly evocative layer of signification to the parallel when at the end of May 2003, speaking to a study abroad class that sociologist Linda Carty and I brought to the Mona campus of the University of the West Indies, he indicated that many of the physical locations occupied today by tourist resorts and free-trade zones are actually the sites of former colonial plantations. The plantation seems still to be with us in the symbolic rebirth suggested by Witter's observation. But it remains with us also materially in the concrete repercussions of its disappearance. The great Caribbean exodus of the second half of the century, which continues unabated to this day, may be understood as the direct result of the decline of the plantation. Paradoxically, just as its insertion into the core of Caribbean life occurred at a great cost of pain and human suffering, the decline of the plantation too has taken its toll on the lives of the less empowered populations of the region, leading to much unemployment, poverty, emigration, and diasporic uprooting. The section that follows, through a look at the paradoxical situation in which the plantation placed a free black woman in eighteenth-century Surinam, explores the significance of the work of Cynthia Mc Leod as an Antillean intellect who returns to the plantation machine to uncover little known patterns of maroon subversion.

Intellects as Maroons

Cynthia Mc Leod's novel *De Vrije Negerin Elisabeth: Gevangene van kleur* has scored a high mark with readers in Holland and Surinam, where it has remained as a bestseller since its original publication in the year 2000. A first English translation of it, entitled *The Free Negress Elisabeth: Prisoner of Color* (2004), has now become available from a publisher in Mc Leod's native Paramaribo, making it possible for readers without a command of Dutch to access, through the story that the book tells, an indispensable chapter of the Caribbean experience. Born in 1936, Mc Leod is the daughter of Johan Ferrier, the last governor and first president of Surinam. With the reception of this work, Mc Leod has added to the celebrity that her first novel *Hoe duur was de suiker* (The High Price of Sugar) (1987) had garnered her. Dealing with a family feud among Jewish colonists in late eighteenth-century Surinam, including a romantic rivalry between two sisters, Mc Leod's first novel caused a sensation when it came out, rising to the rank of the best-selling book ever in Surinam literary history and conquering readers in The Netherlands where "it had gone through ten printings" by the late 1990s (Kempen 2001:388). Mc Leod's *Hoe duur was de suiker?*, through the medium of fiction, brings into sharp focus the preeminent role of Jews in Surinamese history, a subject that has lately received considerable attention. R. A. J. van Lier years ago offered a useful account, despite its discernible apologia, and more recently Ineke Phaf-Rheinberger provides a succinct and sober overview (Lier 1982:23; Phaf-Rheinberger 2001a).

After delving in the drama of Jewish female protagonists in colonial Surinam over 200 years ago, Mc Leod returns to the same century to exca-vate and reconstruct the life and times of Elisabeth Samson, a real-life black businesswoman who at the time distinguished herself for owning a bountiful number of black slaves, successfully running several plantations and other profitable enterprises, competing with the wealthiest members of Surinamese society, and openly defying the interdictions of the white ruling elite. Contending, with Mc Leod's compatriot Astrid H. Roemer, that "there is no novel without a neighborhood, no writer without a home, and no sentence without the writer's logic. No book without a moral code," I would like to propose that the author of *The Free Negress* intervenes with this novel in the literary arena in a manner not unlike her character's provocation of the estab-lished order of things in the colonial society where life placed her (Roemer 1998:185–186). The choices that Elisabeth made dramatized her battle against a social system that would persist in placing her outside the comfort-ing contours of humanity and citizenship, and in her work of excavation Mc Leod marshals a comparably meaningful impeachment of the intellectual dis-courses that display planetary pretensions in their truth-claims about colonial relations and racial othering globally, leaving unattended the intricate interi-ority of the human experience in places like Surinam. Through her celebration of Elisabeth, whom she no doubt construes as a heroine, Mc Leod reflects the Caribbean person's age-old quest to demand a space of recognition in the realm of thought production about human culture. To a large extent, *The Free Negress* constitutes a compelling statement about the state of Caribbean knowledge, especially of that part of the Antillean world colonially connected to Dutch imperial domination, evincing an impetus discernible in an august line of writers from that linguistic bloc who have occupied themselves decidedly in the task of unearthing, rectifying, and disseminating the history, culture, and ideas of their people. To write the novel, Mc Leod spent over 12 years conducting painstaking research at the Rijksarchief in The Hague as well as at other Dutch archives in Amsterdam and Rotterdam, in addition to other documentary repositories in the German cities of Emmerich and Keulen.

During a lecture at the Cultural Center of the Inter-American Development Bank in Washington, DC, on August 7, 1998, the author revealed the fascinating story of her meticulous pursuit of the historical Elisabeth, an effort that culminated in the production of a scholarly study that the University of Utrecht subsequently published as a monograph (Mc Leod 1993). Among the lessons the author claims to have learned in the course of her investigation, she highlights the realization "that every nation should have ready access to the sources of its own history" lest people end up "forming self-images that are erroneous, based purely on stereotypes," a problem that Surinam painfully exemplifies, in her view, "simply because all the records are in Holland" (Mc Leod 1998:13). She also credits her research with having taught her that "while Black and White codes in Suriname were quite severe on paper during the time of slavery, they were far more relaxed in people's everyday life," enabling free blacks "to do things" that today amount to a legacy (13). Perhaps most importantly, she learned that "race relations were much more complex than one would ordinarily imagine" (13). Differing from the United States and largely from the British West Indian colonies, eighteenth-century Surinam society distinguished among people of mixed ancestry, so-called colored, by assigning varied levels of social value in accordance with each given kind of mixture. Thus the union of a black and a white parent produced a *mulatto* child while the progeny of a black with a mulatto or an Indian was called a *karboeger*, a term, unknown in Holland, coined in Surinam specifically to designate a distinct miscegenation. By the same token the union of a mulatto and an Indian would yield a *mesties*. The combination of a *mesties* with a white would bring about a *casties*, who, in turn, would produce a *pusties* by joining with a white (5). By 1782, merely 11 years after Elisabeth died, the government sought to simplify the country's racial classification system by means of a decree stipulating that thenceforth only three categories would obtain to rank blacks and coloreds: "first, Negroes and karboegers; second, mulattos; and third, *mesties*," rendering all other groups eligible to claim the status of white, "including mesties born in wedlock" (13).

An examination of the specific time and place that gave rise to the peculiar case of Elisabeth makes it difficult to conceive how one might attempt to explain the human experience of the Surinamese drawing merely on one's familiarity with other sites of the colonized world or the selective historical accounts bequeathed by scribes of the colonial ruling structure. Mc Leod's work impresses very intensely upon us that eighteenth-century Surinam requires its own separate scrutiny. By documenting Elisabeth's entrepreneurial drive and success as a functional capitalist, the author has rescued her character from the dismissive brief references in which historians had portrayed her as the fortunate beneficiary of the wealth passed on to her by the industrious and benevolent white businessman whom she had married. The racial and gender baggage inherent in the historians' assumption pressupose considerable incredulity concerning the chance that a woman—a black one at that—could amass her own fortune. Mc Leod significantly evokes Elisabeth as a complexly textured character, her personality made impure by her display of traits that we might wish we did not see in order to like her better. Elisabeth seeks perhaps too obsessively the approval of the white elite of Paramaribo, the pursuit of an invitation to the traditional New Year's reception at the Governor's Palace becoming practically her life's goal. She finally does get the invitation after she practically purchases a white husband—at a price ever so dear—that she felt she needed in order to attain the respectability of a proper lady in colonial Paramaribo. After the death of her common law spouse, the white army officer of the Society of Surinam, Carl Otto Creutz, whom she loved and was genuinely loved by, we learn that she refrained from pressing him to legalize their union of love since it seemed certain that he would have had to forfeit his military career had he challenged the long-standing norm that a white could not marry a black (377).

Once her beloved passes away, the matter of her gaining a social standing that accords with her economic position fills her with a sense of urgency. A woman in her fifties, she only has within her reach white men in their thirties who will make for an odd couple with her. First comes Christoph Polycarpus Braband, a sickly and impoverished caretaker and church organist hopelessly in her debt and unable to catch up with his arrears. Presented with an offer that he could not refuse, Braband agrees to petition the local authorities for their marriage. During her exile years in Holland and through her friendship with lawyer Wouter Landman in The Hague, she learned that Dutch jurisprudence had no formal prohibition of interracial matrimony. Surinamese society had simply abided by a ruling instituted by the colony's ninth Dutch Governor Cornelis van Aerssen Sommerlsdijk, who ruled from 1683 to 1688 when he died at the hands of mutinous soldiers. Though he lived in concubinage with the daughter of an Amerindian chief, he prohibited any form of cohabitation between blacks and whites in the colony (Phaf-Rheinberger 2002:97–98). Since the interdiction had remained unchallenged, the local authorities had never, until Elisabeth and Braband requested their permission to marry, needed to verify the legal solidity of their ordinance. Unable to approve or deny the petition, they refer the case to the metropolis and the petitioners have to wait until the ruling comes from Holland.

By the time the favorable decision comes, the groom, afflicted with a bad cough and tightness of the chest, is dead. But Elisabeth will not relent, and soon another bachelor comes her way, Daniel Harmanus Zobre, an uncaring, opportunistic, and dishonest army lieutenant 17 years her junior who, with nothing but his whiteness to show for, immediately realizes the financial wisdom of accepting Elisabeth's modest proposal. As her lawfully wedded husband, he will automatically become principal owner of her estate. Elisabeth and Harmanus enter their request for a marriage license on December 11, 1767 and receive approval the following day. They become man and wife, but despite her crossing the last social barrier impeding her ascent to respectability, she is snubbed for three additional years. She continues to suffer the bitter realization that only Harmanus receives invitations to the Palace and other exclusive social circles. An invitation including her name does come ultimately, for the New Year's reception of January 1, 1771, just over three months before she dies.

Having made it to the Palace, to the overt displeasure of the very people whose company she has sought, Elisabeth comes face-to-face with a thick wall of scorn and rejection. The proper ladies at the gathering would not even deign to make eye contact with her, blatantly displaying their resentment at her trespassing their zone of racial exclusivity. This does not exclude those who have habitually gone to Elisabeth's to procure on credit the wares, furniture, jewelry, and silks with which to embellish their homes and their bodies. The experience proves unbearable to Elisabeth when she comes into awareness of the futility and folly of her yearning for the approval of a constituency that she did not really respect. Overtaken by an overwhelming discomfort, nauseated and fainting, she darts out of the Palace halfway through the festivity. In the days that follow, Elisabeth grows despondent, her health increasingly deteriorating, a result, we gather, of the debilitating psychosomatic impact of her disappointment at the Palace. By weaving into her plot the trappings of such causality, Mc Leod seems intent on having the reader's eyes turn to the deployment of hatred by the white elite of Paramaribo as the primary cause of Elisabeth's death. The novel's denouement no doubt succeeds at eliciting the reader's compassion toward the protagonist, the same way one seldom fails to grieve over the plight of the main character in an ancient Athenian tragedy even while recognizing the flaws that may account for his or her downfall.

She suffers humiliation at the end, and one wishes her pride and self-respect had helped her avert that moral calamity by making her less covetous of the company of her foes. Her own sister Nanette has telling words in this regard when she, visiting Elisabeth on the day of the event at the Palace and seeing the zeal and anticipation with which she prepared for the big night, indicates that were she to have the same opportunity that Elisabeth now had, she would under no circumstances "consort with those people" (429). This comment by Nanette points to Mc Leod's interest in complicating the character of Elisabeth, who lacks the political tact to realize that, though well spoken, better read than her white counterparts, free born, skilled at playing the harpsichord, and wealthy, she could not afford to overlook the fact that her blackness placed hurdles in her path in a society that had to be negrophobic because its very existence depended on the dehumanization of blacks on the plantation and in the cities. The white authorities in Surinam forbade the wearing of shoes by slaves, regulated the clothing styles or kinds of fabric that manumitted blacks could wear, and went as far as to stipulate that a free black found guilty of a serious crime would revert to slavery. Besides, just as blacks—dehumanizingly dominated on the plantation and the household—ensured the colony's prosperity and well-being, the blacks too—when engaging in insurgent action through the maroon bands that pervade the plot of the novel, constitute its principal source of stress, causing economic and social instability.

With blacks as pervasively identified as an inimical entity for colonial Surinamese society, one wonders, as does Nanette, what could have possibly caused Elisabeth to presume that she could, without getting crushed, take sides in a quarrel between Governor Johan Raye and any of the principal colonial families whose animosity he incurred shortly after his arrival in Surinam in December 1735. When the governor has an altercation with the Peltzers, she happens to be close by at a gathering where she overhears them casting aspersions on him. Unmindful of her own tenuous position, Elisabeth thinks it her civic duty to inform the governor about the disparaging comments being spread about him. It turns out that when the governor confronts the culprits, revealing the source of his information, they deny the charge and, in feigned dismay, proceed to discredit the value that the word of blacks could have against respectable white citizens. Assuming the role of the injured party, presumptive victims of her calumny, they begin legal action against Elisabeth, with Van Meel, the head of the local court, spitefully leading the way. As if throwing her to the lions, the governor moves not a finger as she goes to trial for her criminal offense, is found guilty, and receives a sentence of banishment from the colony for life. She goes to Holland and can only come back home nearly two-and-a-half years later thanks to the good offices and considerable investment of army Captain Frederick Coenraad Bosse, her older sister Maria's wealthy white husband who genuinely loves Elisabeth as if she were his daughter. Through Bosse's commercial contacts in Holland the young exile is able to live well away from home and to monitor the progress of the appeal of her sentence.

Elisabeth's ambivalence regarding the sociopolitical significance of her location as a free-born black who has had the exceptional good fortune of receiving a good education and living the pampered life of a white child contributes to the depth of her character. Before and after her exile she has ample opportunity to ascertain the antipathy of the colonial elite against her, but at the same time she cannot conceive of a future outside the contours of white society. Mc Leod here makes no concession to the flattening effect of a prevailing ideological desire that would fault Elisabeth for her lack of a sense of solidarity with her black brethren in captivity or a clearer stance of racial self-affirmation in militant response to the colony's white supremacist logic. Rather, the author seems interested in urging us to grasp the difficulty of the character's quandary given the powerful force of her peculiar circumstances that would seem to preclude clear-cut articulations of social identity. She invites us, in effect, to enter Elisabeth's world free from anachronism, unencumbered by the political sensibility that we have inherited from the twentieth-century success of anticolonialist struggles in the Third World as well as battles for civil rights, social justice, and democratic inclusion of ethnoracial minorities in Europe and the United States. She urges us to assess Elisabeth's options in her context, a given moment in the discrete drama of colonial domination as it was experienced in the Antillean world.

Mc Leod's invitation to us to consider Elisabeth in the specificity of her own predicament corresponds to a compulsion discernible in the overall corpus of writings from Surinam and the rest of the Caribbean to do justice to the particularity of the human experience of the region in discursive representation. Perhaps literary figures and intellectuals from the part of the region colonially linked to The Netherlands reflect the desire to bring into visibility the distinctness of their historical and cultural legacy to an even greater degree because their societies, by virtue of the lesser global status of the languages they speak, enjoy the least international recognition among Caribbean societies. As a result, their literary and intellectual productions enjoy the least dissemination outside of their immediate linguistic bloc. To help outside readers better locate the achievement of Mc Leod's intervention it might come in handy here to attempt a rapid overview, drawing primarily from scholarly sources and compilations available in English and at times in Spanish (Debrot 1963; Howes 1966; Voorhoeve and Lichtveld 1975; Rutgers 1998; Kempen 1998; Lampe 2000; and Phaf-Rheineberger 2001b). Like its Spanish-speaking, Francophone, and English-speaking counterparts the Dutch Caribbean has seen a remarkable efflorescence of literary creativity since the first half of the twentieth century in connection with various stages of nation-building dynamism and cultural self-affirmation for each respective society there. However, this area makes for a more complicated linguistic map than the other Caribbean blocs, especially for the purposes of outlining its literary production. In his early overview of the literature of "The Netherlands Antilles" Cola Debrot noted "the complicated situation of having a folk literature that is expressed in two languages (Papiamentu on the Leeward Islands and English on the Windward Islands) and a written literature that makes use of three languages, Spanish, Dutch, and Papiamentu" (Debrot 1963:1905). Written literature in Curaçao begins in Spanish, the island being first conquered by Spain in the sixteenth century, and it thrives until well into the twentieth century as we can gather from John de Pool's *Del Curaçao que se va* (Vanishing Curaçao) (1936), which Debrot praised as "one of the most important books of our literature" (Debrot 1963:1908; Echteld 2001). By the same token, the literature of the "Dutch Windward Islands," namely Saba, St. Eustatius, and Sint Maarten, which are actually leeward geographically speaking, occurs primarily in English, as is illustrated by the poetry collection edited by Wycliffe Smith *Winds above the Hill* (1982), which the Sint Maarten–based Nigerian scholar Fabian Badejo in the late 1990s referred to as "the first and only anthology of Windward Islands verse" (1998:677). Badejo describes the linguistic situation by saying that St. Martiners, for example, "speak English at home, study in Dutch at school, socialize in Spanish, and in addition know Papiamentu" from their frequent contact with schools in Aruba and Curaçao (1998:676). Several poets, none of whom writes in Dutch, have gained visibility in Sint Maarten over the last decades: from Wycliffe Smith, to Charles Borromeo Hodge, to vigorous Lasana Sekou, a poet and essayist associated with the House of Nehesi Publishers, who also practically "dominates the literary panorama" of those small islands (Lampe 2000:240). Sekou's work is characterized by a "pan-Caribbean outlook" that advocates regional unity and cultural self-affirmation.

When we speak of the Dutch Caribbean, then, we must be mindful of the inaccuracy of that designation. Among the other Antillean islands with a Dutch connection, namely Aruba, Bonaire, and Curaçao, Aruba—an autonomous territory since 1986—has produced first-rate poets, among whom Peña Lampe, Federico Oduber, and Henry Habibe stand out. Lampe died in the 1960s, the victim of political violence. Oduber's work shows an existential bent, and Habibe's is socially and politically informed. Among fiction writers, Dennis Henriquez has achieved the greatest distinction outside his homeland. When in 1992 he published in Dutch the novel *De Zunndistraat*, the first part of a trilogy dealing with the writer's youth in Orangestad, the capital of Aruba, his reputation as an important writer was established in Holland, where he lives, as do Oduber and Habibe, a fact worthy of note in-so-far as it highlights a characteristic of Caribbean literature in general, namely that most of the region's major writers find it difficult to live and work in their native lands (Lampe 2000:238).

Bonaire is the birthplace of novelist and short-story writer Diana Lebacs, who writes in Dutch, cultivating the field of literature for young adults, and playwright Pacheco Domacassé, who writes in Papiamentu. Both Lebacs and Pacheco reside in Curaçao, intra-Caribbean migration being another distinguishing feature of the mobility of writers from this region, a condition that they share with workers skilled and unskilled. Bonaire is also the birthplace of Cola Debrot, a member of the white minority who distinguished himself as a physician, lawyer, politician, and man of letters. In his early thirties he published the important novel *Mijn zuster de negerin* (My Black Sister) (1935), a foundational text among writers using Dutch as their literary language, a work that explored the implications of the pervasive cohabitation that created blood ties between white masters and black slaves in colonial Antillean society. Through several other volumes of fiction, poetry, and essays, and through such initiatives as the editorship of the journal *Antilliaanse Cahiers*, Debrot remained a major cultural force in the region even as he continued to rise on the political scale, culminating in his becoming governor of the Netherlands Antilles on September 10, 1962. He occupied that post on May 30, 1969, when "the great workers' revolution broke out promoting demands of social and racial equality in Curaçao" (Lampe 2000:239). Following the upheaval of 1969, Debrot retired from politics and opted to settle permanently in Holland (239).

The literature produced in Curaçao quantitatively outshines the bodies of writing coming from the other so-called Dutch-speaking Antillean islands. There many of the finest poets have written in Papiamentu as we can see in the *oeuvres* of the mestizo Pierre Lauffer, deemed "the greatest of Curaçao poets," and Elis Juliana, the country's most popular poetic voice, about both of whom Debrot over four decades ago intimated that if they wrote "in English or Spanish" they "would enjoy an international reputation" (Lampe 2000:235; Debrot 1963:1913). One of Juliana's latest poetry collections, *Un mushi di haiku* (1993) is now available in a bilingual English-Papiamentu edition. Two of the haikus in the slim volume impress on the reader the immediacy of climatic conditions for people in the poet's part of the world:

Muchu yobida
ta duna kunakeru
menos kosecha

[Too much rainfall will
cause the poor farmer to reap
a meager harvest]

and

Sèptèmber lamá
i bientu ta kuminsa
kastigá tera

[September seas and
howling winds have begun
to castigate the land.]
(Juliana 2003:9, 20)

Arguably the most memorable slave insurrection registered in the annals of Dutch Caribbean colonial history took place in Curaçao in 1795, with black rebels Tula and Carpata standing out as leaders of the rebellion. The event has recurred as a leit motiv in the island's literary production, as it does in the contemporary poetry of Yerba Sekou and Gibi Basilio. Among fiction writers, Guillermo Rosario, an advocate of Curaçao's African heritage, wrote the first important novel in Papiamentu about the uprising. Subsequently, the mulatto Edgar de Jongh has devoted a novel in Dutch to the revolt while the white Karel de Haseth has dedicated to it one in Papiamentu (Lampe 2000:235–236). To some extent, the literature produced by the descendants of slave masters has also leaned toward subversiveness if mostly of an existential rather than a political kind. Of the two names that stand out in this connection, Boeli van Leeuwen and Tip Marugg, the former has the more peculiar personal history. A member of the colonial aristocracy of Curaçao, Leeuwen spent the war years studying in Holland and Spain. After working as a lawyer in Venezuela, in 1956 he entered the administration of the Dutch Caribbean territories, eventually rising to the rank of secretary of the administration of the Dutch Antilles. Upon his retirement in 1983, he changed his life radically, breaking with the conventions of his class, and went to live in the poor quarters of Willemstad, Curaçao, where he began a practice as a pro Deo lawyer (Lefevere 2002:57–58). Leeuwen has written poetry, a novella, a film script, and six novels, one of which, *Het teken van Jonah* (1988), has appeared in English translation as *The Sign of Jonah* (1995). His first novel, *De rots der struikeling* (1959/1960) (The Rock of Offense) had appeared in Mexico in a Spanish translation as *La piedra de tropiezo* (1964). The latter novel is as prolific in biblical references and blasphemous expletives as the former, and the existential bent ("Kierkegaardian inspiration") that Debrot found in the former seems to accord with the eschatological search that Andre Lefevere identifies in the latter (Debrot 1963:1932; Lefevere 2002:60). Marugg's first novel, *Weekendpelgrimage* (Weekend Pilgrimage) (1957), earned the author recognition in The Netherlands, causing Dutch critic Pierre Dubois to say that, "Because of its subtle appreciation of what is essentially a world problem, this book ought to be translated in a world language" (cited in Debrot 1963: 1931). The novel piercingly explores the difficult psychological location of white Curaçaoans who must carve for themselves a space of native identity in a society increasingly identified with the cultural legacy of blacks and other minorities of color. After spending a whole week in a factory subjected to the depersonalizing pressure of large-scale industrial production, the first-person narrator over the weekend sets out to regain human contact and personal freedom by cruising restaurants, bars, and cafes, interacting with individuals of various class extractions but showing a distinct predilection for the company of individuals from the lower rungs of society, such as Shandi, a grave digger whose touch he believes will prove salutary for him.

We come next to the poet, fiction writer, and cultural activist Frank Martinus Arion, easily Curaçao's most dynamic literary figure. The author of four major novels, the best known of which, *Dubbelspel* (1973), has become available in English translation under the title *Double Play* (1998), Arion writes as an advocate of workers, a defender of the African heritage in Antillean culture, a critic of European colonialism, and a promoter of Papiamentu. His texts reflect also a pervasive engagement with the whole of the Caribbean world. We discern this in the intra-Caribbean linkages exhibited by the lives of the main characters in *Double Play*. Witness the background of Janchi, who, the son of a Venezuelan father, "belonged to the people of Bolivar"; the birthplace of Chamon Nicolas, namely the windward island of Saba; and the largely Dominican origin of the Campo Alegre women, one of whom, Micha, has an eventful encounter with the fickle Bubu Fiel (Arion 1998a:61, 111, 138–141). A similar regional bent is evident in the wealth of references to Aruba, Surinam, Cuba, Jamaica, Guyana, Barbados, and Grenada in just a few pages of Arion's latest novel *De Laatste Vrijheid* (The Last Freedom) (1995) as the characters of Aideline and her husband set out from their "small house just outside Willemstad" to know the "area well because the educational system of their islands had basically isolated them from the rest of the Caribbean and South America" (Arion 1998b). Having headed the Language Institute of the Netherlands Antilles for many years, during which he set out to standardize Papiamentu spelling and foment literary creation in the vernacular, Arion wrote a doctoral dissertation that traces the roots of Papiamentu back to Africa: "The Kiss of a Slave: Papiamentu's West African Connections" (University of Amsterdam 1996) (Lampe 2000:236). Though a promoter of Papiamentu, he has written his novels in Dutch, restricting the use of the vernacular to volumes of poetry and other short forms. One thinks of the explanation offered by the narrator in *Double Play* of the intellectual advantage Chamon Nicolas has over his peers, stressing that he, on account of his command of English, "had access to an extensive world of literature, of which the uneducated Antillean, who speaks and reads only Papiamentu, was completely deprived" (Arion 1998a:113). The observation corresponds fairly accurately to Arion's overall assessment of the Creole speaker's diminished access to the world of learning as a result of measures implemented in 1907, which excluded Papiamentu from the schools and established Dutch as the official and only language of print communication. With Dutch reigning as the language of "the reading culture," an uneven scenario ensued that allowed for a situation that still exists at present and which explains the choices implicit in Arion's own oeuvre. His case, he suggests, accords with the general literary community in Curaçao, where the "bigger" forms such as the novel occur in Dutch—since "writing has to do with reading" and that is "the reading language"—while poetry and folklore find expression in Papiamentu (Arion 1998b:538). Arion offers, perhaps as a saving grace, his view of the creolization of the official language that he has witnessed in his own work, when, while writing poetry in Dutch he has found himself "looking for the rhythms and expressions" of the vernacular, in effect, "looking for Papiamentu" (Arion 1998b:541).

We now return to Cynthia Mc Leod's homeland, the continental Caribbean nation of Surinam, whose colonial history began with English domination in the 1640s and the ensuing development of a plantation economy by the settlers and the introduction of black slaves in 1650 by Lord Willoughby of Parham, who received property rights to the colony from Charles II in 1663 while he also served as governor of Barbados. English domination ended in 1667, when the Dutch stepped in and asserted their colonial hegemony, and the change of imperial guard on the land was ratified through the 1667 Treaty of Breda. The memorable Aphra Behn, who chose Surinam as the setting of her 1688 novella *Oroonoko*, had occasion to lament the English loss in that deal; musing that "had his late Majesty [King Charles II], of sacred memory, but seen and known what a vast and charming world he had been the master of in that continent, he would never have parted so easily with it to the Dutch" (Behn 1992:115). The economic potential of New York—then called New Amsterdam or New Netherlands—which the English got in exchange for Surinam, had apparently not yet become evident to distant observers like Behn. The Dutch quickly established plantations on their newly acquired colony whose population, apart from the native inhabitants, consisted of over 500 black slaves and under 200 whites at the time of the transition. By 1705 the number of plantations cultivating sugar, coffee, cocoa, and cotton had risen to 591 and the enslaved African population to some 50,000. By 1826 Surinam planters had purchased around 325,000 Africans at auction in Paramaribo, while the number of Europeans seldom rose above 3,000 (Hoogbergen 1990:69). When we consider that, among the whites, the proportion of men to women generally stayed at 18 : 1, the inexorability of interracial sexual unions becomes clear (Mc Leod 1998:5). That disproportion accounts for the emergence of the "Surinamese marriage," the practice whereby soldiers and other functionaries coming from Europe to participate in military campaigns against the Maroons or render some other service to the colony would pair up with unfree black females who would serve as their spouses for the duration of their tenure there. Examining the dynamics of the "marriage" of Scottish soldier John Gabriel Stedman and the slave Johanna, which he himself records in his famous *Narrative of a Five Years Expedition Against the Revolted Negroes of Surinam* (1772–1777), published in 1790, Ineke Phaf-Rheinberger has delved into the sociocultural implications of that tradition (Phaf-Rheinberger 1992).

Surinam's literary production, as compared with that of the Dutch Antillean islands surveyed earlier, corresponds in some ways to the larger size of its population of 205,000 inhabitants, exceeding the number of 163,000 living in the six Antilles altogether (Oostindie 1990:235). Modern Surinamese literature, then, reflects the inescapable memory of a colonial past in which the white settlers seem to have gone to extremes to exert their power in the face of their numerical inferiority vis-à-vis the enslaved population and the challenge presented to their power by the "revolted Negroes" who had begun deserting plantation life and running away to the bushes in the Surinamese interior from the period of English rule through the mid-nineteenth century. For nearly two centuries, until the abolition of slavery in 1863, Maroon troops would occasionally raid plantations, abducting slaves, murdering overseers, and destroying property. Throughout that time, the colonial regime would respond by sending military patrols "to the jungle to hunt the Maroons, capture them and destroy their villages and fields," until "the last expedition in search of runaway slaves" recorded in 1862 (Hoogbergen 1990:72, 92). The eighteenth century, and specifically the period spanning the life of Elisabeth Samson, witnessed Maroon-related hostilities with particular intensity. At any rate, some "750 mercenary soldiers from Europe" would be on call "to keep the slave population under control" at any time during the period (Hoogbergen 1990:70).

With that history as its backdrop one can understand that literary production would occur in response to the tension inherent in the clash of competing traditions, the official culture bequeathed by the white colonial minority expressing itself naturally in Dutch and the downgraded culture created by former slaves and other oppressed constituencies, a numerical majority, which uses Sranan and other vernaculars to communicate. Julius Gustaaf Arnout Koenders (1886–1957), the founding editor of *Foetoe-boi* (1946–1956), a monthly that promoted Creole language and culture, holds a place of high esteem as a pioneer in a series of initiatives that sought to redress the inferior rank to which the country's educational system had relegated the expressive forms of the non-white majority. The author of numerous poems and didactic prose pieces, Koenders distinguished himself primarily by his ardent defense of Sranan Tongo and the wisdom of folk traditions. Contemporaneous with Koenders, the essayist and revolutionary political activist Anton de Kom (1898–1945), who advocated social justice in Surinam and in Holland during the Nazi period, causing him to end his days at the concentration camp of Neuengamme, authored the ground-breaking historical essay *Wij slaven van Suriname* (We Slaves of Surinam) (1934), a vigorous indictment of the colonial domination of his country by Spain, England, and, most of all, Holland.

De Kom wrote forcefully, the prose quivering with the author's deep sense of moral indignation, about the cruel oppression perpetrated by white settlers in the past, and about the inhumane, uncaring, and unfair social system that opprobrious beginning has given rise to in the modern period. Zed Books in London published an English translation of de Kom's text in 1987, a Spanish version having already appeared in 1981 in Cuba's Casa de las Americas. De Kom spells out the ideological bent of his intellectual project in a section entitled "History of the Homeland," some of whose sentences bear quoting:

> When we, black kids, children or grandchildren of slaves, learned national history in the schools, the lessons dealt, naturally, with the undertakings of white warriors . . . .the revered Tilburgse brothers, and we studied the heroic exploits accomplished by Piet Hein, de Ruiter, Tromp, de Evertsen, and Banckert . . . We, who would receive slaps on the hand with a ruler as punishment for daring to speak our own language, Sranan Tongo, within school grounds, had to applaud enthusiastically the insubordination of Claudius Civilis or the courageous desertion of William the Silent. We, who would in vain search in our history books for the names of the insurgents Bonni, Baron, and Joli Coeur, would try our best to learn by heart the names . . . of the Dutch governors under whose rule our ancestors came to the country as slaves. And the system yielded result . . . I remember how, as children, we used to feel proud our white classmates consented to play with us . . . To such a degree had the history contained in our textbooks impressed on us the stamp of our inferiority . . . Thus, the present book seeks to awaken a sense of self-respect in the people of Surinam, and also, to show the injustices and the errors committed by the Dutch in their pacifying efforts through centuries of slavery. (de Kom 1981:38–39)

Koender's stress on recovering Creole culture and Anton de Kom's reevaluation of the country's history with an emphasis on the humanity of the oppressed contributed to fueling a rethinking of the national experience especially among students living in Holland. The children of whites had traditionally gone to study in the Netherlands, and records show a small number of black Caribbean people there in the eighteenth century, precisely during the period when Mc Leod's novel places Elisabeth at The Hague, but following emancipation, education became the main objective for blacks and mulattos to travel to the metropolis (Oostindie 1990:232, 235). By 1946 an estimated 3,000 Surinamers resided in the Netherlands and by the late 1980s the number would rise to some 200,000, while only some 400,000 remained in their Caribbean homeland (238, 231). The recognition of the need to rearticulate the national experience brought together around 1950 a number of students living in Amsterdam to form the advocacy organization *We Eagie Sanie* (Our Own Things), one of whose leading figures, the lawyer Eddy Bruma, returned to Surinam to promote the cause of independence. Part of his activism involved writing poetry and plays in Sranan Tongo with an eye on rais-ing consciousness among the common people. Characteristic of his works is a poem entitled "A Warm Night's Dream," which evokes the figure of a white woman who is said to have drowned the child of a female slave during a boat trip on the river because she found its incessant cry irritating. Another is the play *Basya Pataka* (The Tough Overseer) about the dealings of a black foreman on the plantation who appears equally detached from his masters and from the slaves whom he supervises. Both written in Sranan, they illustrate Bruma's constant concern for historical reflection as a means to develop political consciousness (Voorhoeve and Lichtveld 1975:164–181, 181–190).

Proving that it was possible to achieve distinction writing primarily in Creole, the poet Henry de Ziel, using the nom de plume of Trefossa, published his first poem in 1951 in *Foetoe-boi*, the magazine edited by Koenders, to whom he dedicates his 1957 book *Trotji*, a volume of 19 poems in Sranan with Dutch translations by J. Voorhoeve and an introduction by Surinamese man of letters Albert Helman. Trefossa showed a remarkable commitment to exploring the expressive possibilities of the "despised vernac-ular" and uncovering its history. He edited the pioneering Creole writings of Johannes King (1830–1899), a member of the Matuari group who taught himself to read and eventually became a Moravian preacher, writing his prophetic visions in Sranan. A fine poet, Trefossa received the acclaim of the· Surinamese nationalists who congregated in Wie Eegie Sanie, and he succeeded in demonstrating the power of the vernacular "as a full-fledged literary lan-guage," contributing also to fueling the poetic output of several compatriots who "turned to poetry in their efforts to express the nascent feelings of nationhood during the 1960s and early 1970s" (Kempen 1998:634). Trefossa's closest counterpart in intensity and dedication to Creole expres-sion, Johanna Schouten-Elsenhout, a poet of great lyrical power, had no con-tact with the literary establishment when her first volumes of verse and sayings appeared in print in the 1960s when she was already in her fifties. The title of "Grandma Moses" of Surinamese letters conferred upon her by her fellow writers, suggests that she enjoys a rank of public veneration compara-ble to that of Louise Bennett in Jamaican literary history (Voorhoeve and Lichtveld 1975). Following in the footsteps of Trefossa and Schouten-Elsenhout, R. Dobru (pseudonym of Robin Ewald Raveles) became by "far the best known of the 1960s generation of writers who achieved great popu-larity" among massive audiences "greatly contributing to the enhanced status of Creole" (Kempen 634).

The first Surinamese writer to have achieved renown was Lou A. M. Lichtveld, known by the pseudonym of Albert Helman, who came from a large well-to-do family of part-Amerindian origin. A polyglot, he spent his formative years in Surinam and Holland and lived at various times in the United States, Spain, Mexico, Italy, and Tobago. Beginning with his first novel in 1926 *Zuid-Zuid West* (South by Southwest), he published in many genres and wrote mostly for a Dutch audience. He reached such prominence in Holland that for a time he served as Minister Plenipotentiary of the Royal Netherlands Embassy in Washington, DC. Literary scholar Wim Rutgers describes Helman, along with Debrot, as isolated "forerunners who scarcely met with response or critical praise in their own countries" (Rutgers 1998:545). But despite his social profile, Helman still reflected the lure that history has for the Caribbean writer. His writings delve into the deplorable conditions of the Surinam aborigines, and his novels *De stille plantage* (The Silent Plantation, 1931) and *Laaiende Stilte* (Silence in Flames, 1952) reflect his fascination with seventeenth-century slave society in Surinam. Both also reveal Helman's attraction to Aphra Behn's *Oroonoko*, which he translated into Dutch, providing a critical apparatus and a biography of the author (Phaf-Rheinberger 2001b: 473). *De Stille plantage* evokes the period of Sommerlsdijk's rule as governor of Surinam, a period to which Helman would return late in his career in a 1983 historical essay entitled *De faltering van Eldorado* (The Torture of Eldorado) (Phaf-Rheinberger 2002:97). On the whole, Helman, like Debrot, enjoyed the support of a primarily European readership that absorbed him in Dutch literary history probably within the realm of the "exotic" (Rutgers 1994:187). But both he and Debrot left a meaningful legacy that examined the effects of colonial history on their personal lives and their own position amidst the multiracial makeup of their Caribbean homelands.

Any overview of Surinamese writing would have to include the short-fiction writer Hugo Pos, the author of six collections since his "remarkable literary debut at the tender age of seventy one, in 1985," after completing a successful career as an international lawyer of war crimes, having served as Surinam's attorney general and as vice president of the International Court of Law at the Hague (Rutgers 1994:190). Michael Slöry, a socially commit-ted Marxist poet, is said to have "discovered Creole" in the 1960s, and Bea Vianen authored the notable 1969 novel *Sarnini, hai* (Hello, Surinam) which features a racially mixed female protagonist—offspring of a black father and a Hindustani mother—who confronts the throes of patriarchal impediments. Thea Doelwijt has achieved distinction as an author of fiction works and performance texts, and Astrid Roemer has given vent to concerns about the condition of women in Surinam as well as to the cultural and exis-tential challenges met by people of Caribbean descent in the Netherlands. The late Edgar Cairo, a remarkable Creole poet and playwright, in 1969 pub-lished *Temekoe* (Headache), the first novel written entirely in Sranan Tongo, a text that dramatizes a young man's troubled relationship with his father, and Ellen Ombre, a short-fiction and autobiographical travel writer, has explored the sociocultural contrast between Caribbeans and Europeans, while also reflecting on the contemporary remnants of the triangular trade that once linked Holland, Africa, and the Caribbean. Finally, to add just one name to this rapid and necessarily incomplete overview, Henri Ferrier, the brother of our own Cynthia Mc Leod, first achieved distinction with his 1968 psychological novel *Átman*, which explores the multiethnic composition of Surinam's population, particularly in regard to the integration of people of Asian descent.

As this scanty overview of Surinamese and Dutch Antillean letters indicates, Mc Leod belongs to a vibrant intellectual tradition among whose most salient emphases are the affirmation of Creole heritages, the exploration of the colonial past, and the unearthing of the lesser known aspects of the history. The daughter of a governor and president and the product of an elite social circle, Mc Leod does not exhibit the political involvement of an Anton de Kom, whose subversive activities and anticolonialist advocacy brought him persecution, incarceration, and finally death. But both authors equally share the conviction that accessing one's history is an urgent and necessary matter, and while *The Free Negress* does not evoke the story of a liberator, in the sense that de Kom invoked the names of Maroon insurgents like Boni, Baron, and Joli Coeur, the narration of Elisabeth's life in contrapuntal relationship with a sequence of Maroon raids on Paramaribo plantations invites the reading of her individual clash with the colonial power structure as a parallel insurgency. A plantation colony for sugar, coffee, cotton, and cocoa, Surinamese society dealt with the impending threat of Maroon attacks until abolition in 1863, and the eighteenth century that provides the temporal frame for Elisabeth's life was the hey-day of black slavery. Mc Leod paints a character who knows that bondage is an unfortunate social condition that says nothing about the human dignity of an individual. When we first meet her in the novel, we find her scolding her manumitted little sister for her lingering slave behavior, her using "the Negro gate" to come to the house (Mc Leod 2004:14). Regarding slavery as circumstantial, she expects her siblings to display the conduct of the free person immediately upon their manumission, hence, her proceeding to rename them in order to remove the labels of their former condition (18). Elisabeth's self-esteem irritates the sensibility of those white colonists who regard her as putting on airs of whiteness, wishing for her to acknowledge her inferiority on account of her blackness even though she was born free. When he visits the public square in Paramaribo as a newcomer, Carl Otto Creutz hears rumors about Elizabeth's thinking that "she is white." At a funeral ceremony for the late Governor De Cheusses, Carl Otto also hears news about Maroon attacks on two nearby plantations (41).

The Maroon attacks prompt Carl Otto's first expedition to fight the assailants, and his return, his campaign having failed and having fallen ill in the unwelcoming bushes, prompts the start of his relationship with Elisabeth who nurses him back to health. After they fall in love, each separation is caused by his military duties involving specifically a counterinsurgency opration, and the recurring cause of disquiet in the city involves Maroon attacks on the plantations (113). Elisabeth's trial, resulting from her proud refusal to confess to a charge of perjury because of her report on the Peltzers and resulting in her exile to Holland, brings added disturbance to the quiet of the colonial structure. While in Holland, she continues to receive news from Carl Otto about his forays into the Maroon-dominated forests, and continues to learn about European assumptions about her blackness—the constant surprise at her learning and musical skills—while drawing lessons from the fact that she could have a "white maid" (134), elicit romantic devotion from a white male lawyer at The Hague (183), and be valued as exotic company in a white setting where, as a mere individual, she represents no threat (200, 204). When vindicated by the court in Europe, Elisabeth returns to Surinam, where she concentrates on increasing her assets while her lover continues his military duties against the Maroons, the two parallel lines of action coming together when a Maroon raid includes one of Elisabeth's own plantations (298–301).

Sensitive to European society's model of women's domesticity, Elisabeth grieves over the informality of her relationship with Otto and yearns to have a child by him, death coming to him before that can happen (356). Her beloved gone, Elisabeth pursues her plan to marry a white to assert her equality legally, even at the expense of her fortune, which would pass to the control of her husband. It takes two years for judicial authorities in the colony to establish that the age-old prohibition against the marriage of a black and a white had no backing in existing Dutch jurisprudence. After her loveless and economically sacrificial marriage happens, the intensity and frequency of Maroon attacks increase, with the names of the historical figures of Boni, Baron, and Joli Coeur invoked by de Kom recurring more often in the narrative. The governor's decision to create a Corps of Free Negroes to enhance the colony's ability to fight the Maroons and the arrival of the Palace invitation that Elisabeth believes will grant her the legitimacy she aspires to get within the colonial status quo come in the narrative within close proximity of each other (428). The latter ends in the disillusionment that destroys her health, and we can only conjecture what the former must have prompted meaningful changes, but both events powerfully impact on the plantation order. The entrance of free blacks into the military order of the colonial structure brought into existence a scenario that subverted the logic that condemned blacks to the condition of targets of the law. Now they could also be its enforcers, and that, plus the role of economic variables, must have sped up the process leading to the 1863 emancipation. Concomitantly, Elisabeth invested her fortune and her life in forcing the colonial regime to recognize her personhood despite the chagrin caused by her blackness. The character of Elisabeth, therefore, functions as a domestic Maroon, an agent of the plantation regime who advances her difficult insurgency by working from within to bend the logic of plantation society, and Mc Leod serves as the subversive Antillean intellect who chooses to delve into the complexity of the region's history to show that, just as for the likes of Elisabeth there was no easy walk to freedom, for today's learner there can be no easy path to understanding the Antillean world.

CHAPTER 3

Caliban's Dilemma: A Disabling Memory and Possible Hope

Tout botpipel yo se botpipél
All boatpeople are boatpeople,

—Féix Morriseau-Leroy
(1998:149)

COLUMBIAN LANGUAGE AND THE TRAUMA

The deployment of Caliban has served numerous aesthetic and ideological purposes in the intellectual history of the West and the Third World. A wide-ranging examination of "Caliban's three-and-three-quarter century odyssey through the briers and thorns of interpretation and adaptation . . . [in] various media" makes this claim abundantly clear (Vaughan and Vaughan 1991:278). An existing compilation of critical approaches to Caliban as a literary character in the history of British and American letters would seem to show no less (Bloom 1992). The English poet Robert Browning uses Caliban as a vehicle for the poet's sense of failure of the soul of man in the spiritual world he understood to be forming itself as the world around him. The character is a meditative being who from his island location in Setebos reacts to his surroundings: "One hurricane will spoil six good months' hope / He hath a spite against me, that I know / Just as he favors Prosper, who knows why?" (Browning 1951:507). With comparable poetic license, the French man of letter Ernest Renan explored the character of Caliban in two of his "philosophical dramas," *Caliban, suite "De la Tempête"* (1878) and *L'eau de Jouvence, suite de "Caliban"* (1881), texts which, according to Toumson, move indistinctly across the disciplines of history, philosophy, literature, and criticism, ranging an "epistemological domain" that combines the intellectual activities of speculation and creation (Toumson 1981:509, 511). In the first text, Caliban rebels against Prospero to satisfy his craving for freedom against the sober counsel of Ariel, who says to him "You forget that it is because of Prospero that you are a man, that you exist" (Renan 1949:382). Once in power, he becomes an ally and protector of Prospero, and in the end he accepts the wisdom of the closing prayer that extols the aristocracy as the creator of "language, law, morality, and reason" as well as its uplifting "the inferior races" which, "like the emancipated negro, immediately show a monstrous ingratitude toward their civilizers" (435). The second "drama," representing Prospero as "the superior reason momentarily deprived of its authority over the inferior parts of humanity," stages a return to power of the former master through the use of a magical water that restores youth (440). By the time Prospero finally dies, he has earned the respect of Caliban who admits that "what we are we are because of you," and he assures him with these words: "Master, you will be obeyed," which helps Prospero to die with "a smile on his lips" (518,520).

Motivated by Renan, his compatriot Jean Guéhenno wrote a 1928 essay in which he had Caliban embody the rise of the proletariat (Guéhenno 1928). But when he revisited the topic in 1956, after having seen the ravages of two European wars, and now seeing, "socialism" as "the reign of Caliban," he criticized his own initial desire "to let Caliban speak" and ended by positing Stalin, Hitler, and Mussolini as "Caliban's avatars" (1969:29, 44, 46). On the other side of the Atlantic, the critic Max Dorsinville in 1974 used the image of Caliban to represent the rise of "post-European writers" from a number of minor, regional, national, or ethnic literatures whose texts enacted "a possible synthetical stage of reconciliation between Caliban and a reeducated Prospero" (Dorsinville 1974:211). In the decades that followed, the figure of Caliban recurred so frequently that it came often to be seen as suspect by scholars who deemed it monomaniacal (Dash 1989:xiii). The critic Gayatri Chakravorty Spivak has expressed pause about the Third World attraction to Caliban "as an inescapable model" (Spivak 1999:17). Specifically as the figure relates to the Caribbean, a scholar has decried *The Tempest's* "allegories of male collaboration," which she characterizes as a "homoerotic masculinist paradigm" that excludes women, among its various limitations and inherent biases (Kuzinski 1997:286, 288, 298). Interestingly, though, still in 2004 a scholar thought that the play offered "resources for new social imaginings, new social actors, new ways of thinking," in the Caribbean (Goldberg 2004:147).

I propose to argue that the figure of Caliban remains unrivaled as a signifier of the tensions existing at the core of the human experience in the Caribbean. Though invented by the Elizabethan William Shakespeare, the Western poet par excellence whom Harold Bloom's feverish fancy has rendered "inventor of the human," Caliban still commands value as a native topos that points to the epicenter of historical complexity in the Antillean world. Foreign birth notwithstanding, the figure competes unabashedly with the most genuine of the region's symbols, qualifying unequivocally as a Caribbean "cultural synecdoche" (Palencia-Roth 1997:21). It matters little that Bloom should zealously wish to guard Shakespeare against "mock scholars moaning about neocolonialism" who have turned Caliban into "an African-Caribbean heroic Freedom Fighter" (Bloom 1998:662,663). Reproaching Caribbean appropriations of Caliban by "bespoilers of *The Tempest*," he ridicules their treatments as "not even a weak misreading;

anyone who arrives at that view is simply not interested in reading the play at all. Marxists, multiculturalists, nouveau historicists—the usual suspects— know their cause but not Shakespeare's plays" (662). As the cantankerous quality of his dismissal indicates, Bloom's ideological veil enfeebles his vision, hampering his ability to see exactly what kind of use Antillean artists and scholars have made of the Bard's play. Rather than advancing interpretive readings of *The Tempest*, the likes of Aimé Césaire, George Lamming, Roberto Fernández Retamar, and Kamau Brathwaite have mined the text for its rich ore of historically relevant symbols for the Caribbean. The play has lured them because of its wealth of metaphorical possibilities, its payloads of cultural and political paradigms whose deployment can prove enormously fruitful in eliciting the storms and calms that have shaped the Caribbean as a differentiated culture area.

It is Bloom's rabid Eurocentrism, no doubt, that makes him gape in disbelief at the audacity of the so-called bespoilers of *The Tempest* to utilize the priestly Shakespearean text in their Third World disquisition. Conversely, however, a certain zeal for the cultural authenticity of their symbols may cause Third World spokespersons to deny Caliban the power to connote their reality given the European extraction of the figure. They may also object on the basis of the differential ethnology implicit in the coinage of Caliban's name. We know that Shakespeare made up the name as a near anagram of the word "cannibal," the appellation used by Michel de Montaigne in the essay "On Cannibals," from his famous collection *Essais* (1580), to designate a society of New World natives. A copy of the 1603 English rendition of *Essais* found copiously annotated among Shakespeare's papers indicates that the Bard had indeed read Montaigne's text (Fernández Retamar 1974:17). Certainly, also, in creating the character of Caliban to pose as Prospero's antagonist in *The Tempest*, Shakespeare drew on the ideological baggage that at the time located the New World "savage" in a sort of moral antipodes vis-á-vis the "civilized" Christian, hence the unflattering coarseness displayed by the character in the play.

But one can argue against the objections by Third World voices just as one would against Bloom's. One could contend that, problematic as it may be, the birth of Caliban brings along a fair degree of possibilities for nativization. Montaigne, for instance, did not simply echo the binary relation that assumed a moral dichotomy in the cultural disparity between Christian Europe and the newly conquered territories that had received the name of West Indies. The French sage did not succumb to the enticement of the contrastive ideology then current. With mordant irony, Montaigne took advantage of the distance between the two cultural poles to venture a critical glance at the presumed superiority of sixteenth-century Europe with respect to the people who had fallen in the course of the colonial transaction. His essay did not demonize the indigenous population of the Americas. Instead, it scoffed at the common practice of every individual to call "barbarism whatever is not his own practice" (Montaigne 1957:152). Montaigne criticized the scornful attitude of Europeans who rushed to place New World natives on a plane morally beneath them, while remaining "so blind to our own faults" (155). In that sense, the French author steered clear of the Columbian tradition that by the sixteenth century had already reified the conquered peoples of the Americas, relegating them ontologically to a subhuman level, stressing their anthropophagy as a salient marker of their identity. Through that denormalizing ideological maneuver, the conquerors established the rationale that justified their domination of the "savage." That thought pattern served an invaluable function. Used to advantage initially by the Spanish pioneers of the colonial transaction, it warranted the physical violence deployed against the aborigines in each of the lands newly explored and colonized.

By intervening in the Columbian tradition through the creation of a character informed by Montaigne's evocation of New World "cannibals," Shakespeare rendered the Caribbean and Caliban rhetorically inseparable. Columbus inaugurated in his diary the language that gave rise to all subsequent nomenclature to refer to the region and its people. The diary applies the terms "caribes" and "caníbales" interchangeably to those indigenous populations that most decidedly resisted the voracious encroachment of the Spanish conquerors beginning on October 12, 1492. In due time the stigmatizing web of Columbus's language enveloped a whole archipelago, a coastal region, and the sea that delimited them. The word Caribbean, derived from the name "caribes" which the Admiral used to designate the natives, whom he also called "cannibals," meaning "eaters of human flesh," in time came to refer to the Antillean archipelago along with the coastal zones that mark the boundaries of the region and the sea that sustains the islands. At the end of that discursive cycle the Spaniards had conveniently resolved their labor scarcity to complete the colonial enterprise, as Palencia-Roth has noted (1997:18). Given the undercurrent of genocidal violence that lies at the root of the Columbian nomenclature, one cannot ignore the plea by Colbert Nepaulsingh that urges us to rethink the colonial names for the Caribbean region and its people. Regarding the Columbian terminology as a stumbling block that obstructs the efforts to explain the Antillean world as an autonomous culture area, Nepaulsingh emphatically calls upon concerned scholars to adopt a "new name for the Caribbean" (Nepaulsingh 1998:14; 1996a:5–10). He proposes the term "New World Islands," entreating us also to abandon "continental modes of thought" and their attendant "idea that the continents are by definition superior to islands" (Nepaulsingh 1996b:8).

This book however, cannot abide by this colleague's recommendation first because its stress on "islands" would seem to restrict the reach of the appellation to the insular Caribbean excluding the Atlantic coast and those continental territories such as Surinam, Guiana, Guyana, and Belize that share with the archipelago a common historical structure and whose Caribbean identity is indisputable. As the preceding sections of this book ought to have shown, I have employed the different names interchangeably: Caribbean, West Indies, and Antillean world to identify the region, while allowing for the conceptual openness that would make the terms elastic enough to transcend the tellurian geography and, in keeping with the migratory dispersion of the region's population across the globe, to encompass the cultural geography created by Caribbeans elsewhere.

Besides, though sharing Nepaulsingh's disquiet about the troubling baggage contained in the Columbian nomenclature, I see a grave risk in any project aimed at correcting colonial misnomers. I believe we need to preserve the erroneous language insofar as it contains clues that preserve the memory of the Antillean world's catastrophic beginning. The misnomers help keep alive the memory of the misconduct that brought them into being. Europe's intrusion in the region unleashed a process of naming, renaming, and misnaming whose pugnacity paralleled the military raids on the indigenous populations there. I doubt that one could come upon a sensible way of evading the problematic heritage of the Columbian discourse without seeming to dissolve the Caribbean's inescapable—albeit painful—ties to the West. The effort to liberate the region from the linguistic violence of the colonial transaction might inadvertently privilege a civil parlance that would lessen the gravity of the Antillean world's traumatic start. We cannot epistemologically afford to deflate the harshness of that past, the grim images that stand out as we perform the unsavory act of remembering: Taino women raped, Taino men disemboweled, indigenous temples of worship reduced to ashes by the invader's torch, and countless uprooted Africans doomed permanently to slavery's social death. The existing Columbian vocabulary easily evokes the shock of the Caribbean's beginning with all of its baleful brutality: the cracks of the whip, the hangings, and the compulsory inferiorization included. Through it, we can also better value the actions occasionally taken by the besieged natives, from self-immolation in hopeless battle, to straightforward suicide, to running away to the mountains as a means to assert their contested human dignity. The Caribbean as we know it began by undergoing what Brathwaite has termed a counter-Renaissance. Brathwaite uses the term to designate the deplorable dark side of the European renaissance, a period during which Western capitals witnessed dazzling achievements in sculpture, painting, architecture, and literature while simultaneously exporting death and destruction to peoples overseas.

Understanding the Caribbean past as "a history of catastrophe," Brathwaite has advocated a "literature of catastrophe to hold broken mirror up to broken nature" (Brathwaite 1985:456–457). Similarly, I would argue for an approach to Caribbean reality that marches head-on toward the epicenter of the trauma as the best way to capture the gist of the human experience in the region and to grab at the crux of the evasive notion of Caribbeanness. A receptacle of good and evil, a crucible of human histories, a confluence of disparate legacies, the Caribbean, as Carpentier proclaimed, boasts great originality in cultural expression. But that does not alter the fact that the constituent elements of Caribbean culture correspond to the convergence of distinct heritages that coincided in the region during the conquest and colonization. Africa, Europe, and the aboriginal Americas then and there encountered one another in a dreadful embrace, resulting in torrential bloodshed. The blood that ran fertilized the soil of the islands and the coasts, giving rise to the creolizing process whence the Antillean world would emerge as a new product in the history of human culture. But the advent of that new cultural entity responded primarily to an instigation by Western imperial expansionism. Elsewhere I have argued that "the West literally created the Caribbean" following the dynamic unleashed by the conquest starting in the fifteenth century (Torres-Saillant 1997:5).

As an Amsterdam-based Surinamese writer, the late Edgar Cairo stressed the patent form in which the baggage of the past reflects itself daily on the lives of contemporary Caribbean people. His novel *Dat vuur der grote drama's* (That Fire of Great Dramas) (1982) explores the inextricable connection of the Dutch-speaking Caribbean and the Netherlands through the centuries. The text dramatizes the difficulty of evading a former colonial life, the legacy of slavery included, whose burden oppresses the individual experience of "each contemporary Caribbean person who has left the colony and settled in the 'mother' country" (Rutgers 1998:551). Of course, recognizing the interconnection between the metropolis and the colony or former colony should in no way lead to doubts regarding the fundamental difference between the Netherlands as site of imperial departure and the dominated Dutch Caribbean as site of colonial arrival. By no means should one view the Caribbean as a mere cultural extension of the European nations that marshaled the colonial transaction no matter how many points of contact we might identify between here and there. When the most memorable Caribbean thinkers and artists have set out to stress the distinct contours of their identity they have often had recourse to accentuating their substratum of difference with respect to the Christian West (Torres-Saillant 1997:5).

The phenomena that combined in the region to produce Caribbean culture resulted in a peculiar contraption that harbored two seemingly contradictory qualities: inevitable derivativeness and stark authenticity. Similarly, the grievous historical experience that befell the region from 1492 onward, the fractured past that seems to repeat itself ad infinitum, has not rendered the Antillean person unable to imagine a restorative future reality. Despite the ethnic and linguistic fragmentation occurring in countries like Suriname, for instance, poets still envision the presence of wholeness. Robin Ewald Raveles (1935–1983), who used the *nom de plume* R. Dobru in his writings, rendered in his 1965 poem "Wan bon/Een boom" (One Tree) an evidently willful integrative vision. The speaker in one of the stanzas sees: "One tree / so many leaves / one tree" (cited by Kempen 1998:634). In another stanza, the nature imagery gives way to ethnic signifiers to rephrase the vision of unity "One Suriname / so many hair types / so many skin colors / so many tongues / one people" (cited by Rutgers 1998:548). Hopelessness regarding the region's geographical and historical balkanization has not taken hold of Caribbean thought pervasively. Even among those who, like the Surinamese poet Henry de Ziel, better known by his pseudonym as Trefossa, had to abandon their native soil to find refuge in the metropolis, one finds an adamant affirmation of their world. Trefossa's poem "Kopenhagen" presents us with a speaker beholding the famous Edvard

Eriksen statue of a mermaid sitting on a rock. Instead of distracting him from the home country, that European figure is culturally transfigured in his eyes, with the siren turning into the legendary Watramama, the water deity from Surinam's folklore. The first stanza has the bedazzled speaker address the sculpture thus: "What is this by the sea? / see—see! / Watermama, is that you sitting on/that stone?" (Trefossa 1998:519). With similar obduracy, an impressive number of voices uphold pan-Caribbean, unitary worldviews culturally and otherwise. Themes connected to visions of regional unity recur, for instance, in the English-language writings coming from Saba, St. Eustace, and Sint Maarten, the three territories that make up the Dutch Caribbean Windward Islands (Badejo 1998:679). By the same token, the publication in Sranan Tongo of Brathwaite's poetry volume *Rights of Passage* (1967), translated by D. France Oliviera as *Primisi-ô* (1997), represents a telling gesture of the prevailing intent to imagine the Antillean world holistically. That the translator should choose to render the text into a vernacular language rather than into Dutch manifests a desire to access the sort of cultural autochthony that Brathwaite himself has explored through his commitment to the search for an authentically Caribbean way of saying (Kempen 1998:642).

CALIBAN'S CARIBBEAN CONTINGENCY

I subscribe to the use of Caliban as a vehicle via which to delve into the depths of Caribbean life in a manner that unabashedly confronts the tensions, contradictions, and frustrations inherent in the public history of the region. A critical glance at Caliban can enable us to organize a set of themes and variations on Caribbean society's past, present, and future. My use of Caliban as cultural synecdoche for the region will differ from previous treatments that have focused on Caliban's trajectory of anticolonial insurgency and resistance. Prompted by the forceful eloquence with which Lamming's *The Pleasure of Exile* evoked Caliban through the combined virtues of courage, brilliance, and nobility of heart displayed by the figure of Toussaint Louverture, punctuated by the exultation of a parallel magnanimity he recognized in the intellectual legacy of C. L. R. James ("the greatest" of all Caribbean teachers), a discursive tradition took root that from then onward regarded Caliban almost exclusively as a positive revolutionary force. Lamming has remained faithful to his original vision of the Antillean leader as a somewhat anointed individual. In later years, many of the region's political utopias having gone awry, this focus has stressed the role of the artist and the thinker as a force of liberation. Regarding, "cultural production as a necessary alternative to the violence of Caribbean history," Lamming continues to posit the notion of the "artist imagining a new future upon the cemetery of the past" (Nair 1996:144). Lamming belongs to a generation of politically devout Antillean thinkers and artists. That older generation consists of the likes of Dominican painter Silvano Lora, who never renounced his socialist ideas in spite of the political apathy brought about by the fall of the Berlin wall, and the Haitian sociologist Gérard Pierre-Charles, who returned to Haiti after decades of exile in his later years, never stopped believing in his country's possibilities to create a new society based on the principles of equality and social justice, and remained an active participant in the political process until his recent death. When I last met Pierre-Charles, at a conference on "the border" organized by the Ministry of Defense in Santo Domingo in July 2003, I proposed to him that we promote a reevaluation of Caribbean heroes in order to foreground the duality and often the contradictions attributable to their legacy. But he did not think such a project a good idea for a reason that I found disarming, namely that our people already have exposure to too many bad things said about them, and he did not see what service we would be rendering by telling them that even those compatriots whom they think worthy of worship are no good.

While I am sensitive to the seriousness of the caution expressed by Pierre-Charles, which I interpret as an injunction that Antillean intellects ought to refrain from playing into the further spiritual disempowerment of their people, I insist that the debunking of Caribbean heroes can be promoted if it teaches something generically about the problematic nature of heroes, including, and perhaps especially, the heroes worshiped by the metropolitan societies that mock Antillean hero worship. But we cannot remain unmindful about the possibly deleterious effect of allowing the trope of "romance" to guide the logic of our remembering when we look at events and actors in the Caribbean past, especially in light of the supposition that the region may have "managed to fuse competing revolutionary and reactionary paradigms in its discourses about itself" (Edmonson 1999:10). While sharing the concern implicit in the caution by Pierre-Charles, I insist on a way of seeing Caliban's trajectory that will enable us to honor the times when he has behaved as a friend and resent those when he has behaved inimically. Therefore, my approach does not refrain from emphasizing his inconsistencies, which bespeaks a willingness to focus on historical contingency— the accident-prone texture of human events—as a means to apprehend the complexity of the Caribbean experience. I concur with the hermeneutic power of Caliban as a metaphor that captures "our cultural situation," as proposed by Férnandez Retamar, but I would prefer to restrict its application to the culture area of the Caribbean while he applied it to the whole of Latin America and the Caribbean (Fernández Retamar 1974:30–31). I circumscribe its use to the Antillean zone of the hemisphere because I believe that discrete culture areas warrant their own differentiated symbols, and I would argue that the Caribbean merits a specific understanding in terms of its difference from the Latin America mainland no less than from Europe. This holds true despite the dual identity of Cuba, the Dominican Republic, and Puerto Rico, which, by virtue of the linguistic link, simultaneously share the cultural orbits of the Antillean world and of Latin America, moving between the poles that Milan Kundera has called "mediating contexts" (1991:48). I myself have examined the Caribbean's distinct contours as a differentiated cultural zone in spite of its inexorable links to Africa, Europe, and Latin

America (Torres-Saillant 1997). I would add that the relative marginality of Dominican, Puerto Rican, and even Cuban literatures in the panoramic vistas woven by mainland Latin American scholars may have to do with a reticence provoked by the peculiar texture of Caribbean writing. The academics in charge of constructing the Latin American canon find the texts from the Spanish-speaking islands difficult to accommodate fully in the socioaesthetic and cultural framework that informs their tabulation.

Another reason for limiting the use of Caliban to a symbolization of the Caribbean is the connection of Shakespeare's *The Tempest* to events in the region. Roger Toumson points to a Caribbean news item that reached England in 1609 as one of the catalysts for the Bard's composition of the play. In that year, in the course of an expedition headed for Virginia, a ship that had become separated from the rest of its fleet capsized near the coast of one of the islands forming the Bermudas cluster. The crew members managed to find refuge on the island and several months thereafter succeeded on their own in arriving in Virginia, from where they were sent back to England (Toumson 1981:27–28). Because of the dramatic texture of the incident, whose details resembled the events of a fictional adventure story, the shipwreck fostered abundant literary coverage. The Bermudas occurrence then created the context that motivated Shakespeare to write the plot of *The Tempest*; since the Bermudas were then and have since then remained associated with the Antillean world, it may be said that, textually speaking, the character of Caliban was born in a Caribbean cradle.

A native of the Caribbean, Caliban accords with the region's reality in the contingent nature of their common trajectory. Caliban's problematic legacy translates, as it were, into a failure of leadership in the Antillean world. This chapter begins with the working hypothesis that Caliban may have lost the fight with his formidable domesticator, Prospero, the awesome magician, having allowed the oblique and sinuous Ariel to confound him. He may also have lost the fight against himself, proving incapable to distance himself from the forces and patterns of conduct that have historically oppressed his people. We can begin to flesh out the foregoing hypothesis by appealing to the prism of the literary imagination to evoke the genesis of things Caribbean. Skipping the initial arrival of the Admiral on the Amerindian shore, we may go back to a crucial point of origin. The conquest and colonization started in Santo Domingo—or Quisqueya, to honor one of the indigenous names for the island that subsequently became known as Hispaniola. At that incipient Antillean moment, the fleeting instant during which the native Tainos and the invading Spaniards were still equal, skirmishes and more sizable battles took place on the island. But as the unequal relations of force increased their gap, warfare gave way to genocide. Around the year 1513, in the district of Xaragua, one of the five chiefdoms that comprised the political units of the island, the first great massacre took place.

The episode involved the death of Queen Anacaona, the widow of Chief Caonabo and sister to the late Bohechio, from whom she inherited the rule of Xaragua. Along with her died all the men and women of her court as well as all the guests she had convened "to receive, celebrate, and give their reverence to the *Guamiquina* of the Christians" (Las Casas, cited by Wilson 1990:133). The title "*Guamiquina*," a Taino word for Lord, referred to the distinguished visitor Governor Fray Nicolás de Ovando, who had given the queen to understand that he came in peace, hence the generous hospitality bestowed upon him and his 300 Spanish soldiers in Xaragua on that fateful day. Then at one point, after having enjoyed Taino food, drink, entertainment, and cordial conversation, Governor Ovando gave the lethal order. The swift motion of swords, spears, and shields started, and the deafening gunpowder smothered the screams of the astonished natives. Thus did violence put an end to Spanish-Indian communication. The mass murder perpetrated by Ovando's troops inaugurated the tradition of silencing the interlocutor to the advantage of monologic expression. Insofar as "Xaragua was the last stronghold of pre-Hispanic power on Hispaniola," its genocidal destruction meant the completion of a context wherein the word would only command respect when uttered by the voice of the masters (Wilson 1990:134).

In 1880, poet and educator Salomé Ureña de Henríquez, the reputed founding mother of Dominican poetry, published the long narrative poem *Anacaona* to commemorate the courage of the martyred queen and pay tribute to the human dignity of the Tainos who fell victim to the gory onslaught of the "strange visitors / whom the sea hurled on the island's shore" (Ureña 1989:185). Narrated in the third person and aiming for epic loftiness in content and diction, the text celebrates the spirit of resistance attributable to the indigenous population while lamenting the loss of the edenic world that the Spanish fractured upon their arrival in 1492. Ironically, Ureña felt too deep a sense of kinship with the Hispanic heritage that nineteenth-century Dominican society boasted to launch a really radical indictment of Spanish violence. A mulatto who occupied a place of distinction among the country's literati, she harbored too much admiration for Spain's legacy in the New World to take issue with the colonial transaction systemically. The poem depicts the carnage of Xaragua as a deviation. Anacaona and her people die on account of the individual iniquity of Governor Ovando. Other than such isolated instances of misconduct, the Spanish retain their essential goodness. The noble spirit of Columbus remains unaltered throughout the poem. To commit to this portrayal, Ureña had to overlook the historical fact that the Admiral himself had unleashed grievous violence against the Tainos prior to the killing in Xaragua. Columbian violence explained the death of Caonabo and Anacaona's widowhood. But the poet insists in exalting the "discoverer." Witness the unfavorable picture she draws of Columbus's squire Francisco Roldán Ximeno, who led a rebellion against his boss to demand a greater share of the gains amassed by the island's authorities from the colonial enterprise. A pertinent stanza in the poem says: "Infamous Roldán who withheld from Columbus / the tribute of love and respect that was due him / furiously raising his seditious voice / marshaled his troops in baneful revolt / with the myriad tedious turmoil that followed breaking the heart of the great Genoese" (Ureña 1989:234).

As an ideological, historical, and literary counterpoint, nearly a century after the text by Ureña appeared, the Haitian poet Jean Métellus published his dramatic poem *Anacaona* (1986), which offers an alternative evocation of the Taino queen and the devastation of Xaragua. As one would expect, Métellus updates the historical content of the poem. The text represents Ovando's treacherous slaughter as an action consistent with the political and economic logic of the conquest rather than as a deviation stemming from the moral deformity of an individual functionary. We gather from the poem that the destruction of Xaragua occurred because the Spanish authorities wished to avert the possible alliance between the two ethnic groups that shared the common brunt of colonial subjection on the island. Métellus has Governor Ovando warn that "Ce serait une catastrophe si jamais se / produisait la moindre collusion entre / Indians et Négres" [It would be catastrophic if ever / the slightest alliance / of Indians and blacks occurred] (1986:150). The Spanish commander moans over the frequency with which black slaves have already escaped to the mountains and their ensuing hostility against the colonial regime (150). Conversely, the Taino queen is aware of the condition of blacks on the island, and she voices her solidarity with their cause. Whether or not the historical Anacaona identified with the plight of blacks, the awareness that Métellus gives her is at least consistent with the demands of verisimilitude. For blacks had arrived in Santo Domingo in July 1502, in the same fleet that brought Ovando as governor of the island, when the Catholic monarchs Ferdinand and Isabella gave him the rule of their first colony in the western hemisphere. Also, within a year of their arrival, black slaves had begun to run away to the mountains and to interact with the Indians, much to the chagrin of Governor Ovando (Deive 1989:20). The interethnic solidarity that Métellus assigns to the character of Anacaona, then, has a measure of historical plausibility. Shortly before the queen dies, she expresses the wish that she could add to her glory the tittle of "Champion of the black and Indian maroons" (Métellus 1986:155).

While Ureña nostalgically recreates in her text the memory of a lost world, Métellus seeks to infuse the events of Xaragua with the genesis of a legacy of resistance against colonial oppression in the Caribbean. The Dominican poet in that sense looked solely to the past while the Haitian poet has his eyes set on the future. The closing lines in the text by Métellus allude clearly to the insurrections that Indians and blacks would subsequently embark upon in their quest to shake off the chains of their subjection. The character of Yaquimex, who acts as a sort of collective conscience of the Taino community, announces the determination of his people to "head for Bahoruco," reach the mountaintops where their "African brothers" have already gone, and launch from there their common offensive against "these monsters ejected by the sea" (154, 156, 158). They thus will avenge the death of their queen and their compatriots. The poem's ending, charged with righteous emotion and anticipating the liberation struggles that draw near, make for a pervasive optimistic outlook. The last two lines "L'Afrique est venue / Aya bombé, Aya bombé" (Africa is here / Better dead than slave) would seem to connect this moment of potential insurgency with the black slave rebellion that almost three centuries later would dismantle the French colonial structure in Saint Domingue.

No doubt Ureña sins of ideological naiveté in the problematic intent to repudiate the Xaragua massacre without condemning the political and economic project that informed the conquest and colonization of Quisqueya by the Spanish. However, despite enjoying access to the added perspectives afforded by the fact that he wrote almost a century later, Métellus sins no less woefully insofar as he succumbs to the temptation to evoke the history one would have wished rather than the one that actually happened. The sad historical fact is that the genocidal action perpetrated by Ovando did not trigger a movement that would subsequently advance the cause of equality and justice. History did not register the revolutionary virtues that the poem would attribute to the descendants of the Xaragua victims. Just as Ureña's poem in the late nineteenth century misrepresented historical data to flatter Columbus, Propero's progenitor, so did Métellus's late twentieth-century poem misrepresent the known facts to flatter the Taino leadership, ancestors of Caliban. An uprising did occur in the mountains of Bahoruco around 1519 led by the young warrior Guarocuya, a member of the conquered Taino nobility. But that insurrection had hardly a glorious outcome. The event did not bequeath a legacy that could inspire subsequent freedom fighters in the Caribbean.

For many generations, Guarocuya, better known as Enriquillo, a diminutive of his Christian name Enrique, has enjoyed great prestige in the historiography of Hispaniola. The Dominican author Manuel de Jesus Galván, in a novel entitled *Enriquillo: novela histórica* (1882), which became a classic of *indigenista* literature in Latin America, almost single-handedly established the tradition that venerates Guarocuya as a heroic standard-bearer of equality and justice. Haitian schoolbooks also subscribed to the historiographical lore that celebrated "le cacique Henri" as a "vaillant défenseur de sa race opprimé" whose "tenacité avait triomphé de l'injustice" (Dorsainvil 1934: 24, 26). But the resolution of the Bahoruco rebellion would not seem to justify the apotheosis of Enriquillo. One should note that Galván's novel, like the poem by Ureña, manages to extol Guarocuya's armed struggle against the colonial authorities without challenging the raison d'etre of the conquest itself. His text also explains the injustice that the Tainos fought against as caused by isolated acts of cruelty committed by individual Spaniards. The venerable José Martí, who got to sing the praises of the book in a letter to the author that editors have conventionally used as a prologue in the successive reprints of the novel, failed to catch the insidious duplicity that informed Galván's evocation of the Bahoruco rebellion. We owe to the Dominican poet and historian Pedro Mir an interpretation of Guarocuya's story that sets the record straight.

The second chapter of Mir's *Tres leyendas de colores* explores the Taino leader's trajectory, from his upbringing as the protégé of a Spanish landowner named Valenzuela who nurtured him and saw to his education in a Franciscan convent. Baptized with the Christian name Enrique, he received the socialization befitting a Spanish lad (Mir 1978:130). The death of his good master Valenzuela, whose heir treated Enriquillo with contempt, removing the privileges he had previously enjoyed, awakened the young Taino to the lugubrious plight of his people. In time he led a band of native insurgents to the mountains of Bahoruco, starting an insurrection that for 15 years the colonial regime would not defeat. Mir minimizes the personal nature of Enriquillo's grievance, reasoning that, whatever its catalyst, the action of the young warrior ceased to be personal once his community validated his leadership, putting their lives on the line in order to advance the cause he had articulated for them (Mir 1978:145). However, Enriquillo proved unworthy of that trust. He lacked the moral mettle of authentic leadership. When the Spanish authorities, whom he had defeated militarily, sent as emissary the spiritual guide who had instructed him in the catechism as a child, he could not resist. The spiritual offensive was too formidable, and shortly thereafter he brought his troops down from the mountains, the Spanish having offered to restore his social privileges, including the added distinction of addressing him thenceforward as Don Enrique. The prodigal son of the colonial regime then signed an infamous peace treaty whereby his mighty guerilla forces would from then on employ their martial adroitness in the service of the Spanish power structure. Their service included pursuing other insurgents who challenged the colonial regime and capturing runaway black slaves at a price per capita (Mir 1978:156).

Viewed through the prism of the Shakespearean triad, Enriquillo's political inconsistency follows these stages. A momentary loss of privilege brought him into opposition to Prospero, causing him to locate himself in the role of the dissenting native, namely Caliban. But, Hispanized and Christianized by an earlier socialization, his instincts placed him closer to the sensitivity of Ariel. The Ariel that informed his neutralized conscience got the best of him. As soon as Prospero restored his blessing, the Taino chief quickly gave in to the allurement of his former condition. Yet, the chameleon-like nature of his trajectory did not disqualify him for the heroism ascribed to him in the history textbooks. Mir expressed no surprise at the glorification of Enriquillo, which even today holds some sway over the national imaginary in Dominican society. Deconstructing Galvan's psychopathology, Mir understood that the architects of official Dominican discourse elevated the Taino chieftain as an immaculate symbol of Dominican nationality because of their own ideology and class positioning. Simply put, a historian or a novelist with Ariel's mentality will most likely identify with the Ariels of the past. For instance, Galván's glorification of Enriquillo perfectly matched his support of the 1861 annexation of the Dominican Republic to the Spanish crown. He belonged to an entrenched Creole oligarchy that was willing to exchange their nation's sovereignty for the preservation of their social privilege. As Mir has succinctly put it, Galván was a modern-day Enriquillo (cited by Torres-Saillant 1997:166).

UNKEPT PROMISES, PRECARIOUS HOPE

The legacy of Enriquillo and the kind of leadership he represents, which has abounded in Caribbean history from the start of the colonial transaction to the present, might dissuade any hopeful outlook on the history of the region. Yet despite the dismal background that the ambivalence of Caliban encapsulates, the Caribbean imagination has tenaciously resisted the temptation to give in to intellectual pessimism. Often connected with a persevering compulsion to assert the unity and future well-being of people in the various nations of the Antillean world, that optimistic vision has remained vibrant to this day in voices like that of Frank Martinus Arion, the prominent Curaçao an writer. Arion embraces an intransigent Caribbeanism, one that he poses adamantly against those Caribbean personalities who have succumbed to despair, who have doubted the region's potential, or who have allowed them to publicly scorn any of the national communities that make up the larger Caribbean family. He resents the fact that at times it seems that Antilleans would much rather relocate to Europe and the United States than work to raise the quality of life in their home countries to the level of those places. For instance, he laments the case of Stanley Brown, a Curaçao an political leader who in the 1960s advocated decolonization, emancipation, and independence from Dutch rule. Apparently overwhelmed by a series of setbacks, Brown has ended up wishing to retire to a life in exile (Arion 1998c:449).

Arion sadly discovers even the much admired Cuban patriot and man of letters José Martí among Caribbean detractors. Martí authored in the late nineteenth century an essay filled with deprecation toward the people and culture of Curaçao. He spoke of the women on the island in this fashion: "The shepherdesses here are anemic mulattas, formless negresses, and tattered crones busy at fixing smoke-dried sardines by the estuary's bank" (Martí 1964:129–130). Martí also reproached the "yellowish" countenance of Curaçao's population, in whose semblance he found "Not that noble bronze, that most natural bodily hue evident in souls annealed by good fire,—but that earth-like swarthiness born of a slovenly childhood, a questionable ancestry, an idle mind, a sedentary life" (133). Finally, Martí describes the island's ethno-linguistic situation in these dismissive terms: "There they go, a degenerate race, a sickly race, speaking—all too rapidly—with the lush fluidity of the tropics, an ignoble and peculiar tongue, an incorrect and peculiar mixture of Castilian and Dutch, a tongue whose very name reveals it whole: Papiamentu" (Martí 1964:130). Arion pairs Martí's derisive depiction of the people and culture of Curaçao with a more recent declaration by Boeli van Leeuwen, one of the island's most prominent living men of letters, that he dad no interest in any civilization other than that produced by the West through the fusion of Judeo-Christian and Greco-Roman element (Arion 1998:448). Not without anguish, of course, Arion fulminates against the likes of Brown, Martí, Leeuwen, declaring them unprepared to love the Caribbean as it really is.

Arion's indictment would have to go also to various other salient Antillean literary figures not included in his brief survey who have berated their people.

The prominent Puerto Rican intellectual Antonio S. Pedreira published in 1934 the essay *Insularismo*, which attributed an unfavorable pathology to the Puerto Rican population. Pedreira contended that the island condition, insularity, stifles the mind, the meager geographical expanse leading to a shrinking of people's vision, even while he argued for the need to "believe in ourselves so we can invent ourselves" (Pedreira 1973:31–32, 44, 157). The distinguished playwright and short-fiction writer René Marqués wrote a long essay, "El puertoriqueño dócil" (1962) to establish "the docility of the Puerto Rican" in response to his compatriots who had "insistently and childishly denied" that aspect of the national psyche when a well-known North American literary critic, while teaching briefly at the University of Puerto Rico, wrote an essay asserting that "the Puerto Rican is docile" (Marqués 1976:36). The renowned Dominican statesman and author Juan Bosh advanced in his 1950 book *Trujillo: causas de una tiranía sin ejemplo* a historical phenomenology that attributed to his compatriots serious congenital disadvantages. He affirmed at the outset that the social breakdown of the Dominican people began at birth, with the society's coming into being as if from a "poisoned womb" (Bosh 1959:14). More recently, the Haitian poet and fiction writer René Depestre, who from his first book of poems in 1945 to the 1980s distinguished himself as an eloquent spokesperson for the cultural and political vindication of the Caribbean vis-á-vis the Christian West, has joined the ranks of the detractors. Renouncing his previous struggles, he has devoted himself to cultivating an erotic literature marked by self-indulgent frivolity while evoking a touristic vista of Haitian history and culture to cater to his European readership's taste for the exotic. Clearly, then, the position of V. S. Naipaul, the famous Trinidadian author whose book *The Middle Passage* (1962) denied the Caribbean a legitimate place in history, belongs in a tradition that preceded him and continues to this day. But the knowledge of the inimical tradition has not disheartened radical optimists like Arion, who has sought to combat the foregoing disparagement by identifying historical roots as well as ecological and cultural bases that would counterbalance it. Thus Arion tells the story of his continuous search for the "Great Curassow," a bird indigenous to Curaçao that many for long thought extinct. When the search puts him on the tracks to a living specimen that an quaintance of his has spotted on his ranch, Arion reads into that happy outcome "the road to Caribbeanness" leading symbolically to regional integration. As he accepts the ride that will take him to the ranch where the elusive *korsou grandi* awaits, he closes his reflection in this hopeful, forward-looking tone: "I threw the groceries in his car and started for the Caribbean" (Arion 1998:452).

The radical optimism that still pervades much of Caribbean thought, an obstinate outlook that militantly holds on to a constructive vision of the region, serves as a protective shield against the frustration likely to emanate from the catastrophe and the fragmentation brought about by a bad history and an unreliable leadership. It serves also as an ideological response to the discourse of apathy that stresses exceedingly the national, ethnic, linguistic, and geographical balkanization of the Antillean world. A medley of four major European languages, numerous Creole tongues, various distinct national experiences, and a host of political systems converges in the region, making it a tapestry woven from threads of seemingly irreconcilable colors. Diverse forms of interaction with disparate Western capitals have similarly given rise to a polymorphous scenario regarding the nature of the rapport between Caribbean world and their former colonial overseers. Compounding this fractious scenario is a historical awareness of colonialism as the *primum mobile* of the human experience in the area. The legacy still persists of a past shaped by specific types of exchange among the Western director societies that vied for economic and political control of the region. The seventeenth-century disputes between Spain and Holland, followed by the imperial competition between Spain and France that led to the partition of the island into two colonial units, still affect the difficult interaction of Haitians and Dominicans on Hispaniola today (Klooster 1997:8; Moya Pons 1993:22). The friction between Spain and the United States dictated Puerto Rican life from 1898 onward, just as much of what has become of Cuba has roots leading directly back to clashes of imperial titans, namely the Spanish-America War of 1898 and U.S.–Soviet Cold War hostilities after the 1959 Cuban Revolution. Given its peculiar history as a site of contention for world powers, as an "imperial frontier" to use a phrase coined by Bosh, the Caribbean has witnessed external forces whose historical footprints lurk patently on the precarious rapport that still occasionally thwarts projects of regional collaboration.

Quisqueya's Unreliable Caliban

The celebration of resistance, the cult of the Maroon, the study of the folk, and the prevailing emphasis on social history by Caribbean thinkers and artists constitute ways of coping ideologically with historical dependency, that is, with the fact that events at home should follow a logic dictated by the behavior of particular empires abroad. Orienting them is no doubt the desire to produce conceptual frameworks that might reveal a narrative of Caribbean agency despite the preeminence of the sequence of events that so prominently feature outside imperial forces as leading actors. But, while motivated by a search for a vision of wholeness for the region, the archeological impulse to unveil Caribbean agency has often come unaccompanied by a critical examination of that agency, hence the need for the present exploration of the recurring indelicacy of the region's native leadership. This line of inquiry would thus ask whether the anti-Caribbean harshness of such prominent men of letters as Leeuwen, Naipaul, and Depestre might not be regarded as an intellectual stance with kinship to a reneging leadership that, beginning with Enriquillo in the early 1500s, has become a fixture of Caribbean political history. I would argue, in other words, that equally crucial to the advancement of a vision of wholeness for the Caribbean is a study of the history of Caliban's perversity. Only by realistically assessing the frequency with which he has gone astray can we hope to uncover salutary paths conducive to his redemption for the good of the region.

Quisqueya, the island shared by the Republic of Haiti and the Dominican Republic, known also as Santo Domingo as well as Hispaniola, provides a useful setting for a study of Caliban's trajectory. Here we may focus on the paradigms that have captivated the imagination of the ideologues responsible for the prevailing definitions of nation. The clash of titans on the hemisphere provides the pertinent context between the late nineteenth century and the early twentieth century, during that moment of imperial transition when the Spanish crown grumblingly exited in deference to the American eagle. Concretizing the foreign policy figure known as the Monroe Doctrine, North American might put an end to the Spanish imperial presence in Latin America. That political turning point had a noteworthy impact on the state of mind of the region's intelligentsia, which extended to Hispaniola, given the peculiar cultural positioning of the Spanish-speaking Caribbean in relation to Latin America. Many Latin American literati fell into a state of intellectual depression, which manifested itself in a frantic affirmation of Hispanic culture and a rejection of North American values. Concomitantly, they asserted and celebrated the cultural homogeneity of all the Spanish-speaking countries of the hemisphere. They abhorred the encroachment of the United States for its potential to undermine the cultural and moral values that held their countries together. Naturally, a less flattering view of Iberian unity would reveal the bitter drama of genocidal oppression shrouded by the *hispanidad* or *latinidad* they so passionately defended. Eugenio María de Hostos, the eminent Puerto Rican social theorist whose ideas influenced Dominican thought, described the conquest of the Americas by Spain as one of the "greatest services" ever rendered to humanity from the beginning of time (Hostos 1969:169).

The fall of the last vestiges of the Spanish Empire in the Americas exacerbated the Latin American intelligentsia's passion for their Iberian heritage. Confronted with the reality of U.S. domination of the hemisphere, they developed a discourse of defense of their Latin cultural background, which they regarded as a system of values that was diametrically opposed to the nordic ethos that informed the United States. The text that most eloquently captured the uneasiness that vexed the Latin American intelligentsia at the time was the essay *Ariel* (1900) by the Uruguayan José Enrique Rodó. Composed as an oration delivered by an "old and venerated" teacher known as Prospero, as a farewell address to his young pupils at the end of the school year, the essay draws its symbology directly from Shakespeare's *The Tempest* while it converses intertextually with the philosophical drama *Caliban* (1871) by Ernest Renan. The speaker sits close to a bronze statue of Ariel, "genie of the air" who stands "in the symbolism of Shakespeare's play, for the noble and winged side of the spirit," who has the mandate of "rectifying in superior men the tenacious vestiges of Caliban, symbol of sensuality and baseness" (Rodó 1971:26). The speech sustains an impassioned celebration of Western European humanistic values—the foundation of the latinidad that Spain had generously bestowed on Iberian America—envisioning with horror a time when the region might succumb to nordomania and become delatinized (Rodó 1971:102). For Rodó the gravest danger lay in the utili-tarian drive of American democracy, which fosters "equality in mediocrity" (77, 101). The United States, the embodiment of Caliban, appears as the champion of utilitarianism, materialistic pursuits, and vulgarizing ideas of equality, as a threat, that is, to the love of beauty, disinterested cultivation of the intellect, and the highest values of the human spirit encompassed by Ariel.

The Eurocentric, undemocratic, and even racist ideas posited by Rodó—witness his echoing the notion that equated cranial size with the intellectual capacity of the "thinking races" (140)—found no objection in Hispaniola. Thinking retrospectively, one could contend that Haitian and Dominican intellectuals ought to have found it easy to distance themselves from the monotonous sob of their Latin American colleagues. Their island's varied ethnicity and catastrophic history should have alerted them immediately to the falsity of both the presumed homogeneous heritage shared by all nations in the region and the proclaimed moral purity of the Latin heritage. But they did not see the glaring disparity. Rather, they joined the hemispheric plaint. They proceeded to evoke nostalgically the virtues of Spanish and French culture respectively while they warned against the danger hovering over the area should North American values advance their way. In propounding their dichotomous view regarding the cultural options available to their nations, they subscribed emphatically to Eurocentric definitions of Dominicanness and Haitianness. The Haitian intelligentsia—black and mulatto spokesper-sons alike—adhered vehemently to a European civilizational model. Only with the emergence of the "ethnological movement" promoted by Jean Price-Mars, J. C. Dorsainvil, and Arthur Holly at the beginning of the twentieth century did cultural discourse appear that ascribed value to the country's African heritage (Nicholls 1996:11–12). Similarly, the founding fathers of Dominican cultural discourse, namely José Gabriel García, Manuel de Jesús Galván, Federico García Godoy, and Américo Lugo invariably subscribed to a definition of national identity that construed Dominicans as heirs of Iberian values dating back to the conquest and colonization.

Haitian pronouncements on the moral opposition between the competing heritage of the Latin and Germanic sides of America date back at least to the 1870 publication of Demesvar Delorme's *Les théoriciens au pouvoir*, which divided the hemisphere culturally into the Germanic North and the Franco-Iberian South, the population of the latter constituting "a biological progeny of Latin Europe" (Delorme 1975:579). Delorme argued that France, which he described as a salutary receptacle of the highest human values, would have to promote "the advancement of her civilizing and expansive tongue" in order to offset the cultural advance of the United States in the Americas (582). The need to stress the North-South polarity often required the adjust-ment of basic historical data. That would explain why, for instance, precisely at a moment when famous compendia like the one by Joseph Arthur de Gobineau on the mental inequality of human races successfully promoted negrophobia throughout Europe, Delorme should feel compelled to deny the existence of racial prejudice in Europe (Dash 1996:17). Frédéric Marcelin, another subscriber to the standing dichotomy between Anglo-Saxon materialism and Latin humanism, also exonerated European thought of any racist overtones (Dash 1996:176; Hoffmann 1984:73). At times the standing dichotomy manifested itself as a virulent opposition to the United States, as the poem entitled "Yankisme," in Masillon Coicou's 1892 collection *Poésies nationales* plainly illustrates.

EXOGENOUS PARADIGMS

The foregoing scenario points to an intellectual elite pressured by their own theoretical choices to ignore the memory of destruction extant on the island—the atrocities perpetrated by the French colonists in Saint Domingue included—and to avoid hearing the blatantly negrophobic pronouncement that pervaded Western discourse in the nineteenth century. The need to sanitize the humane legacy that the island was said to have received from Latin Europe stemmed from the lack of an analytical model capable of circumventing the binary opposition of the Anglo-Saxon North and the Latin South. The Haitian literati were simply too far removed from their native cultural roots to consider invoking autochthonous paradigms in their conceptualization of national identity. Even Antenor Firmin, famous for his nationalist commitment, could elicit the description Duraciné Vaval made of him, namely that he was "a European soul in a Haitian heart" (Vaval 1933:233). C. L. R. James observed that for over a century after independence Haitian leaders persisted in producing a "replica" of European civilization in the Antilles (James 1963:393). James illustrated his assertion by citing the twentieth-century case of Constantin Mayard, a Haitian ambassador to France, who, anxious to persuade his listeners of the commonality between Haiti and France, went as far as to stress that the Haitians were descendants of the French in every respect, ethos, blood, language, institutions, body, and soul included (393).

The Haitian and Dominican intellectual elites, then, had no reason to disagree with the moral creed and the culturology propounded by Rodó. They too possessed the sort of mind-set that would find virtue in the symbol of Ariel, a creature of refined sensibility, bright and free, removed from the mundane demands of commerce and work. Their affinity with that symbol, of course, also revealed their scorn for workers, non-European cultures, and the lower classes. The oppressed masses, in Rodó's model, occupied a station akin to that of the detested Caliban. Despite the patriotic ardor of their rhetoric, they showed very little sympathy toward the majority of the population, which on both sides of the island was made up of the poor. Similarly, they found little to admire in the products and cultural forms coming from below, from the subaltern sectors of the population. The Dominican scholar Pedro Henríquez Ureña, who in a 1904 essay extolled Rodó as the most brilliant stylist in the Spanish language, had the exceptional foresight to distance himself from the reactionary political philosophy expressed by *Ariel*. He realized that Rodó was addressing an ideal youth, the elite, among the intellectuals, hardly ever referring to the "imperfect lives of our countries" (Henríquez Ureña 1960:24). He also expressed a measure of pause concerning some of Rodó's "harsh judgment" on the United States, and, unlike the Uruguayan author, he praised the egalitarian streak in the American political creed, given his view of the "modern concept of democracy" as the key to all "future evolutions" (Henríquez Ureña 1960:27).

But such isolated critiques aside, Dominican intellectuals for the most part fell under the spell cast by Rodó's *Ariel*. The critic Diógenes Céspedes has shown that *arielismo* had enormous appeal among the overwhelming majority of men and women of letters in the country. By 1901, one year after the Uruguayan edition of the book, the first foreign edition of *Ariel* appeared in Santo Domingo (Céspedes 1994:118–119). Céspedes has aptly argued that the *arielista* passion had come to satisfy a concrete material need of Dominican intellectuals. "Arielismo" came in handy as "a practical instrument" at the service of "their own survival" in a nascent power structure that, as it desperately sought the trappings of modernity, threatened to displace "romantic" intellectuals (114, 140–141). By the same token, the antidemocratic impulse of Rodó's rhetoric provided Dominican intellectuals with a convenient vehicle of conceptual transition that enabled them to enlist without conflict in the ranks to the Trujillo dictatorship. They, the privileged few, were also the deserving, who could not tolerate a condition that would reduce them to a level of equality with the brute masses. "In other words, the new intellectuals found in the Trujillo dictatorship the *arielista* State incarnate: quality vs. the tyranny of the numbers" (Céspedes 1994:125–126).

Scorn for the masses pervades the pronouncements of the Dominican intelligentsia in the nineteenth century. The literary patriarch Félix María del Monte wrote verses aimed at repudiating the religious practices, dances, and other festivities suspected of having ties with African roots, which almost invariably occurred among the lower strata of the population (Del Monte 1979:246). By 1862 the authorities in Santo Domingo would promote police ordinances that forbade all activities associated with worship of folk religions (Deive 1992:163). Even the eating habits of the lower classes provoked the ire of the intelligentsia. The mulatto José Ramón López in the 1890s published a scathing critique of the cuisine and feeding practices of Dominican peasants, whom he chided as a "race of fasting creeps" (López 1975:48–52). One could argue, in fact, that the negrophobia that characterized Dominican intellectuals in the nineteenth century and through most of the twentieth century had to do primarily with their rabidly antipopular sensibility since blackness, for the most part, corresponded most markedly to the phenotype of the country's masses rather than to the light-skinned elites.

Much to their credit, some important Haitian thinkers did pronounce themselves energetically against negrophobic racism. Texts such as the play *Ogé ou le préjugé de couleur* (1841) by Pierre Faubert, the essay *L'egalité des races humaines* (1895) by Antenor Firmin, and the essay *De la rehabilitation de la race noire par la République d'Haiti* (1900) by Hannibal Price offered compelling responses to the "Caucasian presumptions" and the "Aryan phantasmagoria" voiced by a good many nineteenth-century Western thinkers. But their pronouncements did not necessarily entail an acceptance of the neo-African cultural forms found in the everyday lives of ordinary Haitians. In no way would they embrace the cultural expressions of the masses. Witness the fortune of vodou, the religion observed by the overwhelming majority of the Haitian people. The intellectuals usually described that form of worship as an objectionable bunch of "diabolical practices," to put it in the words of Delorme (1975:569). Committed to a foundational discourse on nation, Delorme deluded himself in expecting that vodou would soon disappear. He expressed the belief that with the foreseeable spread of public education throughout the country's geography and in the extent to which Haitian society firmed up its adherence to an effective system of moral precepts, that popular religion would die quickly away. But the Catholic Church did not sit idly to wait for that faith to vanish, hence the formation of the "Anti-Voodoo League" which enlisted the support of men of letters such as Ahemar Auguste and Elie Benjamin. The periodical *La Croix* came into being with the mission, vigorously announced in the inaugural issue of March 14, 1896, to assist in the national campaign to eradicate vodou (Paen 1977:124).

This militant aversion to the spiritual expression of the Haitian masses in the words and the actions of the intelligentsia becomes less shocking when we recall that the tendency to repudiate vodou and the other cultural forms produced by the folk date back to the most venerable leaders of the independence movement, including Toussaint Louverture, Jean Jacque Dessalines, Alexandre Pétion, and Jean Pierre Boyer, to name the most prominent among the mulattos and the blacks (Nicholls 1996:70). The mulatto elite regarded the folk religion as a "redoubt of barbarism and superstition" (91). Typically, the mulatto ruler General Fabré Nicolas Geffrard vowed to wage an all out war against vodou when he came to power following the fall of Faustin Soulouque. After signing a concordat with the Vatican in 1860, Geffrard urged his compatriots to engage in the general effort to eradicate from the Haitian soil the last vestiges of barbarism, slavery, superstition and its scandalous practices (Nicholls 1996:184).

Nearly a century and a half later, the ruling elites, knowledgeable about the political benefit to be reaped from populism, developed clever ways of hiding their contempt for the people without legitimizing folk culture. For instance, the authoritative regime of François Duvalier, who arguably exceeds all previous tyrants in the amount of harm done to the Haitian people, came to power wielding a discourse of black affirmation. An offspring of the *noiriste* current in Haitian thought, Duvalier endeavored to use vodou as an ideological-spiritual arm of his gruesome dictatorship (Nicholls 1996:228). To make his project work, however, he founded it necessary to use lethal violence against a number of hougans who refused to collaborate with the regime (234). Besides, the tyrant did not revoke the 1935 legislation that made the practice of vodou illegal (xxv). Haitians would have to wait until the 1987 constitution for their religion to receive approval by the State.

It appears, then, that Duvalier's rapport with vodou entailed no particular respect for the spiritual expression of the folk but merely a recognition of its possible utility to help consolidate his totalitarian regime. Nor did his government overlook other opportunities for populist politics. In 1964 the Duvalier government adopted the black and the red as the official colors of the Haitian flag, thus reviving the bicolor standard that Dessalines had designed when proclaiming the independence of Haiti in 1804. Duvalier thus managed to show his government identifying with the symbols of the revolutionary struggles marshaled by the slaves of Saint Domingue in the glorious past (Nicholls 1996:234–235).

The Creole language too suffered the antipathy of the Haitian intelligentsia. Only with the 1987 constitution did it receive accreditation as an official language along with French. No direct Dominican counterpart exists for this linguistic phenomenon since the Spanish-speaking part of Hispaniola, like Cuba and Puerto Rico, did not produce a vernacular that differed radically from the European mother tongue. But one can perhaps recognize a distant parallel in that most Dominican writers have historically shunned the distinguishing features of Dominican Spanish. In their creolized version of the language of Castille, Dominicans achieve a distinct sound, tempo, rhythm, and often a peculiar syntax that set their tongue apart from the other Hispanophone Caribbean islands and the Latin American mainland without precluding understanding and effective communication between them and users of the language in other nations. The reticence to draw on the discrete linguistic behavior of the Dominican people may have to do with the belief, promoted largely by the traditional intelligentsia, that the native features of Dominican Spanish are actually "errors," hence the writers' almost frenetic desire to adhere to the strictest standards of correctness, causing them often to excise all the features of their country's linguistic specificity. For fear of localisms, which often smack of misuse to many Dominican writers, they end up settling for a standard diction that makes them culturally unrecognizable.

The linguistic situation of Haiti shows more easily discernible elements than the Dominican case. There the predominance of Creole as the main language of the majority of the population had become evident at least by 1905, when a minister of education first ventured to propose its adoption as the language of instruction in the country's public schools (Alexandre 1993: 189–191). But, just as Martí despised the Creole of Curaçao, Papiamentu, so have Haitian intellectuals disdained the nation's Creole, the language of their people, while at the same time singing hyperbolically the praises of the French tongue. Firmin, for instance, contended that no other language had exhibited the aptitude of French to express the notions of liberty, justice, and human dignity" in as truly a "penetrating way" (Firmin 1975:664). In keeping with the foregoing discussion, then, one could fairly include as part of the unfortunate lot that has befallen the Dominican people and the people of Haiti the calamity of often having voices that loathe them dominating the public discourse that purports to define their culture. Here, returning to our controlling metaphor, we witness a scenario in which Caliban has either lost the use of his voice, having proven an unworthy match for Ariel's duplicity, or has decided, aping Prospero's conduct to the letter, to usurp a fraudulent position of leadership wherefrom he casts aspersions on the community he had vowed to represent. Caliban's behavior results from contradictory impulses. On the one hand, he wishes to hold on to his position of power over the constituency that put him there, but as he becomes astute in the business of governing he learns to cater to other forces, more powerful than his people, and accepts the realization that to preserve his privilege he may have to change his allegiance. He, who rose with the mandate to dismantle the structures whereby Prospero had kept him captive, found paradoxically that he could preserve his privilege by ignoring his initial promise and by copying the actions of his former captor.

ANATOMY OF DISILLUSIONMENT

The Haitian poet Georges Sylvain (1866–1925) once characterized the historical experience of his people in a manner that one might also apply to the Dominican side of the island. He spoke of a recurring pattern consisting of a series of "exultations of popular sentiment, to then change, with every new leadership that rises to power, from the most ecstatic effusion of hope to the most hopeless disillusionment" (Sylvain 1979:14). One would concur that the pattern describes the history of all Hispaniola beginning with Enriquillo's disappointing performance when he rose to power. A glance at the present would suggest that the pattern has proven enduring. The case of Dessalines reveals a history of liberation that culminates in authoritarian rule. Incontestably heroic as leader of the anticolonialist revolt of the Saint Domingue slaves and subsequent founder of the Haitian Republic, Dessalines also inaugurated the native tradition of Caribbean dictatorship. Abusing his power and showing a flair for cruelty, he implemented a development model that in many respects replicated the slave economy, which the uprising had come to dismantle. He also proclaimed himself emperor. The painter Edouard Duval Carrié delves into the irony of that history in his work "Le Nouveau Familier," a portrait of Dessalines who appears sitting with his legs vulgarly spread. He wears the eerie black spectacles that became a trademark of the Tonton Macoutes, the paramilitary terrorist band that Duvalier employed to maintain all dissidence in check. Carrié's portrait painfully connects Duvalier to Dessalines, drawing a long line of dictatorial kinship.

Henry Christophe, another great hero of Haiti's revolutionary saga, reached the pinnacle of the grotesque in uncritically aping the luxuriousness and pomp of European courts. Having come to power in 1806 as chief of the North, when Dessalines died and the government bifurcated, with the South going under the command of the mulatto Alexander Pétion, Christophe crowned himself king in 1811. This black leader of the Revolution did not hesitate to commit atrocities against his people, whose condition resembled their previous slavery. According to General Pamphile de Lacroix, who at the time authored a report on Haiti for presentation to Napoleon Bonaparte, under Christophe's rule farm workers could not leave the area designated for their labor without a written authorization from their foreman (Lacroix 1995:411). Though far less picturesque than Christophe, Pétion had no lack of authoritarian flair. Declaring himself president-for-life, he invested himself unreasonably in the pursuit of French approval. He consented to an arrangement whereby Haiti would pledge to indemnify French planters for the loss of their plantations and their privilege in the course of the slave uprising that culminated in the new country's independence. France would receive compensation also for the expenses incurred to send troops to Saint Domingue to try to defeat the insurgents and preserve the slave economy (Nicholls 1996:51). The subsequent government led by Jean Pierre Boyer reunified North and South under one rule and marched on the Spanish speaking side of the island to bring the whole of Hispaniola under one sole juridical order, with Port-au-Prince as its seat of government. Boyer's unification scheme was initially well received when it occurred in 1822, but the financial debt to the French that his administration had inherited from Pétion led him to implement unpopular and unreasonable fund-raising measures that hurt the commercial class of Santo Domingo. A separation movement emerged that succeeded in rallying widespread support for its cause, which materialized in the declaration of Dominican independence in 1844 (Moya Pons 1972:38, 45).

One should not ignore the implications of the fact that Boyer, just as Pétion, arrived in Hispaniola from France to fight the insurgents and return them to abject slavery. They both came as French soldiers with the invading army commanded by General Leclerc against the black rebels. General Lacroix's report to Napoleon contained a profile of Boyer that described him as a "visceral enemy of Toussant's regime," as a "good Frenchman," and someone capable of playing a crucial role "as intermediary in the advances that we might make to the rebels" (Lacroix 1995:390). Ironically, despite the circumstances of their arrival in Saint Domingue, Boyer and Pétion moved in time to occupy positions of power as leaders of the people whose desire for freedom they came to crush. Here we see another pattern that recurs in the Caribbean whose political history often provides a stage for Ariel's ubiquity to put on a show. We see myriad political turncoats who have relished in the embrace of God and the devil. Their type recurs in Caribbean history more often than Férnandez Retamar's *Calibán* would acknowledge. On the Dominican side, Buenaventura Báez and Máximo Gómez come to mind. Both served as officers of Her Majesty, the queen of Spain, and fought Dominican nationalists from 1861 to 1865, a period when the Spanish army invaded the Dominican Republic to consolidate the Caribbean country's annexation to the Madrid government after a Creole oligarchy surrendered their nation's sovereignty to its former colonial master. The Spanish Empire gave Báez the title of Field Marshall for his service fighting the patriots who took up arms against the invaders and their Creole allies. However, no sooner had the Dominican nationalist forces won the war for the restoration of independence than Báez had made himself palatable to compete in the political arena as a presidential candidate, reaching his goal in less than three years. Gómez, for his part, remained as a soldier of the Crown till the end and had to leave Dominican soil when the nationalists won, landing in Cuba, which still lived under Spanish colonial rule. There he experienced a change of heart. He identified with the Cuban struggle for independence, joining the nationalist forces against Spain and achieving distinction as a commander of the liberation army. For many, the service he rendered to the anticolonialist struggle in Cuba erases his annexationist record in his home country. But I contend that leaving the two facets of Gómez's public history standing side by side, unreconciled and unresolved, can put us in closer contact with the pervasive contingency of human events in the Caribbean.

The foregoing discussion points to only a few of the memorable cases of turncoats, conflicting legacies, antipopular leaders of the people that crowd Caribbean history. Caribbean leaderships, with an acute case of moral ambivalence, make Caliban suspect. Evoked as symbol of the leader in the region, Caliban exhibits multiformity and a series of mutations so rapid that none can predict the ideological path he will take. Caliban has worn the trappings of Ariel at times and appeared indistinguishable from Prospero at other times. Nor has race or class origin mattered much to explain his conduct. Blacks, mulattos, and whites have acted alike, in keeping with the legacy of the Indian Enriquillo. Similarly, those coming from the gutter have no less misconduct to their credit than the offspring of privilege. The Haitian Faustin Elie Soulouque, who proclaimed himself emperor, and the Dominican Ulises Hureaux, who ruled tyrannically for over 15 years, both shared blackness and humble origins. Yet, they exhibited neither less corruption nor greater regard for the well-being of the oppressed masses of their countries than their well-to-do and light-skinned counterparts.

The best known twentieth-century tyrants from Hispaniola, the Dominican Trujillo and the Haitian Duvalier, came from deprived backgrounds. Yet, they perpetrated the most odious regimes against their compatriots. Like other tyrannical miscreants in human history, they displayed great depravity in trampling the bodies and souls of their people throughout their prolonged dictatorships. Duvalier attained popular appeal by presenting himself as a champion of black Haitian culture. But his branch of négritude soon revealed itself as nothing but "an Antillean form of Fascism, a totalitarian neo-racism whose main victims [were] the millions of black peasants and black workers of Haiti" (Depestre 1974:69). Trujillo, for his part, was the grandson of Erciná Chevalier, a Haitian woman who had settled on the Dominican side of the island. However, he ordered a horrendous massacre of Haitian migrant workers at the border in October 1937, and his government made rabid anti-Haitianism a prominent feature of official discourse on Dominican identity. Duvalier and Trujillo illustrate the gamut of contradictions and inconsistencies that the history of leadership—intellectual and political— presents us with in the Caribbean. Caliban has changed colors, exchanged allegiances, and changed his mind too often for one to tell his story in a smooth, forward-looking narrative. His Protean behavior makes him difficult to place, leaving the observer at a loss for race, ideology, or class signs that could help to make an intelligent guess regarding what his next step will be.

THE COLONIAL BORDER TODAY

A brief reference to Sint Maarten/Saint Martin, a Caribbean island that has earned description as "the smallest piece of territory anywhere to be shared amicably by two sovereign powers," comes in handy to speak of Hispaniola, the other territory in the region to harbor two distinct polities (Gravette 1989:111). The piece of land that Columbus in 1493 called San Martín—characteristically disdaining its aboriginal name of "Sualovenga" or Isle of Salt—changed colonial hands several times. Eventually the Mount Concordia Treaty of March 23, 1648 established it as the shared colonial property of the Dutch, who secured the south, and the French, who retained the north (Kruythoff 1964:15). The borderline that separates Sint Maarten from Saint Martin, dating from 1816, encourages travelers to venture into the other side with greeting messages that say "Welcom aan de Nederlandse kant" as they come from the north and "Bienvenue en partie française" as they leave the south. The phonemes "kant" and "partie," in Dutch and French respectively, would seem to suggest a humble sense of polity that acknowledges itself as a fraction of a larger whole. Similarly, referring to one's land as "part" admits to a certain incompleteness, a certain inextricability from the whole.

The polite coexistence of the subjects of Holland and France in Sint Maarten/Saint Martin, which contrasts with the fractious rapport of Haitians and Dominicans in Hispaniola, has rarely attracted the attention of students of the Caribbean region (Bellegarde-Smith 2000:26). Yet, as the only islands in the Caribbean that are juridically split by international borders, the two territories would seem almost enticingly to invite comparison. The mere pitting of the two cases against each other would alone suffice to suggest areas of inquiry that promise to deepen our understanding of border experiences and the enduring significance of the colonial legacy in shaping the everyday lives of people in the Caribbean. Equally steeped in the existential quagmire spawned by the conquest and domination of the colonial transaction beginning in 1492, the two islands did not differ meaningfully in their quotient of historical trauma. History did not spare Sualovenga of the turbulent events endured by Quisqueya and the rest of the Caribbean. The section often described as the Dutch Windward Islands, the Caribbean bloc where Sint Maarten/Saint Martin is located, also lived its "checkered history since 1493," with "much raising and lowering of national flags" through the centuries of colonization, as stated by John and Dorothy Keur in their book *Windward Children*, where we read this scenario: "They have undergone raids by privateers and buccaneers; wars and depredations . . . have suffered hurricane destruction and drought—have survived slavery and its abolition" (cited by Kruythoff 1964:10).

Sint Maarten and Saint Martin still belong juridically to European powers, having never launched successful independence campaigns. A cynical outlook could perhaps celebrate the island's retention of its colonial status especially in light of the failure of national projects in several societies of the region, where scholars have shown that non-independent territories exhibit far higher standards of living than their independent counterparts (Ramos and Rivera 2001). Unlike the disparate and uneven economies of Haiti and the Dominican Republic, Sint Maarten and Saint Martin have reached a sort of continuum of productive life across the two sides of the border. Already, by the early 1960s, when the rest of the region had barely begun to regard tourism as a potentially viable industry, an observer could note the island's surrender to the leisure and pleasure economy. The following description, hailing the island's colonial status, finds on both sides a seamless tourist paradise:

> [Enjoying] freedom under the banners of the Netherlands and France, . . . the island offers an abundance of leisure, interrupted, at will and desire. . . . by pastimes. Formalities and red tape have been chiseled down to a wafer, so as not to embarrass the visitor at any time of his visit. There are no import duties, no excise tax. (Kruythoff 1964:64)

The whole island having been made economically uniform, the border that separates Sint Maarten from Saint Martin is rendered devoid of economic significance. As such, it offers no promise of material betterment to people from one side who migrate to the other. Similarly, secure in markers of sovereignty dictated and guaranteed by European flags—by two countries that are signatories of the European Union—the two societies that share the island have little need to construct border-based ideas of nation. They have no compulsion to weave doctrines of patriotism that draw on the multiple discursive uses to which disempowered foreigners can be put. Colonial powers can at times display a mutual cordiality that sharply contrasts the zeal with which dependent sovereign countries go about policing the boundaries of their weak, vulnerable states. Curiously, the lesser their ability to protect their territories from the economic, political, and strategic impositions of the director societies that serve as their overlords, the greater their vehemence to safeguard the contours of the nation from the imagined danger of feeble immigrants, who cross the border as devalued workers ready to supply labor needs in the most depreciated strata of the job market. On the other hand, the leadership of the societies that share the nonindependent island of Sint Maarten/Saint Martin, lacking direct control of the structure of their polity, have little use for devising discourses of national belonging with unduly reliance on the border as outskirts of the space of citizenship. As they have experienced it, the border lacks symbolic power as a locus that harbors the kernel of national belonging. Their historical context has not evolved into a geopolitical juncture conducive to attributing a patriotic essence to the threshold that divides one society from the other. The definition of the border espoused by General José Miguel Soto Jiménez, minister of the Armed Forces of the Dominican Republic, as "the epidermis of our nationality" or as "the most lacerating spot of our patriotic practice," would find hardly any application in the Franco-Dutch island (Soto Jiménez 2004:4, 7). In this nonindependent Caribbean society, unlike in Hispaniola, ruling elites do not have at their disposal a manipulation of border history capable of cultivating distant memories of past traumas or of raising alarm about its potential for harming the health of the nation.

Conversely, the two nations of Hispaniola appear locked in a difficult embrace from which they have no foreseeable possibility of coming loose while the border that divides them juridically seems relentless in its capacity to incite strife between the two nations. Haiti, a country whose ruling elites have shown little regard for securing the most basic implements of social stability and material well-being to the population, has denied the citizenry the option of pursuing their dreams and aspirations in their homeland, hence the massive emigration of people, often through the perilous means one associates with those emigrants known generically as "the boatpeople." The Dominican Republic, on the other side of the border, has become the immediate destination of destitute Haitian migrants. Expelled by the greed, indifference, and corruption of ruling classes that hold their people in contempt, economically uprooted Haitian migrants cross to the Dominican side to subject themselves to no lesser quotients of abuse and overall dehumanization. The Dominican Republic, for its part, fraught by a chronic legacy of government corruption, unsuccessful development models, and overall socioeconomic options imposed by the demands of international capitalism with little regard for local consequences, has learned to perform the act of protecting national sovereignty by decrying the foreign influence of Haitian migrants even as it consents to receive the culturally transformative influence of U.S. media, Euro-North American tourism, free industrial zones, and indiscriminate foreign investment in areas of the country's economic life formerly reserved for the Dominican State. By the same token, the country has resigned itself to embracing the questionable strategy of exporting large portions of the population as a necessary variable of the thrust to achieve or maintain economic stability.

To exacerbate the foregoing scenario, Dominican public discourse, as propounded by political, military, and intellectual leaders, finds itself conceptually linked to a manner of imagining the contours of the nation that is rooted in colonial cartography. Strangely, while proudly tracing the advent of the Dominican State to the independence proclaimed on February 27, 1844, Dominican society has remained seduced by a manner of remembering the past that upholds the colonial heritage unabashedly as a pillar of nationhood. Thus, while on July 8, 2003, when he delivered the opening address to a three-day seminar on the border, the Dominican Republic had existed as a sovereign State for only 159 years, General Soto Jiménez characterized the "Dominican history" of the border as

"nearly 400 years of conflict" starting with "the 17th century insertion on the Western part of the island of a small group of French adventurers, who had before then operated from their base at Turtle Island, through the great stress caused by Haitian immigration to our territory in the last years of the twentieth century." (Soto Jiménez 2004: 610)

Like many intellects and politicians before him, Soto Jiménez conceives the national memory regarding the border in a way that ties the narrative of Spain's territorial disputes with France, its imperial competitor on the colony of Santo Domingo as of the mid-seventeenth century, seamlessly to the recent Republican history of conflict on the Haitian-Dominican border. The general thus illustrates a historiographic desire that refuses to delink the narrative of the Dominican people from the experience of their original colonial masters, insisting on identifying the Dominicans of the Republican period with the Spaniards of the colonial era.

A similar historiographical desire has obtained in other Caribbean instances of border disputes such as the conflict between Guyana and Surinam over rights to oil deposits involving the Courentyne River that divides the two countries which poses problems because the former colonial masters left unresolved the question of which side of the river constitutes the border (Singh 2002). By the same token, an eighteenth-century treaty between Britain and Spain still recurs in the conversations between Guatemala and Belize officials as they try to advance their claims regarding the precise location of the line marking the territorial separation between the two countries. On the basis of that colonial accord between the two imperial nations, Guatemala in 1999 proceeded to claim sovereignty rights over more than 50 percent of the territory currently occupied by Belize. The claim has been formulated before, and contestation of their territory partly explains why, although establishing their self-government in 1964, having advocated separation from Britain, Belizeans had to delay until 1981 their formal independence, which Guatemala would not recognize until 10 years later. What these examples suggest is that the political imaginary that fathoms the geography of these various nations in the Antillean world has inherited a colonial way of configuring each country's sovereign territory. This would seem an odd phenomenon since it suggests a conceptual loyalty to the physical space of the imperial power that formerly dominated what is now an independent nation. Separations from a former colonial power would seem incomplete if one inherits the conflicts, disputes, and animosity that occupied the former masters.

Inheriting the inter-imperial enmities of former masters has debilitating consequences for the relationship among Caribbean societies in that it reduces the possibilities of regional collaboration. The 1777 Aranjuez Treaty formally defined the boundaries dividing Santo Domingo from Saint Domingue, but the line vanished in 1795 when Spain ceded to France its portion of the island of Hispaniola. By February 1844, when Dominicans declared their independence, Haitian families had for long occupied the lands west of the San Juan Valley, which were physically located on the Spanish side of the line drawn by the two empires. The Republican governments on both sides of Hispaniola, then, had the option of conceiving the national geography as what it was at the moment of independence. The 1937 genocide whereby the Trujillo dictatorship made Dominican society culpable of a horrendous crime against humanity presumably to liberate a national territory from foreign usurpation would not have happened had Dominican statesmen conceived the geographical contours of the nation devoid of conceptual loyalty to the colonial territory of the former Spanish colony. Throughout the first decades of the twentieth century Dominican leaders claimed the Haitian-occupied lands as Dominican because they had been Spanish. When in 1911 a government functionary condemned the presence of Haitian residents on these lands, he literally characterized it as "a violation of the Aranjuez Treaty" (Montolío 1911:11). The genocidal massacre of 1937, whereby Trujillo resolved an anxiety evinced by his predecessors, showed how high a moral cost Caribbean societies can pay by adhering to colonial ways of conceiving their territories and themselves. The colonized remembering has been at the heart of the Haitian-Dominican conflict, which has influenced the very texture of Dominican ways of configuring the country's national history, the ethnoracial identity of the population, the representation of the borderland as a site of national dilution, and the homogeneous and exclusionary views on nation that have prevailed in the country.

Homo Migrans

Caliban's problematic legacy has added to the burden of the unsavory colonial past. As a result, the contemporary Caribbean, often the site of economic injustice, political oppression, and corruption, has large portions of the population reduced to poverty and helpless neglect. No wonder that emigration has become the strategy par excellence for people to wrestle with the demands of survival. Leaving the Antillean world has become a norm. The speaker in the poem "Nabel String" by Merle Collins suggests that people leave "because things not so good / and something better is always somewhere else" (Collins 1998). The former Haitian ambassador to Washington, Jean Casmir, describes the current historical moment in the region as one in which "the whole population savors expectantly the opportunity to migrate to the rich countries. Migration is probably the only survival strategy shared by all social groups. No government seems capable of arresting the current depopulation and, at the same time, sustaining, directing, or accelerating social change internally" (Casimir 1997:257). One could argue that Caliban, though sharing responsibility for the decline of contemporary Caribbean societies, has also suffered destitution. This view would advise us to look for Caliban not only among leaderships controlling power structures but also among the downtrodden who leave their homelands in order to secure their material well-being. Victim as well as victimizer, Caliban heads the inefficient and perverse State that has made almost every Caribbean country dependent on tourism—the economy of sand, sun, and sex that has virtually replaced agricultural production—while he also wears the pained countenance of the expelled, the excess workers who venture across the ocean in pursuit of receding job markets. In other words, the desperate passengers of Haitian "boats," Dominican "yolas," and Cuban "balsas" who regularly defy the dangers of the unharvested sea for a chance at a decent life represent the other face of Caliban. I contend that in that face lies the Caribbean's greatest repository of hope. As the experience of the diaspora may foster a new kind of agency, Caliban may undergo a sort of spiritual rebirth that might put him on the path to a restorative future.

The title story in Ana Lydia Vega's collection *Encancaranublado* has three archetypal characters, representing distinct Caribbean national experiences, who end up sharing a fragile boat in the middle of the ocean. A Haitian man named Antenor, seeking to escape his country's asphyxiating poverty, has put to sea in a fragile skiff that seems unlikely to withstand the severe movements of the waves and the long journey on his way to Miami, Florida. He has no reason to look back:

> The putrid mangoes, emblems of diarrhea and famine, the war cries of the macoutes, the fear, the drought—it's all behind him now. Nausea and the threat of thirst once the meager water supply runs out—this is the here and now. For all its menace, this miserable adventure at sea is like a pleasure cruise compared to his memories of the island. (Vega 1995:1)

From out of nowhere come the Dominican Diógenes and the Cuban Carmelo to join Antenor's eerie voyage. Their common wretchedness induces a sense of circumstantial solidarity, which subsequently withers as they begin to taunt one another recalling national antipathies from their fractious Caribbean historical experience. Their ventilating feelings coming from their insidious legacies escalates to near physical aggression, causing their boat to capsize. Just before they are to fall to their deaths out of the boat, a U.S. ship comes to their rescue. Once under the protection of an American captain, "Aryan and Appolinean," our three Antilleans receive instructions from the mouth of a fellow Caribbean, a Puerto Rican sailor member of the crew, who reminds them that in order to eat they would have to work "and I mean work hard. A gringo don't give anything away. Not to his own mother" (Vega 1995:6). Evidently an allegory of the plight of contemporary Caribbeans, the story presents us with the dark side of transnational mobility from the islands, an ironic realization of the Antillean Confederation gone awry. Haiti, the Dominican Republic, and Cuba meet Puerto Rico on the American ship. They share a common dependency on and a common subservience to the United States. They also share the compulsion to leave home to ensure their material survival.

Another story from the same collection by Vega, "El día de los hechos," depicts a possible outcome of the legacy of animosity between Haitians and Dominicans once they meet in the diaspora. The Dominican émigré in Puerto Rico, Filemón Sagredo, loses his life at the hand of his Haitian nemesis Félicien Apolon, who has tracked him down in the neighboring island to avenge an age-old offense. The fatal resolution of Félicien shooting Filemon brings closure to several generations of conflicts between their respective families in a feud nurtured by a long history of Haitian-Dominican tensions (Vega 1987:21–27). The events related in the story suggest the possibility that the interethnic conflicts that have hampered regional cohesion at home might follow Caribbean migrants abroad to the detriment of unitary projects in the diaspora. However, the alternative outcome appears no less plausible. Something in the shared uprooting of Haitians and Dominicans who must leave home for a chance to dream would seem most conducive to stimulating pan-Caribbean solidarity. The majority of Haitians residing in the United States arrived after 1957, during the repressive regimes of Papa Doc Duvalier and his son Jean-Claude. The combination of factors that propelled their emigration included political persecution, administrative corruption that resulted in a continuous decline in the quality of life, and the progressive deterioration of the national economy (Laguerre 1984:21).

Concomitantly, the massive exodus of Dominicans began in the 1960s, following the death of Trujillo whose firm control of foreign travel by Dominican nationals had kept the number of emigrants low. A military coup against a democratically elected president, a popular armed uprising to restore the constitutional order, and a U.S. invasion later, Joaquin Balaguer, who had served as a puppet president when Trujillo died, came back to power as president on June 1, 1966. Balaguer not only resorted to unrestrained political repression, murdering and incarcerating most prominent dissidents, but his regime also embraced economic policies that restructured the job market, displacing low-skill urban workers and farmers. For economic and political reasons, then, leaving home became the thing to do for Dominicans who could. Also contributing to fuel the instinct to escape was the prevailing sense of hopelessness that dominated the country. How could the people hope in light of the bitter fact that, despite the struggle, the sacrifice, the many lives lost for the cause of freedom and equality, the Trujillo power structure had returned with the backing of the United States and wearing the guise of a democracy. Then came also the 1965 immigration law, which increased the number Caribbean migrants who could enter the United States every year. That combination of push and pull factors catapulted Dominicans massively to the North American mainland, triggering a migratory flow that has continued unabated (Torres-Saillant and Hernandez 1998:30–31).

Dominicans and Haitians represent the epitome of the condition that the contemporary Caribbean person faces: a scenario where compulsory exile shapes the people's visions of tomorrow. The Haitian Creole poet Félix Morisseau-Leroy has evoked that fateful predicament in the poem "Botpipél," which dramatizes his people's compulsion to leave home: "We are all in a drowning boat / it happened before in St. Domingue / We are the ones they call boat people / . . . We set out in search of jobs and freedom / Piled on cargo boats—direct to Miami/They began calling us boat people" (Morisseau-Leroy 1998:149). One of the poem's closing stanzas stresses the equalizing force of diasporic uprooting: "We don't raise our voices or scream / But all boat people are equal, the same / All boat people are boat people" (149). The scenario evoked by Morisseau-Leroy, discrete national specificities not withstanding, also describes the plight of Cuban *balseros*, Dominican *yoleros*, and all others for whom staying in the native land has become hazardous to their well-being.

Occupying the space of the diaspora has not come without a measure of ontological discomfort, stemming most likely from the sense that one has lost a homeland without necessarily gaining another. The listless, circular, transnational mobility that many scholars have been pastoralizing since the 1990s may in the Caribbean case result from this ontological discomfort. Luis Rafael Sánchez has explored the Puerto Rican side of the phenomenon in his often quoted lyrical essay "The Flying Bus." The easy travel between here and there—which because of modern aeronautics Puerto Ricans can now experience the Atlantic Ocean as a "blue pond"—paradoxically points to a split with potentially sad consequences (Sánchez 1987:24). The flight between New York and San Juan provides Sánchez with a stage that displays much of the angst of the national condition of his people: "Puerto Ricans who cannot breathe in Puerto Rico but catch a lung-full in New York can achieve a ballpark average of four hundred . . . Puerto Ricans who want to be there but must remain here . . . Puerto Ricans who live there and dream about being here" (24). The essay's closing sentence succinctly describes the predicament evoked here, namely "the relentless flow of a people who float between two ports, licensed for the smuggling of human hopes" (25).

But irrespective of how one construes the psychology and existential drama behind the back-and-forth mobility that Sánchez investigates in his essay, the Antillean person must cope with the fact of having to trade home for elsewhere. Apart from the devastating legacy of the colonial past, the responsibility for the compulsory dispersion may fall partly on the shoulders of a leadership that the governed have neglected to hold accountable. The aforementioned poem by Merle Collins suggests a sort of suicidal leniency on the part of the people who have to leave: "Because the landless somehow becoming / more landless yet but still loving / some leader because of a memory" (1998:91). They leave grumblingly, though, resenting their virtual banishment, and continuing to hurt on account of the homeland. Their emotional attachment to their native soil, exacerbated by the hostility that might meet them in the receiving society, may induce in them an ambivalent state of mind regarding the here and there dialectic. The Surinamese writer Astrid H. Roemer has articulated one of the manifestations of the ambivalence in a passage from her book *Nergens ergens* (Nowhere, Somewhere 1983):

> I have a love-hate relationship with Suriname. Hate because history shows how I ended up here. My ancestors were dragged here by force and emigrated under false pretenses. They suffered and never bequeathed Suriname as their native country to their offspring . . . yet I love Suriname because I was born there . . . Holland's material wealth was gained partly at the expense of my native land.

After five generations of legitimate oppression I have the right to choose to
which country I belong. I have chosen Holland, even though Holland has not
chosen me. (Cited by Rutgers 1998:552)

We cannot lose sight of the salutary potential inherent in the ontological
discomfort of the Antillean emigrants. The awareness that their compulsory
exile, and the grievous suffering therein, occurred on account of the ineptitude and indignity of their homeland ruling elites makes them judgmental
and vigilant about their history and culture. The diasporic experience induces
a desire to supervise Caliban, scrutinize his behavior, control the quality of
his service, reward and censure him according to dessert. The diasporic experience provides Caliban himself with a second chance to think through his
career and seek to repair the damage. As a site of ontological renewal, the
diaspora may bring about a change of direction in the history of Caribbean
leadership while the governed accept their responsibility to hold the leaders
accountable. The Caribbean diaspora, in putting legacies under the lens,
might sponsor the overhauling of official nationalist discourses and fraudulent patriotisms encouraged by entrenched ruling elites. The logic born out
of the diasporic experience would create conditions in which the denouement of Vega's "El día de los hechos" would seem inconceivable. At the level
of popular culture, for instance, we see the opposite trend. Diverse groups
from the English-speaking West Indies, where the politically unifying West
Indian Federation project failed miserably, have managed to privilege
regional over national interest in their joint celebration of Carnival. Currently
over 40 U.S. cities have Carnival celebrations that stress regional symbols,
suggesting a meaningful "potential of Caribbean unity and identity" (Belcom
1998:191). Referring to the most famous Carnival celebration, the one held
on Labor Day in Brooklyn, New York, sociologist Patricia Belcom says that
"On Eastern Parkway there are no Jamaicans, no Bajans, no Trinidadians—
we are all 'Caribbeans'. We benefit from our solidarity as we learn to leave
parochial squabbles behind" (1998:193).

The diasporic experience, in the best of circumstances, awakens Caribbean
communities to the similarity of their condition irrespective of national
region. Haitian and Dominicans, *boat people* and *yoleros*, learn to recognize
themselves as sharing the brunt of the failure of leadership most immediately
responsible for their expulsion from both sides of Hispaniola. The folk wisdom of Tibon, a character in Edwidge Danticat's novel *The Farming of Bones*
(1998) captures the essence of the political economy that explains why people at the bottom of the social ladder in Haiti end up enduring pain as
migrant workers in the Dominican Republic's sugar fields: "They have so
many of us here because our country—our government—has forsaken us.
Poor people are sold to work in the cane fields so our country can be free of
them" (1998:177–178). That same logic explains why so many Dominicans
live in the United States, Puerto Rico, Europe, and elsewhere. It explains also
why the Dominican State so ardently continues to cherish the privilege of
exporting excess workers. One gets the sense that diaspora Haitians and

Dominicans recognize themselves as victims of a common depravity. Historian Bernado Vega has pointed to the momentum that turns the two nations of Hispaniola into emigrant communities: "While Haitians attempt to reach Florida in small boats, Dominicans try to ride their *yolas* across the Mona Canal to get to Puerto Rico, 'Ambafiles' are the Haitians who, though wishing to emigrate, fail to make it to their preferred destinations: the United State or Canada. In New York neighborhoods Haitians and Dominicans, outside Hispaniola, interact for the first time" (Vega 1998:420). The rapprochement that the diaspora facilitates has repercussions back in the island. For over two decades now, historian Frank Moya Pons has insisted on the appreciable impact that Dominican migrants have had on notions of nationhood, race, and cultural identity in the home country (Moya Pons 1996:24–25). In their periodic visits to the native land, Dominican émigrés bring with them a new awareness of ethnic tolerance and cultural diversity with clear implication for their rapport with Haitians. U.S. journalist Michelle Wucker has observed the appeal of *gaga*, a religious music born of Haitian-Dominican cultural fusion in the *bateyes*, for Dominicans returning from New York. At Palave, the scene of a *gaga* festival, the journalist noted the fallowing: "The Haitian meets Dominican and blends with New York. Haiti is no longer on the other side of the border across the water. They are here in the cane fields that have long represented the center of conflict between the Dominican Republic and Haiti. The two worlds have fused into one" (Wucker 1999:251)

CALIBAN REFORMED: A VISION OF THE FUTURE

The diasporic experience has the double potential to encourage regional solidarity in the Caribbean and to reform Caliban. Through a process of cultural remittance to the islands and the coasts, émigré Caribbean communities can exert a rectifying influence in the home countries. They might thus manage to counteract the politics of fragmentation put in practice by the ruling elites. Ironically, the original expulsion from their homelands in the region and the rigors of the struggle for survival in societies not always hospitable can, with luck and contingency, eventually liberate the migrant from the polarizing logic stimulated by the sending State when defining the contours of national identity. Emancipated from the supervision of the State in the home country and only precariously inserted in the cultural logic of the State in the receiving society, the diaspora is in a position to access a strange privilege, namely that of coldly calculating the terms of its allegiance to State authority. In the diaspora the contractual implication of State affiliation becomes discernible. With the opportunity to negotiate its allegiance to State authority transactionally, the diaspora enjoys the privilege of having the chance to forge the truest form of citizenship, one in which the subject participates actively in drafting the terms of his or her affiliation in the ancestral homeland as well as in the host country.

Because émigré Caribbean communities have become important to most national economies in the Antillean world, States in the region have increasingly shown an interest in cultivating and preserving their loyalty. In places such as Haiti and the Dominican Republic the financial support sent by the émigrés to their relatives back home constitutes one of the two or three principal sources of revenues. Through a peculiar flip of the sociohistorical coin, the diaspora, initially a social formation expelled from the region as excess labor, becomes an economic force that the sending society then begins to take into account. One should think that this economic force in time will turn into political power, that is, when the diaspora, aware of its own importance, begins to demand change in the homeland while it continues to advocate for diversity, inclusion, and social justice in the host society. One can envision a time in the not too distant future when the diaspora will wield the power to barter. Already some Haitian and Dominican scholars have highlighted the growing influence of the diaspora on the public affairs of the societies on both sides of Hispaniola (Laguerre 1997; Torres-Saillant 1999). Since both émigré communities have undergone migratory processes that have made it imperative for them to forge alliances across ethnic lines, one can expect them to be able to undermine elements of ethnic and racial antipathy in the public discourse that defines national and cultural identity at home. Similarly, the diaspora's sociopolitical training in the struggle for equality and social justice in the United States and Europe may perhaps reach the homeland in the form of social and cultural remittances. The émigrés, that is, may foster in their respective native lands an enhanced concern for the observance of human rights, respect for diversity, and democratization of political and economic life. The diaspora's bartering may effectuate Caliban's political rebirth.

The notion of a reborn—or rehabilitated or reformed—Caliban will make historical sense in a context where we see the diaspora engaged in revising the ideologies and cultural myths that have both fostered intra-Caribbean division and ensured the impunity of failed leaderships. The more Caliban learns to care genuinely for his people in his particular nation in the Antillean world, the more he will commit himself to regional agendas. Embracing the right attitude, of course, presupposes the ability to imagine the nation in ways that transcend the geographical contours sanctified by State definitions. Transnational definitions of fatherland (motherland, homeland, etc.) come naturally to diasporas. A Haitian émigré in the Dominican Republic, the poet Jacques Viau Renaud possessed a diasporic vision. His poem "I Am Trying to Speak About My Homeland" conceives of Haiti and the Dominican Republic as "two complementary grounds / cardinal points of my sadness / fallen from the mariner's compass / like two lovers torn from their embrace" (Viau 1985:91). The son of Alfred Viau and Elaine Renaud, Jacques was born in Port-au Prince on July 28, 1941. He arrived in Santo Domingo at the age of six, when his family, having fallen out of favor with the political regime, sought refuge in the Dominican side of the island. During the 1965 uprising, Jacques joined the Dominican patriots who fought to restore the democratically elected government. With only 23 years of age, having attained the rank of Deputy Chief of Comando B-3, he received a mortar shot wound that within days put an end to his life. He and the other patriots had to fight a formidable enemy, namely the U.S. soldiers who came to the aide of the antidemocratic corporate and military elite that had violently deposed a constitutionally elected president. In making the ultimate sacrifice on behalf of Dominican democracy, Viau corporealized the vision of nationality expressed in the poem cited earlier. Other pertinent lines in the text further stress the speaker's double loyalty to both the Dominican and the Haitian side of Hispaniola: "I've been trying to tell you about my homeland / my two fatherlands / my one island / which long ago some men split apart / over there, where they parked to dig up a river" (Viau 1985:95).

That Jacques Viau's father should have enlisted in the service of the Trujillo dictatorship when he came from Haiti escaping political persecution should disturb no one. Alfred Viau went as far as to write texts that praised the tyrant unconditionally, seeming even to justify the massacre of thousands of Haitian and Dominican-Haitian migrant workers at the borderlands in October of 1937. His perplexing intervention in the aggression of the regime against his people surfaces as an unpleasant juxtaposition over the admirable trajectory of his son who gave his life for the human dignity of people on both sides of the border. The juxtaposition alerts us to the complexity of past events and the baffling nature of agency in the Caribbean. The counterpoint of Jacques Viau and his father Alfred accentuates the problematic of Caribbean history and culture: a canvass of discontinuities, regressions, disorderly advances, and seeming contradictions, in short, a heap of happenings that hardly amounts to a coherent narrative with any semblance of linearity. The human experience as it has taken place in the Caribbean defies the modes of analysis that too ardently espouse dichotomies and polarities. Jacques and Alfred Viau, the son who gives his life to protect human dignity across ethnicities and the father who sells his services to tyranny and ethnic antipathy, are both equally Caribbean. They both represent recognizable faces of Caliban. We should not overlook the seeming contradiction, and any application of the paradigms we draw from *The Tempest*—Harold Bloom's discouragement notwithstanding—should account for the problematics of history in the Antillean world. In that respect, much of the Caribbean cultural history that centers around Caliban might need adjustment to enhance its usefulness. Too often the literature, from Fernández Retamar and Lamming onward, portrays Caliban exclusively as a symbol of resistance and cultural self-affirmation in the Caribbean. The bibliography portrays him as inherently benign, the moral and political opposite of the oppressive colonial master Prospero. This chapter, deeming Jacques Viau and his father Alfred as equally indicative of Caliban's historical trajectory, has sought to chart a different path. This meditation starts from an acceptance of the distressful challenge posed by the moral and political metamorphoses exhibited by Caliban in history. It accepts the realization that neither oppression nor being black or Indian has made much of a difference in guiding the conduct of Caribbean leaders. The native and his descendants, from Enriquillo to Duvalier to their successors, have not shown greater zeal to look after the interests of the disinherited or promote equality and justice in their society than the invader and his descendants when in control of the State.

I would argue that representations of Caliban that transcend moral polarities can empower citizens of the Caribbean with the skepticism necessary to remain watchful of the conduct of leadership in the Antillean world's contemporary history. At the same time, we should amplify the expressive reach of the Shakespearian paradigm to encompass leaders in Prospero's lineage who may have rendered salutary service to the cause of human dignity in the region. We should foster schemes of thought that transcend the moral essentialisms of class, ethnicity, and cultural background. A slave-descendant whose depravity has increased the misfortune of the oppressed in the Caribbean ought not to enjoy reverence nor prestige over an offspring of the colonial masters who has a verifiable record of earnestly looking after the best interests of the population. The novel *De eerste Adam* (The First Adam, 1966) by Leeuwen explores the predicament of the children of white colonists as they interact with their black compatriots. In commenting on the novel in an essay on Dutch Caribbean literature, Wim Rutgers contextualizes that predicament indicating that they, mostly in Europe, tend to feel out of place in the old world, hence their return "home" to face their contrapuntal reality. "A restless searching springs from their attempts to define their own position on the island with regard to the non-white majority. In doing so, they isolate themselves, confronting the feeling of superiority of their parents" whose actions "toward the black citizens" they simply reject (Rutgers 1998:549). As the reference to Leeuwen's novel illustrates, literature has evoked the drama of the children of colonial privilege. One could perhaps read much of the poetry of Saint-John Perse in that light. But the phenomenon still awaits adequate historiographical accounting. The cases of individuals coming from the ranks of the colonial power structure who delinked from imperial logic in order to join the oppressed in their fight for social justice await a narrative of their own. Their humanistic legacy deserves attention. The Caribbean's historical memory ought to reserve a place of honor for the likes of Father Antón Montesinos, a priest of the order of St. Dominic who nearly a decade prior to Enriquillo's insurrection denounced the immorality of the colonial transaction, confronting the authority of Governor Diego Colón and the entire power structure. He first condemned the "cruelty and tyranny" perpetrated against the Taino population of Santo Domingo and then intransigently resisted, with unremitting backing from his vicar Father Pedro de Córdoba, the colonial government's pressure to make him recant (Las Casas 1985:441–442, 444–445).

I propose, then, a new interpretation of the history of Caribbean leadership that would evince, for instance, the moral superiority of Montesinos and Cordoba over the likes of Enriquillo. Such an interpretation would assess leaders on a case-by-case rather than class-by-class basis, thus sharpening the people's eye's to recognize instances of both depravity and magnanimity. Such a framework would deprive Caliban of the a priori privilege he has usurped. The people would not love him merely "because of a memory," and he would have to answer for the intent and the consequences of his actions. This interpretative approach, I believe, could make an intellectual contribution to a process that should culminate in a reformation of Caribbean leadership. I propose a way of imagining Caliban's trajectory in which the historiographical work itself discourages the passivity of the governed and empowers them with the analytical tools and the appropriate mental demeanor to expect and demand a new kind of leadership. The scholarship itself would be invested in fostering a political stage in which rotating the ruling elites would not suffice. To be deemed new the leadership would have to show itself as more just, more efficient, more humane. It would need to display a better caliber than its predecessors. The intellectual discourse, then, would champion the effort to reeducate the Caribbean imaginary so as more accurately to identify friends and enemies irrespective of skin color or class origin. Historians and cultural critics of the Caribbean, in other words, have a crucial role to play in bringing about the rehabilitation of Caliban.

Since one of the saddest elements of Caliban's unfortunate track record involves a behavior that fosters intra-Caribbean tension—the incorporation of ethnic antipathies in the official discourse of national identity—any progress made toward his reformation can be expected to further unitary and holistic visions of the region. Hispaniola, therefore, offers an ideal stage for the enactment of tensions pertinent to the possibility of both Caribbean unity and renewal of leadership. Hispaniola sits stubbornly as a stumbling block on the path of regional coherence. Dominican and Haitian nationalist discourses have construed the human experience on both sides of the island as antithetical and mutually exclusive. Paradoxically, the irreconcilability of the two official narratives, with their focus on contradistinction with respect to the other, highlights a contradictory rapport. They are as inextricable as they might seem incompatible. Haiti and the Dominican Republic appear as contrasting texts: different languages, divergent forms of worship, dissimilar links to the West during the colonial transaction, and disparate trajectories leading to the birth of the nation. Moreover, following Dominican independence, the moment when the Spanish-speaking residents of Santo Domingo chose to delink from the jurisdiction of the Haitian State that had unified the island under one rule, military clashes between Haitians and Dominicans occurred. The actual war between them as different nations came to exacerbate a history of border conflicts inherited from the colonial period, namely the territorial disputes between France and Spain regarding the geographical limits of their contiguous colonies of Saint Domingue and Santo Domingo from the late seventeenth century onward. That context explains the emergence of oppositional logic as an element of national and cultural self-definition in the discourse of the intelligentsia especially on the Dominican side of the island.

There is little doubt, however, that Haitians and Dominicans, as coparticipants of the historical experience that ushered in the colonial transaction in the Caribbean, are equally decisive for the possibility of a restorative, unitary vision of the region. They share the island that inaugurated the plantation, aboriginal genocide, black slavery, racial mixture, religious syncretism, nativization of European languages, and sociopolitical creolization. With the early uprisings of Tainos and Africans as well as the rise of *manieles* or *palenques* as alternatives to plantation society, Hispaniola gave to the world the figure of the Maroon to serve as both model of social action and trope of discourse. Historically speaking, the original encounter of Prospero and Caliban, mediated by Ariel, took place on this island that the Tainos called Quisqueya. The culture and history of the Caribbean as we know it, then, began here. As Ür-Caribbean, inaugural site of the Antillean experience, Hispaniola poses a terrible challenge that constantly defies the slogans of cohesion that abound in the intellectual tradition that Glissant has denominated Caribbean discourse. The challenge consists in finding a way of reconciling the contrasting texts of Haiti and the Dominican Republic without imposing unwarranted versions of harmony nor simplistic expectations of unity. Caribbean discourse faces the task of weaving two disparate national narratives into one common tapestry while at the same time fairly appraising the specificities stemming from the distinct colonial traumas experienced by people on both sides of the island. Without first completing that task, pan-Caribbean visions of regional coherence would seem unconvincing if not deceptive.

Glissant's *Discours antillais* (1981) and Bénitez-Rojo's *La isla que se repite* (1989) make impressive attempts at identifying a controlling logic, a pervasive metaphor that suits the complexity of Caribbean history and culture. At a discursive level, they both accomplish their intellectual goals in that they organize bodies of knowledge around the rules of metaphor. They concern themselves less with extratextual reality: political history, social outcomes of past events, historical memory. They do not take on the trauma of our catastrophic history: the hurt, the depravity, the betrayal. They do not tackle the disquieting disappointment that characterizes the contemporary Caribbean, the background that explains the dispersion of Antilleans to foreign shores in search of jobs, dignity, and hope. The analytical paradigms stemming from cultural studies circles, such as the notion of the "black Atlantic" advanced by Paul Gilroy (1993), do not account for the specificity of Caribbean events or the unique texture of the region's traumas. Similarly, the dynamics stressed by the abundant and growing body of writings produced under the aegis of postcolonial studies have seldom shed meaningful new light on historical, cultural, or political dynamics in the region.

The moment seems right, then, for paying another visit to Shakespeare's triad, given especially the Caribbean roots of *The Tempest*. Caliban's enduring appeal has to do primarily with the historical rootedness of the metaphor. In the year 2005, writing nearly three decades after Fernández Retamar published his *Calibán* (1972), we can now afford a closer, more critical, more skeptical look at the implications of Caliban's leadership. We now know more about the instances of his failure, his negligence, his mendacity. We may also have a diaspora prepared to shame him, to reeducate him, to make him vow that he will seek to repair the damage. Three additional decades of disappointments have made us less sanguine about celebrating Caliban, the leader of the people. The lyrical evocation that pervades Fernández Retamar's text finds us, as we ponder on the legacy of misconduct of Caribbean leaders, devoid of candor. History is the story of things that actually happened irrespective of how unsavory the results may have been for us. We may frown at the unfavorable outcome for us of particular past events. But we cannot change what actually was. Our power lies in the ability to change our understanding of things past with an eye on affecting the future. When we identify past wrongs and wrongdoers, we might learn enough to promote behavioral modifications in the present so as perhaps to elicit a restorative future, hence the belief that by updating our understanding of Caribbean traumas through the examination of failed native leadership we may reach the point of stimulating improvement and making hope tenable. The Caribbean imagination, empowered by the experience and the learning of its diaspora, can chart new historical ground. By essaying new—albeit painful—interpretations of the culture and history underlying the present state of affairs in the region (not by merely coining neologistic vocabularies nor wielding new tropes to signal familiar knowledge), Caribbean discourse has a chance to restore cultural self-confidence and historical possibility. But a truly new inquiry into Caribbean history and culture necessitates a measure of intellectual disruption. Problematizing the familiar metaphors and tropes to penetrate the core of the trauma in the history and culture of the region presupposes a willingness to dissect the ideologies and myths that have dominated analysis of the human experience in the Antillean world. The focus on Caliban's ideological duplicity and moral deformity along with his legacy of insurrection and resistance accords with that willingness.

The idea here is that Caribbean discourse should become emancipated just as Caliban in repairing his historical misconduct ought to overcome his ontological dependency. With excessive and lethal frequency, Caliban has justified himself by simply brandishing his opposition to Prospero. Proclaiming his difference with respect to his former master has mattered more than showing virtues of his own. Needless to say, he has often failed even at that meager feat. But on the whole, he has hardly needed to show concrete proof of his commitment to the well-being of his society. Nor has he suffered the consequences of his dereliction of duty or even his crime. The Caribbean has a long history of impunity for leaders who commit atrocities and then leave power. A list focusing solely on Hispaniola would include the Trujillo family, Balaguer, Jean-Claude Duvalier, and Raoul Cedras. Unlike the other three, Balaguer did not even need to abandon the scene of his crime. After his initial escape from the Dominican Republic following the death of Trujillo in 1961, he came back shortly thereafter, gaining the presidency in 1966. Neither the thousands of political murders committed by his regime between 1966 and 1978, nor the corruption of his governments up to 1996, nor his complicity in the genocide of Haitians at the border when he served as henchman of the dictatorship in 1937 ever caused him any discomfort, and he ended up dying in the comfort of his own bed.

The thought that he will have to pay for his wrongdoing would orient the actions of the new Caliban. The vigilance of the governed would help to keep him honest. Aware that the oppositional stance with respect to Prospero will not suffice, he would have to make a more creative, more genuine, greater effort to individuate his worth. Concomitantly, intellectual production around historical development and cultural identity would do well to pay heed to Brathwaite's proposal beginning decades ago when he posited an alternative model of Caribbean self-definition. Drawing on the Shakespearean paradigms, Brathwaite summoned Caliban to delve deeply into the realm of his own self in search of native roots. That descent into self, Brathwaite contended, could give Caliban access to the subterranean plane where his mother Sycorax lies buried. Addressing the matter of Caliban's derivative, oppositional, and therefore dependent ontology, Brathwaite speculates that if instead of learning to "curse" Prospero in the master's own language, Caliban "had listened to his mother's voice; if he could speak her [sic] in their language / He might have had a better chance when the chance for revolt came his way" (Brathwaite 1983:35). Sycorax does not appear as a physical presence in Shakespeare's text, and that invisibility suggests further symbolism to Brathwaite. In other words, her absence has protected her resources, which remain submerged as historical subtext and cultural potentiality (Brathwaite 1984:44). To reach his mother, to reap the benefit of a legacy that because of its long concealment has managed to preserve its vitality, he has to reconnect with the autochthonous heritage of his ancestry.

Consistent with Brathwaite's instructions to assist in the rehabilitation of the leader in the region, the intellectual discourse that follows Caliban's trajectory as cultural synecdoche of the Caribbean might enhance its focus on the wavy course described by his career. As the foregoing pages insistently highlight, Caribbean history, as encapsulated in the fluctuation of agents and events, follows a zig-zag path that defies the narrative logic discernible in the teleology of either Hegelian or Marxist dialectics. Brathwaite's alternative paradigms would seem to contribute an analytical model capable of accounting for the Caribbean's fluctuating pattern of mobility and unassailable careers of the leadership. In 1990 father Jean Bertrand Aristide—Titid to the people—rose to visibility in Haiti with a message of justice and equality, illuminating Haitian society as a beacon of hope. Today, a coup d'état having overthrown him and a U.S. invasion having restored him, he has lost his shine and possibly also his moral rectitude, as reports about his huge mansion and spectacular land acquisitions and the conditions of his second removal from power would suggest. On the other side of the island, events have taken a no less magical turn. Ninety-three-year-old Balaguer, blind and hardly able to walk, with a record of murder and corruption that few organized crime clans could equal, not only held in his hands enough power to decide political elections in the country, but in September 1997 the multipartisan legislature in the Dominican Congress proclaimed him "Great Builder of Dominican Democracy." The year before Balaguer, representing the Trujillo oligarchy, held hands with Juan Bosh, a reputed democrat who had opposed Trujillo and Balaguer, flanked by young political leaders whom the dictator and his heir had rendered orphans and widows, standing next to the military chiefs who had killed their parents and their spouses, forging an alliance called "Patriotic Front" to bring Leonel Fernández, candidate of the Dominican Liberation Party, to the presidency of the country, and block the most popular leader in the race, José Francisco Peña Gómez, who had Haitian ancestry. Such history, which reads like experimental fiction, needs a method that can fit the sinuosity, of events in the Antillean world.

Brathwaite has proposed the notion of tidalectics, which is a theorically luring paradigm that promises to account for the uncanny, for trauma, and stasis, for hope and catastrophe in the Caribbean. Tidalectics accords with the wavy movement of Antillean events, the dialectics of the tides, "the movement of the water backwards and forwards as a kind of cyclic, I suppose, motion, rather than linear" (Mackey 1991:44). Conceived from the perspective of a centripetal approach to the philosophy of history of the Caribbean, detached from Western teleological inexorability, Brathwaite's tidalectics avoids simplification and distortion. Perhaps here the complexities of the human experience in the region have found an autochthonous paradigm befitting its sinuosity. Constructed from a Caribbean positionality, the model provides the porous framework required to assess the seemingly contradictory ordering of events in the region. Tidalectics can perhaps help to harmonize the hallucinating Haitian-Dominican rapport in Hispaniola, thus pointing to the possibility that we might confidently tackle the development of a coherent and believable theory of Caribbean unity in history and letters. Should we find the fit between the two contrasting narratives on both sides of Hispaniola, the foundation for a pan-Caribbean vision of wholeness will have been promisingly laid.

Epilogue: A Century of Caribbean Diaspora

A person of Antillean descent who is aware of the checkered history of the past 500 years, of the vastness and complexity of the human species that inhabits the amplitude of the planet, and of the countless occasions when projections of the future have disappointed those daring to prophesy, would reasonably be disinclined to venture visions of things to come. But, in view of the massive mobility of people from and across the various points of the globe at the start of the new millennium, it takes effort to overcome the temptation to predict that diasporic actions, ideas, and forms of utterance will shape the lives of societies in the century we have just entered. Particularly for the Caribbean, an observer looking at the development projects and options currently within reach of governments in the region, there would seem to be nothing in the offing that can offer grounds for believing that structural changes and social transformation will come in the foreseeable future to those societies with the result that emigration will lose currency as the primary mode for the less empowered portions of the population there to seek assurance of a fighting chance in the struggle for survival and the aspiration to lead productive lives.

The seriously asymmetrical exchange stemming from the current phase of the global economy has exacerbated the dependency of the Antillean world on the larger economies of the West, diminishing the possibilities of at least working toward self-sufficiency. The airwaves in Jamaica are dominated by foreign mass media to such a degree that it takes considerable perseverance to find a local program on national television. *Life and Debt*, the film by Stephanie Black, harrowingly documents the process whereby formerly thriving local industries have declined or perished as a result of external pressure coming from the international banks and global corporations. Globalization has not brought about in the Antillean world a situation in which, for instance, Dominican *sancocho* can flow easily to Puerto Rico, which in its turn can ship *cuchifritos* back to the Dominican Republic, while both receive succulent *ajiaco* from Cuba, and the three of them export their culinary ingenuity to the world market. Rather, it sponsors a state of affairs in which the three societies are asked to remove economic barriers to foreign investment so that international capital can move in and accumulate unencumbered, meaning that they will open their doors to *Burger King* (Torres-Saillant 2004: 224–225). In this asymmetrical exchange, Antillean societies end up having to buy from abroad the things that they used to be able to make, decreasing the number of people whom they can employ and reducing the purchasing power of their currency. The exchange rates are dictated by the providing countries who also happen to control the logic and the priorities of the global economy. A slice of the logic and priorities in question is made available in Black's documentary through the words of Stanley Fisher, deputy director of the International Monetary Fund, who justifies the encroachment of the global corporations into the local market at the expense of native industries by positing that the "Jamaican consumer has a right to have the same products that people in other parts of the world have." Such being the mind-set governing the economic thinking of the protagonists of the world system into which the Caribbean must exist, the kind of development, based on self-sufficiency, that would enable the countries in the region to provide social guarantees to the population, making it desirable for people to remain home, seems unlikely to materialize. As a result, emigration seems fated to remain an inescapable trend, and the Antillean population abroad will continue to grow.

Whatever the future may bring, however, already the Caribbean population has, as if pushed by a powerful centrifugal force, spread widely across the globe. Kevin A. Yelvington reminds us that Edward Wylmot Blyden, whose defense of the black heritage in the nineteenth century brought him distinction, was a native of the Virgin Islands who moved to West Africa. At the time a contingent of Jamaica Maroons went to establish a settlement in Sierra Leone. By the end of the century French West Indians took government posts in French dominated West Africa, and in the 1950s Rastafarians from Jamaica went to Ethiopia as colonists (Yelvington 2004:33). Similarly, Haitian anthropologist Michel Laguerre has traced a Haitian presence in the United States going back at least to the mid-eighteenth century, when the place was still called Saint Domingue. The notable names include Pierre Toussaint, who came to New York in 1787, worked as a hairdresser, and became known for his religious devotion and charity, leaving behind so salient a legacy that nearly 100 years after his death Cardinal Spellman submitted his name for canonization to the Vatican. Also memorable, William de Florville, known as Billy the Barber, became President Lincoln's personal barber and confidant. The 1915 occupation of Haiti by the United States increased the flow of Haitians to North America, and some joined the Marcus Garvey movement. When occupation ended in 1934, a good many U.S. soldiers who had Haitian mistresses, wives, and children, brought them to the United States when they returned home. To illustrate the meaningful presence of Haitians in the United States, Laguerre mentions the huge crowd that went to welcome President Magloire when the Haitian statesman received an honorary doctorate from Fordham University in 1955 (Laguerre 1984:166–169). Two years later, François Duvalier would climb to power in Haiti, shortly thereafter creating political, economic, and social conditions that would unleash an exodus that has remained unabated, with the United States and Canada as principal destinations but spreading also to other places in the Americas and Europe.

The growth of the Caribbean population in the United States may be suggested by noting that by 1998 the Hispanic subsection alone exceeded five million residents, with nearly a million among those having been born in the host country (Duany 1998). That at least 40 U.S. cities hold Trinidad-style carnival celebrations every year, with the largest occurring on Labor Day weekend in Brooklyn, New York, should be emblematic of a major Anglophone West Indian presence in North America (Belcom 1998:191). At the start of the present century, the United Kingdom hosted nearly a million West Indians from the former British Caribbean, the arrival of the *SS Empire Windrush* at Tilbury Docks on June 21, 1948 marking the watershed moment. Census data report that by 2001 there were over 362,000 British-born West Indians, who look back with warmth to their respective ancestral homelands in the Caribbean but who recognize Britain as their home (Peach 2004:625, 633). By the same token, the Surinamese and Dutch Antilleans living in Holland in 2000 boasted a registered population of nearly half-a-million strong, the majority a product of push-and-pull factors emerging most visibly after World War II (Blakely 2004:599–600). Mass emigration especially from Surinam, which alone in 1975, the year of the country's independence from the Netherlands, amounted to 36,537, has "had serious consequences for the country's post-independence development" (Oostinde 1990:231). Like its counterparts in the United Kingdom, this Caribbean population in Holland exhibits little prospects for return to the ancestral homeland.

As to Antilleans in France, many came to the *Métropole* during and after World War II, but they were probably less distinct to the larger society than were their counterparts in the other Western nations. Along with immigrants from the Antilles, France hosted arrivals from Senegal, Cameroon, Benin, Gabon, among other Western African countries, in addition to Vietnam, North Africa, and the other regions that form part of *la francophonie*. Perhaps more than any other colonial power, France has invested considerable effort in policies known as adaptation, assimilation, insertion, and integration with the purpose of engineering the acculturation of immigrant minorities irrespective of their origin. Their common denominator as non-Europeans mattering more than their ethnic particularities as individual groups, French society has regarded their cultural difference as something to erase rather than to acknowledge. The fiction writer Gisèle Pineau, who was born in Paris in 1956, recalls that when she had a problem with her white classmates in the Kremlin-Bicêtre suburb where she grew up, the quickest taunt that would come to their lips was "Négresse, retourne dans ton pays, en Afrique!" (Makward 2003:1202). The salient marker of her despised difference was blackness, not Caribbeanness, hence the injunction to return to her "country in Africa." Given the homogenizing climate in which the young Gisèle was growing, one can understand her parents' decision never to use Creole at home and to omit their Guadeloupean cultural background from her education, something that in retrospect Pineau "for a long time" resented because she felt "they had made a 'Negropolitan'" of her (Makward

2003:1203; Veldwachter 2004:182). Pineau's father had answered from Guadeloupe the June 18, 1943 "appeal" by General De Gaulle urging patriots to defend the fatherland then besieged by the Nazi invaders. After the war, he stayed with the French Army, and in Paris the family lived in a state-owned housing designated for "subordinate civil servants," located in a suburb of the capital city where in her formative years Pineau found herself as the only black girl in her class and the only "black to walk the street under the scornful eyes of the whites," who did not see a French citizen when they looked at her (Sourieau 2003:172).

What Pineau as a writer made out of what racist French society did to her permits a positive reading of the outcomes that the dispersion of Antilleans outwardly to the globe may possibly bring. Her father at one point in her childhood found it necessary to go back to Guadeloupe and bring his mother to live with them in Paris. Gisèle discovered her roots through her grand-mother, Man Ya, whom she at first scoffed because the old woman did not speak French, spoke an unintelligible tongue, and simply stood out too sharply against the Parisian setting where the family lived. But in time the old woman became her bridge to the Guadeloupean and thereby the Antillean heritage that Pineau came later to recognize as a source of intellectual and moral strength. When Pineau learned to respect what her grandmother rep-resented culturally to her and she learned to listen to the stories that Man Ya would constantly tell her, an entirely unknown civilization, the Antillean world, opened itself to her. Pineau comes very close to suggesting that it was her grandmother, through exposing her to storytelling, who inclined her to the literary craft. When Pineau became a writer, her grandmother Man Ya turned into a crucial and recurring figure in her work, first in her novel for young adults *Un papillon dans la cité* (1992) and, most frontally, *L'Exil selon Julia* (1996), a novel in which she set out to explore "how an old woman from the Antillean countryside lands in Paris and meets her 'Negropolitan' grandchildren" (Veldwachter 2004:181). Her award-winning novel *La Grande Drive des esprits* (1993), which she herself describes as a work of rootedness ("l'enracinement" [Makward 2003:1211]), provides Pineau with a venue to locate herself comfortably in the thick of Caribbean culture by drawing on a combination of Guadeloupean folk traditions and her own experience of biculturality. Aware of her father's successful response to De Gaulle's patriotic appeal in 1943, one is tempted to find much significance in the chapter of the novel entitled "Glory," as rendered by the good translation of Michael Dash, which starts the passage downhill of the main character Léonce. When he answered to the call of the fatherland "to her children" (France the "battered mother, always so good to her colony"), Léonce did not qualify to serve on account of his club-foot (Pineau 1999:133).

Pineau's exploration of Man Ya as a cultural source and key to the Antillean world matters enormously for any discussion of the intellectual his-tory of the Caribbean insofar as it confers validity to the knowledge and the expressive forms that may be found in the region's oral traditions, allowing for an illiterate peasant woman to occupy the position of authority. The author thus contributes to diversifying the funds of knowledge that need to be deemed crucial in understanding the human experience in the Antillean world. Similarly, aware that numerous works exist that present the enslaved black as a "plantation zombie" and "ungendered being," but convinced that the sex of captives counted a great deal since "the destiny of men and of women differed very much," Pineau paired up with coeditor Marie Abraham (who "worked primarily on the historical matters") to assemble *Femmes des Antilles: Traces et voix* (1998), a massive compilation that commemorates the sesquicentennial of the abolition of slavery by simply allowing "women to have their say and display their humanity" (Makward 1204–1205). The first-person narratives gathered in the volume illustrate the difficult location of enslaved women, who were "in some way a bridge between the world of the whites and the world of the blacks" (1205). Recalling that the master could at any moment sexually possess a *négresse*, who could then have mulatto children by him, Pineau urges us to consider the ways the master's open access to the black woman's body could have affected her marital relationship with her black male companion, stressing the error of supposing that women and men lived the same experience. Pineau's preface states that these women "lived with men who were marked by this history, who were raised by these women who century after century repeated the same gestures in order to instill fierceness in their little men so that they would finally decide to take possession of the lands of the Antilles" (Pineau and Abraham 1998:14).

Comparable to Pineau in her determination to put her writing to the service of expanding the horizons of Caribbean knowledge is the novelist and short-fiction writer Edwidge Danticat, who left Haiti at the age of 12 and settled in Brooklyn, New York, where she grew up and lived with her parents until her recent marriage and relocation to Miami. An American Book Award winner, Danticat has enjoyed remarkable literary success since the 1994 publication of her first novel *Breath, Eyes, Memory*, a book that draws on the typical patterns of the immigrant narrative but complicates the form by interlacing the young protagonist's experiences in New York with the call of the land of origin. Through reconnecting with maternal aunts and grandmother, thereby accessing a world of creole culture and folk wisdom, the young protagonist moves closer to her center and is on the way to achieving wholeness. The following year Danticat published *Krik? Krak!*, a collection of stories set in recognizable moments of the historical experience of Haitians, including "New York Day Women," which takes on the challenges and opportunities that Haitian immigrant women encounter as they navigate the precarious job market accessible to them in the United States. The "Epilogue" stages a conversation between the narrator and her "muses of history," namely the women for whom she has to speak and who thereby empower her with a voice. The opening story, "Children of the Sea," spoken in the middle of the ocean by a first-person narrator to the beloved on the other shore during the horror of his futile travel along with "thirty six deserting souls," evokes the frequent and tragic sea journeys of Haitian "boatpeople" throughout the last decades of the twentieth century. The second story,

"Nineteen Thirty Seven," locates the action in the midst of the carnage perpetrated by the Trujillo regime against Haitian and Haitian-Dominican residents of the border towns in 1937, announcing a subject to which Danticat would devote full treatment in the 1998 novel *The Farming of Bones*. Wrenchingly and lyrically evoking the massacre, the novel deserves the appraisal of the *Time* reviewer who described it as "a book that, confronted with corpses, has the cold-eyed courage to find a smile" (Farley 1998:78).

Having conquered the U.S. literary market before the age of 30, Danticat has escalated her zealous engagement with Hatian history and her ancestral culture. Her latest major novel, *The Dew Breaker* (2004), centers around a man who has lived for decades as a loving father and family man in the East Flatbush section of Brooklyn but whose dark past links him irretrievably as a cold-blooded culprit to the cruel torture and murder chambers of the Duvalier dictatorship in the 1960s. Before the publication of that novel, however, Danticat had expanded her agenda of dissemination to include a collection she put together to spotlight the works of other Haitian literary artists and thinkers living abroad, namely *The Butterfly's Way* (2001) in whose preface she identifies herself as a diasporic citizen: "My country, I felt, was something that was being called the tenth department. Haiti has nine geographic departments and the tenth was the floating homeland, the ideo-logical one, which joined all Haitians living in the *dyaspora*" (Danticat 2001: xiv). Her work of intellectual advocacy has also involved writing books on Haiti for the young, such as *Behind the Mountains* (2002), a narrative that tells the story of 13-year-old Celianne's passage from her native village in Haiti through her adaptation to immigrant life after she meets with her father in Brooklyn. Pervasively the author manages to sprinkle the story with his-torical information and regularly imbues the girl's surroundings with the trappings of Haitian culture and everyday life. Probably aimed at reaching readers of all ages, Danticat's travelogue *After the Dance* (2002), a text evocatively subtitled "A Walk Through Carnival in Jacmel, Haiti," narrates the author's return to her native hometown, 20 years after her settlement in the United States, during the carnival celebration. A distinct feature of this evocation is the narrative voice's combination of surprise and intuited familiarity before the spectacle that unfolds in front of her eyes. The Jacmel festivity triggers thought and emotion in the observer who gradually becomes participant. The exposure to Danticat's account of her physical and mental travel through carnival in her hometown persuades the reader that Jacmel, perhaps unknown until the reading of this text, compares in importance to Rio and other famed sites of carnivalesque frenzy.

Both Pineau and Danticat have achieved their market success as writers in the West whose books, issued by major presses, quickly attain international visibility and garner translations into several languages. Their literary careers in that respect compare with those of other writers from the Caribbean dias-pora who have achieved distinction. Similarly, in the United States Antigua-born Jamaica Kincaid and Dominican-descended Julia Alvarez have become household names. A comparable development may be seen in Britain, where

Pauline Melville, born in Guyana, and Caryl Phillips, born in St. Kitts, both of whom immigrated early in their childhood, established themselves as writers, and now enjoy wide acclaim. To mention at least one more case, one might add the spectacular career of Zadie Smith, the London-born child of a Jamaican mother and an English father, whose best-selling first novel *White Teeth* (2000) became a publishing sensation and was quickly adapted for a BBC-TV mini-series. Living and writing in Madrid, the Cuban-born Zoé Valdez has authored several novels that have caught the attention of Hispanophone readers and have been translated into other languages. By the same token, two of the most prominent cultural critics associated with the rise of cultural studies and postcolonial perspectives, Stuart Hall and Paul Gilroy, were born in Jamaica.

On the surface we may be witnessing in the foregoing scenario the end of the vernacularization of Caribbean literature and thought production with respect to the Western-dominated worldwide intellectual market. By vernacularization, a usage suggested by its root, the noun *verna*—"home-born slave"—I mean a relegation to a rank of cultural and intellectual marginality. A vernacular in this sense constitutes the language of the less empowered in its relationship with its linguistic superior, paralleling the unequal statuses of the master and the slave. In the eyes of the master the words of the captives did not even constitute a language. When Columbus brought a few Tainos back with him in his first return trip to Spain in 1493 he wished for them to "learn to speak" rather than merely to acquire Spanish as a foreign language. The lesser prestige enjoyed by Caribbean vernaculars—the various creoles emerging out of the linguistic fusion propelled by the colonial transaction— has to do simply with their having originated in the bosom of disempowered populations. That is why, for instance, Frank Martinus Arion can locate Papiamentu outside the family of "reading languages." The comment by Diana Lebacs at a Caribbean symposium held in New York City at The Americas Society in May 2003 contributes yet another layer of complexity to the language question for writers coming from her linguistic bloc of the Caribbean. After explaining that Papiamentu did not open doors of communication to writers outside their small islands, she went on to add that Dutch did not much help either in light of the precarious position of that language vis-à-vis the major Western tongues, recalling the mordant remark of someone who had described Dutch as "the Papiamentu of Europe." Mc Leod's effort to publish in Surinam an English version of her novel on Elisabeth Samson is no doubt an attempt to diminish the deleterious effect of the lesser rank of Dutch among the imperial languages of the West.

The Caribbean as a culture area has experienced vernacularization even when literary artists and thinkers have expressed themselves dexterously in the major European languages. The marginal status accorded to the region's societies by the protagonists of the intellectual world market vernacularizes the utterances of the region's voices, rendering them less desirable both for exportation in their original languages and translation into other languages. Pedro Mir, the late poet laureate of the Dominican Republic, and his compatriot Aída Cartagena Portalatín, the country's most important woman of letters in the twentieth century, both wrote perfect, standard, imperial Spanish, just as the major Haitian thinker Jean Price-Mars and his compatriot Marie Viau Chauvet, a first-rate novelist, both wrote impeccable French. But their utterances have neither traveled widely within the Hispanophone and the Francophone worlds in the languages they wrote them nor elicited major translations into other languages to expand their spread to greater portions of the global readership. Existing translations into English, for instance, have come out of small presses or through particular arrangements involving the collaboration of devoted compatriots. By the same token, Andrew Salkey's works or those of Jan Carew, written in the most meticulous King's English, have not reached significant resonance throughout the Anglophone world. The employment of the major imperial languages, then, has not for the most part mitigated the grievous vernacularization of the Caribbean word.

With the rise to global visibility of the texts of Alvarez, Kincaid, Phillips, Smith, and the like, writing, as they do, from the center of the West, and published, as they are, by corporate firms that have the capacity to propel their words widely across the planet's geography, the representation of the Antillean experience may be said to have finally attained the international centrality it deserves. As a result of the migratory process that, referring specifically to her country, Louise Bennett captured poignantly in the lines "I feel like me heart gwine burs' / Jamaica people colozin / Englan in reverse," the Caribbean has entered the Western metropolis (Bennett 1966:179). The West now will find it increasingly harder to deploy its willful ignorance of the humanity of people in the Antillean world. After a reading at Syracuse University on April 25, 2005, the award-winning Dominican-American poet Rhina P. Espaillat praised the accomplishments of Julia Alvarez by stressing the fact that, as a result of reading the novelist's *In the Name of Salomé* (2000), which evokes the life of the woman poet who founded modern Dominican literature, thousands of people worldwide who otherwise would not have heard of Salomé, now know about her. Espaillat put it succinctly by saying that Alvarez "has put Dominican culture on the map." Indeed, by carving their niche in the capitals of the intellectual production of the core countries—England, France, Spain, Holland, and the United States—diaspora voices have begun to creolize the imagination of the metropolitan centers, with the foreseeable result that the West may rehabilitate its conventionally inimical portrayal of the Antillean world, recognizing its unquestionable humanity and its rightful belonging within the sphere of history. No doubt, this development calls for a different sort of figuration of the Antillean world. Studies of "the region" now need to encompass the tellurian geography of the archipelago and the continental rimlands where Caribbean societies are physically located plus the cultural and existential geography created by generations of emigrants whose experiences fueled the genius of Samuel Selvon in such foundational texts as *The Lonely Londoners* (1956) and whose offspring include the authors of the books that now vie for attention in the display windows of major metropolitan bookstores.

The rise to visibility of Caribbean diasporic voices, however, does not come without its complications. In the extent to which the international success of the Western-based writers and thinkers might have the effect of supplanting their homeland-based counterparts in the ability to speak influentially about the human experience of the Antillean person, the present development could usher in a mixed blessing. At the end of April 2005 in the program of the Santo Domingo International Book Fair, the Belgian scholar Rita De Maeseneer presented a paper on the subject of Dominican literature of the last decade, at the start of which she explained that for practical purposes she had circumscribed her inquiry to those authors whose works had reached the Belgian market through Dutch translation. Ironically, my Belgian colleague's choice had the unintended effect of excluding all works written in the Dominican Republic since only those U.S.-based authors whose books have come out of major presses had the muster to travel geographically and translinguistically. The symbolism of this exclusion points to the asymmetry in the power of communication exhibited by the two bodies of writing involved: the one produced by voices of the Antillean world and the one produced by their diasporic compatriots. A search at any major metropolitan research institution, such as the main branch of the New York Public Library, can graphically illustrate the asymmetry. Prodding the electronic catalogue for Dominican, Haitian, and Puerto Rican authors, for instance, the search will most likely yield the following outcomes. Under "Dominican" Junot Díaz and Angie Cruz will emerge sooner than any title by Manuel Rueda and Manuel del Cabral. "Haitian" will trigger references to Edwidge Danticat a lot more quickly than to Jacques Stephen Alexis or Marie Viau Chauvet, while "Puerto Rican" will bring up Esmeralda Santiago long before such classics as the poet Julia de Burgos or the playwright René Marqués will have a chance to surface.

At first, the scenario herein described might appear to bring nothing new to the conversation since Caribbean intellects have always spoken about their culture and history and about their people's place in the world from "abroad." Suffice it to mention the cases of C. L. R. James, Césaire, Lamming, and Fanon. Similarly, Anton de Kom and Albert Helman had their say outside their Dutch-speaking Caribbean homelands. Already in the latter half of the nineteenth century the Cuban Martí and the Puerto Rican Betances had set the pattern for the course that the Antillean intellect would follow as consummate exile. The Aruban writer Denis Henriquez would go as far as to describe his literary peers as "nomads, if not physically, at least mentally," languishing in "a world that isn't theirs," and, in the case of those coming from Aruba, Bonaire, and Curaçao, "in a language that isn't theirs either," with the result that they end up "flying as exotic birds into the cage of an alien culture" (Henriquez 2004:59). However, one should observe an important distinction. Caribbean intellects writing "abroad," but retaining their native lands as their existential ground and as the center of their political sphere, differ significantly from those who, having been socialized in the metropolis and been required to construct there their idea of home, do not have the Caribbean easily at their disposal to place it at the center of their existential and political being. Thus, Lamming and Brathwaite have both returned to Barbados in their later years. But one could argue that physical return need not happen for the individual to retain his or her Caribbean ground. The evocation of the region one finds in many of Naipaul's texts reveals his rootedness in the Caribbean in spite of himself, even if he never returns to Trinidad, and this qualifies him as an Antillean intellect working "abroad."

The diaspora intellect does not live "abroad." The identity location of Selina Boyce, the young protagonist in Paule Marshall's *Brown Girl, Brownstones* (1959), makes this palpable. Like Marshall herself, Selina must regard Barbados as her parents' country, especially her father's, since her mother Silla, has decided to stay permanently in the United States. Linking with the ancestral homeland serves for the young protagonist the purpose of better positioning herself socially and culturally in the American society. Home is something she must build in the diaspora. Beginning with the main character in her novel *Annie John* (1983) by Jamaica Kincaid, herself a literary and existential product of the diasporic experience, the oeuvre of this reputed author dramatizes a process of constructing one's idea of home precisely in contradistinction to the values of the ancestral homeland. The title poem in the collection *The Other Side* (1995) by Alvarez depicts Dominican society as a site of darkness from whose demonic pull the poet needs to exorcise herself so as better to realize herself in her craft and womanhood as an American. Yolanda Martínez-San Miguel's readings of the works of writers ancestrally connected to the Hispanic Caribbean highlight the diversity of figurations involved in the act of imagining home from a diasporic location. As in the case of Nicholasa Mohr, at times Antillean intellects might feel the need to embrace a detachment from ethnic familiarity in order to liberate the imagination for ancestral "evocation" through their writing (Martínez-San Miguel 2003:333).

The Caribbean diaspora has experienced the sort of uprooting that creates, in the words of Rushdie, "radically new types of human beings: people who root themselves in ideas, rather than places, in memories as much as in material things" (Rushdie 1991:124). On the whole, having the representation of the Antillean world in the hands of diasporic intellects who do not root themselves culturally or politically in "the region," may lead to their strategic use of their privileged position at the center of the Western intellectual industry to continue the work of upholding the humanity and the historical groundedness of their people, as Pineau and Danticat have done. But they could also, wielding greater might than their counterparts in the region, resort to the deployment of "borrowed eyes" to look at their parents' homelands, adding to the long tradition of inimical representation that the Caribbean has endured for over five centuries. However, the best outcome could also happen, namely the emergence of an influential cadre of intellects who will not judge their ancestral homelands more harshly than they do the Western societies where they live and work, but who recognize their diasporic citizenship as one that entails a "double duty (with accountability both here and there)" (Radhakrishnan 1996:212). This would mean that they will use their ascendancy to continue to combat the conceptual aggression that Western discourse recurrently deploys against their people while also holding institutions and policy makers in "the region" accountable to the need to create economically and socially hospitable societies governed by the principle of justice and equality and mindful of the human dignity of the less empowered.

WORKS CITED

Adorno, Theodor W. "On Popular Music." *Cultural Theory and Popular Culture: A Reader*. Ed. John Storey. London: Edward Arnold, 1994.

AFIHC [American Family Immigration History Center]. www.ellisislandrecords.org. Accessed 2002.

Ahmed, Aijaz. *In Theory: Classes, Nations, Literatures*. Delhi: Oxford University Press, 1994.

———. "Postcolonialism: What's in a Name?" *Late Imperial Culture*. Ed. Roman de la Campa, E. Ann Kaplan, and Michael Sprinker. London: Verso, 1995. 11–32.

Alegría, Ciro. *El mundo es ancho y ajeno*. 8th ed. México, D. F.: Editorial Diana, 1964.

———. *Broad and Alien is the World*. Trans. Harriet de Onís. London: Merlin Press Limited, 1973.

Alexandre, Guy. "La relación francés/créole en Haiti: Trato, función, evolución y perspectivas." *Francophonie et Caraibe/Francofonía y Caribe*. Ed. Jacques Leylavergne. Santo Domingo: Casa de Francia, 1993. 185–192.

Alexis, Jacques Stephen. *El compadre General Sol*. Colección Literatura Latinoamericana. Havana: Casa de las Américas, 1974.

Alig, Wallace B. "Man with a Hammer." *Américas* 5.5 (May 1953): 6–8, 43–45.

Allen, Ray, and Lois Wilcken, eds. *Island Sounds in the Global City: Caribbean Popular Music and Identity in New York*. New York: New York Folklore Society and Institute for Studies in American Music of Brooklyn College, 1998.

Alonso, Carlos J. *The Burden of Modernity: The Rhetoric of Cultural Discourse in Spanish America*. New York: Oxford University Press, 1998.

Alvarez, Julia. *In the Name of Salomé*. Chapel Hill: Algonquin Books of Chapel Hill, 2000.

Appiah, Kwame Anthony. "Is the 'Post-' in 'Post-colonial' the 'Post' in 'Postmodern?' " In MacClintock, Mufti, and Shohat. 420–444.

Araújo, Nara. *Visión romántica del otro (Estudio comparativeo de "Atala" y "Cumandá," "Bug-Jargal" y "Sab")*. México. D.F.: Universidad Autónoma Metropolitana, 1998.

Arends, Jacques, and Matthias Perl, eds. *Early Suriname Creole Texts: A Collection of 18th-Century Sranan and Saramaccan Documents*. Frankfurt am Main: Vervuert Verlag, 1995.

Arion, Frank Martinus. "The Great Curassow or The Road to Caribbeanness." *Callalloo* 21.3 (1998c): 447–452.

———. *Double Play: The Story of an Amazing World Record*. Trans. Paul Vincent. London: Faber and Faber, 1998a.

———. "An Interview with Frank Martinus Arion." By Charles H. Rowell. *Callaloo* 21.3 (1998b): 538–541.

Arnold, A. James, ed. *A History of Literature in the Caribbean*. Vol. 2: English and Dutch-Speaking Regions. Amsterdam and Philadelphia: John Benjamins Company, 2001.

Arnold, A. James, ed. *A History of Literature in the Caribbean*. Vol. 3: Cross-Cultural Studies. Amsterdam and Philadelphia: John Benjamins Publishing Co., 1997.

Ascencio, Michaelle. *Lecturas antillanas*. El Libro Menor No. 166. Caracas: Academia Nacional de la Historia, 1990.

Ashcroft, Bill, Gareth Griffiths, and Helen Tiffin. *The Empire Writes Back: Theory and Practice in Postcolonial Literatures*. London and New York: Routledge, 1989.

————, eds. *The Postcolonial Studies Reader*. London and New York: Routledge, 1995.

Atwood, Margaret. "Travels Back." *Maclean's* 86 (January 1973): 28, 31, and 48.

Auerbach, Erich. *Mimesis: The Representation of Reality in Western Literature*. Trans. William R. Trask. Princeton: Princeton University Press, 1953.

Averill, Gage. " 'Toujou sou konpa': Issues of Change and Interchange in Haitian Popular Dance Music." In Guilbault. 68–69.

Badejo, Fabian A. "Introduction to Literature in English in the Dutch Windward Islands." *Callaloo* 21.3 (1998): 676–679.

Bajeux, Jean-Claude, ed. *Mosochwazi Pawòl Ki Ekri An Kreyòl Ayisyen/Anthologie de la littérature créole haïtienne*. Port-au-Prince: Editions Antilia, 1999.

Baker, Francis, and Peter Hulme, eds. *Cannibalism and the Colonial World*. Cambridge: Cambridge University Press, 1998.

Balboa Troya y Quesada, Silvestre de. *Espejo de paciencia*. Ed. Angel Aparicio Laurencio. Miami: Ediciones Universal, 1970.

Balutansky, Kathleen M. "Naming Caribbean Women Writers: A Review Essay." *Callaloo* 13.3 (1990): 539–550.

Bangerter, Lowell A. *The Bourgeois Proletarian: A Study of Anna Seghers*. Bonn: Bouvier Verlag Herbert Grundman, 1980.

Barradas, Efrain. *Para leer en puertorriqueño: Acercamiento a la obra de Luis Rafael Sánchez*. RioPiedras: Editorial Cultural, 1981.

————. "Luis Rafael Sánchez." *Spanish American Authors: The Twentieth Century*. Ed. Angel Flores. New York: H.W. Wilson, 1992. 795–797.

Baudrillard, Jean. *Simulacra and Simulation*. Trans. Sheila Faria Glaser. Ann Harbor: University of Michigan Press, 1994.

Baugh, Edward. "Postcolonial/Commonwealth Studies in the Caribbean: Points of Difference." *Postcolonizing the Commonwealth: Studies in Literature and Culture*. Ed. Rowland Smith. Waterloo, Ontario: Wilfrid Laurier University Press, 2000. 11–17.

Behn, Aphra. *Oroonoko, The Rover, and Other Works*. Ed. Janet Todd. London: Penguin Books, 1992.

————. *Oroonoko and Other Writings*. Ed. Paul Salzman. Oxford World Classics. Oxford and New York: Oxford University Press, 1994.

Belcom, Patricia. "All Ah We Is One: Caribbean Carnival in New York." *Caribbean Connections: Moving North*. Ed. Catherine A. Sunshine and Keith O. Warner. Washington, DC. Network of Educators of the Americas, 1998. 191–194.

Bell, Betty Louise. "Burying Paper." *Here First: Autobiographical Essays by Native American Writers*. Ed. Arnold Krupat and Brian Swann. New York: The Modern Library, 2000. 30–40.

Bell, Howard H., ed. *Black Separatism in the Caribbean, 1860*. By James Theodore Holly and J. Dennis Harris. Ann Arbor: The University of Michigan Press, 1970.

Bellegarde-Smith Patrick. "Alas de un ave, contraste en las culturas políticas en la Española: una perspectiva haitiana." *Del Caribe* 32 (2000): 26–29.

Benítez-Rojo, Antonio. *The Repeating Island: The Caribbean and the Postmodern Perspective*. Trans. James Maraniss. Durham and London: Duke University Press, 1992.

————. "El Caribe en el siglo XXI. Un proyecto de investigación." *Memorias: IV Seminario Internacional de Estudios del Caribe*. Ed. Instituto Internacional de Estudios del Caribe. Barranquilla: Fondo de Publicaciones de la Universidad del Atlántico, 1999. 11–20.

Benjamin, Walter. *Illuminations*. New York: Schocken Books, 1969.

————. "The Work of Art in the Age of Mechanical Reproduction." *Literary Theory: An Anthology*. Ed. Julie Rivkin and Michael Ryan. Malden and Oxford: Blackwell Publishers, 1999. 282–289.

Bennett, Louise. *Jamaica Labrish*. Kingston: Sangster Book Store, 1966.

Benson, Eugene, and L. W. Conolly, eds. *Encyclopedia of Post-colonial Literatures in English*. London and New York: Routledge, 1994.

Bercovitch, Sacvan. "Hawthorne's A- Morality of Compromise." *Representations* 24 (1988): 1–27.

Berrian, Brenda F. *Awakening Spaces: French Caribbean Popular Songs, Music, and Culture*. Chicago: University of Chicago Press, 2000.

Berrou, Raphael, and Pradel Pompilus. *Histoire de la littérature haïtienne illustrée par les textes* . Port-au-Prince: Editions Caraibes, 1975. 2 vols.

Bhabha, Homi K. *The Location of Culture*. London and New York: Routledge, 1994.

Birbalsingh, Frank, ed. *Frontiers of Caribbean Literature in English*. New York: St. Martin's Press, 1996.

Bishop, Joseph Bucklin. *Theodore Roosevelt and His Time Shown in His Own Letters*. Vol. 23 of *The Works of Theodore Roosevelt*. New York: Charles Scribner's Sons, 1926.

Blakely, Allison. "African Diaspora in the Netherlands." In Ember, Ember, and Skoggard. Vol. 2. 593–602.

Bloom, Harold, ed. *Caliban*. Major Literary Characters. New York: Chelsea House, 1992.

————. *Shakespeare: The Invention of the Human*. New York: Riverhead Books, 1998.

Bogues, Anthony. *Caliban's Freedom: The Early Political Thought of C.L.R. James*. London and Chicago: Pluto Press, 1997.

Bonafoux, Luis. *Betances*. San Juan: Instituto de Cultura Puertorriqueña, 1970.

Bosch, Juan. *Trujillo: Causas de una tiranía sin ejemplo*. Lima: Populibros Peruanos, 1959.

————. *De Cristóbal Colón a Fidel Castro: El Caribe, frontera imperial*. Madrid: Ediciones Alfaguara, 1970.

Brathwaite, Kamau. "Caribbean Culture: Two Paradigms." *Missile and Capsule*. Ed. Jurgen Martini. Bremen: University of Bremen, 1983.

————. *The Development of Creole Society in Jamaica: 1770–1820*. Oxford: Clarendon Press, 1971.

————. *The Colonial Encounter: Languages*. Mysore, India. The Center for Commonwealth Literature and Research University of Mysore, 1984.

————. "Metaphors of Underdevelopment: A Poem for Hernan Cortez." *New England Review and Bread Loaf Quarterly* 7.4 (1985): 453–476.

————. "An Interview with Edward Kamau Brathwaite." By Nathaniel Mackey. *Hambone* 9 (1991): 42–59.

————. "Words by Kamau Brathwaite." Kamau Brathwaite and the Caribbean Word: A North-South Counterpoint Conference. Bronx, New York. Hostos Community College, City University of New York. October 24, 1992.

————. *Middle Passages*. New York: New Directions, 1993.

Brereton, Bridget. "Regional Histories." In Higman. 308–342.

Breton, André. "Préface." *Cahier d'un retour au pays natal.* By Aimé Césaire. Paris: Editions Présence Africaine, 1983. 77–87.

Briton, Celia M. *Edouard Glissant and Postcolonial Theory.* New World Studies. Charlottesville and London: University Press of Virginia, 1999.

Brooks, Cleanth, R. W. B. Lewis, and Robert Penn Warren, eds. *American Literature: The Makers and the Making.* 2 vols. New York: St. Martin's Press, 1973.

Browning, Robert. *Selected Poetry of Browning.* Ed. Keneth L. Knickerbocker. New York: The Modern Library, 1951.

Buck-Morss, Susan. "Hegel and Haiti." *Critical Inquiry* 26 (Summer 2000): 821–865.

Bundy, Andrew. "Introduction." *Selected Essays of Wilson Harris: The Unfinished Genesis of the Imagination.* London and New York: Routledge, 1999. 1–34.

Cabral, Manuel del. *Obra poética completa.* 2nd ed. Santo Domingo: Editora Alfa y Omega, 1987.

Cadet, Jean-Robert. *Restavec: From Haitian Slave Child to Middle-Class American (An Autobiography).* Austin: University of Texas Press, 1998.

Calderón, Hector, and José David Saldivar, eds. *Criticism in the Borderlands: Studies in Chicano Literature, Culture, and Ideology.* Durham and London: Duke University Press, 1991.

Campbell, Mavis C. *The Maroons of Jamaica, 1655–1796: A History of Resistance, Collaboration, and Betrayal.* Granby, MA: Bergin and Garvey, 1988.

Carpentier, Alejo. *El reino de este mundo.* Santiago, Chile: Editoria Universitaria, 1967.

———. *Vision de América.* Barcelona: Editorial Seix Barral, S.A., 1999.

Carreras, Carlos N. *Betances, El Antillano proscrito.* San Juan: Club de La Prensa, 1961.

Carrol, Lewis. *Alice's Adventures in Wonderland and through the Looking Glass.* Philadelphia and Toronto: The John C. Winston Company, 1923.

Casimir, Jean. *La invención del Caribe.* San Juan: Editorial de la Universidad Puerto Rico, 1997. Spanish version of *La Caraïbe: Une et divisible.*

Castaños Alés, Enrique. "Un caso aislado: la investigación interdisciplinaria de Frank Rebajes." http://www.013.infonegocio.com/818/rebajes1.htm (1996). Revised version of article published in the Málaga newspaper *Sur* August 20, 1989.

Castellanos, Juan de. *Elegías de varones ilustres de Indias.* Biblioteca de Autores Españoles. Ed. D. Buenaventura Carlos Aribau. Madrid: Real Academia Española, 1944.

Castor, Suzy. *Migración y relaciones internacionales (El caso haitiano-dominicano).* Santo Domingo: Editora Universitaria UASD, 1987.

Castro-Gómez, Santiago, and Eduardo Mendieta, eds. *Teorías sin disciplina, latinoamericanismo, poscolonialidad y globalización en debate.* México: University of San Francisco/Miguel Angel Porrúa Grupo Editorial, 1998.

Cervantes Saavedra, Miguel de. *The Ingenious Gentleman Don Quixote de la Mancha.* Trans. Samuel Putnam. New York: The Viking Press, 1949.

Césaire, Aimé. 1960. *Toussaint Louverture: La revolution française et le problème colonial.* 2nd ed. Paris: Présence Africaine, 1961.

———. *La tragédie du roi Christophe.* Paris: Présence Africaine, 1963.

Céspedes, Diógenes. *Política de la teoría del lenguaje y la poesía en América Latina en el siglo XX.* Santo Domingo: Editora Universitaria UASD & Ediciones Librería La Trinitaria, 1994.

Chamberlin, J. Edward. "The Language of Kamau Brathwaite." *The Art of Kamau Brathwaite*. Ed. Stewart Brown. Bridgen: Seren, 1995. 33–51.

Chaturvedi, Vinayak, ed. *Mapping Subaltern Studies and the Postcolonial*. London and New York: Verso, 2000.

Chow, Rey. "How (the) Inscrutable Chinese Led to Globalized Theory." *PMLA* 116.1 (January 2001): 69–74.

Christie, Agatha. *A Caribbean Mystery*. London: Collins, St James's Place, 1964.

Churchill, Winston S. 1957. *A History of the English-Speaking Peoples*. 4 vols. New York: Dorset Press, 1990.

Claypole, William, and John Robottom. *Caribbean Story*. Book One: Foundations. New Edition. Essex: Longman Caribbean, 1989.

Cliff, Michelle. *No Telephone to Heaven*. New York: Plume, 1996.

Cohen, Jeffrey Jerome, ed. *The Postcolonial Middle Ages*. New York: St. Martin's Press, 2000.

Collins, Merle. "Nabel String." In Sunshine and Warner. 90–91.

Collins, Merle. *Rotten Pomerack*. London: Virago Press, 1992.

Columbus, Christopher. 1969. *The Four Voyages*. Trans. and ed. J. M. Cohen. London: The Cresset Library, 1988.

Columbus, Christopher. *The Log of Christopher Columbus*. Trans. Robert H. Fuson. Camden, Maine: International Marine, 1987.

Cooppan, Vilashini. "W(h)ither Post-colonial Studies? Towards a Transnational Study of Race and Nation." *Postcolonial Theory and Criticism*. Ed. Laura Chrisman and Benita Parry. Cambridge: D.S. Brewer, 2000. 1–35.

Cornevin, Robert. *Le théatre haïtien: Des orgines à nos jours*. Ottawa: Leméac, 1973.

Coser, Stelamaris. *Bridging the Americas: The Literature of Paule Marshall, Toni Morrison and Gayl Jones*. Philadelphia: Temple University Press, 1995.

Costello, Ray. *Black Liverpool: The Early History of Britain's Oldest Black Community 1730–1918*. Liverpool: Picton Press, 2001.

Courtney, W. S. *The Gold Fields of Santo Domingo*. New York: Anson P. Norton, 1860.

Craton, Michael. "Forms of Resistance to Slavery." In Knight. 222–270.

Cuevas, Mapi M., and William G. Lamb. *Holt Physical Science*. Austin: Holt, Rinehart and Winston, 1994.

Cugoano, Quobna Ottobah. *Thoughts and Sentiments on the Evil of Slavery*. Ed. Vincent Carretta. New York: Penguin Books, 1999.

Cundall, Frank, and Joseph L. Pietersz. *Jamaica under the Spaniards*. Kingston: Institute of Jamaica, 1919.

D'Aguiar, Fred. "Introduction." *The West Indies and the Spanish Main*. By Anthony Trollope. New York: Carroll and Graf Publishers, 1999. v–viii.

Dabydeen, David. "West Indian Writers in Britain." *Voices of the Crossing: The Impact of Britain on Writers from Asia, the Caribbean and Africa*. Ed. Ferdinand Dennis and Naseem Khan. London: Serpent Trail, 2000. 59–75.

Daldianus, Artemidorus. *Interpretation of Dreams (Oneirocritica)*. Trans. Robert J. White. Park Ridge, NJ: Noyes Press, 1975.

Danticat, Edwidge. *The Farming of Bones*. New York: Soho, 1998.

———, ed. *The Butterfly's Way: Voices from the Haitian Diaspora in the United States*. New York: Soho Press, 2001.

Dash, Michael. "Introduction." *Caribbean Discourse: Selected Essays*. By Edouard Glissant. Trans. J. Michael Dash. Charlottesville: University Press of Virginia, 1989. xi–xlv.

Dash, Michael. *Edouard Glissant*. Cambridge Studies in African and Caribbean Literature. Cambridge: Cambridge University Press, 1995.

———. *Haiti and the United States: National Stereotypes and the Literary Imagination*. 2nd. ed. New York: St. Martin's Press, 1996.

———. *The Other America: Caribbean Literature in a New World Context*. New World Studies. Charlottesville and London: University of Virginia Press, 1998.

Dawes, Neville. *Prolegomena to Caribbean Literature*. Kingston: Institute of Jamaica, 1977.

De La Campa, Román. "Resistance and Globalization: Antonio Benítez-Rojo and Edouard Glissant." *A History of Literature in the Caribbean*. Vol. 3. Ed. A. James Arnold. Amsterdam and Philadelphia: John Benjamins Publishing Company, 1997. 87–116.

Debrot, Cola. "Literature of the Netherlands Antilles." *Panorama das literaturas das Americas*. Vol. 4. Ed. Joaquin de Montezuma Carvalho. Angola: Ediçao do Municipio de Nova Lisboa, 1963. 1897–1935.

Deive, Carlos Esteban. *Los guerrilleros negros: Esclavos fugitivos y cimarrones en Santo Domingo*. Santo Domingo: Fundación Cultural Dominicana, 1989.

Deive, Carlos Esteban. *Vodú y magia en Santo Domingo*. 3rd. ed. Santo Domingo: Fundación Cultural Domincana, 1992.

Del Monte, Félix María. "Cantos dominicanos." *Poesía popular dominicana*. Ed. Emilio Rodríguez Demorizi. Santiago: UCMM, 1979. 244–246.

Delano, Amasa. *Delano's Voyages of Commerce and Discovery*. Ed. Eleanor Roosevelt Seagraves. Stockbridge, MA: Berkshire House Publishers, 1994.

Delorme, Demesvar. *Les théoriciens au pouvoir*. Excerpts in Berrou and Pompilus, Vol. 1. 544–592.

Dennis, Ferdinand, and Naseem Khan, eds. *Voices of the Crossing: The Impact of Britain on Writers from Asia, the Caribbean, and Africa*. London: Serpent's Tail, 2000.

Depestre, René. *Pour la révolution, Pour la poésie*. Collection Francophonie Vivante. Québec: Lémec, 1974.

Devèze, Michel. *Antilles, Guyanes, La Mer des caraïbes de 1492 à 1789*. Paris: Sociëté D' Edition D' Enseignement Supérieur, 1977.

Diederich, Bernard, and Al Burt. *Papa Doc: Haiti and Its Dictator*. 1969. Maplewood, NJ: Waterfront Press, 1991.

Dirlik, Arif. "The Postcolonial Aura: Third World Criticism in the Age of Global Capitalism." In MacClintock, Mufti, and Shohat. 501–528.

Dolan, J. F., H. T. Mullins, and D. J. Wald. "Active Tectonics of the North-Central Caribbean: Oblique Collision, Strain Partitioning, and Opposing Subducted Slabs." *Active Strike-Slip and Collisional Tectonics of the Northern Caribbean Plate Boundary Zone*. Special Paper 326. Boulder: Geographical Society of America, 1998.

Donne, John. *John Donne: A Critical Edition of the Major Works*. Ed. John Carey. Oxford: Oxford University Press, 1990.

Dorsainvil, J. C. *Manuel d'Histoire d'Haiti*. Port-au-Prince: Imprimerie Henri Deschamps, 1934.

Dorsinville, Max. *Caliban Without Prospero: Essay on Quebec and Black Literature*. Erin, Ontario: Press Percepic, 1974.

Douglass, Frederick. *Life and Times of Frederick Douglass Written by Himself*. 1882. New York: Collier Books, 1962.

Duany, Jorge. "Blurred Frontiers: The Socioeconomic Impacts of Transnational Migration on the Hispanic Caribbean and the United States." Paper presented at conference "One Hundred Years of Transformation: The Caribbean and the United States, 1898–1998." Lehman College, City University of New York, Bronx, New York. October 13–15, 1998.

Duarte, Rosa. *Apuntes de Rosa Duarte: Archivo y versos de Juan Pablo Duarte*. Ed. E. Rodríguez Demorizi, C. Larrazabal Blanco, and V. Alfau Durán. 2nd. ed. Santo Domingo: Secretaría de Estado de Educación Bellas Artes y Cultos, 1994.

Dunn, L. C., and Theodosius Dobzhansky. *Heredity, Race, and Society*. New York: Mentor Books, 1946.

Eagleton, Terry. *The Idea of Culture*. Malden, MA: Blackwell, 2000.

Echteld, Liesbeth. "Curaçaoan Literature in Spanish." In Arnold, 2001. 505–512.

Economist. "The Triumph of English: A World Empire by Other Means." *The Economist* (December 22, 2001): 65–67.

Edgar, Andrew, and Peter Sedgwick. *Key Concepts in Cultural Theory*. London and New York: Routledge, 1999.

Edmondson, Belinda J., ed. *Caribbean Romances: The Politics of Regional Representation*. New World Series. Charlottesville and London: University of Virginia Press, 1999.

Eltis, David. "The Slave Economies of the Caribbean: Structure, Performance, Evolution, and Significance." In Knight. 105–137.

Ember, Melvin, Carol R. Ember, and Ian Skoggard, eds. *Encyclopedia of Diasporas: Immigrant and Refugee Cultures Around the World*. 2 vols. New York: Kluwer Academic/Plenum Publishers, 2004.

Encyclopédie ou dictionnaire raisonné des sciences, des arts et de métiers par une société de gens de lettres. Vol. II. Ed. Denis Diderot and Jean Le Rond D'Alembert. Paris, 1751.

Engerman, Stanley L., and B. W. Higman. "The Demographic Structure of Caribbean Slave Societies in the Eighteenth and Nineteenth Centuries." In Knight. 45–104.

Eversley, Shelley, et al. "Twentieth-Century Literature in the New Century: A Symposium." *College English* 65.1 (2001): 9–32.

Farley, Christopher John. "Smiling amid Corpses." *Time* (September 7, 1998): 78.

Faulkner, William. *Essays, Speeches, and Public Letters*. Ed. James B. Meriwether. New York: Random House, 1965.

Fehervary, Helen. *Ana Seghers: The Mythic Dimension*. Ann Arbor: The University of Michigan Press, 2001.

Fernández Retamar, Roberto. "Caliban Speaks Five Hundred Years Later." In McClintock, Mufti, and Shohat. 163–172.

Fernández Retamar, Roberto. *Calibán: Apuntes sobre la cultura en Nuestra América*. 2nd. ed. México, D.F.: Editorial Diógenes, 1974.

Ferré, Rosario. *Maldito amor*. México, D. F.: Editorial Joaquín Mortiz, 1986.

Ferrer Gutiérrez, Virgilio. *Luperón: Brida y espuela*. La Habana: Carasa y Ca., 1940.

Finkel, Michael. "Desperate Passage." *The New York Times Magazine* (June 16, 2000): 50–53, 66–67, 78, 82–83, 94, 99.

Firmín, Anténor. Excerpts in Berrou y Pompilus. Vol. 1. 635–665.

Fishburn, Evelyn. "Caliban: America as the Other." *Encyclopedia of Latin American Literature*. Ed. Verity Smith. London and Chicago: Fitzroy Dearborn Publishers, 1997. 158–159.

Foner, Nancy. *From Ellis Island to JFK: New York's Two Great Waves of Immigration*. New York: Russell Sage Foundation/Yale University Press, 2000.

Foucault, Michel. *Histoire de la sexualité*. Tome III. Le Souci de soi. Paris: Gallimard, 1988.

Franco, Franklin J. *La era de Trujillo.* Santo Domingo: Fundación Cultural Dominicana, 1992.

Frey, John Andrew. *A Victor Hugo Encyclopedia.* Westport, CT: Greenwood Press, 1999.

Froude, James Anthony. *The English in the West Indies or the Bow of Ulysses.* London: Longmans, Green, and Co., 1888.

Fukuyama, Francis. *The End of History and the Last Man.* New York: The Free Press, 1992.

García López, José. *Historia de la literatura española.* 17th ed. Barcelona: Editorial Vicens-Vives, 1972.

García Márquez, Gabriel. *El general en su laberinto.* Bogotá: Editora La Oveja Negra, 1989.

———. "Caribe Mágico." *The Archipelago: New Caribbean Writing.* Special issue of *Conjunctions* 27 (1996): 9–12.

———. *El amor en los tiempos del cólera.* 1985. Barcelona: Mandadori, 1999.

Gerbi, Antonello. *The Dispute of the New World: The History of a Polemic 1750–1900.* Revised and Enlarged Edition. Trans. Jeremy Moyle. Pittsburgh: University of Pittsburgh Press, 1973.

Gerzina, Gretchen. *Black London: Life Before Emancipation.* New Brunswick: Rutgers University Press, 1995.

Gikandi, Simon. *Writing in Limbo: Modernism and Caribbean Literature.* Ithaca: Cornell University Press, 1992.

Gilroy, Paul. *The Black Atlantic: Modernity and Double Consciousness.* Cambridge, Massachusetts: Harvard University Press, 1993.

Glissant, Edouard. *Le discours antillais.* Paris: Gallimard, 1981.

———. *Monsieur Toussaint.* Paris: Editions Du Seuil, 1986.

———. *Caribbean Discourse: Selected Essays.* Trans. J. Michael Dash. Charlotesville: University Press of Virginian, 1989.

Goldberg, Jonathan. *Tempest in the Caribbean.* Minneapolis and London: University of Minnesota Press, 2004.

Goldie, Terry: "Edward W. Said." *Encyclopedia of Contemporary Literary Theory: Approaches Scholars, Terms.* Ed. Irena R. Makaryk. Toronto, Buffalo, and London: University of Toronto Press, 1993. 461–463.

González, Nancie L. *Prospero, Caliban, and Black Sambo: Colonial Views of the Other in the Caribbean.* Department of Spanish and Portugese Working Papers No. 11. College Park: University of Maryland, 1991.

Grainger, James. *The Sugar Cane.* 1764. *The Poetics of Empire: A Study of James Grainger's "The Sugar Cane."* By John Gilmore. London and New Brunswick: The Athlone Press, 2000.

Gravette, A. Gerald. *The Netherlands Antilles.* New York: Hippocrene Books, 1989.

Greenbaum, Toni. "Frank Rebajes." *Messengers of Modernism: American Studio Jewelry 1940–1960.* Ed. Martin Eidelberg. Paris-New York: Montreal Museum of Decorative Arts and Flammarion, 1996. 70–73.

Guehenno, Jean. *Caliban parle.* Paris: Grasset, 1928.

———. *Caliban et Prospero.* Paris: Gallimard, 1969.

Guérin, Daniel. *Les Antilles decolonisées.* Introduction par Aimé Césaire. Paris: Présence Africaine, 1956.

Guerra y Sánchez, Ramiro. *Sugar and Society in the Caribbean.* New Haven and London: Yale University Press, 1964.

Guerra, Gustavo Tatis. "Alfonso Múnera Cavadía: Un historiador en el corazón del Caribe." *El Universal* (Colombia). July 31, 2001. 5A.

Gugelberger, Georg M. "Postcolonial Cultural Studies." *The Johns Hopkins Guide to Literary Theory and Criticism.* Ed. Michael Groden and Martin Kreiswirth. Baltimore and London: The Johns Hopkins University Press, 1994. 581–585.

Guilbault, Jocelyne. *Zouk: World Music in the Caribbean.* With Gage Averill, Edouard Benoit, and Gregory Rabess. Chicago and London: The University of Chicago Press, 1993.

Guillén, Nicolás. *Obra poética.* Vol. I. Ed. Angel Augier. La Habana: Editorial Letras Cubanas, 1980.

Habermas, Jürgen. 1998. *La constelación posnacional: Ensayos políticos.* Trans. Pere Fabra Abat, Daniel Gamper Sachse, and Luis Pérez Díaz. Biblioteca del Presente. No. 11. Barcelona: Paidós, 2000.

Hall, Douglas. *In Miserable Slavery: Thomas Thistlewood in Jamaica, 1750–86.* Kingston: The University of the West Indies Press, 1999.

Hall, Stuart, *Portrait of the Caribbean* TV Documentary BBC 1992.

———. "Cultural Identity and Diaspora." *Colonial Discourses and Post-Colonial Theory: A Reader.* Ed. Patrick Williams and Laura Chrisman. New York: Columbia University Press, 1994. 392–403.

———. "The Local and the Global: Globalization and Ethnicity." In MacClintock, Mufti, and Shohat. 173–187.

Hall, Stuart, and Paddy Whannel. 1964. *The Popular Arts.* Boston: Beacon Press, 1967.

Hall, Stuart, and Tony Jefferson, eds. *Resistance through Rituals: Youth Subcultures in Post-War Britain.* London: Hutchinson, 1976.

Harney, Stephano. *Nationalism and Identity: Culture and the Imagination in a Caribbean Diaspora.* London and Kingston: Zed Books and the Press-University of the West Indies, 1996.

Harpelle, Ronald D. *The West Indians of Costa Rica.* Montreal and Kingston: McGill-Queen's University Press and Ian Randle Publishers, 2001.

Harris, J. Dennis. *A Summer on the Borders of the Caribbean Sea.* 1861. In Bell. 67–184.

Harris, Wilson. *Selected Essays of Wilson Harris: The Unfinished Genesis of the Imagination.* Ed. Andrew Bundy. London and New York: Routledge, 1999.

———. *The Whole Armour* & *The Secret Ladder.* London: Faber and Faber, 1973.

Hawking, Stephen W. *A Brief History of Time: From the Big Bang to Black Holes.* Toronto: Bantam Books, 1988.

Hegel, Georg Wilhelm Friedrich. *The Philosophy of History.* Trans. J. Sibree. New York: Dover Publications, 1956.

Henna, José Julio. "Al pueblo norteamexicano." *Las ideas anexionistas en Puerto Rico.* Ed. Aaron Gamaliel Ramos. Río Piedras: Ediciones Huracán, 1987. 65–72.

Henríquez Ureña, Pedro. *Obra crítica.* México, D.F.: Fondo de Cultura Económica, 1960.

Henriquez, Denis. "Sombras del sol." *El artista caribeño como guerrero de lo imaginario.* Ed. Rita De Maeseneer and An Van Hecke. Madrid and Frankfurt am Main: Iberoamericana/Vervuert, 2004. 55–61.

Henry, Paget. *Caliban's Reason: Introducing Afro-Caribbean Philosophy.* London and New York: Routledge, 2000.

Hernández Franco, Tomás. *Yelidá.* San Salvador: Ediciones Sargazo, Talleres Gnáficos Cisrieros, 1942.

Hernández, Ramona, and Silvio Torres-Saillant. "Dominican Quiddities in the U.S. Academy." *Punto 7 Review: A Journal of Marginal Discourse.* 3.1 (Fall 1996): 1–10.

Hesse, Mary. "Laws and Theories." *The Encyclopedia of Philosophy*. Vol. 4. Ed. Paul Edwards. New York: Macmillan and The Free Press, 1967. 404–410.

Heward, Edmund. *Lord Mansfield*. Chichester and London: Barry Rose (Publishers) Ltd., 1979.

Higman, B. W. "Modes of Dissemination." In Higman c. 687–708.

Higman, B. W. a "The Development of Historical Disciplines in the Caribbean." In Higman a. 3–18.

Higman, B. W., ed. *General History of the Caribbean*. Vol. VI. Methodology and Historiography of the Caribbean. London and Oxford: UNESCO Publishing/MacMillan Caribbean, 1999b.

Hilden, Patricia Penn. *When Nickels Were Indians: An Urban Mixed-Blood Story*. Smithsonian Series of Studies in Native American Literatures. Washington and London: Smithsonian Institution Press, 1995.

———. "Til Indian Voices Wake Us . . ." *For the Geography of a Soul: Emerging Perspectives on Kamau Brathwaite*. Ed. Timothy J. Reiss. Trenton and Asmara: Africa World Press, 2001. 403–430.

Hodge, Merle. *Crick-Crack, Monkey*. 1970. Caribbean Writers Series. Oxford: Heinemann, 1981.

Hoffmann, Léon-Francois. *Essays on Haitian Literature*. Washington, DC: Three Continents Press, 1984.

Hogan, Patrick Colm. *Colonialist and Cultural Identity: Crises of Tradition in the Anglophone Literatures of India, Africa, and the Caribbean*. Albany: SUNY Press, 2000.

Hoggart, Richard. 1957. *The Uses of Literacy: Changing Patterns in English Mass Culture*. Boston: Beacon press, 1966.

Holly, James Theodore. *A Vindication of the Capacity of the Negro Race for Self-Government and Civilized Progress*. 1857. In Bell. 17–66.

Hoogbergen, Wim. "The History of the Surinam Maroons." *Resistence and Rebellion: Old and New*. Ed. Gary Brana-Shute. Studies in Third World Societies No. 42. Williamsburg, VA: Department of Anthropology, College of William and Mary, 1990. 65–102.

Hooks, Bell. *Yearning: Race, Gender, and Cultural Politics*. Boston: South End Press, 1990.

Hostos, Eugenio María de. *Obras completas*. 2nd. ed. Vol. 10. San Juan: Editorial Coquí, 1969.

———. *America:The Struggle for Freedom (Anthology)*. Ed. Manuel Maldonado-Denis. San Juan: City University of New York, Institute of Hostosian Studies, and University of Puerto Rico, 1992.

Howard, Jean E. "The New Historicism in Renaissance Studies." *English Literary Renaissance* 16 (1986): 13–43.

Howes, Barbara, ed. *From the Green Antilles: Writings of the Caribbean*. New York: Macmillan, 1966.

Hugo, Victor. *Hans of Iceland. Bug-Jargal. Claude Gueux*. Chicago: Hooper, Clarke, & Co., 1900?

Hulme, Peter. *Colonial Encounter: Europe and the Native Caribbean, 1492–1797*. London and New York: Methuen, 1986.

———. "Introduction: The Cannibal Scene." *Cannibalism and the Colonial World*. Ed. Francis Barker, Peter Hulme, and Margaret Iverse. Cambridge: Cambridge University Press, 1998. 1–38.

Humboldt, Alexander von, and Aimé Bonpland. *Personal Narrative of Travels to the Equinoctial Regions of America during the Years 1799–1804*. Trans. from the French and ed. by Thomasina Ross. Vol. III. London: Henry G. Bohn, 1853.

Hurbon, Laënnec. "Ideology in Caribbean History." In Higman a. 136–161.

Isaacs, Jorge. *María*. Bogota: Editorial Sol 90, 2001.

James, C. L. R. *The Black Jacobins: Toussaint Louverture and the San Domingo Revolution*. 2nd. ed. New York: Vintage Books, 1963.

———. "The West Indian Intellectual." *Froudacity*. By J. J. Thomas. London: New Beacon, 1969. 23–49.

———. "Haiti, History of." *Encyclopedia Britannica*. 15th ed. 1979. Micropaedia. Vol. 8. 550–552.

Jameson, Fredric. *Postmodernism, or The Cultural Logic of Late Capitalism*. Durham: Duke University Press, 1991.

———. *The Jameson Reader*. Ed. Michael Hardt and Kathi Weeks. Oxford and Malden: Blackwell, 2000.

Jefferson, Thomas. *The Life and Writings of Thomas Jefferson*. Ed. Adrienne Koch and William Peden. New York: The Modern Library, 1944.

Johnson, Charles. *Middle Passage*. New York: Simon and Schuster, 1990.

Joseph, Margaret Paul. *Caliban in Exile: The Outsider in Caribbean Fiction*. New York, Westport, and London: Greenwood Press, 1992.

Juliana, Elis. *Haiku in Papiamentu/Un mushi di kaiku*. Trans. Hélène Garrett. Edmonton: The University of Aberta Press, 2003.

Jussawalla, Feroza, and Reed Way Dasenbrock, ed. *Interviews with Writers of the Post-Colonial World*. Jackson and London: University Press of Mississippi, 1992.

Katzner, Kenneth. *The Languages of the World*. 3rd. ed. London and New York: Routledge, 2002.

Kempen, Michiel van. "Vernacular Literature in Surinam." *Callaloo* 21.3 (1998): 630–644.

———. "The Literary Infrastructure of Surinam: Problems and Changes." *A History of Literature in the Caribbean*. Vol. 2. English- and Dutch-speaking regions. Ed. A. James Arnold. Amsterdam and Philadelphia: John Benjamin Publishing Company, 2001. 387–395.

Kleist, Henrich von. "Betrothal in Santo Domingo." In *German Romantic Novelas*. By Henrich von Kleist and Jean Paul. Ed. Frank G. Ryder and Robert M. Browning. Foreword by John Simon. The German Library. Vol. 34. New York: Continuum, 1985. 136–165.

Klooster, Wim. *The Dutch in the Americas: 1600–1800*. Providence, Rhode Island: The John Carter Brown Library, 1997.

Knight, Franklin W. *General History of the Caribbean*. Vol. III. The Slave Societies of the Caribbean. London and Basingstoke: UNESCO Publishing and Macmillan, 1997.

Kom, Anton de. *We Slaves of Surinam*. Trans. Arnold J. Pomerans. London: Zed Books, 1987.

———. *Nosotros, esclavos de Surinam*. La Habana: Casa de las Américas, 1981.

Krise, Thomas, ed. *Caribbeana: An Anthology of English Literature of the West Indies, 1657–1777*. Chicago and London: The University of Chicago Press, 1999.

Kruythoff, S. J. *The Netherlands Windward Islands*. 3rd. ed. Oranjestad, Aruba: De Wit Inc., 1964.

Kundera, Milan. "The Umbrella, the Night World, and the Lonely Moon." *The New York Review of Books* (December 19, 1991): 46–50.

Kutzinski, Vera. "The Cult of Caliban: Collaboration and Revisionism in Contemporary Caribbean Narrative." *A History of Literature in the Caribbean.* Vol. 3. Cross-Cultural Studies. Ed. A. James Arnold. Amsterdam and Philadelphia: John Benjamins Publishing Co., 1997. 285–305.

Labat, Jean Baptiste. *The Memoirs of Pére Labat 1693–1705.* Trans. and abridged by John Eaden. With an Introduction by Philip Gosse. London: Frank Cass and Company, 1970.

Lacan, Jacques. "The Mirror Stage as Formative of the Function of the I as Revealed in Psychoanalytic Experience." *Literary Theory: An Anthology.* Ed. Julie Rivkin and Michael Ryan. Malden and Oxford: Blackwell Publishers, 1998. 178–183.

Lacroix, Pamphile de. 1819. *La Revolution de Haiti.* Ed. Pierre Pluchon. Paris: Editions Karthala, 1995.

Laguerre, Michel S. *American Odyssey: Haitians in New York City.* Ithaca and London: Cornell University Press, 1984.

———. "The Role of the Diaspora in Haitian Politics." *Haiti Renewed: Political and Economic Prospects.* Ed. Robert J. Rotberg. Washington, DC: Brookings Institution Press, 1997. 170–182.

Lamming, George. *The Pleasures of Exile. 1960.* Foreword by Sandra Pouchet Paquet. Ann Arbor: The University of Michigan Press, 1992.

———. "Concepts of the Caribbean." In Birbalsingh 1996. 1–4, 5–9.

Lampe, Armando. "Por la aparición de 'Double Play.' " *Revista Mexicana del Caribe* 5.10 (2000): 233–240.

Laquerre, Michel. *American Odyssey: Haitians in New York City.* Ithaca: Cornell University Press, 1984.

Lara, Oruno D. *Breve historia del Caribe.* Trans. Wilma Moreno de Rosentul and Víctor Hugo Yánez. El Libro Menor 223. Caracas: Academia Nacional de La Historia, 2000.

Laraque, Paul, and Jack Hirschman, eds. *Open Gate: An Anthology of Haitian Creole Poetry.* Trans. Jack Hirschman and Boadiba. Willimantic, CT: Curbstone Press, 2001.

Las Casas, Bartolomé de, Fray. *Historia de las Indias.* Vol. II. Hollywood, Florida: Ediciones Continente, S.A., 1985.

Lazarus, Neil. "Introducing Postcolonial Studies." *The Cambridge Companion to Postcolonial Studies.* Ed. Neil Lazarus. Cambridge: Cambridge University Press, 2004. 1–16.

Leeuwen, Boeli van. *The Sign of Jonah.* Trans. André Lafevere. Sag Harbor, NY: The Permanent Press, 1995.

Lefevere, Andre. "Boeli van Leeuwen's *The Sign of Jonah:* Escathology in the Dutch Caribbean." *Sisyphus and Eldorado: Magical and Other Realisms in Caribbean Literature.* Ed. Timothy J. Reiss. Trenton and Asmara: Africa World Press, 2002. 57–70.

Lewis, Gordon K. *Main Currents in Caribbean Thought: The Historical Evolution of Caribbean Society in Its Ideological Aspects.* Baltimore and London: The John Hopkins University Press, 1983.

Lier, R. J. J. van. "The Jewish Community in Surinam: A Historical Survey." *The Jewish Nation in Surinam.* Ed. Robert Cohen. Amsterdam: S. Emmering, 1982. 19–27.

Lizardo, Luis Francisco. *Palma Sola: La tragedia de un pueblo.* Santo Domingo: Instituto de Formación Curricular, 1982.

Loomba, Ania. *Colonialism/Poscolonialism.* London and New York: Routledge, 1998.

López de Jesús, Lara Ivette. *Encuentros sincopados: El Caribe contemporáneo a través de sus prácticas musicales*. Série Pensamiento Caribeño. México, D.F.: Siglo XXI Editores, 2003.

López Morales, Humberto. "The History of Literary Language." *A History of Literature in the Caribbean*. Vol. 1. Ed. A. James Arnold. Amsterdam and Philadelphia: John Benjamins Publishing Co., 1994. 9–23.

López, José Ramón. *La alimentación y las razas*. El Gran Pesimismo Dominicano. Santiago: Universidad Católica Madre y Maestra, 1975. 29–68.

Lovejoy, Arthur O. *The Great Chain of Being: A Study in the History of an Idea*. Cambridge, MA: Harvard University Press, 1936.

Lovelace, Earl. *The Wine of Astonishment*. 1982. Oxford: Heinemann, 1986.

Mackaye, Percy. *Caliban by the Yellow Lands*. Garden City, NY: Doubleday, Page and Company, 1916.

Mackey, Nathaniel. "An Interview with Edward Kamau Brathwaite." *Hambone* 9 (1991): 42–59.

Makward, Christine. "Entretien avec Gisèle Pineau." *The French Review* 76.6 (2003): 1202–1215.

Marqués, René. *The Docile Puerto Rican*. Trans. Barbara Bockus Aponte. Philadelphia: Temple University Press, 1976.

Márquez, Roberto. "Raza, Racismo e Historia: 'Are All My Bones From There' " *Latino(a) Research Review* 4.3 (2000): 8–22.

Martí, José. *Obras completas*. Vol. 19. La Habana: Editorial Nacional de Cuba, 1964.

———. *Obras completas*. Vol. 4. La Habana: Editorial Nacional, 1963.

———. *Selected Writings*. Ed. and Trans. Esther Allen. New York: Penguin, 2002.

Martínez-San Miguel, Yolanda. "De ilegales e indocumentados: Representaciones de la migración dominicana en Puerto Rico." *Revista de Ciencias Sociales* 4 (January 1998): 147–171.

———. *Caribe Two Ways: Cultura de la migración en el Caribe insular hispánico*. San Juan: Ediciones Callejón, 2003.

Marx, Karl. "Democratic Pan-Slavism." *Collected Works of Karl Marx and Frederick Engels*. Vol. 8. New York and Moscow: International Publishers and Progress Publishers, 1977. 362–371.

Mayor, Federico. "Preface." *General History of the Carebbean*. Vol. 1. Ed. Jalil Sued Badillo. Paris, London, and Oxford: UNESCO Publishing and Macmillan Publishers, 2003. vi–viii.

Mc Leod, Cynthia. *De vrije negerin Elisabeth: Gevangene van kleur*. AB Schoorl, Netherlands: Vitgevery Conserve, 2000.

———. *The Free Negress Elisabeth: Prisoner of Color*. Trans. Sean F. Taylor and Monique S. Pool. Paramaribo-Zuid, Suriname: The Waterfront Press, 2004.

———. *Elisabeth Samson: Ern vrije zwarte vrouw in het achttiende-eeuwse Suriname*. Utrecht: Universiteit Utrecht, Vakgroip Culturele Anthropologie, 1993.

———. *Celebrating the Extraordinary Life of Elisabeth Samson*. Encuentros No. 27. Washington, DC.: Inter-American Development Bank Cultural Center, 1998.

———. "Elisabeth Samson: Celebrating an Extraordinary 18th Century Free 'Negresss.' " Paper presented at the Gilder Lehrman Center for the Study of Slavery, Resistance & Abolition. Center for International and Area Studies. Yale University, New Haven, CT. March 26, 1999.

McClintock, Anne, Aamir Mufti, and Ella Shohat, eds. *Dangerous Liaisons: Gender, Nation, and Postcolonial Perspectives*. Minneapolis and London: University of Minnesota Press, 1997.

McCullough, David. *Brave Companions: Portraits in History.* New York: Simon and Schuster, 1992.

Melville, Herman. *Benito Cereno. 1855. Shorter Novels of Herman Melville.* Introduction by Raymond Weaver. New York: Liveright Publishing Corp, 1942.

Melville, Pauline. *The Migration of Ghosts.* London: Bloomsbury, 1998.

Métellus, Jean. *Anacaona.* Collection Monde Noire Poche. Paris: Editions Hatier, 1986.

Milne, Dew, ed. *Modern Critical Thought: An Anthology of Theorists on Theorists.* Malden and Oxford: Blackwell Publishing, 2003.

Milz, Sabine "Edward W. Said." *The Johns Hopkins Guide to Literary Theory and Criticism.* 2nd ed. Ed. Michael Groden, Martin Keiswirth, and Inre Szeman. Baltimore and London: The Johns Hopkins University Press, 2005. 824–831.

Mintz, Sidney W. *Sweetness and Power: The Place of Sugar in Modern History.* New York: Penguin Books, 1986.

Mir, Pedro. *Cuando amaban las tierras comuneras.* México, D.F.: Siglo XXI Editores, 1978.

———. 1969. *Tres leyendas de colores: Ensayo de interpretación de las tres primeras revoluciones del Nuevo Mundo.* 2nd. ed. Santo Domingo: Editora Taller, 1978.

———. *Countersong to Walt Whitman and Other Poems.* Trans. Jonathan Cohen and Donald D. Walsh. Washington, DC: Azul Editions, 1993.

Montaigne, Michel de. *The Complete Works of Montaigne.* Trans. Donald M. Frame. Stanford: University of California Press, 1957.

———. *Ensayos.* Tomo 1. Buenos Aires: Ediciones Orbis, 1984.

Montes Huidobro, Matías. "Prólogo." *El Laúd del desterrado.* Ed. Matías Montes-Huidobro. Houston: Arte Público Press, 1995. vii–xix.

Montolío, Andrés Julio. *Resumen de una cuestión* (diferendo domínico-haitiano). Santo Domingo?: n.p., 1911.

Moore-Gilbert, Bart. "Homi K. Bhaba." *The Johns Hopkins Guide to Literary Theory & Criticism.* 2nd ed. Ed. Michael Groden, Martin Keiswirth, and Inre Szeman. Baltimore and London: The Johns Hopkins University Press, 2005. 111–113.

———. "Gayatri Chakravorty Spivak." *The Johns Hopkins Guide to Literary Theory & Criticism.* 2nd ed. Edited Michael Groden, Martin Keiswirth, and Inre Szeman. Baltimore and London: The Johns Hopkins University Press, 2005. 882–884.

Morales Padrón, Francisco. *Jamaica española.* Sevilla: Escuela de Estudios Hispano-Americanos de Sevilla, 1952.

Moreno Fraginals, Manuel R. *El ingenio: El complejo económico social cubano del azúcar.* Tomo 1.1760–1860. La Habana: Comisión Nacional Cubana de la UNESCO, 1964.

———. *The Sugar Mill: The Socioeconomic Complex of Sugar in Cuba, 1760–1860.* Trans. Cedric Belfrage. New York and London: Monthly Review Press, 1976.

Morisseau-Leroy, Félix. "Botpipèl." In Sunshine and Warner. 148–149.

Morrison, Toni. *Playing in the Dark: Whiteness and the Literacy Imagination.* New York: Vintage, 1993.

Moya Pons, Frank. *The Dominican Republic: A National History.* New Rochelle, NY: Hispaniola Books, 1995.

———. *La dominación haitiana: 1822–1844.* Santiago: UCMM, 1972.

———. "Las tres fronteras: Introducción a la frontera domínico-haitiana." *La cuestión haitiana en Santo Domingo.* Ed. Wilfredo Lozano. Santo Domingo: FLACSO/North-South Center University of Miami, 1993. 17–32.

———. "Dominican National Identity: A Historical Perspective." *Punto 7 Review: A Journal of Marginal Discourse* 3.1 (1996): 14–25.

———. *Breve historia contemporánea de la República Dominicana*. México, D.F.: Fondo de Cultura Económica, 1999.

———. "Plantation History of the Caribbean." Unpublished manuscript.

———. "The Establishment of Primary Centres and Primary Plantations." *General History of the Caribbean*. Vol. II. New Societies: The Caribbean in the Long Sixteenth Century. Ed. Peter C. Emmer. London and Basingstoke: UNESCO Publishing/Macmillan, 1999. 62–78.

———, ed. *Atlas de los Recursos naturales de la República Dominicana*. Santo Domingo: Secretaría de Estado de Medio Ambiente y Recursos Naturales, 2004.

Müller, Heiner. *The Task*. In *Hamletmachine and Other Texts for the Stage*. Ed. and trans. Carl Weber. New York: Performing Arts Journal Publications, 1984. 80–101.

Mullins, Henry T., et al. "Carbonate Platforms along the Southeast Bahamas-Hispaniola Collision Zone." *Marine Geology* 105 (1992): 169–209.

Múnera Cavadía, Alfonso. *El fracaso de la nación: Región, clase y raza en el Caribe Colombiano (1717–1810)*. Bogotá: Banco de la República/El Ancora Editores, 1998.

———. "El ilustrado Francisco José de Caldas y la creación de una imagen de la nación." *Cuadernos de Literatura* 4.7–8 (1998): 36–49.

———. "Cartagena, centro simbólico del Caribe." *Memorias: IV Seminario Internacional de Estudios del Caribe*. Barranquilla: Fondo de Publicaciones de la Universidad del Atlántico, 1999. 5–8.

Munro, Dana G. *Intervention and Dollar Diplomacy in the Caribbean: 1900–1921*. Princeton, NJ: Princeton University Press, 1964.

Naipaul, V. S. "Foreword." *The Middle Pasage*. New York: Vintage Books, 1981.

———. 1962. *The Middle Passage*. New York: Vintage Books, 1981.

Nair, Supriya. *Caliban's Curse: George Lamming and Revisioning of History*. Ann Harbor: The University of Michigan Press, 1996.

Nardin, Jean–Claude. *La mise en valeur de l'ile de Tabago, 1763–1783*. Paris: Mouton, 1969.

Nepaulsingh, Colbert I. "Thing Fall Apart; The Center Cannot Hold." *Latino Review of Books* (Winter 1998): 13–17.

———. "A New Name for the Caribbean." *Latino Review of Books* (Spring 1996a): 5.10.

———. "Islands and Continents." *Latino Review of Books* (Fall 1996b): 8–10.

Nicholls, David. *From Dessalines to Duvalier: Race, Colour and National Independence in Haiti*. Revised Edition. New Brunswick, NJ: Rutgers University Press, 1996.

O'Neill, Eugene. *Selected Plays by Eugene O'Neill*. Introduction by José Quintero. Book Club Edition. New York: Nelson Doubleday, 1979.

Oostindie, Gert J. "Prelude to the Exodus: Surinamers in the Netherlands, 1667–1960s." *Resistance and Rebellion in Surinam: Old and New*. Ed. Gary Brana-Shute. Studies in Third World Societies No. 42. Williamsburg, VA: Department of Anthropology, College of William and Mary, 1990. 231–258.

Ortiz, Fernando. *Cuban Counterpoint: Tobacco and Sugar*. Trans. Harriet de Onís. New York: Vintage Books, 1970.

Ortiz, Martha. "El país no tiene respuestas para un gran terremoto." *El Caribe* (April 10, 2001). "Ciencia." Internet Edition.

Osterhammel, Jürgen. *Colonialism: A Theoretical Overview*. Trans. Shelley L. Frisch. Princeton, New Jersey, and Kingston, Jamaica: Markus Wiener Publishers and Ian Randle Publishers, 1997.

Otero Garabis, Juan. *Nación y ritmo: Descargas desde el Caribe*. San Juan: Ediciones Callejón, 2000.

Paen, Marc. *L'illusion heroique: 25 ans de capoise 1890–1915*. Vol. 1. 2nd. ed. s.n.: Imprimerie H. Deschamps, 1977.

Palencia-Roth, Michael. "Mapping the Caribbean: Cartography and the Cannibalization of Culture." *A History of Literature in the Caribbean*. Vol. 3. Cross-Cultural Studies. Ed. A. James Arnold. Amsterdam and Philadelphia: John Benjamins Publishing Company, 1997. 3–27.

Palés Matos, Luis. *Selected Poems/Poesía selecta*. Trans. Julio Marzán. Houston: Arte Público Press, 2000.

Paquet, Sandra Pouchet. "Foreword." *The Pleasures of Exile*. By George Lamming. Ann Arbor: The University of Michigan Press, 1992. vii–xxvii.

Parker, Michael, and Roger Starkey, eds. *Postcolonial Literatures*. New York: St. Martin's Press, 1995.

Peach, Geri. "Caribbeans in the United Kingdom." In Ember, Ember, and Skoggard. Vol. 2. 624–634.

Pedreira, Antonio S. *Insularismo*. San Juan: Editorial Edil, 1973.

Phaf-Rheinberger, Ineke. a "The Portuguese Jewish Nation: An Enlightenment Essay on the Colony of Surinam." In Arnold, 2001a. 491–503.

———. "Introduction." In Arnold, 2001b. 471–477.

———. "Plantation Emblems in the Dutch Seventeenth Century: Albert Helman's Contrastive Analysis." *Sisyphus and Eldorado: Magical and Other Realisms in Caribbean Literature*. Ed. Timothy J. Reiss. Trenton and Asmara: Africa World Press, 2002. 91–101.

———. "Actualizando a Stedman: El retorino del matrimonio surinamés." *Dispositio* 17.42–43 (1992): 135–163.

Phillips, Michael D., ed. *Snapshots of Belize: An Anthology of Short Fiction*. Belize: Cubola Books, 1995.

Pineau, Gisèle. *The Drifting of Spirits*. Trans. Michael J. Dash. London: Quarter Books, 1999.

Pineau, Gisèle, and Marie Abraham eds. *Femmes des Antilles: Traces et voix cent cinquante ans après l'abolition de l'ésclavage*. Paris: Stock, 1998.

Pollard, Arthur. *Anthony Trollope*. London, Henley, and Boston: Routledge and Kegan Paul, 1978.

Pollard, Arthur, ed. 1973. *Webtser's New World Companion to English and American Literature*. New York: Popular Library, 1976.

Polo, Marco. *The Travels of Marco Polo {The Venetian}*. Ed. Manuel Komroff. Garden City, New York: Garden City Publishing Co., 1930.

Pratt, Mary Louise. *Imperial Eyes: Studies in Travel Writing and Transculturation*. London and New York: Routledge, 1991.

Prengaman, Peter. "Toll in Island Flooding Rises to More than 860." *Washington Post* (May 27, 2004). A11.

Prestol Castillo, Freddy. *El Masacre se pasa a pie*. 5th. ed. Santo Domingo: Ediciones Talles, 18982. See also 11th ed. Ed. Biblioteca Taller Permanente. Santo Domingo: Taller, 1998.

"Prudent Dominican Leader: Joaquín Balaguer." *The New York Times* (May 19, 1970).

Purchas, Samuel. *Hakluytus Posthumus or Purchas His Pilgrimes*. Vol. 16. Glasgow: James MacLehose and Sons, 1906.

Puri, Shalini. *The Caribbean Postcolonial: Social Equality, Post-Nationalism, and Cultural Hybridity*. New York: Palgrave MacMillan, 2004.

Quayson, Oto. *Postcolonialism: Theory, Practice or Process*. Cambridge: Polity Press, 2000.

Quintero Rivera, Angel G. *Salsa, sabor y control: Sociología de la música tropical*. México, D.F.: Siglo XXI Editores, 1998.

Rabess, Gregory. "Cadence: The Dominican Experience." In Guibault. 90–107.

Radhakrishnan, Rajogopalan. *Diasporic Mediations: Between Home and Location*. Minneapolis and London: University of Minnesota Press, 1996.

Raleigh, Sir Walter. *The Poems of Sir Walter Raleigh: Collected and Authenticated*. Ed. J. Hannah. London: George Bell and Sons, 1891.

———. "Discovery of Guiana." *Voyages and Discoveries*. By Richard Hakluyt. Edited, abridged, and introduced by Jack Beeching. London: Penguin Books, 1972. 386–413.

Ramanujan, A. K. "Is there an Indian Way of Thinking? An Informal Essay." *India through Hindu Categories*. Ed. Mckim Marriott. New Delhi, Newbury Park, and London: Sage Publications, 1990. 41–58.

Ramnarine, Tina K. *Creating Their Own Space: The Development of an Indian Caribbean Musical Tradition*. Kingston: University of The West Indies Press, 2001.

Ramos, Aaron Gamaliel, ed. *Las ideas anexionistas en Puerto Rico bajo la dominación norteamericana*. Rio Piedras: Huracán, 1987.

Ramos, Aaron Gamaliel, and Angel Israel Rivera, eds. *Islands at the Crossroads: Politics in the Non-Independent Caribbean*. Kingston and Boulder: Ian Randle Publishers and Lynne Rienner Publishers, 2001.

Reiss, Timothy J., ed. *Sisyphus and Eldorado: Magical and Other Realisms in Caribbean Literature*. Trenton and Asmara: Africa World Press, 2002.

Reiss, Timothy J., ed. *Music, Writing, and Cultural Unity in the Caribbean*. Trenton and Asmara: World Africa Press, 2005.

Renan, Ernest. *Oeuvres complètes*. Tome III. Drames Philosophiques. Ed. Henriette Psichari. Paris: Calmann-Lévy, Editeurs, 1949.

Renk, Kathleen J. *Caribbean Shadows and Victorian Ghosts: Women's Writing and Decolonization*. Charlottesville and London: University of Virginia Press, 1999.

[Report] *Report of the Commission of Inquiry to Santo Domingo*. Commissioners B. F. Wade, A. D. White and S. G. Howe. Washington, DC: U.S. Government Printing Office, 1871.

Reyes Angelita. "The Caribbean." *Global Voices: Contemporary Literature from the Non-Western World*. Ed. Arthur W. Biddle et al. Englewood Cliffs, NJ: Blair Press, 1995. 11–22.

Rhys, Jean. *Wide Sargasso Sea*. 1966. New York: W.W. Norton & Co., 1982.

Richards, David. "West Indian Literature." *Encyclopedia of Literature and Criticism*. Ed. Martin Coyle et al. Detroit and New York: Gale Research Inc., 1991. 1198–1209.

Richardson, William. *Melville's "Benito Cereno"*. Durham, NC: Carolina Academic Press, 1987.

Robins, Nick. "Loot." *Resurgence* No. 210 (January/ February 2002): 12–16.

Robinson, Carey. "Maroons and Rebels (a Dilemma)." *Maroon Heritage: Archeological, Ethnographic and Historical Perspectives.* Ed. Kofi Agorsah. Barbados, Jamaica and Trinidad/Tobago: Canoe Press, 1994. 86–93.

Rodó, José Enrique. *Ariel.* 1900. Madrid: Espasa-Calpe, 1971.

Rodríguez Herrera, Esteban. "Estudio crítico preliminar de 'Cecilia Valdés.' " *Cecilia Valdés o La Loma del Angel.* By Cirilo Villaverde. Habana: Editorial Lex, 1953. xxi–lxviii.

Rodríguez Julia, Edgardo. *Las tribulaciones de Jonás.* San Juan: Ediciones Huracán, 1981.

Rodríguez, Objío, Manuel. *Gregorio Luperón e historia de la Restauración.* Vol. II. Santiago: Editorial El Diario, 1939.

Rodríguez, Richard. 1982. *Hunger of Memory: The Education of Richard Rodríguez (An Autobiography).* Toronto: Bantam Books, 1983.

Roemer, Astrid. "Writing Back in the Diaspora: Surinamese Ethnic Novels." *Presencia criolla en el Caribe y América Latina/Creole Presence in the Caribbean and Latin America.* Ed. Ineke Phaf. Frankfurt am Main and Madrid: Vervuert/Iberoamericana, 1996. 37–43.

———. "Dangerous Liaison: Western Literary Values, Political Engagements, and My Own Aesthetics." *Winds of Change: The Transforming Voices of Caribbean Women Writers and Scholars.* Ed. Adele S. Newson and Linda Strong-Leek. New York: Peter Lang, 1998. 179–187.

Roggiano, Alfredo A. *Pedro Henríquez Ureña en los Estados Unidos.* State University of Iowa Studies in Spanish Language and Literature No. 12. Mexico, D.F.: Iowa University, 1961.

Roosevelt, Theodore. 1913. *An Autobiography.* Vol. 22 of *The Works of Theodore Roosevelt.* New York: Charles Scribner's Sons, 1925.

Rossi, Jr., Máximo. *Praxis, historia y filosofía en el siglo XVII: Textos de Antonio Sánchez Valverde (1729–90).* Santo Domingo: Taller, 1994.

Ruprecht, Alvina, and Cecilia Taiana, eds. *Latina America, The Caribbean, and Canada in the Hood: The Reordering of Culture.* Ottawa: Carleton University Press, 1995.

Rushdie, Salman. *Imaginary Homelands: Essays and Criticism (1981–1991).* New York: Penguin Books, 1991.

Rutgers, Wim. "Dutch Caribbean Literature." *Callaloo* 21.3 (1998): 542–555.

Rutgers, Wim. "Dutch Caribbean Literature." *Caribbean Writers/Les auteurs caribéens.* Ed. Marlies Glaser and Marion Pausch. Amsterdam and Atlanta: Rodopi, 1994. 185–196.

Sachdev, Rachana. "Sycorax in Algiers: Cultural Politics and Gynecology in Early Modern England." *A Feminist Companion to Shakespeare.* Ed. Dympna Callaghan. Malden and Oxford: Blackwell Publishers, 2000. 208–225.

Said, Edward W. *Culture and Imperialism.* New York: Alfred A. Knopf, 1993.

———. "Edward Said's Reflections on Exile." C-Span Booknotes. Host Brian Lamb June 17, 2001a.

———. "Globalizing Literary Studies." *PMLA* 116.1 (January 2001b): 64–68.

Sánchez Valverde, Antonio. *Ensayos.* Biblioteca de Clásicos Dominicanos. Santo Domingo: Ediciones de la Fundación Corripio, 1988.

Sánchez, Luis Rafael. *La guaracha del Macho Camacho.* Barcelona: Editorial Argos Vergara, 1982.

———. "The Flying Bus." Elpidio Laguna-Díaz. *Images and Identities: Puerto Ricans in Two World Contexts.* Ed. Asela Rodríguez de Laguna. New Brunswick and Oxford: Transaction Books, 1987. 17–25.

————. *Macho Camacho's Beat.* Trans. Gregory Rabassa. Normal, IL: Dalkey Archive Press, 2001.

————. "¿Porqué escribe usted?" *Desde La Biblioteca* (Instituto Tecnológico Metropolitano-Medellin) 21 (2003): 41–59.

Sancho, Ignatius. *Letters of the Late Ignatius Sancho, An African.* Ed. Vincent Carretta. New York: Penguin Books, 1998.

Sanderson, Ivan T. *Caribbean Treasure.* New York: Pyramid Books, 1965.

"Santo Domingo." *Encyclopaedia Britannica.* Vol. XXIX. Eleventh Edition. 1910. 194–195.

Savory, Elaine. "Returning to Sycorax/Prospero's Response: Kamau Brathwaite's Word Journey." *The Art of Kamau Brathwaite.* Ed. Stewart Brown. Bridgend, Wales: Seren, 1995. 208–230.

Schmidt-Welle, Friedhelm, ed. *Ficciones y silencios fundacionales: Literaturas y culturas poscoloniales en América Latina.* Madrid and Frankfurt am Main: Iberoamericana and Vervuert, 2003.

Schulman, Ivan A. "Prólogo." *Cecilia Valdés.* Por Cirilo Villaverde. Caracas: Biblioteca Ayacucho, 1981. ix–xxvii.

Scobie, Edward. *Black Britannia: A History of Blacks in Britain.* Chicago: Johnson Publishing Company, 1972.

Séjour, Victor. "The Mulatto." 1837. *The Norton Anthology of African American Literature.* Ed. Henry Louis Gates, Jr. and Nellie Y. McKay. New York: W.W. Norton, 1997. 286–299.

Selvon, Samuel. *The Lonely Londoners.* 1956. Essex: Longman Group, 1985.

Senior, Olive. *Gardening in the Tropics.* Toronto, Ontario: McClelland & Stewart, 1994.

Senior, Olive. ed. *Encyclopedia of Jamaica Heritage.* St. Andrew, Jamaica: Twin Guinep Publishers, 2003.

Serbin, Andrés. *Caribbean Geopolitics: Toward Security Through Peace?* Trans. Sabeth Ramirez. Boulder and London: Lynne Rienner Publishers, 1990.

Shetty, Sandhya, "Masculinity, National Identity, and the Feminine Voice in *The Wine of Astonishment.*" *The Journal of Commonwealth Literature* 29.1 (1994): 65–79.

Short, John Rennie. *New Worlds, New Geographies.* Syracuse: Syracuse University Press, 1998.

Silvera, Makeda. "Caribbean Canadian Writers: A Literary Forum." In Ruprecht and Taiana. 93–109.

Simon, John. "Foreword." *German Romantic Novelas.* Ed. Frank G. Ryder and Robert M. Browning. New York: Continuum, 1985. vii–xv.

Singh, Rickey. "Historic End to Age-Old Belize-Guatemala Border Row." *Guyana Chronicle* (September 18, 2002). Online.

Smart, Ian. *Central American Writers of West Indian Origin: A New Hispanic Literature.* Washington, DC: Three Continents Press, 1984.

Smith, Adam. *An Inquiry into the Causes and Nature of the Wealth of Nations.* Ed. Edwin Cannan. New York: The Modern Library, 1994.

Sokal, Alan, and Jean Bricmont. *Fashionable Nonsense: Postmodern Intellectual's Abuse of Science.* New York: Picador USA, 1998.

Soto Jiménez, José Miguel. "La frontera en la agenda de seguridad, defensa y desarrollo nacional del Estado dominicano en el siglo XXI." *La Frontera: Prioridad en la agenda nacional del siglo XXI.* Ed. Secretaría de Estado de las Fuerzas Armadas. Santo Domingo: Editora de las Fuerzas Armadas Dominicanas, 2004. 3–16.

Sourieau, Marie-Agnès. "Afterword." *Exile According to Julia*. By Gisèle Pineau. Charlottesville and London: University of Virginia Press, 2003. 171–187.

Spivak, Gayatri Chakravorty. *A Critique of Postcolonial Reason: Toward a History of the Vanishing Present*. Cambridge, MA: Harvard University Press, 1999.

———. "Can the Subaltern Speak?" *Colonial Discourse and Postcolonial Theory: A Reader*. Ed. Patrick Williams and Laura Chrisman. New York: Colombia University Press, 1994. 66–111.

Stowe, Harriet Beecher. 1852. *Uncle Tom's Cabin*. New York: The Modern Library, 2001.

Stuempfle, Stephen. *The Steelband Movement: The Forging of a National Art in Trinidad and Tobago*. Philadelphia: University of Pennsylvania Press, 1995.

Suárez Díaz, Aida. *El Doctor Ramon Emeterio Betances: su vida y su obra*. San Juan: Ateneo Puertorriqueño, 1970.

Suckling, James. "The Supermodels of Cuba." *Cigar Aficionado: The Good Life Magazine for Men* (June 2003): 60–70.

Suk, Jeannie. *Postcolonial Paradoxes in French Caribbean Writing: Césaire, Glissant, Condé*. Oxford: Clarendon Press, 2001.

Sundquist, Eric. "Melville, Delany, and New World Slavery." *Literary Theory: An Anthology*. Ed. Julie Rivkin and Michael Ryan. Malden and Oxford: Blackwell Publishers, 1998. 827–848.

Sunshine, Catherine A. *The Caribbean: Survival, Struggle, and Sovereignty*. Washington, DC: EPICA, 1985.

Sunshine, Catherine, and Keith Q. Warner, eds. *Caribbean Connections: Moving North*. Washington, DC: Network of Educators on the Americas, 1998.

Sylvain, Georges. *Confidences et melancholies*. 1898. Port-au-Prince: Imprimiere Henri Deschamps, 1979.

Thomas, J. J. 1889. *Froudacity*. Introduction by C. L. R. James. London: New Beacon Books, 1969.

Todorov, Tzvetan. *The Conquest of America. The Question of the Other*. Trans. Richard Howard. New York: Harper and Row, 1984.

Torres-Saillant, Silvio. Dominicans as a New York Community: A Social Appraisal." *Punto Review: A Journal of Marginal Discourse* 2.1 [New Format] (1989): 7–25.

———. "The Dominican Republic." *No Longer Invisible: Afro-Latin Americans Today*. Ed. Minority Rights Group. London: Minority Rights Group, 1995. 109–138.

———. *Caribbean Poetics: Toward an Aesthetic of West Indian Literature*. Cambridge: Cambridge University Press, 1997.

———. *El retorno de las yolas: Ensayos sobre diáspora, democracia y dominicanidad*. Santo Domingo: Ediciones Librería La Trinitaria & Editora Manatí, 1999.

———. "Before the Diaspora: Early Dominican Literature in the United States." *Recovering the U.S. Hispanic literary Heritage*. Vol. 3. Ed. María Herrera-Sobek and Virginia Sánchez Korrol. Houston: Arte Público, 2000. 250–267.

———. "Caliban's Betrayal: A New Inquiry into the Caribbean." *For the Geography of a Soul: Emerging Perspectives on Kamau Brathwaite*. Ed. Timothy Reiss. Trenton and Asmara: World Africa Press, 2001. 221–243.

———. "The Limits of Globalization: Caribbean Higher Education and the Borders that Remain." *The Challenge of Public Higher Education in the Hispanic Caribbean*. Ed. María J. Canino and Silvio Torres-Saillant. Princeton: Markus Wiener, 2004. 211–226.

Torres-Saillant, Silvio, and Ramona Hernández. *The Dominican Americans.* The New Americans. Westport, CT.: Greenwood Press, 1998.

Toumson, Roger. *Trois Calibans.* Havana: Casa de las Américas, 1981.

Trefossa [Henry de Ziel]. "Kopenhagen." *Trotfi Puema* (Amsterdam, 1957). Reproduced in *Callaloo* 21.3 (1998): 519.

Trollope, Anthony. *The West Indies and the Spanish Main.* 1860. New York: Carroll and Graf Publishers, 1999.

———. *An Autobiography.* Ed. David Skilton. London: Penguin Books, 1996.

Trouillot, Michel-Rolph. *Silencing the Past: Power and the Production of History.* Boston: Beacon, 1995.

Ureña de Henríquez, Salomé. *Anacaona.* 1880. *Poesías completas.* Biblioteca de Clásicos Dominicanos. Santo Domingo: Ediciones de la Fundación Corripio, 1989.

Usherwood, Stephen. "The Abolitionist's Debt to Lord Mansfield." *History Today* 31 (1981): 40–45.

Vargas Llosa, Mario. *La fiesta del chivo.* Madrid: Alfaguara, 2000.

Vaughan, Alden T., and Virginia Mason Vaughan. *Shakespeare's "Caliban": A Cultural History.* Cambridge: Cambridge University Press, 1991.

Vaval, Duraciné. *Histoire de la littérature haïtienne ou "L'âme noire."* Port-au Prince: Fardin, 1933.

Vega, Ana Lydia. "Cloud Cover Caribbean." Trans. Mark McCaffrey. *Rhythm & Revolt: Tales of the Antilles.* Ed. Marcela Brown. New York: Plume/Penguin, 1995. 1–6.

———. *Encancaranublado y otros cuentos de naufragio.* 3rd ed. San Juan, Puerto Rico: Editorial Antillana, 1987.

———. "Ana Lydia Vega." *Spanish American Authors: The Twentieth Century.* Ed. Angel Flores. New York: H.W. Wilson, 1992. 875–876.

———. "Ana Lydia Vega." *Encyclopedia of Latin American Literature.* Ed. Verity Smith. London and Chicago: Fitzroy Dearborn Publishers, 1997. 749–752.

Vega, Bernardo. *Trujillo y las fuerzas armadas norteamericanas.* Santo Domingo: Fundación Cultural Dominicana, 1992.

———. *Trujillo y Haiti.* Vol. 1. Santo Domingo: Fundación Cultural Dominicana, 1998.

Veldwachter, Nadège. "An Interview with Gisèle Pineau." *Research in African Literatures* 35.1 (2004): 180–186.

Venables, Robert. *The Narrative of General Venables (with an Appendix of Papers Relating to the Expedition to the West Indies and the Conquest of Jamaica, 1654–1655).* Ed. C. H. Firth. The Royal Historical Society. London, New York, and Bombay: Longman, Green and Co., 1900.

Verne, Jules. *The Mysterious Island.* New York: Airmont Publishing Company, 1965.

Viau, Jacques. *Jacques Viau: Poeta de una isla.* Ed. Antonio Lockward. Santo Domingo: Ediciones CEDEE, 1985.

Villaverde, Cirilo. *Excursión a Vuelta Abajo.* Biblioteca Básica de la Cultura Cubana. La Habana: Consejo Nacional de Cultura/Ministerio de Educación, 1961.

Voorhoeve, Jan, and Ursy M. Lichtveld, ed. *Creole Drum: An Anthology of Creole Literature in Surinam.* Trans. Vernie A. February. New York and London: Yale University Press, 1975.

Walcott, Derek. "The Sea is History." *Frontiers of Caribbean Literature in English.* Ed. Frank Birbalsingh. New York: St. Martin's Press, 1996. 22–28.

———. "A Frowsty Fragrance." *New York Review of Books* (June 15, 2000): 57–61.

———. *The Haitian Trilogy.* New York: Farrar, Strauss and Giroux, 2002.

Walder, Dennis. *Post-Colonial Literatures in English: History, Language, Theory.* Oxford: Blackwell Publishers, 1998.

Wallerstein, Immanuel. *The End of the World as We Know It: Social Science for the Twenty-First Century.* Minneapolis and London: University of Minnesota Press, 1999.

Wambu, Onyekachi, ed. *Empire Windrush: Fifty Years of Writing about Black Britain.* London: Phoenix, 1999.

Watlington, Francisco. "The Physical Environment: Biogeographical Teleconnections in Caribbean Prehistory." *General History of the Caribbean.* Vol. 1. Ed. Jalil Sued-Badillo. Paris, London, and Oxford: UNESCO Publishing and Macmillan Publishers, 2003. 30–92.

Webster's New Universal Unabridged Dictionary. 1983 Edition.

Welles, Summer. 1928. *Naboth's Vineyard: The Dominican Republic (1844–1924).* Mamaroneck, NY: Paul P. Appel, 1966.

Wild, Anthony. *The East India Company: Trade and Conquest from 1600.* London and New Delhi: Harper Collins, 1999.

Williams, Eric E. *Capitalism and Slavery.* Chapel Hill: University of North Carolina Press, 1944.

Wills, Gary. *"Negro President": Jefferson and the Slave Power.* Boston and New York: Houghton Mifflin Company, 2003.

Wilson, Edwin, and Alvin Goldfarb. *Living Theater: An Introduction to Theater History.* New York: McGraw-Hill Book Co., 1983.

Wilson, Samuel M. *Hispaniola: Caribbean Chiefdoms in the Age of Columbus.* Tuscaloosa. London: The University of Alabama Press, 1990.

Wucker, Michele. *Why the Cocks Fight: Dominicans, Haitians, and the Struggle of Hispaniola.* New York: Hill and Wang, 1999.

Yelvington, Kevin A. "African Diaspora in the Americas." In Ember, Ember, and Skoggard. Vol. 1. 24–35.

INDEX

Dorsainvil, J.C., 210, 216
Dorsinville, Max, 200
Douglass, Frederick, 58, 127–130
Drake, Francis, 22
Dryden, John, 72
Du Bellay, Joachim, 110
Duany, Jorge, 245
Dubois, Pierre, 190
Ducasse, Jean, governor of Saint Domingue, 168
Dunn, L.C., 6
Durand, Oswald, 25
Duvalier, François, 219, 220, 230, 235, 244
Duvalier, Jean-Claude, 146, 230, 239

Eagleton, Terry, 39
East India Company, 18, 81, 82, 118, 145, 164
Echteld, Liesbeth, 187
Edgar, Andrew, 30
Edgell, Zee, 121
  Beka Lamb., 121
  In Times Like These, 121
  The Festival of San Joaquin, 121
Edmonson, Belinda J., 206
Eliot, George, 76
Elsewhere/yoretime, 99, 100
Eltis, David, 176
Empson, William, 158
Encyclopedia Britannica, 63–64
  entry on "Santo Domingo," 1910 edition, 63–64
Engels, Fredrich, 75
  The Origins of the Family, Private Property, and the State, 75
Engerman, Stanley L., 174
England, 8, 16, 47 (tributary to Caribbean culture)
Enriquillo, Indian chief, 8, 34–35, 210–212, 223, 235, 236
  Guaroruya, his Taino name, 210
Equiano, Olaudah, 95
Espaillat, Rhina P., 250
Estefan, Gloria, 30
Ethnic studies, 2, 94–96
ethnoracial pluralism, Caribbean familiarity with, 28
Eubulus, chief commissioner of the theoric fund, 53
Europe, 2, 7
Everly, Shelley, 101–102

Fabens, Joseph W., 58
Fanon, Frantz, 43, 91, 152, 162
  Peau noire, masques blancs, 91

Farley, Christopher John, 248
  Time review of *The Farming of Bones*, 248
Faubert, Pierre, 218
  Ogé ou le prejugé de couleur, 218
Faulkner, William, 131
Fehervary, Helen, 124
Fellini, Federico, 55
  Satyricon, 55
Fernández de Oviedo, Gonzalo, 111
Fernández, Leonel, 15, 241
Fernández Retamar, Roberto, 91, 148, 201, 206, 222, 235, 238
  Calibán, 91, 148, 222, 238
Ferré, Rosario, 181
  "Isolda en el espejo," 181
  Maldito amor, 181
Ferrer, Ibrahim, 45
Ferrer Gutiérrez, Virgilio, 144
Ferrier, Henri, 196
  Átman, 196
Firmin, Antenor, 217, 218, 220
  L'égalité des races humaines, 218
Fischback, Ephraim, 89–90
Fisher, Stanley, 244
Florville, William de, known as Billy the barber, 244
Foner, Nancy, 100
Fornet, Ambrosio, 98
Foucault, Michel, 44, 76
  History of Sexuality, 76, 158
FOX, television network, 120–121
  reality show, *Temptation Island*, set in Belize, 120–121
France, 8, 16, 47 (tributary of Caribbean culture)
François, Jean, 169
Free Associated State of Puerto Rico, 23
Freire, Paulo, 91
  Pedogogia do oprimido, 91
Freud, Sigmund, 74
Frey, John Andrew, 116
Froude, James Anthony, 18, 21, 74, 113–115
  The English in the West Indies, 114–115
Fukuyama, Francis, 2
  The End of History, 2

Gage, Thomas, 16
Galeano, Eduardo, 47, 91
  Las venas abiertas de América Latina, 91
Galván, Manuel de Jesús, 76, 210, 211, 216
  Enriquillo: novela histórica, 76, 210
García, Cristina, 93
García Godoy, Federico, 216
García, José Gabriel, 216

Quintero Rivera, Angel "Chuco," 36, 38, 103, 162
on conceptualizing joy, 38
Quitman, John A., Governor of Mississippi, 175

Rabess, Gregory, 31, 32
Radhakrishnan, Rajogopalan, 91, 252
Radio City Music Hall, 45
Raleigh, Sir Walter, 22, 118–120
advocating colonization of Guyana, 22
"Discovery of Guiana," 118, 119
Ramanujan, A.K., 89
Ramnarine, Tina K., 32
Ramos, Aaron Gamaliel, 18, 48, 146, 159, 160, 225
Rastafarianism, 112, 152
Raynal, Abbé, 34
Rebajes, Francis, 59–62
Reglamento de Jornaleros, 174
Reiss, Timothy J., 30, 79
Music, Writing and Cultural Unity in the Caribbean, 30
Renan, Ernest, 74, 199, 200, 215
Caliban, suite "de la Tempete," 199, 215
L'eau de Jouvence, suite de "Caliban," 199
Renaud, Elaine, 234
Rg Veda, 89
Rhodes, 29
Rhys, Jean, 153, 172
Wide Sargasso sea, 172
Richards, I.A., 158
Richardson, William, 126
Richepanse, Antoine, General, 170
Rivera, Angel Israel, 18, 48, 159, 225
Rivera, Tomás, 96
Rizal, José, 161
Road Movies, 45
Robespierre, Maximilien de, 73, 125
Robins, Nick, 82
Robinson, Carey, 34
Robottom, John, 25
Rochambeau, General, 170
Rodney, Walter, 152
Rodó, José Enrique, 215–218
Roemer, Astrid H., 4, 6, 26, 182, 195, 231
Nergens ergens, 231
relationship to Western thought, 4
Rodríguez Herrera, Esteban, 151, 152
Rodríguez Julia, Edgardo, 146, 166
Rodríguez, Nestor, xii
Rodríguez Objío, Manuel, 144
Rodríguez, Richard, 79–82, 85
Hunger of Memory, 85
Roggiano, Alfredo A., 59

Roman, Jules, 74
Roosevelt, Theodore, U.S. President, 62, 63
Autobiography, 63
intervention in the Dominican Republic, 62–64
Rossi, Jr., Máximo, 111
Roumain, Jacques, 43, 152
Rueda, Manuel, 251
Ruiz de Burton, Maria Amparo, 96
The Squatter and the Don, 96
Rushdie, Salman, 41, 160
Rutgers, Wim, 187, 195, 204, 232, 236
Ryswick, Treaty of, 1697, 22
Franco-Hispanic conflict in Hispaniola, 22

Saco, José Antonio, demographic concern over slavery, 175
Saget, Nissage, 144
Said, Edward W., 2, 6, 54, 92, 98, 102, 103, 156
Saillant, Delfin, 57
Saillant, Don Pedro, 56
Saillant, María Amparo, 57
Saldívar, Jaime David, 100
Criticism in the Borderlands, 100
Salgari, Emilio, 60
Salkey, Andrew, 250
Salnave, Sylvan, 144
Samana Bay, 23
contested Dominican territory, 175
conveted by colonial powers, 23
Samper, Miguel, 111
San Pedro de Macorís, Dominican city, 51
Sánchez, Luis Rafael, 48, 49, 104, 142, 153, 231
La guaracha del macho Camacho, 48, 142
Sanchez Valverde, Antonio, 111
La América vindicada, 111
Sancho, Ignatius, 81, 83
Sanderson, Ivan T., 11, 12
definition of the Caribbean, 11
Sankatsing, Glenn, 39
Santiago, Esmeralda, 251
Santos Febres, Mayra, 87, 161
São Tomé, 29
Saramaccan, Surinamese creole, 24, 26
spoken by Bush Negroes, 24
Savory, Elaine, 42
Schoelcher, Victor, 143
Les colonies françaises, 143
Schomburg, Arthur, 95
New York Public Library branch named after, 95
Schouten-Elsenhout, Johanna, 153
Schulman, Iván, 152

Printed in the United States
62745LVS00004B/1-96